Great Debates in Medical Law and Ethics

Palgrave Great Debates in Law

Series Editor
Jonathan Herring, Professor of Law, University of Oxford

Company Law
Lorraine Talbot

Contract Law
Jonathan Morgan

Criminal Law
Jonathan Herring

Employment Law
Simon Honeyball

Equity and Trusts
Alastair Hudson

Family Law
Jonathan Herring, Rebecca Probert & Stephen Gilmore

Gender & Law
Rosemary Auchmuty (ed.)

Jurisprudence
Nicholas J McBride & Sandy Steel

Medical Law and Ethics
Imogen Goold & Jonathan Herring

Land Law
David Cowan, Lorna Fox O'Mahony & Neil Cobb

The European Convention on Human Rights
Fiona de Londras & Kanstantsin Dzehtsiarou

Great Debates in Medical Law and Ethics

Second Edition

Imogen Goold
Associate Professor of Law and Fellow
St Anne's College, Oxford

Jonathan Herring
Professor of Law and Fellow
Exeter College, Oxford

macmillan education   palgrave

First edition published 2014
This edition published 2018 by
PALGRAVE

Palgrave in the UK is an imprint of Macmillan Publishers Limited,
registered in England, company number 785998, of 4 Crinan Street,
London N1 9XW.

Palgrave® and Macmillan® are registered trademarks in the United States,
the United Kingdom, Europe and other countries.

ISBN 978–1–352–00228–7

This book is printed on paper suitable for recycling and made from fully
managed and sustained forest sources. Logging, pulping and manufacturing
processes are expected to conform to the environmental regulations of the
country of origin.

A catalogue record for this book is available from the British Library.

A catalog record for this book is available from the Library of Congress.

CONTENTS

INTRODUCTION

The aim of this book is to introduce some of the key debates around the question of how we should regulate medicine. It is necessarily a book about both law and ethics, because medicine can have a deeply personal impact on individuals as well as a profound impact on the community. Abortion, euthanasia, consent to treatment and medical negligence, to name but a few, are all aspects of medical practice that provoke fierce debate precisely because of their potential effect on people's lives. In this book, we introduce you to both the legal and ethical aspects of these debates to help you understand just why people hold such strong beliefs about them. We endeavour not to take a particular stance, but instead present the case for each side of the debate and draw out the areas of contention. We offer explanations of why the law takes the positions it does, and outline the criticisms that have been made in response and the various ethical questions that are relevant to the debate.

Many of these debates are complex and vexed, as they involve tensions between religious beliefs, respect for individual autonomy, and the desire to protect the vulnerable in our society. Almost every medical issue is also affected by concerns about rationing, and how we balance the needs of everyone against the interests of the people most directly affected. In such a slim volume, it would be impossible for us to explore all the nuances of these debates, but we hope by presenting an overview of the relevant laws and ethical stances we can give you the tools to think deeply about these areas of debate.

There are many ways to approach these questions. We might take the view that individual autonomy is the most important value, and then our views will flow from there. Or we might say that the law's primary goal should be to help people live the best, healthiest life. Or perhaps we would start from the position that the needs of the many should outweigh those of the few. We can then take these general principles and begin to apply these to the areas of debate. Alternatively, we can think about why some areas are so difficult, such as the emotional aspects of having a child, or the unknowable consequences of dying. In addition, some might think that it is most important that the law takes an ethical stance, while others will advocate legal certainty or a commitment to general legal principles as the best guide to what the law should be. In this book, we bring together all of these approaches to help you see different ways of looking at each of the areas of contention, and the many things that must be considered when we think about how the law should regulate the role of medicine in people's lives.

Throughout this book, we have tried to avoid taking a firm position on the issues under discussion until the end of each section, preferring to help you come to your own conclusions. One of the things students (and in fact many people) find especially difficult about medical law and ethics is explaining *why* they feel as they do about an issue. Often, we have intuitions about an issue in this area, or a long-standing belief – such as an opposition to abortion, or support for euthanasia – but we are not sure why we feel this way. We would encourage you to try to unpack your views about a topic by referring to some of the ethical arguments we have outlined. See where you agree, and where you disagree, then try to think about why you disagree on a particular point. This will help you work out why you feel as you do, or perhaps even lead you to change your mind.

We have included a list of further reading at the end of each chapter. On each of the topics we cover here there is a wide range of views, and sometimes very heated disagreement. The arguments are often detailed and subtle, and we would encourage you to read beyond just our text to help you delve deeper into the issues. In an area where so many of the areas of debate have personal resonance for many people, you will want to reach your own conclusions on the questions we explore here, and we hope this further reading will help you to do so.

CASES

LEGISLATION

CHAPTER 1

General Ethical Theories

INTRODUCTION

It is interesting how many law degree courses and textbooks are entitled 'Medical Law and Ethics'. It would be unthinkable to write a textbook on medical law or design a course on it without including a discussion of general ethical theories, often as the opening chapter or seminar. Indeed, that is exactly what we have done with this book. But our colleagues don't do that with other subjects on the legal curriculum. Books on contract law, land law or constitutional law, for example, do not tend to emphasise ethical principles in the same way. It would look odd to have a book entitled 'Tort Law and Ethics', although that is de rigueur for medical law.

In one sense it is not surprising that medical law and medical ethics are linked. After all, we would not want the law to be requiring medical professionals to act in an unethical way. Indeed, we would hope that the law would reflect and reinforce the general moral principles which should guide doctors. It is also an acknowledgement that medical professionals will be seeking to comply with both their legal and ethical requirements at the same time. It therefore makes sense that they should be integrated.

On the other hand it is important to realise the differences between the way the law works and the way ethics work. First, generally the law sets down the minimum that must be done to avoid committing a legal wrong. Ethics, by contrast, is often asking a different question and is seeking to ascertain what is the ideal moral behaviour in these circumstances. If you like, the law tells you how not to be a devil, while ethics often asks what it means to be an angel.

Second, the law must be enforced in courts. This means it must be susceptible of legal proof. Its requirements and regulations tend, therefore, to focus on matters capable of evidence in a courtroom. Ethicists do not worry about proof and are more likely to discuss matters (such as motive) which are less capable of objective assessment.

Third, the law must be capable of providing guidance. People need to know in advance what the law requires. For medical professionals, ethical issues often arise in an emergency and so the law's requirements need to be relatively straightforward and simple to follow. This is less of a concern for ethicists, who in their analysis will want to tease out every ambiguity in providing an authoritative discussion. In brief, legal regulations tend to be short and somewhat crude, lacking the length and sophistication that a full ethical analysis can provide.

In this chapter we shall explore the ethical foundations of medical law. We shall look at four important issues, examining some of the key themes in medical ethics: autonomy; paternalism; utilitarianism; and relativism. Inevitably these topics are huge and there is much that could be said.

Debate 1

Is respect for autonomy the most important ethical principle?

This question is particularly appropriate in a liberal, pluralist society. As such a society, we place considerable importance on people freely forming and following their own choices about how to live.[1] In simple terms, we don't like being told what to do. To some degree the legal system takes the approach advocated by John Stuart Mill, that we should have the maximum freedom to make choices about our own lives, but not to the extent that others' similar degree of autonomy should be impinged upon. According to Mill, the 'only purpose for which power can be rightfully exercised over any member of a civilised community, against his will, is to prevent harm to others'.[2] This reflects the principle of autonomy. Each person should be free to develop and live out their vision of the 'good life'.

This approach has also found favour with many contemporary writers on ethics. Ronald Dworkin has argued that people have a right, and a responsibility, to 'confront the most fundamental questions about the meaning and value of their own lives for themselves, answering to their own consciences and convictions'.[3] The alternative would be for the government, or the law, to tell people how they should choose to live. Most people think that is unacceptable.

In this debate we will explore whether respect for autonomy should be the most important ethical principle. To get you thinking, here is a scenario to consider:

Scenario to ponder

Mildred suffers from body dysmorphic disorder. This is a recognised condition which causes people to feel a part of their body is alien to them and they strongly wish to have it removed. Mildred detests her legs. She asks a doctor to remove them. She emphasises it is her body and she should be able to do what she wants to with it. She relies on the principle of autonomy to claim the doctor should be permitted to remove her legs.

---

[1] J. Savulescu, 'Editorial: Death, us and our bodies: personal reflections' (2003) 29 *Journal of Medical Ethics* 127, 128–29.

[2] J.S. Mill, *On Liberty* (Cosimo Classics, 2005 [1859]), 6.

[3] R. Dworkin, *Life's Dominion* (HarperCollins, 1993), 166–67.

Why is Autonomy so Important?

The freedom to make our own choices is important because what we choose, and the goals and values we have, are themselves important to us.[4] Further, as Will Kymlicka rightly points out, 'freedom of choice, while central to a valuable life, is not the value which is centrally pursued in such a life' – it is the projects that we value that are important, and therefore freedom to choose to pursue them is crucial to our being able to live fulfilled lives.[5] We need to be allowed to choose to pursue them, not to have other goals and values that we do not value forced upon us. That is true even if the goals that are imposed upon us are worthwhile.

Freedom to make our own choices is also important because, in doing so, we are able to experiment with life, as John Stuart Mill argued, and to grow in the process by testing our ideas about what we want, re-evaluating and thereby determining which projects will make our lives go best. In addition, exercising these capacities of choice and reasoned decision making is in itself an aspect of self-fulfilment, because in exercising them we improve them. As Mill stated:

> The human faculties of perception, judgment, discriminative feeling, mental activity, and even moral preference, are exercised only in making a choice. ... The mental and moral, like the muscular powers, are improved only by being used.[6]

For each of these reasons, interventions that override this capacity to choose may decrease our quality of life, and should be presumed to be objectionable. This capacity should be overridden only where sufficient justification can be found.

What is Autonomy?

The basic idea behind autonomy is straightforward. It is about people being free to determine for themselves how they wish to live their lives. This is why, for example, a law forbidding consensual same-sex activity would infringe the principle of autonomy. It would prevent people pursuing activities they want to do. However, the concept is far more complex than it at first appears. We will now explore some of the ambiguities around it.

Autonomy and capacity

Autonomy requires that we respect the choices that people make, but only if they are 'autonomous choices'. What does that mean? Antonia Cronin suggests:

> Autonomy is the capacity of persons to reflect critically upon their first-order preferences, desires, wishes and so forth and then readiness to accept or attempt

---

[4] One limitation on this liberty is that individuals should not be allowed to give up their autonomy (e.g. by entering into slavery). See, for example, D. Archard, 'For our own good' (1994) 72 *Australasian Journal of Philosophy* 283, 291.

[5] W. Kymlicka, *Contemporary Political Philosophy* (Clarendon Press, 1990), 210.

[6] J.S. Mill, *On Liberty* (Cosimo Classics, 2005 [1859]), 34.

to change these in the light of higher-order preferences and values. By exercising such a capacity, persons define their nature, give meaning to their lives and take responsibility for the kind of person they are.[7]

But to other commentators this is far too demanding. Consider, for example, Simon reaching out for his tenth chocolate truffle. In one sense he has chosen to eat ten chocolates, and that was his autonomous choice. Imagine, however, that his friend Thia grabbed the chocolates away at the last minute. Thia might argue that Simon had recently started a diet and determined to eat fewer calories. She might say she was acting in Simon's autonomy interests in promoting his autonomous decision to eat healthily. Indeed, she might refer to Cronin's quote and say that she was promoting Simon's 'higher-order preference' (to eat healthily) over his 'desire' (to taste the delicious chocolate).

We will be exploring this issue further in Chapters 3 and 4. But for now notice that even if you decide to respect someone's decision, it is not always clear what their decision is, or which decision you should respect.

What is the difference between autonomy and liberty?

It can be helpful to distinguish between autonomy and liberty, or between positive and negative autonomy as it is sometimes called. It is one thing to say 'I should be left alone to do what I want with my life' (liberty or negative autonomy) and another to say 'I should be enabled to do what I want with my life' (autonomy or positive autonomy). This distinction is especially important in the area of medical treatment.

The law certainly protects liberty strongly. If you do not consent to medical treatment, a doctor cannot force that treatment upon you (provided you have the capacity to refuse treatment). However, this does not mean you have the right to demand certain treatment.[8] In short, the law may strongly protect your right to say 'no' to treatment, but it does not give you the right to demand it.

However, debates over autonomy can be more complex than this. Some commentators believe that the state can have a duty to enable people to pursue their life goals in some circumstances.[9] Disabled people have the right to have their disability accommodated; those with infertility may have a right of access to assisted reproduction; children may have the right to education so that they have the skills they need; and so on. What is generally agreed, however, is that the right to be left alone (liberty) is more strongly protected than the claim that you should be given the services you need to fulfil your goals (autonomy).

---

[7] A. Cronin, 'Transplants save lives, defending the double veto does not: a reply to Wilkinson' (2007) 33 *Journal of Medical Ethics* 219, 220.

[8] A point emphasised in *R (Burke) v GMC* [2005] EWCA Civ 1003.

[9] J. Raz, *The Morality of Freedom* (Oxford University Press, 1982).

Autonomy and bodily integrity

Is there a difference between autonomous decisions involving your body and those not? Consider these two cases. Su wants to attend an anti-Brexit march, but cannot as a cordon of police have blocked off access to the march. Tom wants to attend the march, but is grabbed by police and put onto a train home. Both are having their autonomy interfered with; but does the fact that the interference with Tom's involved a touching of his body make it a more serious invasion of his rights? Many think so and writers commonly use the idea of bodily integrity to capture this idea. You might think that bodily integrity is simply a strong form of the autonomy right: it is bad to interfere in someone's decisions about how to live, but it is particularly bad if it involves touching them. Or you may think it is a separate right. This latter view has some merit because even if a person lacks capacity (e.g. they have very severe dementia) we don't think people should touch them without good reason. Not everyone is convinced by the emphasis on bodily integrity: does it presuppose an assumption about being independent and self-contained that privileges a stereotype about what a good body is like or how people should be?[10]

Perfectionism

Does autonomy protect the right to pursue any goal that does not harm others? Most theories of autonomy would answer this question 'yes'. You should have the right to engage in trainspotting, gambling or nude sunbathing if you wish, however foolish or even immoral others may regard these activities to be, with one proviso. That is, that in your activities you do not harm others. Joseph Raz, however, takes a different view. He argues: 'Autonomous life is valuable only if it is spent in the pursuit of acceptable and valuable projects and relationships.'[11] He therefore limits protection of autonomy to 'valuable' projects. Notably, he also supports the state's being under an obligation to assist people in realising their autonomous plans. This is clearly a more acceptable view if autonomy is limited to worthwhile projects. The difficulty for Raz is in determining what is a worthwhile project. Is listening to the music of Justin Bieber a worthwhile project? Is casual sex? People will have different views on these questions.

Relational autonomy

A powerful critique of traditional understandings of autonomy has come from those who support relational autonomy.[12] This is a complex body of writing, and we can summarise its central themes only briefly. Supporters

---

[10] J. Herring and J. Wall, 'The nature and significance of the right to bodily integrity' (2017) 76 *Cambridge Law Journal* 566.

[11] J. Raz, *The Morality of Freedom* (Oxford University Press, 1982), 312.

[12] See, e.g., J. Herring, *Relational Autonomy and Family Law* (Springer, 2014); J. Herring, 'Forging a relational approach: best interests or human rights?' (2013) 13 *Medical Law International* 32 for more discussion of the concept.

of relational autonomy argue that people understand themselves and their goals in relational terms. In other words, most (or maybe all) people live in families or communities. It does not therefore make sense to talk of someone living their vision of the 'good life', because this is tied up with the interests of others. Relational autonomy theorists criticise traditional versions of autonomy for being too individualistic in imagining everyone as isolated individuals pursuing their own goals, and not recognising that in fact we operate relationally. This means we cannot always get what we want; we need to pursue the relationships we want, which come with commitments. A good example is family life. Families cannot exist if every person does what they want all the time. Inevitably there is give and take, and one person gets to do what they want one day and another person another day. As long as this operates in a fair way and one person does not dominate, family life works in a way which benefits all. This kind of approach, relational autonomy supporters argue, can apply more widely. We cannot always get what we want, but we promote relationships which value each person and are fair. So in the medical context it is not a straightforward case of asking 'What does this patient want?', but rather considering the patient within the context of the relationships in which they live.

WHEN SHOULD WE RESTRICT AUTONOMY?

We will now consider when it may be appropriate to restrict autonomy. Here are some possible arguments.

Beneficence

This is the principle that we should do good to others. In a medical context it requires medical professionals to promote the good of patients. This might come into conflict with the principle of autonomy where a patient is refusing beneficial treatment which is harmful. We will not discuss this further here because it underpins the concept of paternalism which we will discuss in Debate 2 below.

Non-malfeasance

This is the principle that we should not harm others. This also can conflict with autonomy in a case where a patient is requesting treatment that is harmful. Arguably the scenario of body dysmorphic disorder mentioned earlier is one example. This principle will also be discussed in Debate 2 and so we will only discuss it briefly here.

It is worth noting that some commentators argue that the principle of non-malfeasance (not harming others) is a stronger principle than beneficence (doing good for others). Most people readily acknowledge they do not do all they could to help others (they could give more money to charity, for example). However, they may hope that they rarely harm others. In the medical context, where doctors have a special duty to care for patients, this distinction between doing good and not harming may be weaker than in other contexts.

Justice

The concept of justice is complex, and there are many different views on quite what it means. In the medical context it means ensuring that people are treated fairly. One good example where this might infringe autonomy is the area of healthcare rationing. A patient may seek an expensive treatment, but be denied it on the basis that the NHS cannot afford it or that other patients have a greater call on resources than the first patient. As long as the process which determines how healthcare resources are allocated is fair, this may be an acceptable limit.

The interests of others

As we have already mentioned, it is generally agreed that autonomy can be interfered with if what someone wants to do will harm someone else. You cannot rely on the principle of autonomy to drive in excess of the speed limit. However, as the following case shows, this does not mean that a person can be operated on in order to benefit others.

Controversial case

St George's Healthcare NHS Trust v S[13]

A woman in labour was told that she needed a Caesarean section, and that without such an operation she and the foetus she was carrying would die. Despite her refusal to consent, the operation was carried out. The Court of Appeal held this to be unlawful. Great weight was placed on the importance of the right to bodily integrity. Not even the fact that she and the foetus would die without the operation provided a good enough reason to justify carrying out the Caesarean without her consent.

We shall explore these issues further in Chapter 2.

---

[13] *St George's Healthcare NHS Trust v S* [1998] 3 All ER 673.

ARE THERE BETTER ALTERNATIVE PRINCIPLES?

If we were not to rely on the concept of autonomy, what other principles might be used?

Dignity

Some commentators emphasise the importance of dignity. Charles Foster has argued that dignity is the central principle in bioethics. He defines dignity as 'objective human flourishing':[14] it is about thriving as a human. Foster argues that an ethical analysis requires a concept of dignity:[15]

> It is wrong to use the head of a dead person as a football, for medical students to practise vaginal examinations on a woman in permanent vegetative state or to let youths at a Casualty Department gaze lustfully at the undraped body of a seriously brain-damaged girl – even though she enjoys their attention. The wrongness can only properly be described in the language of dignity.

However, many others have been sceptical about whether dignity can be defined in a precise way.[16] What exactly is the 'objective human flourishing' to which Foster refers?

It is clear that dignity is not the same as respecting autonomous decisions, although that may be a part of respecting a person's dignity in some situations. Most supporters of dignity are referring to the special status of people. Human beings are precious, and we should not allow people to be treated as objects. Hence many supporters of dignity argue that people should not sell their organs, because that would demean the special status of the body. Suzy Killmister[17] argues that dignity can be distinguished from autonomy because autonomy concerns self-government, while dignity concerns self-worth. Mary Neal suggests that dignity should:

> reflect a valuing of the sense in which human existence (perhaps uniquely) embodies a union between the fragile/material/finite and the transcendent/sublime/immortal. In valuing us because of, and not in spite of/regardless of our vulnerability.[18]

---

[14] C. Foster, *Choosing Life, Choosing Death: The Tyranny of Autonomy in Medical Ethics and Law* (Hart Publishing, 2009), 6.

[15] C. Foster, 'Human dignity in bioethics and law' (2015) 41 *Journal of Medical Ethics* 935, 936. For a full discussion see C. Foster, *Human Dignity in Bioethics and the Law* (Hart Publishing, 2011).

[16] R. Brownsword, 'Bioethics today, bioethics tomorrow: stem cell research and the "dignitarian alliance"' (2003) *Notre Dame Journal of Law, Ethics and Public Policy* 15.

[17] S. Killmister, 'Dignity: not such a useless concept' (2010) 36 *Journal of Medical Ethics* 160.

[18] M. Neal, 'Not gods but animals: human dignity and vulnerable subjecthood' (2012) 33 *Liverpool Law Review* 177, 186.

The problem is that what seems undignified to one person does not to another. In short, indignity, critics claim, is a label for things people instinctively do not like. And that does not provide a good reason for enforcing dignity as a legal principle.

Ethic of care

The ethic of care has become an influential approach to questions of ethics. Its starting point is that we all have needs that must be met if we are to live. These needs are typically met by the care of others. The provision of care is, therefore, of central importance to life and plays an essential role in society. We cannot live a life where we are not cared for or do not care for another. Yet, despite its central importance, care has been largely ignored in society and by the law.[19] Care work goes unpaid and unrecognised; carers are given few legal rights by virtue of their care; and philosophers construct grand theories that have little meaning in a care-filled life. Autonomy is the prime example of this. The notion of being free to do what one wants is a sick joke to a parent caring for a baby, or someone caring for a demented relative. Most people's lives are marked by fulfilling their obligations to care for others, rather than exercising their free autonomy. Many supporters of ethics of care take a feminist angle on this issue, and argue that the lack of attention paid to care reflects the fact that the majority of care is performed by women.

The ethic of care, therefore, rather than valuing individual freedom, values the interdependency of and mutuality in relationships. Susan Wolf has argued:

> By depicting the moral community as a set of atomistic and self-serving individuals, [liberal individualism] strips away relationships that are morally central. This not only is impoverished, but may also be harmful, because it encourages disregard of those bonds. It is also inaccurate; developing children as well as full-grown adults are profoundly interdependent. Indeed, we are so interdependent that we cannot even understand the terms of moral debate without some community process and shared understanding.[20]

There are two points particularly to bring out about an ethic of care, which mark it out from other approaches. First, it elevates to primary position good caring relationships. So when faced with an ethical dilemma, the question is not: 'What rights do I have?' but rather questions like: 'How can I best express my caring responsibilities?' and 'How can I best deal with vulnerability, suffering and dependence?'[21]

---

[19] J. Herring, *Caring and the Law* (Hart Publishing, 2013).
[20] S. Wolf, 'Introduction: Gender and feminism in bioethics' in S. Wolf (ed.), *Feminism and Bioethics* (Oxford University Press, 1996), 17–18.
[21] I. Gremmen, G. Widdershoven and A. Beekman, 'Ulysses arrangements in psychiatry: a matter of good care?' (2008) 34 *Journal of Medical Ethics* 77.

Second, the ethic of care tends to reject approaches based on grand principles, such as justice, dignity or autonomy. Instead it seeks to find a tailored response to the particular relation and context. So what might be an appropriate caring response in one situation might not be appropriate in another similar cases. Hence an ethic of care of approach often responds to a situation by saying, 'We need to find out more details and talk through the issues with the parties.' This can be a rather frustrating response to some, but it reflects the emphasis the ethic of care places on the particularities of the relationships involved.

Critics of an ethic of care argue that the notion of care is too vague.[22] There is a danger that an ethic of care may glamorise care and ignore the fact that abuse can take place within a caring relationship. This danger may be exacerbated by the downplaying of individual rights within an ethic of care analysis. Many supporters of an ethic of care would accept that more work needs to be done to 'flesh' out the concept, and that it is in the relatively early days of development.

Virtue ethics

Virtue ethics focus on assessing the attitudes motivating a person's actions, rather than on their consequences. It is the character of a person that matters more than what they achieve. James Rachels suggests that a virtue is 'a trait of character, manifested in habitual action, which it is good for a person to have'.[23] The emphasis in virtue ethics approaches tends to be on issues such as compassion – honesty and kindness – rather than on autonomy or justice.

Some virtue ethicists go so far as to suggest that consequences of an act are utterly irrelevant, but others argue that the two tend to go hand in hand. Philippa Foot explains:

> Men and women need to be industrious and tenacious of purpose not only so as to be able to house, clothe and feed themselves, but also to pursue human ends having to do with love and friendship. They need the ability to form family ties, friendships and special relations with neighbours. They also need codes of conduct. And how could they have all these things without virtues such as loyalty, fairness, kindness and in certain circumstances obedience?[24]

Critics complain that a great deal of harm can be done by a well-motivated person. Some terrible things have been done by dedicated and brave people. Further, legal critics claim that the law cannot be based on motivation because it is impossible to assess. It also provides limited guidance to a doctor wanting to know what to do in the face of a particular dilemma. Telling them to be kind or compassionate may not be very helpful.

---

[22] P. Allmark, 'Can there be an ethics of care?' in K. Fulford, D. Dickenson and T. Murray (eds), *Healthcare Ethics and Human Values* (Blackwell, 2002).
[23] J. Rachels, *The Elements of Moral Philosophy* (McGraw-Hill, 1999), 23.
[24] P. Foot, *Natural Goodness* (Oxford University Press, 2001), 44.

Conclusion

As can be seen, there is no straightforward answer to the question of whether we should respect autonomy. In part this is because much depends on what is meant by autonomy: do we mean the liberty to be left alone, or the power to direct our futures? Further, there is uncertainty over what constitutes an autonomous choice that must be respected. There are also other competing values that may be at least as important as autonomy, such as care and virtue. It may be that there are some times in our lives when the freedom to act as we wish is treasured most, and in others the importance of care and protection is valued more. Perhaps what might be widely agreed is that autonomy is important, but it is by no means the only value to be taken into account.

Debate 2

Should doctors act paternalistically?

In the past, the idea of 'doctor knows best' was a prevalent approach to medical decision making, with doctors, rather than patients, making treatment decisions. This approach is known as 'paternalism', because the doctor acts rather like a father making decisions for a child. James Childress has called this the 'arrogant enforcement of "the good" for others'.[25] However, over the past forty years, the principle of respect for autonomy has gained considerable support in medical ethics, while support for a paternalistic model, with doctors making choices on behalf of patients for their own good, has correspondingly waned.[26] Autonomy now informs much of the legal regulation of medical and reproductive practice, which is focused on informing patients and respecting their choices.

Defining Paternalism

A basic definition of paternalism is the restriction of individuals' liberty without their consent, where the justification for doing so is either to benefit individuals or to prevent them from self-harming – what John Kleinig has called 'enforced benevolence'.[27] To benefit someone, in the paternalistic sense, does not mean doing what they wish you to do, but instead acting on your own view of what is harmful to and beneficial for the other person.[28] Paternalism often results where one person considers that they are better placed to determine what is good for someone else, due to the possession of greater knowledge, foresight or experience.[29] Bernard Gert and others suggest that an action is not

---

[25] J. Childress, 'The place of autonomy in bioethics' (1990) 20 *Hastings Center Report* 12, 15.

[26] See, e.g., G. Dworkin, 'Can you trust autonomy?' (2003) 33 *Hastings Center Report* 42, 42.

[27] J. Kleinig (ed.), *Paternalism* (Manchester University Press, 1983), 4.

[28] B. Gert et al., *Bioethics: A Return to Fundamentals* (Oxford University Press, 1997), 198, 203.

[29] E. Loewy, *Textbook of Medical Ethics* (Plenum Medical Book Co., 1989), 68.

paternalistic if the subject consents to the action, nor if the person behaving paternalistically expects the subject's immediately forthcoming consent. For example, it is not paternalistic to pull someone from in front of an oncoming car that they do not see, as it is likely that they would consent to the touching immediately they realised what was happening (unless they were deliberately trying to self-harm). However, this latter form of non-paternalism only holds if it is not possible to ask for prior consent.[30]

Paternalism can range from coercion to merely limits on liberty.[31] In the medical context, coercion is unlikely, although it might happen if a patient is declared incapable of making decisions for himself and is then subjected to a treatment. A doctor might instead act paternalistically by simply making a treatment decision for the patient without consulting him, or not offer him a treatment he might have wanted. Alternatively, the doctor might withhold information or deliberately misinform the patient to press him towards a particular course of action.

PATERNALISM AND AUTONOMY

One of the main objections to doctors acting paternalistically is that this constitutes a failure to respect an individual's autonomy. Usually, the law follows what is known as the 'harm principle', which tells us that we should allow people to make their own choices about how to act, except where their actions will harm or restrict the liberty of other people. The fact that the act is good for those people themselves is not sufficient reason. There are a number of justifications for this position, one of which is, as Mill argued, that allowing individuals the greatest liberty possible best promotes individual development.[32] Mill's idea of individuality also encompasses a right to be different, so that each person may choose to live their life as they choose.[33] If we accept this view, we accept the empirical claim that individuals are best placed to make choices that are good for them, and therefore that allowing individuals to make their own choices will best promote their interests. We explored more reasons why respect for autonomy is important in Debate 1 in this chapter.

JUSTIFICATIONS FOR PATERNALISM

If autonomy is recognised as so important why, then, might a doctor want to act paternalistically?

---

[30] B. Gert et al., *Bioethics: A Return to Fundamentals* (Oxford University Press, 1997), 203.

[31] T.L. Beauchamp, 'Medical paternalism, voluntariness and comprehension' in J. Howie (ed.), *Medical Paternalism, Voluntariness and Comprehension* (Southern Illinois University Press, 1983), 126.

[32] Ibid., 128.

[33] See, e.g., M. Charlesworth, *Bioethics in a Liberal Society* (Cambridge University Press, 1993), 20.

Bad decisions

One reason is that the doctor might think that the patient is making a bad decision given the risks it entails. Let us use an example to explore this:

Scenario to ponder

A patient, Ian, is suffering from late-stage cancer and has a month to live. There is a new treatment that might help him, but it only has a 5 per cent success rate and tends to extend life for only another year. It is also quite unpleasant. A paternalistic doctor might decide that it is not worth it, and that Ian would be better off enjoying his final month, rather than going through the unpleasantness of the treatment that might not pay off. An easeful death now would, in the doctor's view, be preferable to fighting for another year with little chance of success. So the doctor does not tell Ian about the treatment.

One of the things that is wrong with the doctor acting in this way towards Ian is that medical decisions are usually highly personal and subjective to a great degree. Often in such cases, only the patient can know how best to fulfil their own desires about the course of their life. While many treatments carry risks, a patient could quite rationally regard the risks as worth taking if they give them the chance to live a little longer, if this is what they want. For Ian, the possibility of that extra year with his family might be worth the unpleasantness of the treatment, even if the chance of success is very low. As Mill argues, each person 'has means of knowledge immediately surpassing those that can be possessed by anyone else' to determine what is in the interests of his or her well-being.[34] What kinds of risks we want to take on relative to the benefits they bring is highly personal.

If we flip the example around, we can see another problem with doctors acting paternalistically. Imagine the doctor thinks Ian should fight on to live the extra year, while Ian would prefer to allow nature to run its course now. He has said his goodbyes and made his peace; he is ready. The paternalistic doctor could give him the treatment anyway, or misinform him about the chances or the side-effects to press him into taking it. In this case, the doctor would be pushing Ian to pursue the extra year of life, despite the unpleasantness he will experience as a result. The objection to paternalism here is that coercing people into choices based on beliefs they do not hold, or to pursue goals they do not value, does not in fact benefit them. While there may be some things that are objectively good for people, and longer life might be one of them, if they do not value them then their lives may not be improved by having them – to benefit from them, we have to want them.[35] As Will Kymlicka argues, 'no life goes

---

[34] J.S. Mill, *On Liberty* (Cosimo Classics, 2005 [1859]), 277.
[35] J. Kleinig (ed.), *Paternalism* (Manchester University Press, 1983), 26.

better by being led from the outside according to values the person doesn't endorse. My life only goes better if I'm leading it from the inside, according to my beliefs about value'.[36]

Another example is this:

Scenario to ponder

Following a car accident, Alan requires a transfusion or he will die. However, as a Jehovah's Witness, Alan believes that receiving blood from another person contravenes certain passages in the Bible, and that by doing so he will suffer eternal damnation in the afterlife.[37] He therefore refuses the treatment.

In that scenario the doctor may think that it is clearly in Alan's best interests to receive the treatment. However, from the perspective of Alan's belief, the choice to refuse transfusions is in his best interests. Requiring him to receive a blood transfusion so that he will live may give him some actual benefit, but for him personally it will cause much greater damage. Even aside from debate about the validity of his beliefs, he will be actually harmed in his own mind because his body will have been desecrated, and he would live believing he was damned – both of which will likely have an adverse effect on his quality of life. A paternalistic doctor who gives Alan a blood transfusion against his wishes or without informing him would not be making Alan's life go better for him.

It seems, then, that the paternalistic doctor should actually respect patients' views and allow them to make their own choices. However, there are a number of good arguments in favour of doctors acting paternalistically. In many debates about paternalism, autonomy is held up as the moral 'trump card'.[38] However, arguably, there are other, morally valid competing principles that can justify interventions for someone else's good, such as the principle of beneficence, which we discussed in Debate 1.

One argument, which leads into a range of other justifications for paternalism, is that giving prime place to individual decisions often means that more subtle, unforeseen or longer-term consequences of a choice are not considered when an individual chooses how to act. As Bonnie Steinbock and Ron McClamrock argue, autonomy often trumps other moral concerns because 'it is usually easier to identify benefits than harms, particularly long-term harms'.[39] This might be particularly true in a medical context, where the doctor has more experience of

[36] W. Kymlicka, 'Liberalism and communitarianism' (1988) 18 *Canadian Journal of Philosophy* 188, 183.

[37] R. Macklin, *Mortal Choices: Bioethics in Today's World* (Pantheon, 1987), 13.

[38] M. Charlesworth, *Bioethics in a Liberal Society* (Cambridge University Press, 1993), 12.

[39] B. Steinbock and R. McClamrock, 'When is birth unfair to the child?' (1994) 24 *Hastings Center Report* 15, 41.

seeing the consequences of different treatment options and the impacts they have on patients' lives. For example, an experienced doctor proposes a painful treatment, but the patient refuses it, fearing the pain. The doctor knows many of her patients fear the pain, but all of them are afterwards glad they had the surgery. Might not the doctor in such a case feel that she has the experience to know the patient will be better off with the surgery? However, this is really an argument for the doctor providing more information, rather than making a decision for the patient, because it does not address the essential problems that others are unlikely to know what is good for someone better than the person themselves; nor that people derive value from being able to make their own choices per se.

Lack of capacity and paternalism

Other, perhaps better, justifications for paternalistic interventions can be made when we engage with some of the specific complexities of allowing people to make their own medical decisions. These include issues about what constitutes competence, influences that may affect how we make decisions and the complexity of determining whether expressed desires are the individual's actual desires. We will be exploring these themes further in Chapter 3.

H.L.A. Hart argued that paternalism can be justified if we believe that there are factors that diminish a person's capacity to make free and informed choices.[40] A reduction in our ability to make such choices might be so extensive that we lack the competence to make such decisions, in which case these interventions probably do not fall within the definition of paternalism, because paternalism really only relates to overriding the choices of people with the capacity to make free choices. For example, a person suffering from paranoid delusions might lack control over their decisions, and hence the decisions they make might be regarded as what Gert and others call 'volitional incompetence', where irrational decisions harm the decision maker without a rational belief about a corresponding benefit for anyone.[41] Overriding these decisions would not in fact be paternalism.

However, competence to make decisions is more complex than this simple case. Competence refers to the capacity to understand the benefits and risks in order to be able to make a rational decision (what Gert calls 'cognitive competence'[42]). In fact, as Simon Lee points out, respect for autonomy rests on the assumption that people are rational beings, able to assess information and make choices by weighing the merits of choices that are open to them.[43] People's choices are respected precisely because they have the capacity to make choices that can be respected, because they are reasoned and reflect their desires. However, it is possible to be rational and capable of weighing information and choices generally and yet still lack full competence to make a decision, and this will be especially so

[40] H. Hart, *Law, Liberty and Morality* (Oxford University Press, 1963).

[41] B. Gert et al., *Bioethics: A Return to Fundamentals* (Oxford University Press, 1997), 208.

[42] S. Lee, *Law and Morals: Warnock, Gillick and Beyond* (Oxford University Press, 1986), 64.

[43] S. Lee, *Law and Morals: Warnock, Gillick and Beyond* (Oxford University Press, 1986).

of medical decisions. Here, we are not talking about someone who cannot make a rational decision but about someone whose competence is reduced due to lack of information or the capacity to understand complex medical information.

These factors may lead a patient to make a decision that is not in their best interests, not because they do not wish to be cured but because they are not able to rationalise based on the information before them.[44] For example, let us consider Alan again, but imagine this time he chooses not to have a blood transfusion, not because of his beliefs but because he does not fully understand what a transfusion is. His objective is to live, and he understands that the transfusion will help him live. However, he refuses it because he has been told that there is a very small risk of contracting a disease from the blood – not because he considers the risk too high, but because he does not fully understand the statistics given to him to explain the risk.

This kind of lack of understanding may challenge the anti-paternalistic stance, which rests on the assumption that people make choices that they believe are best for them and that they are best placed to do so. In this instance, Alan's specific choice about the transfusion does not accord with his overall choice – to have treatments that will save him – and he is perhaps not best placed to make the choice because he does not understand the nature of his choice. Another example of this may be a patient who has needle phobia and who, while wanting to have an operation, panics on seeing the needle needed to give the necessary anaesthetic and withdraws consent.[45] That patient's refusal is the result of panic, not a considered decision. Jay Katz illuminates what is happening in this kind of instance by separating self-determination into two components to pose two questions. First, to what extent should an individual's *choices* be respected; and, second, to what extent should an individual's *thinking about choices* be respected?[46] It may be that if Alan's thinking about his choice is problematic or based on lack of understanding, we may justifiably not respect it. For this reason, misconceptions and misunderstanding of information may provide sufficient reasons to justify action on beneficent grounds and to place respecting autonomy below beneficence as a reason to act. Hence, in this kind of case, as David Archard suggests, paternalism may be defensible where people 'misrecognise' what is for their own good, and that others 'do no wrong, indeed do right, in trying to promote what they can better recognise to be for the other's good'.[47] Some of these scenarios may be better understood as cases where a patient lacks

---

[44] See, e.g., *Sidaway v Governors of Bethlehem Royal Hospital* [1985] AC 871, 904–05 per Lord Templeman.

[45] *Re MB* [2007] EWCA Civ 1361.

[46] J. Katz, 'Can principles survive in situations of critical care?' in J. Moskop and L. Kopelman (eds), *Can Principles Survive in Situations of Critical Care?* (D Reidel and Kluwer Academic, 1985), 55.

[47] David Archard premises this position by stating that this applies only where other objections to paternalism are not open, that is where the chooser will not violate a moral rule in making and enforcing the choice, and the good does not require the person to have any belief about its worthwhileness or for the choice to have been made autonomously: D. Archard, 'For our own good' (1994) 72 *Australasian Journal of Philosophy* 283, 290.

capacity, and so autonomy does not apply, rather than cases where paternalism trumps autonomy.

Paternalism and weakness of will

An alternative argument in favour of paternalism is the 'weakness of will' argument; that sometimes people can judge what would be good for them but still choose not to do it.[48] In the medical context, this might include refusing an unpleasant treatment, such as a colonoscopy or chemotherapy, even though the individual knows it will benefit their health. In these cases, Kymlicka argues paternalism may be justified where weakness of will can be overcome by paternalistically providing an incentive for people to make better choices.[49] Such arguments work best when they entail only a small infringement of a person's liberty, and for a goal that it is clear the person actually wants to achieve. The needle-phobia cases are good examples of this sort of situation.

Paternalism and choice

A final, somewhat subtle argument that might justify a doctor's acting paternalistically in some cases rests on the complexity of how people express their choices. One complexity of respecting autonomy that we should take account of is that people communicate their preferences in many ways – in non-verbal form, as well as in written and verbal forms. Sometimes people say one thing but actually mean another. People may need cajoling into something, and may be looking for this in refusing. People may be petulant or aggressive, or bury their heads in the sand because they are afraid. If we focus on only their explicit, present expression of choice and their competence, we may ignore what they are really trying or wanting to say. In each case, there may be a place for paternalistic interventions to promote what appears to be a person's actual desires, even if they cannot express them. This need not extend to coercing a choice, but perhaps might involve recommending counselling before a treatment, or requiring a patient to undergo a cooling-off period. Their liberty is somewhat restricted, with the aim of promoting their interests through determining what they actually want.

Paternalism and conflicting choices

Sometimes, as James Childress suggests, people also express ambivalent or contradictory preferences.[50] By this, Childress means that people give consent and withdraw it, or change their preferences over time. Therefore:

> in discharging our obligations under the principle of respect for autonomy, we not only have to determine whether a patient is autonomous and just what he or she is choosing, we also have to put that patient's present consents and dissents in a broad temporal context encompassing both the past and the future.[51]

---

[48] The chocolate truffles mentioned earlier are an example of this.
[49] W. Kymlicka, *Contemporary Political Philosophy* (Clarendon Press, 1990), 232, Footnote 1.
[50] J. Childress, 'The place of autonomy in bioethics' (1990) 20 *Hastings Center Report* 12, 13.
[51] Ibid.

In some cases, it may be justified to override a current consent paternalistically to determine what the patient's authentic desires are. For example, imagine Alan had not refused a transfusion despite being a Jehovah's Witness, and that although he followed the religion's teachings, in the face of illness he chose to be treated. However, imagine that the doctor knows that for a long time Alan has been committed to refusing a transfusion. If we wanted to respect Alan's choice, the doctor might hold off giving the transfusion for a little while to give him time to be sure of his own mind.

Paternalism and promoting choice

Each of these justifications for limited paternalistic interventions is based on similar thinking – that although paternalism is presumptively objectionable, it may be justified where it actually promotes individuals' ability to make the choices they actually want to make, or will wish to make when they possess full information. However, each still faces considerable challenges in overriding the importance of respecting autonomy. We might also be better seeing many of these situations not as a choice between paternalism and respect for autonomy, and instead as a context in which we need to do more to provide the conditions to help people exercise their autonomy fully. As John Kleinig points out, protecting individual liberty does not require people to be let completely alone:[52] they are still open to be advised and informed; we can still bring our perceptions to bear on them. The difference is that we cannot override their choices with our own.[53] Similarly, Katz argues that clearly defined exceptions to respecting autonomy in medical decision making will enhance, rather than undermine, promotion of self-determination.[54] Katz argues that in medical decision making, things can be done to enhance a person's capacity for thinking about their choices, such as testing their understanding of the information presented to them and engaging them in discussion of why they have chosen as they have.[55] Katz is not arguing that people's choices should not be honoured, even where they are influenced by psychological factors. Rather, he argues that there is a place for engaging with how an individual is thinking about their choices to help them address 'distortions' that may affect their thinking. Katz cites 'ignorance, misconceptions, exaggerated fears, and magical hopes about tests and therapeutic interventions' as influences that can distort thinking about a choice in medicine.[56] In doing so, individuals' thinking can be

---

[52] J. Kleinig (ed.), *Paternalism* (Manchester University Press, 1983), 27.
[53] J.S. Mill, *On Liberty* (Cosimo Classics, 2005 [1859]), 277.
[54] J. Katz, 'Can principles survive in situations of critical care?' in J. Moskop and L. Kopelman (eds), *Can Principles Survive in Situations of Critical Care?* (D Reidel and Kluwer Academic, 1985), 42.
[55] Ibid., 55.
[56] Ibid., 56.

influenced towards 'greater rationality and consciousness' by clarifying uncertainties, dispelling fears and addressing confusions that might arise from previous experiences.[57] In taking time to present information carefully, and listening attentively to patients, a doctor might often be able to take a beneficent stance and encourage patients to choose well, without forcing good upon them when they do not want it. It can also help patients to make the decisions that they may wish to make but do not in the first instance.

CONCLUSION

Nowadays few medical professionals or ethicists would claim to be out-and-out paternalists. The idea that doctors should simply make decisions for patients and that patients must do what they are told has few, if any, supporters. However, as this debate has shown, it is far from clear that paternalism is never justified. In particular, where the patient's autonomy is compromised, the line between acting paternalistically and seeking to comply with a patient's genuine wishes becomes blurred. There are some who would want to hold out against any paternalism and insist on respecting the decision of a patient unless it is quite clear that the patient lacks capacity. Others argue that an impaired decision cannot be used to justify doing something that harms a patient.

Debate 3

To what extent should the law be guided by utilitarianism?

INTRODUCTION

Utilitarianism has its roots in the eighteenth-century work of David Hume, but came to prominence in the nineteenth century following the work of Jeremy Bentham and John Stuart Mill. Bentham's *Principle of Utility* held that in deciding how to act, we should choose the course that appears to best promote the happiness, pleasure or good of all parties who will be affected.[58] An act would conform to this principle if it tended to promote, on balance, greater happiness than pain, taking account of the intensity, duration, certainty and nearness of the pleasure it caused, as well as its likelihood of causing greater subsequent pleasures, whether it might have the opposite effect of producing pain as well, and the number of people it would affect.[59] This form of utilitarianism focuses on the consequences of actions and the happiness they will produce, not for the individual but collectively for all concerned. As Mill noted, 'between his own happiness and that of others, utilitarianism requires [a person] to be as strictly

---

[57] Ibid., 58.

[58] See J. Bentham, *Introduction to the Principles of Morals and Legislation* (Hafner, 1948 [1781]).

[59] Ibid.

impartial as a disinterested and benevolent spectator'.[60] This form of utilitarianism is now known as 'Act Utilitarianism', because it focuses on determining which acts are morally good or bad.

Bentham's early model of utility has been modified and refined in a variety of ways. One refinement is the theory of Rule Utilitarianism, which holds that rather than judge the rightness or otherwise of each particular action, we should compose a set of rules that promote optimal happiness for all. James Rachels has also noted a form of utilitarianism he calls Multiple Strategies Utilitarianism, where we aim to promote the greatest general happiness but can take a variety of approaches to achieve it. Another modification focuses on the satisfaction of preferences as an approach to promoting happiness, and is sometimes referred to as Preference Utilitarianism.

Though they differ in some degree, each version of utilitarianism rests on some conception of general good which must be defined to determine what the good and bad consequences of our actions will be. Between these views there is considerable disagreement about what is meant by 'happiness' or 'good'.

WHAT IS GOOD?

There are three major, competing positions on how we determine what defines value or what is good in life. First, the classical utilitarian view asserts that the good life is determined by the happiness or pleasure of which we are conscious, or, as Peter Singer describes it, the view that 'only some form of desirable consciousness can be intrinsically good'.[61] A proponent of the first view, Henry Sidgwick, argued that the ultimate good can only be conceived of as desirable consciousness, that nothing is good intrinsically, but only as some kind of conscious experience. This need not be a hedonistic approach. For example, Mill argued that human happiness was fulfilled in greater part by the higher pleasures, and argued that some pleasures were more desirable and valuable than others.[62] For example, people would not forgo intelligence for the fulfilment of lower pleasures, because a sense of dignity is an integral part of happiness.[63]

The second view holds that it is what people prefer or demand that determines value. The Desire Fulfilment approach holds that we define the good life not by simple happiness, but by the maximisation of people's preferences or desires; we live the good life when our desires are fulfilled. On this view, nothing has any intrinsic good or bad qualities. Instead, things have value only as they meet our desires. Each desire should be satisfied for its own sake, and the only reason not to satisfy a desire arises where others have competing

---

[60] J.S. Mill, *Utilitarianism* (Bobbs-Merrill, 1956 [1863]), 21.

[61] P. Singer, *Ethics* (Oxford University Press, 1994), 181.

[62] J.S. Mill, 'Higher and lower pleasures' in P. Singer (ed.), *Ethics* (Oxford University Press, 1994), 201–02.

[63] Ibid., 203.

desires.[64] Applying this approach in a utilitarian model, the right act is the one that ensures the greatest number of demands is met, or the fewest are not left unfulfilled. Where these demands compete, some must be subordinated to others.[65]

The third view suggests that we can assemble lists of intrinsically valuable goods the possession of which make a good life. Derek Parfit has called this the Objective List Theory of defining the good life, and it holds that we can compile lists of basic aspects of well-being.[66] These basic goods cause us to experience pleasure and make our lives go well because they have intrinsic value. These things are good or bad for people regardless of whether a person would wish to have or avoid them, because they are good in themselves. Even if they do not produce much pleasure for some, they are no less valuable and important for having a good life. For example, John Finnis in his list of the basic forms of good includes sociability, such as friendship and love.[67]

There is disagreement about which conception of the good should be the basis of utilitarian theory, but we can probably accept that we need to do more than think about what makes us happy. As James Rachels argues, theories that focus only on defining the good life by things that make us feel good 'get things the wrong way round', because they suggest that things are good because they make us happy. Rachels suggests that this is incorrect, that instead things make us happy 'because we already think them good'.[68] Derek Parfit suggests that we might hold that what makes the good life is both possession of things that are intrinsically good *and* having the desire to possess them.[69]

ARGUMENTS IN FAVOUR OF UTILITARIANISM

One argument in favour of utilitarianism is that it matches how most people instinctively think and act. When deciding, for example, what to eat for tea, someone may weigh up the competing merits of taste, healthiness, time required for preparation and expense, and make their decision. Most people hope their actions will promote good consequences and avoid bad consequences. This approach, seeking to produce good consequences, is known as consequentialism. The approach, therefore, mirrors how decisions are generally made.

A linked point to this is that supporters claim it is a practical approach. A medical professional faced with a dilemma between doing either A or B can

---

[64] See, e.g., W. James, 'Good as the satisfaction of demands' in P. Singer, *Ethics* (Oxford University Press, 1994), 207.

[65] See ibid., 210.

[66] D. Parfit, 'What makes someone's life go best?' in P. Singer, *Ethics* (Oxford University Press, 1994), 239.

[67] J. Finnis, 'The basic values' in P. Singer (ed.), *Ethics* (Oxford University Press, 1994), 234.

[68] J. Rachels, *The Elements of Moral Philosophy* (McGraw-Hill, 1999), 104.

[69] D. Parfit, 'What makes someone's life go best?' in P. Singer, *Ethics* (Oxford University Press, 1994).

quickly calculate the good and bad consequences that will flow from each, and decide what is the best option. Alternative approaches, focusing on abstract principles, seem far removed from the real world. The ethereal concepts of promoting dignity, or truth or justice, may seem too abstract compared with the concrete realities of what will or will not benefit a patient.

A final point about consequentialism is that it provides a ready framework for people who disagree. Imagine two doctors disagreeing about whether a patient should be given treatment A or B. If they are consequentialists, they can discuss the good and bad consequences that will flow from the treatment. They may try to persuade each other that they have miscalculated what the consequences are. If, however, they are not consequentialists and one doctor says that to do A will be undignified and the other doctor says it will not, it is not easy to see how their dispute can be resolved. It comes down to base understandings of what is or is not dignified.

OBJECTIONS TO UTILITARIANISM

Utilitarianism asks too much of us

Consequentialist theories like utilitarianism hold that actions should be judged *solely* according to the consequences they produce. For example, classical utilitarian theories argue we should judge actions on whether they increase or decrease pleasure.[70] Utilitarianism also demands complete impartiality in judging the effects of our actions. One of the objections to using utilitarianism to guide us is that such theories ask too much of us. As Dan Brock states, they 'confuse what is morally required or obligatory with what, though praiseworthy, goes beyond the call of duty'.[71]

Susan Wolf seeks to unpack this criticism by raising a number of reasons why these demands are too high. First, consequentialism requires us to commit ourselves to moral saintliness that does not 'constitute a model of personal well-being toward which it would be particularly rational or good or desirable for a human being to strive'.[72] This is because possessing this many moral virtues prevents the saint from possessing enough other, non-moral virtues that contribute to 'a healthy, well-rounded, richly developed character.'[73] All the time the saint must spend doing good deeds for others prevents him from pursuing his own pleasures, such as playing the piano, because he must always make the moral choice and forgo other aspects of life. Wolf argues that his life and character, though worthy, is underdeveloped.[74]

---

[70] See, e.g., J. Bentham, *Introduction to the Principles of Morals and Legislation* (Hafner, 1948 [1781]); J. Rachels, *The Elements of Moral Philosophy* (McGraw-Hill, 1999), 92.

[71] D. Brock, 'Utilitarianism' in T. Regan and D. Van DeVeer (eds), *And Justice for All: New Introductory Essays in Ethics and Public Policy* (Rowman and Allanheld, 1982), 239.

[72] S. Wolf, 'Moral saints' in P. Singer (ed.), *Ethics* (Oxford University Press, 1994), 346.

[73] Ibid., 347.

[74] Ibid.

Wolf's view is intuitively appealing, because it recognises that we do value in our lives things other than doing good for people. We value non-moral virtues both in ourselves and others, which, she points out, is demonstrated by the admiration we have for people who possess non-moral virtues such as wit or athleticism. This common-sense argument alone may not be sound, for as J.J.C. Smart argues, intuitive common sense about matters of ethics does not of itself provide a sound answer to moral questions.[75]

We can use Wolf's position to respond to Smart's view, however, as she points out that non-moral virtues can help to produce general happiness inadvertently – for example, a brilliant musician may make the world happier with his music. But consequentialism would prevent the moral saint from pursuing such virtues, because at each moment when he sits down to practise, though this may in the future promote the general good, among the actions he can choose from it is not the choice that will do so best, and so he cannot practise.[76] Wolf's point is correct if we regard consequentialist theories as directing us to find the best action we can take to promote the good.

We might instead conceive of consequentialism as requiring us, when faced with a choice of actions, to choose the one with the best consequences. If the choices the saint had before him were to play the piano or go to sleep, because it is late at night, then he could play the piano and still be a good consequentialist. However, the problem with this view, which makes Wolf's point remain quite strong, is that consequentialism in this account doesn't show how we restrict what our choices *are*. So this argument will only hold if it also includes some way of limiting the choices we might see as before us, otherwise we could always imagine something virtuous to do that would then have to trump pursuing non-moral virtues, because, as Wolf notes, our potential to act morally all the time is unlimited.[77]

Consequentialism is too demanding also because, by requiring us to sacrifice pursuit of all non-moral virtues that we desire, it inadvertently treats the saint as morally unimportant. His desires and autonomy are not respected, because he is required always to subsume them to the greater good. Society is treated as an end, but he becomes a means to that end because he must always act as the consequences for society demand, not as he would choose if able. As Wolf argues, we should recognise that each person deserves the good things in life, and allow for this in our choices of how to act.[78] That is, we should ask whether it is 'always better to be morally better', and not assume that morality is always the most important goal to pursue.[79]

Another objection to utilitarianism is that it prevents us from favouring people we love by requiring us to be impartial. This would make it difficult for

[75] In Smart's words, 'so much the worse for the common moral consciousness'. See J.J.C. Smart, *An Outline of a System of Utilitarian Ethics*, as cited in J. Rachels, *The Elements of Moral Philosophy* (McGraw-Hill, 1999), 114.
[76] S. Wolf, 'Moral saints' in P. Singer (ed.), *Ethics* (Oxford University Press, 1994), 354.
[77] Ibid., 357–58.
[78] Ibid., 359.
[79] Ibid., 361.

us to maintain relationships, leaving us lonely, as well as preventing the societal benefits of friendships, such as promoting social cohesion. For example, following William Goodwin's example, where we could only save one person from a burning building, consequentialism tells us we should save the person who will most benefit society, not our relatives or friends.[80] Is that putting too little weight on the obligations that arise from relationships?

A third objection is that utilitarianism might demand we take abhorrent actions in the name of the greater good, including ignoring considerations of justice or rights.[81] It could therefore justify wrongfully imprisoning an unpopular celebrity on the basis that the joy the public would feel would outweigh the misery of the celebrity.

Finally, utilitarianism also unreasonably demands that we be what R.M. Hare calls 'archangels', with 'infinite knowledge and clarity of thought and no partiality to self or other human weaknesses',[82] even though people are not able to think purely objectively and impartially, and lack all the information, time and self-subjugating ability they need to make perfect decisions.

CONCLUSION

Utilitarianism carries an appeal for many people because it seems to reflect how we make everyday decisions. It just seems common sense that we should produce good results. However, its appeal lessens when we come to difficult moral dilemmas, where its obligations appear too great and it can produce unpalatable consequences. It seems there can be no denying that it is a useful way of thinking about moral dilemmas, but it should not be used in isolation. It is one tool that an ethicist can use, but arguably should not be the only one.

Debate 4

Is it all a matter of opinion?

It is sometimes suggested that morals and ethics are just a matter of opinion, that we all have different views and we should respect that some people think differently about moral issues. This perspective is often raised when talking about other people's religious views, or the differences between countries and cultures. Such an approach is appealing if we value freedom of thought and action, cultural tolerance and acceptance of the views of others. In philosophy, this is known as 'Simple Subjectivism', a theory of ethics that rejects the existence of objective moral truths and suggests that moral opinions are merely statements or expressions of feelings, which are objectively neither right nor

---

[80] See W. Goodwin, 'The archbishop and the chambermaid' in P. Singer (ed.), *Ethics* (Oxford University Press, 1994), 313.

[81] See further J. Rachels, *The Elements of Moral Philosophy* (McGraw-Hill, 1999), 105.

[82] R. Hare, 'The structure of ethics and morals' in P. Singer (ed.), *Ethics* (Oxford University Press, 1994), 330.

wrong. Another variant is 'Emotivism', which holds that ethical judgements are *expressions* of our moral attitudes, often made to influence others.[83] These are descriptive theories, because they suggest that ethical judgements are simply descriptions or expressions of people's moral attitudes.[84] On both views, everyone's moral and ethical judgements are subjective and therefore equally valid.[85]

However, if we think about this a little more, it leads us to some problematic conclusions. If ethics are subjective then it means that whatever view someone takes, that view is justified by its very subjectivity. Their view is right simply because it is their view, and we must respect that. But the problem is that this means we are precluded from arguing that someone else's viewpoint is incorrect, and from presenting reasons why we think this. In fact, we cannot even have a moral argument of the kind we actually want to have. How can this be so? Simple Subjectivism holds that a moral opinion is merely a statement of opinion on an ethical question.[86] Although such statements may purport to be assertions of some objective moral standard, according to Simple Subjectivism they merely state that the individual approves or disapproves of something. As a result, ethical statements of this kind can never be objectively wrong, unless the person stating them is lying about their feelings. Such statements therefore cannot be contradicted. So if I say that I think murdering people is morally acceptable, you cannot contradict me except to say 'I don't believe you really think that'. From an Emotivism perspective, you could only say 'I understand that that is how you feel', because you could only think that I was expressing my feelings, and perhaps trying to influence you to share them. But if you had thought ethics were subjective, you couldn't actually tell me that I was wrong to think these things.

Even more problematically, if we think that ethics are subjective, then we cannot judge the ethical acceptability of someone else's behaviour, and so have no grounds for preventing them from acting in a way that causes harm. If I decide that killing people is morally acceptable, and you disagree but believe ethics to be subjective, you could not logically say to me 'Don't do that, it's wrong' and expect me to change my mind. You could only accept that we have different opinions on the matter, and there it ends. You would have to respect my viewpoint, even if you disagree with it. In fact, if we really believe that all ethical judgements are subjective and therefore equally sound, we should not even be trying to prove another's view wrong, because we should think the other's view as sound as our own. Therefore, accepting that all ethical judgements are subjective forces upon us a form of tolerance for the views of others that is not actually tolerance. Rather, it is only unthinking acceptance, because the premise removes all grounds for disputing the views of others save that they

---

[83] See, e.g., J. Rachels, 'Subjectivism' in P. Singer (ed.), *A Companion to Ethics* (Basil Blackwell, 1991), 432.

[84] See R. Hare, 'Universal Prescriptivism' in P. Singer (ed.), *A Companion to Ethics* (Basil Blackwell, 1991), 454.

[85] See R. Shafer-Landau, 'Ethical Subjectivism' in J. Feinberg (ed.), *Reason and Responsibility*, 10th edn (Wadsworth, 1999), 513.

[86] J. Rachels, *The Elements of Moral Philosophy*, 4th edn (McGraw-Hill, 2003), 33.

may be lying. This clearly does not accord with how we actually view the opinions of others in some cases, because people often debate matters of morality and ethics, and do not regard one another's views as equally sound. In these instances, each person who is arguing wants to show that the others are wrong and that they should act in a different way.

For the most part, when we criticise another's behaviour as unethical we are not just stating or expressing disapproval and telling others to act as we wish (as Simple Subjectivism and Emotivism would suggest), we are arguing that our view is *preferable* and that therefore that person should refrain from acting as they are. Believing that ethics is subjective fails to account for what people are really trying to do when they make ethical arguments, and this reveals what ethical 'truth' really is. When we argue about ethics and morals, we each present *reasons* in support of our viewpoint, and we are trying to convince the other person that our reasons are the most convincing. Morality and ethics do not lend themselves to the kind of truth found in science, where conclusions are supported by objective data. But this does not mean there are no 'truths' in another sense (although 'truth' is probably an unhelpful term here anyway). A good moral or ethical position is one supported by good reasons. So if you rejected the idea that morality and ethics are entirely subjective, you could then say to me, 'Murder is not OK, because it harms other people.' This is, in fact, how people do argue about morals and ethics. They are not merely shouting their opinions at one another, they are presenting reasons in the hope that their view will convince the other person.

There are good reasons why we need to accept that ethics are not subjective. As James Rachels rightly points out, a certain degree of agreement and certainty about how to behave is required for societies to function effectively.[87] If everyone's subjective views on what constituted acceptable behaviour were equally valid, there would be no certainty about how we should act. Someone might regard murder as morally acceptable, while others might believe that we should not interfere with others' bodily integrity. As one could never know which belief someone held, one could not predict how that person would act. We would have to constantly protect ourselves in case we came upon one of these would-be murderers, making social interaction very difficult.

And in fact, when we think about it, there is a surprisingly large amount on which we *do* agree. Our laws reflect the fact that, mostly, people agree that hurting others, stealing, going back on promises and so on are wrong. The main areas in which we *allow* for disagreement are actions that are self-regarding, such as homosexuality. This is partially because there is space for us to disagree, because we can act privately and not affect others. But on actions that affect other people, we have in fact usually come to a fair amount of agreement, and do not actually regard ethical views on these matters as subjective at all.

---

[87] J. Rachels, *The Elements of Moral Philosophy*, 4th edn (McGraw-Hill, 2003), 23–24.

Conclusion

'You are entitled to your opinion' has become somewhat of a catchphrase in debates in bars and between friends. Indeed, it is common to hear people suggest that morals are just a matter of personal opinion. In this debate we have seen that it is not that straightforward. With a little more thought, most people will accept that there must be some objective moral principles. The view that rape is wrong is not just a matter of opinion. The difficulty is how far we take this. Where is the line to be drawn between which moral principles are objective and which are subjective? That is an issue to which we shall return throughout this book.

Further Reading

Debate 1

C. Foster, *Choosing Life, Choosing Death: The Tyranny of Autonomy in Medical Ethics and Law* (Hart Publishing, 2009).

J. Herring and J. Wall, 'The nature and significance of the right to bodily integrity' (2017) 76 *Cambridge Law Journal* 566.

J. Herring, *Caring and the Law* (Hart Publishing, 2013).

M. Neal, 'Not gods but animals: human dignity and vulnerable subjecthood' (2012) 33 *Liverpool Law Review* 177.

J. Raz, *The Morality of Freedom* (Oxford University Press, 1982).

Debate 2

D. Archard, 'For our own good' (1994) 72 *Australasian Journal of Philosophy* 283.

J. Childress, 'The place of autonomy in bioethics' (1990) 20 *Hastings Center Report* 12.

H. Hart, *Law, Liberty and Morality* (Oxford University Press, 1963).

Debate 3

W. Goodwin, 'The archbishop and the chambermaid' in P. Singer (ed.), *Ethics* (Oxford University Press, 1994).

D. Parfit, 'What makes someone's life go best?' in P. Singer (ed.), *Ethics* (Oxford University Press, 1994).

J. Rachels, *The Elements of Moral Philosophy* (McGraw-Hill, 1999).

S. Wolf, 'Moral saints' in P. Singer (ed.), *Ethics* (Oxford University Press, 1994).

Debate 4

J. Rachels, 'Subjectivism' in P Singer (ed.), *A Companion to Ethics* (Basil Blackwell, 1991).

R. Shafer-Landau, 'Ethical subjectivism' in J. Feinberg (ed.), *Reason and Responsibility*, 10th edn (Wadsworth, 1999).

CHAPTER 2

Consent

INTRODUCTION

The need for consent before a treatment can be given, or a procedure performed, is one of the cornerstone principles of medical law. But while it might seem merely a matter of asking the patient whether she is happy to be treated or not, the reality is less straightforward. It is clear that the patient can give effective consent only if she has capacity, but the definition of capacity is complex. Should someone who refuses treatment on the basis of very strict religious views be treated against his will? Can a woman in the throes of a painful labour give valid consent? How much information should patients be given? Can they be given too much information? And what if they would rather not know? What weight should the decisions of competent children have on decisions about their medical treatment? Are there some procedures that will be unlawful even if the patient gives consent?

These questions, along with many others, have given rise to considerable debate and will be considered in this chapter. Medicine aims to help people who are unwell, and this can lead to a conflict of goals, between respecting patients' autonomy and doing what is most likely to bring them back to good health. The tension between these two goals underpins much of the debate around consent. In this chapter we will examine four areas of particular contention in relation to consent: what constitutes valid consent; overriding refusals of treatment; decisions by children; and procedures which may not be permissible even where free, informed consent has been provided. Before addressing these we will provide an overview of the law on consent.

THE LAW OF CONSENT

It is a fundamental tenet of the law that touching another person without their consent is unlawful. This is as true for doctors as it is for anyone else. As the Court of Appeal made clear in *R (Burke) v GMC*:

> Where a competent patient makes it clear that he does not wish to receive treatment which is, objectively, in his medical best interests, it is unlawful for doctors to administer that treatment. Personal autonomy or the right of self-determination prevails.[1]

---

[1] *R (Burke) v GMC* [2005] 3 FCR 169, para. 30.

Treating a patient without consent can give rise to both criminal sanctions and to actions for civil law battery and negligence. Medical practitioners who treat without consent will also face professional approbation, and possibly sanctions from the General Medical Council.

CRIMINAL LAW

A doctor who touches a patient without consent may be guilty of a battery. If the touching includes a surgical procedure, the bodily invasion could be sufficient to constitute 'grievous bodily harm'.[2] It is, however, rare for criminal charges to be brought against a doctor in such cases, unless there is evidence of some seriously reckless or iniquitous motive. Most of the criminal cases have involved doctors acting with sexual motivation.[3]

CIVIL LAW

Treating a patient without valid consent can expose a doctor to tort actions for trespass to the person (battery) or negligence. If found liable for either tort, the doctor will be required to pay compensation (damages) to the patient who has brought the claim. There are some important differences between a claim brought for a battery or for negligence. The essence of a battery claim is that the patient had not consented to what the medical professional did. The essence of a claim in negligence is that the doctor did not live up to the standards expected of professionals in relation to the provision of information. Note that under a claim of negligence it may be accepted that a patient did consent; the claim is that, nonetheless, insufficient information was given. Another important difference is that for damages to be awarded in a negligence claim, a loss must be shown. If a doctor negligently fails to provide sufficient information, but the operation is a success, only nominal damages will follow. By contrast, in a claim for battery there is no need to show that a loss followed. Damages will be awarded to acknowledge that a person was touched without their consent.

PROFESSIONAL SANCTIONS

The professional bodies have issued some helpful guidance on how doctors should obtain consent from patients. While this guidance is not enforced directly in law, doctors following this guidance could be confident they would be acting within the law. The General Medical Council states:

- The doctor and patient make an assessment of the patient's condition, taking into account the patient's medical history, views, experience and knowledge.

---

[2] Offences Against the Person Act 1861, ss. 18 and 20. Where a patient dies a charge of gross negligence manslaughter can be brought.
[3] *R v Healy* [2003] 2 Cr App R (S) 87.

- The doctor uses specialist knowledge and experience and clinical judgement, and the patient's views and understanding of their condition, to identify which investigations or treatments are likely to result in overall benefit for the patient. The doctor explains the options to the patient, setting out the potential benefits, risks, burdens and side-effects of each option, including the option to have no treatment. The doctor may recommend a particular option which they believe to be best for the patient, but they must not put pressure on the patient to accept their advice.
- The patient weighs up the potential benefits, risks and burdens of the various options as well as any non-clinical issues that are relevant to them. The patient decides whether to accept any of the options and, if so, which one. They also have the right to accept or refuse an option for a reason that may seem irrational to the doctor, or for no reason at all.
- If the patient asks for a treatment that the doctor considers would not be of overall benefit to them, the doctor should discuss the issues with the patient and explore the reasons for their request. If, after discussion, the doctor still considers that the treatment would not be of overall benefit to the patient, they do not have to provide the treatment. But they should explain their reasons to the patient, and explain any other options that are available, including the option to seek a second opinion.[4]

A failure to follow such guidance can lead to sanctions from the professional bodies, including ultimately to a doctor's being struck off and not being permitted to act as a medical professional.

WHAT IS VALID CONSENT?

Valid consent has three essential components. For a person to give valid consent, that person must:

- have capacity to make the decision;
- act voluntarily and free from coercion or manipulation; and
- have sufficient information to make the decision.

We shall be exploring the third of these criteria in Debate 1. The first and second criteria are discussed in Chapter 3.

---

[4] General Medical Council, *Consent: Patients and Doctors Making Decisions Together* (GMC, 2009) © General Medical Council 2014. Reproduced with permission.

Debate 1

How much information must be given before there is consent?

THE LAW

As already mentioned, there are two possible claims that may be made in a case where a doctor has provided insufficient information. The first is that the patient was given insufficient information to consent so that there was a battery. The second is a claim in negligence, based on the claim that the doctor's provision of information fell below the standard expected in the law.

Looking first at the battery claim, all that is needed for a patient to consent is that the patient must understand 'in broad terms the nature of the procedure which is intended'.[5] The Department of Health, in its guide on consent, states: 'To give valid consent, the person needs to understand the nature and purpose of the procedure. Any misrepresentation of these elements will invalidate consent.'[6]

This is a remarkably limited approach for the law to take. Note that there is no need for a patient to be told of the risks, nor even, it seems, the alternative treatments. As long as the patient understands in 'broad terms' what the doctor is to do, there is consent. As a result, it is not surprising that few cases are brought under the law on battery. Far more common is a claim in negligence. So how much information must be given under a negligence claim? The two leading cases are *Chester v Afshar* and *Montgomery v Lanarkshire Health Board*:

Leading case

Chester v Afshar [2004] 4 All ER 587

A journalist, Ms Chester, was suffering from persistent lower back pain. She consulted Mr Afshar, a consultant neurosurgeon. Mr Afshar recommended a particular kind of surgery. Ms Chester agreed to have the operation with Mr Afshar as soon as possible, which was a few days later. There was a dispute over what Mr Afshar said about the risks, but the trial judge preferred the evidence of Ms Chester, which was that Mr Afshar mentioned no risks connected with the operation, except to comment that he 'hadn't crippled anybody yet'. Expert evidence established that in fact there was generally a 1–2 per cent chance of paralysis with this operation, even when carried out faultlessly. Mr Afshar performed the operation in an appropriate way, but sadly Ms Chester suffered severe pain and impairment of movement as a result.

---

[5] *Chatterton v Gerson* [1981] 1 All ER 257, 265.

[6] Department of Health, *Reference Guide to Consent for Examination or Treatment* (DoH, 2009), 13.

The House of Lords determined that Mr Afshar should have told Ms Chester about the risks. Lord Steyn held:

> A surgeon owes a legal duty to a patient to warn him or her in general terms of possible serious risks involved in the procedure. The only quali-fication is that there may be wholly exceptional cases where objectively in the best interests of the patient the surgeon may be excused from giving a warning ... In modern law medical paternalism no longer rules and a patient has a prima facie right to be informed by a surgeon of a small, but well established, risk of serious injury as a result of surgery.[7]

If Mr Afshar had warned Ms Chester about the risks, she would have taken the opportunity to consider whether or not to have the operation and had it at a different time. By a majority of 3:2 she was held able to claim damages.

Leading case

Montgomery v Lanarkshire Health Board [2015] UKSC 11

Nadine Montgomery was in late stages of pregnancy. Her doctor decided that it would be better to proceed with a vaginal birth and not to do a Caesarean section. The doctor did not tell Ms Montgomery of the 9–10 per cent chance of shoulder dystocia, nor offer her the option of a Caesarean section, even though shoulder dystocia can lead to a baby's shoulder becoming stuck during vaginal birth, causing serious complica-tions for both mother and baby. Ms Montgomery went ahead with the vaginal birth and sadly the risk of shoulder dystocia materialised. Her son became stuck during birth, and as a result suffered complex disabilities. Ms Montgomery sued in negligence, claiming that had she been told of the risk and offered the option of a Caesarean Section she would have taken that.

The Supreme Court found in favour of Ms Montgomery. The doctor had been negligent in failing to inform her of the risks of vaginal deliv-ery and not offering her the Caesarean section operation. Lord Kerr and Lord Reed wrote the primary speech and explained that doctors had to take reasonable steps to ensure patients were aware of 'material risks'. By a material risk they meant (i) a risk a reasonable person in the posi-tion of the patient would be likely to attach significance to and (ii) a risk the doctor should reasonably be aware the particular patient would

(Continued)

---

[7] *Chester v Afshar* [2004] 4 All ER 587, para. 16.

Leading case (*Continued*)

attach significance to. Whether a risk was material or not would depend on several factors: 'the nature of the risk, the effect which its occurrence would have upon the life of the patient, the importance to the patient of the benefits sought to be achieved by the treatment, the alternatives available, and the risks involved in those alternatives.'[8] Their lordships applied that to this case and found the 9–10 per cent risk of a serious disability was a risk a reasonable person in Ms Montgomery's position would have attached significance to. Their lordships accepted two exceptions to the general rule that a patient should be told of material risks. The first was the 'therapeutic privilege'. This applied where a doctor believed that telling the patient about the risk would be seriously detrimental to her health. That might be where, for example, informing a patient of a risk would induce a serious panic attack. The second exception was if there was an emergency situation and the doctor did not have time to tell the patient of the risk.

Their lordships also went on to say that not only must doctors inform patients of the material risks, they must offer patients reasonable alternative treatments. Particularly in this case the patient should have been offered the alternative of a Caesarean section.

At the heart of the approach of the Supreme Court was the importance attached to autonomy. Patients should be allowed to make decisions about what treatment to receive. To do this they need to know about the risks attached to treatment and the reasonable alternatives available.

This approach notably departs from that taken in earlier cases, and in particular in *Sidaway v Bethlem*,[9] where, although there was a division of views, the starting point had been the *Bolam* test (see Chapter 4), namely that a doctor should provide information of the kind a responsible body of medical opinion would give. The *Montgomery* and *Chester* decisions depart from *Bolam* in this context by saying that all serious risks must be disclosed, regardless of whether there is a body of professional opinion saying otherwise or what a doctor might think a reasonable patient might want to know.[10]

There is an important limitation to these decisions. That is that it must be shown that if the patient had been told of the risk of (or the alternative available) treatments they would not have had the surgery or, at least, would not

---

[8] *Montgomery v Lanarkshire Health Board* [2015] UKSC 11, para. 94.
[9] *Sidaway v Bethlem* [1985] 1 All ER 643; *Pearce v United Bristol Healthcare NHS Trust* (1998) 48 BMLR 118.
[10] J. Miola, 'On the materiality of risk – paper tigers and panaceas' (2009) 17 *Medical Law Review* 76.

have had the surgery at the time they had done so.[11] You might imagine that in plenty of cases a doctor may have failed to disclose a risk but the patient would have consented to the operation even if they had been told of the risk. In such a case the claim will fail because it will not have been shown that the negligence caused a loss. Similarly, if the risk is not disclosed, but the operation is a success and so there is no harm, there will be no loss and an action will be likely to fail.

What Should the Law be?

To start a consideration of this debate it is worth examining these four views:

1. *Full information approach.* Patients should be given information about every risk associated with treatment. Only with a complete knowledge can they assess all of the risks. This is in line with patient autonomy. The patient should be allowed to decide which risks they are willing to take. It is paternalistic for a doctor to imagine they know better than a patient which risks are sufficiently important for a patient to care about.

2. *Reasonable doctor test.* The doctor should be required to provide information on those risks which a responsible body of medical opinion thinks a patient should be told about. In other words, the standard *Bolam* test (see Chapter 4) should apply. There is no reason why the test for liability in the tort of negligence should be different in a case of information provision than in any other matter. The *Bolam* test recognises that doctors can take different views on what is the appropriate way of dealing with patients, and the law should respect that diversity of views. Doctors are best placed to know what risks are the ones that should worry patients. The error in providing patients with all risks is that patients will be overwhelmed with information. Having a doctor highlight the few key risks is in fact far more valuable for patients than their being given a sheet of paper with hundreds of risks set out.

3. *Reasonable patient test.* The law should require doctors to disclose what a reasonable patient would want to know. This is not likely to be every conceivable risk but should include all important risks. This should not be seen as a matter for professional discretion (as View 2 above would have it) but looked at from the point of view of the patient. This would require a doctor to disclose the important risks, and in addition to disclose any risks that they think the particular patient would want to know about. For example, a patient who is a musician may be more concerned about any potential impact on hand movement than other patients.

4. *Patient-centred approach.* The doctor should allow the patient to set the agenda. Some patients want to know all of the risks and some do not want to know any. Any questions raised by a patient should be answered fully and carefully, but a doctor should not decide what to tell a patient.

---

[11] *Chester v Afshar* [2004] 4 All ER 587.

This approach could fit in with one which sees medical decision making as a 'team effort'. The doctor will advise the patient about the alternatives and the risks and assist the patient to determine what decision they wish to make, given their particular circumstances and values. This can be seen as the approach adopted in *Montgomery*.[12]

These four views give you a flavour of how different people might respond to this debate. We see here some of the issues about the balance between paternalism and autonomy that were discussed in Chapter 1. Do we trust doctors to make the right decision about what risks patients should know, or do we give patients all the information and let them decide?

There is some merit in the point made in View 2 above, that giving patients a sheet of paper (or a one-hour lecture) listing all the potential risks may in fact not be informative at all. We have probably all opened packets of medication with a leaflet in tiny script informing us of hundreds of risks, and simply thrown the leaflet away. In the light of this, it is of interest that a survey of English patients found that 79 per cent felt they had been given the 'right amount of information' about their treatment (even though English law does not require full disclosure).[13] Lords Kerr and Reed were aware of this danger and wrote:

> the doctor's advisory role involves dialogue, the aim of which is to ensure that the patient understands the seriousness of her condition, and the anticipated benefits and risks of the proposed treatment and any reasonable alternatives, so that she is then in a position to make an informed decision. This role will only be performed effectively if the information provided is comprehensible. The doctor's duty is not therefore fulfilled by bombarding the patient with technical information which she cannot reasonably be expected to grasp, let alone by routinely demanding her signature on a consent form.[14]

It might be assumed that View 1 is the view that most promotes informed decision making by patients. However, arguably, a doctor highlighting the main risks may do more to help a patient make an informed choice than overwhelm them with information about every conceivable risk. It may be that the solution lies in a middle path. A doctor must provide a leaflet with all of the risks (or a website address) and verbally inform the patient of the major risks. That way, the patient who wants to know more has ready access to that information. If they choose not to read about all the risks, they cannot complain they were not told about them.

View 4 raises a broader issue which is worth considering further. Should a patient have a right not to know?

---

[12] J. Herring, B. Fulford, M. Dunn and A. Handa, 'Elbow room for best practice? Montgomery, patients' values, and balanced decision-making in person-centred clinical care' (2017) 25 *Medical Law Review* 582.

[13] The Picker Institute, *The Key Findings Report for the 2008 Inpatient Survey* (Picker Institute, 2009).

[14] *Montgomery v Lanarkshire Health Board* [2015] UKSC 11, para. 94.

Is There a Right 'Not to Know'?

Scenario to ponder

Frank gets terribly nervous about operations and spends the weeks before thinking through all the things that could go wrong. When his doctor tells him he needs a minor operation on his throat, he immediately says: 'Please don't tell me what might go wrong, I'll just worry. I am happy to have the operation without knowing.' Should the doctor comply with his wishes?

It seems that many doctors are not willing to let a patient undergo an operation without their knowing of any of the risks. This is understandable: If a doctor discloses a risk and a patient consents nonetheless, the patient has little chance of legal recourse if the risk materialises (assuming the operation was performed properly). However, if the risk does materialise and the doctor has not disclosed the risk, a negligence action seems more plausible. The safest course is to disclose. No legal action could be brought for disclosing a risk which a patient did not want to hear about.

Some commentators have argued that patients have a right not to know.[15] There may be good reasons why a patient does not want to know information, and we should respect that. It may be the patient is worried the information will simply cause them panic; the patient may fear that too much information will overwhelm them and prevent them from making a decision; or they may realise they do not really understand the concept or risk (like many people) and so it would not be helpful to be told about it. Whatever the reason, some commentators argue that we should respect the patient's choice and that forcing unwanted information on a patient breaches their right to privacy. Certainly the courts have recognised that being given information can be harmful. Indeed, in *X County Council v A mother*,[16] Moses LJ held that it was not in the best interests of two children in care to be tested for Huntington's Disease, knowing the information would harm them, without providing any benefits because there is no cure for the condition.

There is, however, a problem with this argument. Can you consent not to know a piece of information if you don't know what it is?! Let us return to Frank. Imagine the doctor complied with his wishes and did not disclose the risks of the operation, one of which was impotence. Further, imagine that unfortunately the risk materialised. Frank might then say, 'When I said I did not want to hear about the risks I imagined you were going to tell me all about things happening to my throat; I had no idea impotence was involved.' But that is the problem. If you don't know what the information is, how can you decide that you don't want to hear it?

---

[15] J. Herring and C. Foster, '"Please don't tell me": the right not to know' (2011) 21 *Cambridge Quarterly of Healthcare Ethics* 12.
[16] *X County Council v A mother* [2013] EWHC 953 (Fam).

This is not necessarily a 'knock down' argument. We might simply say that Frank decided not to learn of the risks, and he cannot complain if there were surprising risks he did not know about. Alternatively, there might be a middle path where, in a case such as Frank's, the doctor should say: 'I will comply with your wishes, but you should be aware some of the risks are not ones you would necessarily expect. Are you sure you don't want to know?'

CONCLUSION

As this debate demonstrates, it is enormously difficult to determine how much information should be given to patients. In part this is because different patients want to be given different levels of information. Some patients do not want to hear anything about risks; some patients want to hear about every risk; and yet others want to hear just about the main ones. There is a need to balance the right of patients to be informed and the right of patients not to know information they do not want to know. Perhaps the answer lies in doctors trying to find out from patients what they want to know and providing them with the level of information they seek. That may, however, be unpopular with doctors, who would like clear guidance on what they should say so that they know for sure what they must do to comply with the law.

Debate 2

Should doctors be allowed to treat competent patients who refuse treatment?

THE LAW

As we have already noted, it is unlawful for a doctor to treat a patient without that patient's consent. That was dramatically revealed in *St George's Healthcare NHS Trust v S*:

Leading case

St George's Healthcare NHS Trust v S[17]

A woman in labour was told that she needed a Caesarean section and that without such an operation, she and the foetus she was carrying would die. Despite her refusal to consent, the operation was carried out. The Court of Appeal held this to be unlawful. Great weight was placed on the importance of the right to bodily integrity.

---

[17] *St George's Healthcare NHS Trust v S* [1998] 3 All ER 673.

One of things that is notable about this decision is that the patient's refusal to treatment was upheld even though without it, she and the foetus would die. The Court of Appeal acknowledged that the woman's decision 'may appear morally repugnant',[18] but that was no reason for overruling her decision. This decision reveals how strongly the right to bodily integrity is protected in the law.

It would not be right to suggest that the right to bodily integrity can never be interfered with. There are limited circumstances in which it is lawful for a person to touch someone without their consent. These include the following:

- The Mental Health Act 1983 permits the treatment of a patient who is detained under that legislation for a mental disorder. Notably this covers cases where a patient has capacity to refuse treatment.
- Everyday touching ('physical contact which is generally acceptable in the ordinary conduct of daily life'[19]) does not require consent. A handshake, or tapping someone on their shoulder to alert them to the fact they have dropped something, would not require consent. This is normally justified on the basis of implied consent (if we go into a public place we impliedly consent to normal touching). If so, it may not properly be an exception to the rule that one cannot be touched without consent.
- If a patient is suffering from a contamination or infection, they can be ordered to be detained by a magistrate under the Public Health (Control of Disease) Act 1984.[20]
- If a person is trying to commit suicide, it is generally thought to be lawful to seek to prevent that happening. In *Savage v South Essex Partnership NHS Foundation Trust*,[21] the House of Lords confirmed that a public authority may be under a positive obligation to protect a person in their care (e.g. a prisoner) from committing suicide.
- In *Secretary of State v Robb*[22] it was suggested that public policy could justify interfering with the rights of self-determination. It is far from clear when this would be so. It seems best to say it could do so in the most exceptional of cases.
- Section 55 of the Police and Criminal Evidence Act 1984 allows intimate searches of a suspect without consent in some circumstances.
- The defence of self-defence in criminal law allows a defendant to use force against another by way of protection.

---

[18] At 957 (Judge LJ).

[19] *Collins v Wilcock* [1984] 3 All ER 374.

[20] The Health and Social Care Act 2008 amended that Act so that all infections and contaminations are now covered.

[21] *Savage v South Essex Partnership NHS Foundation Trust* [2008] UKHL 74.

[22] *Secretary of State v Robb* [1995] 1 All ER 677.

ARE THERE ANY CIRCUMSTANCES IN WHICH DOCTORS SHOULD OVERRIDE A REFUSAL OF TREATMENT?

There may be some cases in which a refusal is that of a person lacking capacity. In those cases it is relatively uncontroversial to say that the refusal can be ignored, and the doctor can either act on earlier capacitous consent or under the Mental Capacity Act 2005 if the treatment is in the best interests of the patient (see Chapter 3).

More interesting is a claim that a person is acting with capacity but that their decision is not autonomous. That argument requires us to look more carefully at what it means to exercise autonomy. Catriona Mackenzie and Wendy Rogers argue that to be able to exercise autonomy, a person needs to:[23]

- *be self-determining*, i.e. 'able to determine one's own beliefs, values, goals and wants, and to make choices regarding matters of practical import to one's life free from undue interference. The obverse of self-determination is determination by other persons, or by external forces or constraints.'[24]
- *be self-governing*, i.e. 'able to make choices and enact decisions that express, or are consistent with, one's values, beliefs and commitments. Whereas the threats to self-determination are typically external, the threats to self-governance are typically internal, and often involve volitional or cognitive failings. Weakness of will and failures of self-control are common volitional failings that interfere with self-governance.'[25]
- *have authenticity*, i.e. 'a person's decisions, values, beliefs and commitments must be her "own" in some relevant sense; that is, she must identify herself with them and they must cohere with her "practical identity", her sense of who she is and what matters to her. Actions or decisions that a person feels were foisted on her, which do not cohere with her sense of herself, or from which she feels alienated, are not autonomous.'[26]

These requirements indicate that an argument might be made that even if a person has capacity to refuse treatment, that refusal might not, in fact, represent a person's autonomous wishes.[27] This will become clearer with a few examples.

Cases where there are competing wishes

In *Re MB*,[28] a woman was in the late stages of pregnancy and needed to be given a Caesarean section operation, without which her life and that of the foetus were in danger. She needed an injection, but she had needle phobia and

---

[23] C. Mackenzie and W. Rogers, 'Autonomy, vulnerability and capacity: a philosophical appraisal of the Mental Capacity Act' (2013) 8 *International Journal of the Law in Context* 37, 49.

[24] Ibid.

[25] Ibid.

[26] Ibid.

[27] A. Maclean, *Autonomy, Informed Consent and the Law: A Relational Challenge* (Cambridge University Press, 2009).

[28] *Re MB* [1997] EWCA Civ 1361.

refused to consent to the injection. The Court of Appeal authorised the giving of the injection without her consent. One way of justifying this would be to say that she lacked consent to refuse the injection because her panic about needles meant she could not weigh up the information to make a decision. Another argument is to say that in this case there were two competing wishes: to be given the Caesarean and not to be given the injection. We cannot meet both of these wishes, and we must decide which is more richly autonomous – in other words, which most reflects the settled decision of the person. In this case we might say that in fact it better respects the wishes of the woman to override her refusal and give her the Caesarean.

Cases where a person's current wishes do not reflect a settled decision

There may be some cases where we are confident that the immediate wishes of the individual are in conflict with their settled wishes. Here we draw on the common experience that we have impulses which do not in fact reflect the values we normally wish to live by and which we greatly regret acting upon. For example, we have decided to eat healthily, but impulsively eat an unhealthy snack. In such a case the decision to eat healthily may be one that is thought about carefully and is fully informed. The grabbing of the snack may be an almost instinctive reaction, not really reflecting our deepest wishes.

It may be that this explains the law's response to suicide. The immediate wish to die may reflect a short period of darkness and not a settled decision to die. Indeed, many of those who attempt suicide but fail express enormous relief subsequently that their decision failed. This kind of argument is most effective where the decision at stake is one of huge importance to the individual with lasting repercussions. Applied in the medical context, it may be that a doctor could determine that a particular decision (e.g. the refusal of the injection in *Re MB*) was simply an instinctive reaction and not a properly autonomous decision.

Cases where a patient is not being the 'real them'

Sometimes there are cases where there is a conflict between the person as they are now and 'the real them'. A good, although controversial, example is people with anorexia nervosa. This is complex issue, and there is not space here to discuss it in the detail it deserves.[29] But in a case where a person is refusing food because they believe they are overweight, some commentators argue that the disease (anorexia) has distorted the person's values and understandings, and that the 'real them' (the person they were before the disease took hold)

---

[29] T. Hope, J. Tan, A. Stewart and J. McMillan, 'Agency, ambivalence and authenticity: the many ways in which anorexia nervosa can affect autonomy' (2013) 8 *International Journal of Law in Context* 20; B. Clough, 'Anorexia, capacity, and best interests: developments in the court of protection since the Mental Capacity Act 2005' (2016) 24 *Medical Law Review* 434.

would not take such a view. We are therefore justified in treating them without their consent so that we can return them to the state they were in before, and so that they are properly able to make a decision. This argument can be used more broadly to justify the Mental Health Act 1983 provisions which allow for compulsory treatment for mental disorders. There is controversy over such argument, because it assumes there is a 'real them' to discover. In the case of a person with a long-term mental condition, we might ask: 'Who is the "real them"?'

In *King's College Hospital NHS Foundation Trust v C and V*,[30] a patient refused dialysis and treatment for a kidney condition. The court accepted that most people would regard the decision as foolish and even immoral. However, they found that the patient, who was said to be 'sparkly' and enjoyed glamour and fine dining, was being true to herself in preferring death to treatment which she found demeaning and unglamorous. Therefore her decision was entirely consistent with her 'real' self.

Undue influence

A similar kind of argument to the one just made can be used in cases where a person is under the influence of someone else. While in extreme cases we might determine that the influence is so strong that the person lacks capacity, in other cases they may retain capacity, even though they are being influenced by another. A good example may be *DL v A Local Authority*,[31] where an elderly couple lived with their son. He was mistreating them in a variety of ways. Social services wished to remove them from their son's care, but they opposed the intervention. The couple were found to have capacity to make the decision because they understood the central issues. Nevertheless, the court made orders protecting them from their son. Although they had capacity, the son was controlling their decision making and 'their' decision was not really theirs.

The interests of others and the public interest

Can the interest of others or the public interest justify overriding a refusal? As we saw in Chapter 1, we generally allow people to make decisions about themselves unless doing so harms others. Yet we allow someone to refuse to donate a kidney, even if as a result someone else will die. So clearly a stronger principle than simply the principle of autonomy is at play in cases involving refusal of treatment.[32]

---

[30] *King's College Hospital NHS Foundation Trust v C and V* [2015] EWCOP 80. See, by contrast, *A Local Authority v Mr and Mrs A* [2010] EWHC 1549.

[31] *DL v A Local Authority* [2012] EWCA Civ 253; *Re D (Vulnerable Adult)* [2016] EWHC 2358 (Fam).

[32] J. Coggon and J. Miola, 'Autonomy, liberty and medical decision-making' (2011) 70 *Cambridge Law Journal* 523.

Supporters argue that this is the principle of bodily integrity. Although the general interest and the interests of others might support restricting autonomy generally, they are generally insufficient to allow an interference in autonomy which involves bodily integrity.

So what might support giving the principle of bodily integrity especial protection? Why is interfering in a person's body a different matter to interfering in other choices? One argument is that our bodies go to the root of identity, they are our very selves, and so an interference in the body is an interference with the very essence of who we are. That argument will not convince everyone. Some people may regard non-bodily matters of more importance than the body. For example, a religious person may say that being prevented from praying is a worse interference with their sense of self than having some of their hair taken without consent.

A second argument for why we should regard bodily interference as particularly serious is that it involves treating another person as an object to be used for the greater good. Some people might say it objectifies people or undermines human dignity. The point is that if you are stopped from doing something you do not want to do, you are not being used by someone else for their gain. Where, however, your organ is removed, you are being used as a mere means to an end. For some (most famously Immanuel Kant) there is a fundamental moral wrong in using people as a means to an end.

It is worth finishing this discussion with an observation that not everyone believes it is right to see bodily interferences as more wrongful than others. Is it right to elevate bodily wrongs as that much more serious than other wrongs? Is exploiting a relationship worse than punching a stranger? It may be better simply to take each interference with autonomy separately, and decide how serious it is and whether the interference can be justified, rather than assuming bodily interferences are necessarily worse than non-bodily ones.

CONCLUSION

Generally, the law takes the right to refuse strongly. Although it is not without exception, the principle that a patient cannot be treated without their consent is strongly protected in the law. The basis for it rests on the contentious claim that an interference with the body is a more serious invasion of the self than other interferences with autonomy. As we have seen, people will disagree over whether that is a correct starting point. This debate has highlighted two circumstances in which it might be justified to treat someone despite their refusal. The first, and more justifiable, is where the refusal is not a genuinely autonomous decision of the patient. The second, and more controversial, would be where there are compelling public policy reasons for overturning a refusal. It may be that you reject both of these arguments and want to hold on to the principle that a patient can never be treated without their consent.

Debate 3

Should children be allowed to make their own decisions about medical treatment?

So far we have been looking at adult patients. But what happens when a patient is a child? Can a child give effective consent? Or is it the parents whose consent is required? Is there a difference between a teenager and a toddler? These are some of the issues we will explore in the following debate.

THE LAW

Where a child is young the law allows a person with parental responsibility to consent to medical procedures, or, if there is a dispute between the parents and the doctors, for the court to declare the procedures lawful.[33] Particularly tricky cases involve older children who may have views of their own. Section 8(1) of the Family Law Reform Act 1969 states that 16 and 17 year olds can give legally effective consent to treatment. But for children under the age of 16 the law is dominated by the decision in *Gillick* (below).

> **Leading case**
>
> *Gillick v West Norfolk and Wisbech Health Authority* [1986] AC 112 (HL)
>
> A circular was issued by the Department of Health and Social Security, informing doctors that they would be acting lawfully if they prescribed contraception to girls under the age of 16, even if they did so without parental consent. Mrs Gillick, a committed Roman Catholic with five daughters, sought a declaration that the circular was illegal.
>
> At the heart of the decision by the House of Lords was the finding that although parents had rights, these existed in order to protect the welfare of children. Parental rights yielded to the rights of the child to make decisions for herself if she had sufficient understanding and intelligence. Therefore, a doctor could provide contraceptive advice and treatment to a child aged under 16, without her parents' consent, if she had sufficient understanding of the issues involved and it was in her best interests to receive the treatment.

This case established the concept of '*Gillick* competent' children. That covers children who have the levels of maturity and understanding to make decisions for themselves.

---

[33] *Great Ormond Street Hospital v Yates* [2017] EWHC 1909 (Fam).

The *Gillick* case concerned the question of whether a mature child could consent. It was generally assumed that the same approach would be taken in a case where a child refused treatment, but rather surprisingly the later cases appear not to have taken that view. The decisions in *Re W (A Minor) (Medical Treatment: Court's Jurisdiction)* and *Re R (A Minor) (Wardship: Consent to Treatment)*[34] are generally taken to indicate that if a *Gillick* competent child has refused to consent to treatment, that refusal can be overridden if consent is provided by either the court or a person with parental responsibility. This was applied in *Re M (Medical Treatment: Consent)*,[35] where a 15-year-old girl refused a heart transplant, stating that she did not want to have someone else's heart. Her mother consented to the treatment. The Court of Appeal authorised the operation, stating that the preserving of the girl's life justified overriding her views.

The law was explained in *Re W (A Minor) (Medical Treatment: Court's Jurisdiction)*[36] in this way: a doctor who wishes to give medical treatment to a child needs a 'flak jacket' to give them legal protection against being sued. This flak jacket can be provided by any of the following:

- a *Gillick* competent child
- a person with parental responsibility
- an order or a declaration of the court.

In short, we have the situation that where a child is sufficiently mature, she has the right to say 'yes' to treatment, but not 'no'. The law was applied in *R (Axon) v Secretary of State for Health (Family Planning Association intervening)*:

Leading case

R (Axon) v Secretary of State for Health (Family Planning Association intervening) [2006] 1 FCR 175

Mrs Axon applied for judicial review of Department of Health guidance which said that medical professionals could provide advice on abortion to children aged under 16, without their parents being notified.

Silber J, following *Gillick*, ruled that there was a duty of confidence owed to young people, and so advice on abortion and other matters could be given without informing their parents. He argued that if confidentiality concerning sexual matters could not be guaranteed, young

(Continued)

---

[34] *Re W (A Minor) (Medical Treatment: Court's Jurisdiction)* [1993] 1 FLR 1, [1992] 2 FCR 785; *Re R (A Minor) (Wardship: Consent to Treatment)* [1991] 4 All ER 177.

[35] *Re M (Medical Treatment: Consent)* [1999] 2 FLR 1097.

[36] *Re W (A Minor) (Medical Treatment: Court's Jurisdiction)* [1992] 2 FCR 785.

people might be deterred from seeking medical advice, and this would have 'undesirable and troubled consequences'.[37] He rejected a claim that under Article 8 of the European Convention on Human Rights parents had a right to be informed of advice or treatment given to their children. He explained that once a child is competent to make decisions for herself, her parents have no 'right to family life' requiring their consent.[38] Even if they did have a right to be told of treatment given to their children, this could be justifiably interfered with in the name of promoting good sexual health among young people.[39]

Challenging the orthodox interpretation of the case law

It may be that despite the official line taken by the courts, in practice the views of children are given weight by doctors. In one much publicised case, a 14 year old, Hannah Jones, refused the heart transplant recommended by her doctors even though without it she was likely to die. The doctors decided to abide by her wishes, although she subsequently decided to accept the transplant.[40] In 2010 there were newspaper reports of a 15-year-old Jehovah's Witness, Joshua McAuley, who died after refusing a blood transfusion. In both these cases the issue was not brought to the courts.[41]

Gilmore and Herring[42] have argued that these recent reports indicate that there are changing attitudes towards competent children, and that the previous case law can be re-examined. They argue that a better interpretation of the judgments in *Re W (A Minor) (Medical Treatment: Court's Jurisdiction)*[43] and *Re R (A Minor) (Wardship: Consent to Treatment)*[44] is that the courts were saying that the children were competent to consent to treatment, but not competent to refuse all treatment. They argue that the courts have therefore yet to deal with a case where a child is *Gillick* competent to refuse all treatment. As a matter of interpretation of the case law, it may be that there is sufficient

---

[37] At para. 66.

[38] It would seem preferable to say that the parent does have a right to family life in connection with the decision, although this right can be interfered with because that is necessary in the interests of the child. After all, if the decision is not to have an abortion, this will have a huge impact on the parents' life.

[39] Although see E. Lee, 'We still need abortion as early as possible, as late as necessary', *Spiked*, 9 July 2004, which highlights the practical difficulties young people face in accessing abortion services.

[40] www.bbc.co.uk/news/uk-14592420.

[41] www.theguardian.com/uk/2010/may/18/jehovahs-witness-dies-refuse-blood-transfusion.

[42] S. Gilmore and J. Herring, '"No" is the hardest word: consent and children's autonomy' (2011) 23 *Child and Family Law Quarterly* 1.

[43] *Re W (A Minor) (Medical Treatment: Court's Jurisdiction)* [1993] 1 FLR 1, [1992] 2 FCR 785.

[44] *Re R (A Minor) (Wardship: Consent to Treatment)* [1991] 4 All ER 177.

ambiguity in the judgments that a later court, seeking to by-pass the standard interpretation of *Re W* and *Re R*, might use the Gilmore/Herring analysis. However, their interpretation of the case law allows a court to determine that a child has capacity to consent to, but not refuse, treatment, something many commentators have found hard to accept.[45] We shall explore that shortly.

WHAT IS GILLICK COMPETENCE?

There has never been an authoritative statement on exactly what a child must demonstrate to be *Gillick* competent, but it seems from the case law that the following are included:

- The child must understand the nature of their medical condition, and the treatment proposed by doctors and any side-effects.[46]
- The child must understand the moral and family issues involved in the decision.[47]
- The child must have experience of life. In *Re L (Medical Treatment: Gillick Competency)*,[48] a 14-year-old Jehovah's Witness was found not to be *Gillick* competent because she had lived a sheltered life and had not been exposed to a variety of different world views.[49]
- The child must be capable of weighing the information to reach a decision. In *F v F*,[50] a vegan girl (L) refused to consent to the MMR injection as it contained animal products. She was found to lack capacity to refuse as she could not weigh up the competing arguments.

There have been concerns raised by the approach of the courts in these cases. First, it seems that the approach taken requires children to be more competent than many adults. For example, the requirement that children understand the moral and family issues involved is not matched in a requirement for adults. Similarly, adult Jehovah's Witnesses do not need to show they have been exposed to a variety of religious views.

Second, there is a concern that children are found to lack capacity because they are not told the information they need. Rather controversially, in *Re L (Medical Treatment: Gillick Competency)*,[51] L was found not to be competent because she did not appreciate the manner of her death if the treatment was not performed. The reason why she did not was because the doctors thought it would cause her undue distress if they were to tell her. It seems highly

---

[45] E. Cave and J. Wallbank, 'Minors' capacity to refuse treatment: A reply to Gilmore and Herring' (2012) 20 *Medical Law Review* 423.

[46] *Re R (A Minor) (Wardship: Consent to Medical Treatment)* [1991] 4 All ER 177.

[47] *Re E (A Minor) (Wardship: Medical Treatment)* [1993] 1 FLR 386.

[48] *Re L (Medical Treatment: Gillick Competency)* [1998] 2 FLR 810.

[49] See also *Re E (A Minor) (Medical Treatment)* [1993] 1 FLR 386.

[50] *F v F* [2013] EWHC 2783 (Fam).

[51] *Re L (Medical Treatment: Gillick Competency)* [1998] 2 FLR 810.

unsatisfactory that a child can be found not competent because the doctors have failed to give her the relevant information that she needs to be competent.[52]

Third, underpinning these concerns is a suspicion that children's rights are not being taken seriously. They are found competent if they say what we want them to say (consent to treatment), but are found to lack competence if they do not say what we want them to say (refusal of treatment). *F v F*[53] (the girl refusing the MMR injection) may be an example of this. It is hard to believe that if she was consenting to the injection there would be a questioning of her competence. This, however, leads us on to the next issue. Is there a difference between consent and refusal?

A DIFFERENCE BETWEEN CAPACITY TO CONSENT AND REFUSAL

As mentioned earlier, Gilmore and Herring believe the case law can be explained on the basis that a child may have the capacity to consent to treatment, but not the capacity to refuse treatment. They discuss a homely example which explains their view. A 10-year-old child falls over in the playground and scrapes her knee. A teacher offers to put a plaster on the scratch. Gilmore and Herring argue that the child may well have capacity to consent, because she understands the treatment and what it involves. She is likely to have had a plaster on her knee before and knows what it does. She has capacity to consent. However, she may not have capacity to refuse to consent, because that would require her to understand the consequences of not putting a plaster on a cut (the risk of septicaemia, the danger of infections, etc.). Indeed, it may be quite common for a child to understand a proposed treatment, but not to understand the alternatives if no treatment is offered.

Opponents of the view argue that we should ask whether a child has capacity to make the decision. Cave and Wallbank argue this must mean the child understands what having the treatment involves, and also what not having the treatment involves, and then decides whether or not to have the treatment.[54] Otherwise a child is not meaningfully making a choice. While their view has much attraction in theory, it would mean that it would be rare that a child could be *Gillick* competent, given the complexity and range of things that might happen if a medical condition goes untreated.

SHOULD A PARENT BE ABLE TO OVERRIDE A GILLICK COMPETENT CHILD'S REFUSAL OF TREATMENT?

This question has proved highly controversial. Let us start with the argument that a parent should not be able to override a competent child's refusal. The claim would be that once we have decided that a child is as competent as an

---

[52] E. Cave, 'Maximisation of a minors' capacity' (2011) 4 *Child and Family Law Quarterly* 429.

[53] *F v F* [2013] EWHC 2783 (Fam).

[54] E. Cave and J. Wallbank, 'Minors' capacity to refuse treatment: a reply to Gilmore and Herring' (2012) 20 *Medical Law Review* 423.

adult, there is no reason to treat that child differently from an adult. An adult has an absolute right to refuse treatment, and so too should a competent child. Although in formal legal terms an age discrimination claim under the Equality Act 2010 cannot be brought by children, it might well be argued that it is simply age discrimination to treat a mature child differently from an adult. Indeed, the current law, which says that a mature child can give a legally effective 'yes' but not a 'no', is simply incoherent. In effect it is saying, 'We will recognise your maturity as long as you say what we want you to say.'

One response to this argument is that it fails to understand what the law is trying to do. *Gillick* was not so much a case about allowing children to consent to treatment as it was about stopping parents from denying their children access to medically appropriate treatment. From this approach, the starting point is that if a doctor wishes to give treatment to a child, they should be able to do so. The law enables this by saying that a doctor can operate if they have the consent of either the child or a parent or the court. It seeks to prevent giving either the child or the parent a veto over appropriate treatment, and does everything it can to enable the doctor to provide treatment. So understood, the law is not about promoting children's autonomy but about promoting their welfare in ensuring they receive medical care. That argument may work as an explanation of the case law, but given the general move in medical law and ethics away from paternalism and towards respecting autonomy, it does not sit well with many commentators.[55]

CONCLUSION

The law on minors and consent to treatment is not in a very happy state. It is not entirely clear what the current law is, and the courts have failed to articulate a clear set of principles upon which to base the law. There is much attraction in the straightforward view that if a child is as mature as an adult, they should have the same rights as an adult. However, when it comes to actual cases, it is understandable that the courts have been extremely reluctant to let a child refuse treatment and die. In such cases, perhaps our natural instincts to protect children trump the rational case to respect their decisions.

Debate 4

Should there be some treatments to which one cannot consent?

INTRODUCTION

In this debate we will consider whether there should be treatment to which a patient cannot consent. To be clear, we are imagining a case where a patient wants a certain form of surgery and the doctor is willing to provide it: in such a case, should the doctor be prohibited from going ahead? One might imagine

---

[55] S. Gilmore and J. Herring, '"No" is the hardest word: consent and children's autonomy' (2011) 23 *Child and Family Law Quarterly* 1.

a patient seeking dramatic cosmetic surgery or asking for the removal of a limb because they have body dysmorphic disorder (BDD), or seeking an unapproved medical treatment. Of course, in these cases, if the doctor does not want to give the patient the treatment they cannot be forced to. But if the doctor is willing, does the law have any justification in preventing it?

The notorious decision in *R v Brown*[56] gives an example of where the law was willing to intervene, despite the consent of the participants. Members of a sadomasochist group were convicted of an assault occasioning actual bodily harm and inflicting grievous bodily harm on other members of the group, even though the activities were consensual. The minority of the House of Lords would have overturned the convictions, primarily on the basis that the activities were in private, were consensual, and caused no proven public harm. However, the majority upheld the convictions, arguing that only where there was a public benefit to allow an activity should people should be allowed to cause each other harm. Surgery and sports were example of publicly beneficial behaviour which should be permitted, but sadomasochism was not.

The case has proved highly contentious, and most commentators are not persuaded by the reasoning. If a person consents to the treatment and no one else is harmed, that person should be allowed to do what they want with their body. However, there may be more to the debates than that. Let us look further at some of the arguments that might be used to restrict what a person can consent to.

ARGUMENTS AGAINST THE RIGHT TO CONSENT TO HARMFUL TREATMENT

Self-harm

We might believe that people should be protected from making foolish decisions. This is the argument in favour of paternalism set out in Chapter 1. We will not repeat the arguments made there. For now we just note that such straightforward paternalism is very much out of vogue in current thinking. Hence many critics of the decision in *Brown* (above) have argued that the majority were simply imposing their own moral views on the defendants.[57] However, consider this quote from Jonathan Herring and Jesse Wall:

> It is a terrible thing to be assessed as lacking capacity when you do not – to have others make decisions on your behalf and set aside your own wishes based on what they think is in your best interests. You lose control over your life. You are no longer in charge of your destiny.

---

[56] *R v Brown* [1994] 1 AC 212. For the significance of this for medical law see S. Fovargue and A. Mullock, *The Legitimacy of Medical Treatment: What Role for the Medical Exception?* (Routledge, 2016).

[57] See J. Herring, *Great Debates in Criminal Law* (Palgrave, 2016), Chapter 5.

It is a terrible thing to be said to have capacity when you do not – to be left to cause yourself and those you love great harm on the basis that you know what you are doing and you are making your own choices, when in fact your decisions are not really yours. To have others harm you and to be told no protection is offered because you have chosen this harm, even though it is against your deepest values, is horrific.[58]

While this is not advocating paternalism, it does highlight the dangers that can arise from being so concerned about not finding a capacious patient to lack capacity that we leave them to suffer harm without justification.

Protecting autonomy

Where the person is seeking dramatic treatment, we might respect their right to harm now in following their wishes, but we may be severely limiting their options in the future. Imagine, for example, a person with BDD who seeks to have their legs removed. A straightforward autonomy argument might say that we should respect that person's decision as it is their choice as regards their body. However, in respecting their autonomy now we are severely limiting that person's autonomy in the future. Without legs, their options will be greatly reduced. It might therefore be claimed that at least where the treatment is going to cause a serious impact on a person's future life options, we should not permit it.

This argument will not have convinced everyone. Many decisions we take will have long-lasting consequences. The decisions to become a parent, to marry, to go bankrupt (or perhaps all three at the same time!) are decisions which can have effects for a whole life. Yet we do not prevent people from making such decisions because they will be limiting their decisions in the future. (Although in reply it might be said that becoming a parent opens up new opportunities in a person's life, while removing their legs seems simply to remove options.)

Raz and autonomy

In Chapter 1 we referred to the view of Joseph Raz that we should only respect those autonomous decisions which are good.[59] We might argue that surgery that causes serious harm is not covered by the right to respect for autonomy. The difficulty with this approach, mentioned in Chapter 1, is that it assumes we can assess which forms of body modification are good or bad. Not long ago many people would have regarded gender reassignment surgery as harmful. Few people would do so now. Is male circumcision a legitimate expression of cultural identity or personal preference, or is it a form of mutilation? If there is no clear consensus on what are good or bad uses of the body, Raz's argument is problematic.

---

[58] J. Herring and J. Wall, 'Autonomy, capacity and vulnerable adults: filling the gaps in the Mental Capacity Act' (2016) 25 *Legal Studies* 698, 698.
[59] J. Raz, *The Morality of Freedom* (Oxford University Press, 1986).

Dignity

To some, the preciousness of the body means that we should not treat it as an object to do with what we will. It is, if you like, a sacred thing. Behaviour which treats the body in a degrading or undignified manner should not be permitted. This would require a line to be drawn between what behaviour is not undignified (presumably ear piercing is not) and what is (presumably clinically unnecessary limb removal is). As we mentioned in Chapter 1, one of the problems with 'dignity' is that different people understand the term in different ways, and the law may feel there is no consensus on what is a dignified use of the body.

Cost

Most people would accept that cost to the National Health Service (NHS) would be a reason for restricting access to treatment not clinically recommended. However, this would be no argument in cases where the patient had arranged the work privately and paid for it themselves. Then the only argument might be that if many doctors were undertaking this work privately, they would be able to spend fewer hours on NHS work.

John Coggon[60] has usefully summarised the requirements for when treatment is lawful in this way:

> For treatment to be lawful it is requisite that:
>
> - It is established to reflect, or at least be consistent with, the patient's personal view of her interests: this may be established through gaining consent, or by reference to proven facts about the patient's values.
> - It is judged by reference to professional opinion to be in the patient's best interests: this will be established by reference to the doctor(s) agreeing that the intervention is indicated as a worthwhile intervention because of the benefits – whether therapeutic or otherwise – that it will provide.
> - It is judged, by reference to principles of sound public decision-making, to be worth funding through the health care system: this will be established by the particular resource allocation model that governs access to treatment.

It is worth noting that on his analysis the autonomy of the patient is only one of the three requirements before it becomes lawful to give treatment.

Autonomy of others

At first sight, allowing one person to mutilate their body does not affect others, but it is a little more complex than this. Two arguments might be

---

[60] J. Coggon, 'Mental capacity law, autonomy, and best interests: an argument for conceptual and practical clarity in the court of protection' (2016) 24 *Medical Law Review* 396, 406.

made. First, it might be said that if we allow harmful surgeries, there is a risk that some people who do not consent will be harmed. This was an issue raised in the *Brown* case (above). There, it was accepted that the group in question was well-organised and that all the members of the group consented.[61] However, the majority said that other groups were less careful, and there was a danger that others who were not fully consenting might be drawn into the issue. The point is that if we allow a harmful activity, while some consenting people will be able to exercise their autonomy and engage in it, others who are not properly consenting may become involved. One response to this is that while some might be nervous about sadomasochist groups self-policing, we can be sure that doctors will carefully counsel any patient requesting harmful treatment, and there is only a tiny risk that patients who are not consenting will be involved.

Second, there is an argument that allowing an option might pressure some people to choose it. That sounds a little odd, but an example will clarify. There are press reports that cosmetic surgery is rampant amongst high-school students in some parts of the US.[62] It is not difficult to imagine in such a scenario that as more and more students choose to have such surgery, others will feel pressured into following suit ('peer pressure'). Even though the pressure will not be such as to mean that people will be robbed of any choice, their freedom to choose becomes compromised.

This is an important argument in this debate. There are two points to consider in response. First, note that it assumes that cosmetic surgery is bad. We would not feel the same concerns if peer pressure was causing people to eat healthily. So it is pressure to behave in a way which is thought harmful which is at the root of the argument. Second, we might question whether peer pressure will ever force people into major surgery which causes permanent harm, such as limb removal.

CONCLUSION

Those who support there being no restrictions on medical surgery, provided both the patient and doctor are willing to proceed, will emphasise the importance of autonomy: 'Our bodies are ours and we can do what we want to with them.' As we have seen, a host of arguments might be put the other way, but many of them can appear to be no more than a dislike of how someone wants to treat their body. These cases are a challenge for autonomy supporters. If you let people make their own choices, are you willing to do so even if they want to cause themselves serious harm?

---

[61] That might be questioned on the facts.

[62] www.telegraph.co.uk/news/worldnews/northamerica/usa/9514215/American-teenagers-resort-to-plastic-surgery-to-beat-bullies.html.

FURTHER READING

Debate 1

J. Herring and C. Foster, '"Please don't tell me": the right not to know' (2011) 21 *Cambridge Quarterly of Healthcare Ethics* 12.

J. Herring, B. Fulford, M. Dunn and A. Handa, 'Elbow room for best practice? Montgomery, patients' values, and balanced decision-making in person-centred clinical care' (2017) 25 *Medical Law Review* 582.

Debate 2

J. Coggon and J. Miola, 'Autonomy, liberty and medical decision-making' (2011) 70 *Cambridge Law Journal* 523.

J. Herring and J. Wall, 'Autonomy, capacity and vulnerable adults: filling the gaps in the Mental Capacity Act' (2016) 25 *Legal Studies* 698.

T. Hope, J. Tan, A. Stewart and J. McMillan, 'Agency, ambivalence and authenticity: The many ways in which anorexia nervosa can affect autonomy' (2013) 8 *International Journal of Law in Context* 20.

C. Mackenzie and W. Rogers, 'Autonomy, vulnerability and capacity: a philosophical appraisal of the Mental Capacity Act' (2013) 8 *International Journal of the Law in Context* 37.

Debate 3

E. Cave, 'Maximisation of a minors' capacity' (2011) 4 *Child and Family Law Quarterly* 429.

E. Cave and J. Wallbank, 'Minors' capacity to refuse treatment: a reply to Gilmore and Herring' (2012) 20 *Medical Law Review* 423.

S. Gilmore and J. Herring, '"No" is the hardest word: consent and children's autonomy' (2011) 23 *Child and Family Law Quarterly* 1.

Debate 4

T. Elliott, 'Body dysmorphic disorder, radical surgery and the limits of consent' (2009) 19 *Medical Law Review* 149.

C. Foster, 'Dignity and the use of body parts' (2014) 40 *Journal of Medical Ethics* 44.

CHAPTER 3

Capacity

Debate 1

How should we define capacity?

INTRODUCTION AND THE LAW

The concept of capacity plays a central role in the law. Those who lack capacity are deemed unable to make decisions for themselves. Decisions are made by others based on an assessment of what is in the best interests of a person lacking capacity. Those with capacity are free to make decisions about their lives, subject to the constraints of the law. No one is permitted to make decisions on behalf of a competent person, unless, for example, they have been appointed as an agent by that person. If you have capacity you can consent to an operation, decide to enter a contract or agree to meet someone. If you do not have capacity then these decisions are made on your behalf.[1]

At the heart of the law's approach is the principle of autonomy. That is, that each person should be free to choose for themselves their version of the 'good life' and to seek to pursue it. Joseph Raz puts it this way:

> [T]he good life is for each of us to live. It is not in anyone's gift. It consists, I have argued, in the wholehearted and successful pursuit of worthwhile relationships and goals. They are goals we have to adopt and pursue. This requires the use of our powers of rational agency.[2]

That is only possible, however, where a person has the ability to decide how they wish to live their life and to put that decision into practice.

The law on capacity is found in the Mental Capacity Act 2005 (MCA). The starting point is the presumption is that a person is competent, unless there is evidence that they are not.[3] In a medical case the burden is on the doctor to

---

[1] R. Fyson and J. Cromby, 'Human rights and intellectual disabilities in an era of "choice"' (2013) 57 *Journal of Disability Research* 1164.
[2] J. Raz, 'The role of well-being', available at http://ssrn.com/abstract=1002585.
[3] MCA, s. 1(2).

demonstrate that the patient lacks capacity on the balance of probabilities.[4] Understandably, when the court is determining whether a patient has capacity, the views of the medical experts carry 'very considerable importance'.[5] But at the end of the day it is for the court, not the doctors, to determine the issue. The issue of who has capacity to make a decision is, therefore, a controversial one. In this debate we will explore how the law should decide capacity. We will take the current law as a starting point and consider the difficulties it raises.

ISSUE-SPECIFIC CAPACITY

A central aspect of the MCA's approach to capacity is that it is 'issue specific'. It is inaccurate to talk of someone generally being 'incompetent' or 'lacking capacity'. Rather, you should ask whether a person has capacity to decide a particular issue. It may well be that a person has capacity to decide some issues but not others. For example, they may be able to decide whether they would like marshmallows on their hot chocolate or not, but lack the capacity to be able to execute a will.

This is an important aspect of the MCA and marks a clear departure from the previous law, which tended to categorise a person in general terms. This approach has been broadly welcomed because it ensures that people are given as much opportunity to make decisions for themselves as possible, and a decision is made on their behalf only where necessary. This is in line with the general principle of autonomy that we should let people make decisions for themselves as much as possible.

THE CAUSE OF INCAPACITY

Section 2(1) of the MCA states:

> [A] person lacks capacity in relation to a matter if at the material time he is unable to make a decision for himself in relation to the matter because of an impairment of, or a disturbance in the functioning of, the mind or brain.

In *A Local Authority v TZ*[6] it was explained that this involves a 'diagnostic test' and a 'functional test'. Under the diagnostic test, it must be found that a person has impairment or a disturbance in the functioning of the brain. Under the 'functional test', it must be determined whether, as a result of the disturbance, a person is unable to make the decision. Importantly, it must be shown that the inability to make the decision results from the impairment. So, a person who has a mental disorder but is unable to make a decision because, say, they are drunk, will not lack capacity because their inability to make

---

[4] *R (N) v Dr M, A NHS Trust* [2002] EWHC 1911.
[5] *A NHS Trust v Dr A* [2013] EWHC 2442 (COP), para. 12.
[6] *A Local Authority v TZ* [2013] EWHC 2322 (COP).

the decision does not result from the mental impairment. Similarly, patients with no mental impairment who refuse all treatment because of their religious belief that God will cure them will not lack capacity even if the doctors try to argue that those patients do not properly understand the reality of their situation. They do not have a mental impairment and so cannot lack capacity to make a decision.

This approach has two main problems with it. First, Peter Bartlett[7] has made a powerful case that this breaches the United Nations Convention on the Rights of Persons with Disabilities. Article 12(2) provides that people with disabilities may enjoy legal capacity 'on an equal basis with others in all aspects of life'. Yet the MCA draws a distinction between a case where a person is deluded because of a mental condition and a case where a person is deluded for some other reason. It is hard to deny that this appears to be a breach of the person's right not to be discriminated against on the basis of mental disorder.

A second problem is that it means that a person whose impairment in reasoning is not the result of a mental condition is left to have their decision respected, even though it may not in fact represent an autonomous decision of their own. We will return to this issue later when we discuss vulnerable adults (below).

THE NECESSARY INFORMATION

For persons to lack capacity, it must be shown that they are unable to make a decision for themselves. Section 3(1) of the MCA explains:

[A] person is unable to make a decision for himself if he is unable –

(a) to understand the information relevant to the decision,
(b) to retain that information,
(c) to use or weigh that information as part of the process of making the decision, or
(d) to communicate his decision (whether by talking, using sign language or any other means).

As this indicates, there are a number of ways in which a person may be said to be unable to make a decision. One is that there is a lack of comprehension: the person is not capable of understanding their condition or the proposed treatment, or the consequences of not receiving treatment.[8] The MCA, however, emphasises that a patient should not be treated as lacking capacity 'unless all

---

[7] P. Bartlett, 'The United Nations Convention on the Rights of Persons with Disabilities and Mental Health Law' (2012) 75 *Modern Law Review* 752.
[8] MCA, s. 2(4).

practical steps to help him' reach capacity 'have been taken without success'.[9] This means that if a person does not understand an aspect of their condition, a doctor should try to help them understand.

That is relatively uncontroversial. What is complex is deciding what information a person needs to understand if they are to have capacity. The person only needs to understand the central aspects of the decision. Macur J, in *LBL v RYJ*,[10] explained that 'it is not necessary for the person to comprehend every detail of the issue ... it is not always necessary for a person to comprehend all peripheral details'. However, this raises the difficult question of what are peripheral details and what are not.

A good example of the difficulties that can arise is the following case:

Leading case

PC v City of York [2013] EWCA Civ 478

PC (a woman with significant learning difficulties) had married a man (NC) while he was in prison for a series of sex offences. NC was due to be released, and he and PC intended to live together. The professionals involved with PC's care were convinced that if that happened, NC would pose a risk to PC. They sought an order that PC lacked capacity to cohabit with NC. The key issue for the court was: 'What did PC have to understand about cohabiting with NC in order to have capacity?' There was general agreement that PC had to understand what living with someone meant, and this she did. However, there was a lack of agreement over whether she had to understand what *living with NC* would be like. The Court of Appeal held that it was necessary for her to understand that. She did not believe that NC had a violent past or that he posed a risk to her. She therefore failed to understand a crucial piece of information. However, the reasoning then took a surprising turn. It had not been shown that it was PC's mental disorder, rather than 'blindness in love' or bad judgement, which had caused her to be unaware of the information about NC, and so the MCA did not apply.[11]

The Court of Appeal in *PC v York* highlighted a distinction between 'person specific' decisions and 'act specific' decisions. Sometimes the courts have taken an 'act specific' approach, where the court determines that the person said to lack capacity (P) understands the nature of the act, even though they do not need to understand the nature of the person they are doing it with. This is the

---

[9] MCA, s. 2.
[10] *LBL v RYJ* [2010] EWHC 2664 (Fam), para. 24.
[11] J. Wall and J. Herring, 'Capacity to cohabit: hoping "everything turns out well in the end"' (2013) 27 *Child and Family Law Quarterly* 417.

approach the courts have taken in relation to marriage: the question is whether P understands what marriage is like, not whether P understands what marriage to X is like. In other cases the courts have taken a 'person specific' approach, meaning that that P must understand the act in relation to the other person. Interestingly, in *PC v York* the Court thought that capacity to cohabit had to be person specific, so PC had to understand what living with NC was like.

The courts have also struggled in dealing with a series of cases in relation to sex. The lower courts have taken the approach that capacity to have sex is act specific.[12] Parker J in London Borough of *Southwark v KA*[13] listed what information needed to be understood to have capacity to consent to sex in general:

(i)   The mechanics of the act.
(ii) That sexual relations can lead to pregnancy.
(iii) That there are health risks caused by sexual relations.
(iv) The ability to understand the concept of and the necessity of one's own consent is fundamental to having capacity: in other words that P 'knows that she/he has a choice and can refuse'.[14]

Controversially, Parker J held that understanding that one's partner should consent is not part of the capacity to consent. This reflects the general approach of the courts that there is no need for P to understand moral issues in relation to sex.

The Court of Appeal *IM v LM & Others*[15] approved this approach, having been heavily influenced by pragmatic considerations to support the approach taken by the lower courts:

> [I]t would be totally unworkable for a local authority or the Court of Protection to conduct an assessment every time an individual over whom there was doubt about his or her capacity to consent to sexual relations showed signs of immediate interest in experiencing a sexual encounter with another person.

These cases reveal two problems. First, it is very difficult to discuss a question such as 'Does this person have capacity to consent to sex?' or 'Does this person have capacity to cohabit?' in the abstract. It is much easier to discuss whether a person has capacity in relation to a particular individual and at a particular time. This is true not just of those with mental disorders. None of us, in reality, have capacity all the time. If we are asleep, drunk or terrified, we may well lack capacity. All the courts can say is that we can imagine circumstances in which a person can make a decision of this kind with capacity, but it does not make sense to talk about whether a person generally has capacity to consent.[16] Indeed the 'issue specific'

---

[12] *A Local Authority v TZ* [2013] EWHC 2322 (COP).
[13] *Southwark v KA* [2016] EWCOP 20. See also *D Borough Council v AB* [2011] EWHC 101.
[14] *A Local Authority v TZ* [2013] EWHC 2322 (COP) explained that if P was engaging in same-sex sexual activity then the last factor did not need to be understood.
[15] *IM v LM & Others* [2014] EWCA Civ 37.
[16] J. Herring, 'Mental disability and capacity to consent to sex' (2013) 34 *Journal of Social Welfare and Family Law* 471.

approach of the MCA indicates they are better avoiding these sweeping judgments. However, those caring for people with mental disorders need clear guidance from the courts. If they are told a person lacks capacity for sex in general,
they can take steps to ensure that no one has sex with that person. The problem is
that if they are told a person has capacity generally to have sex, that does not give
clear guidance on whether they have capacity in a particular situation.

Second, the cases indicate another difficulty. There is a wide range of views
over what a person should understand before they have capacity to consent to
sex or to marry, for example. Indeed there is something unsavoury about the
court's deciding whom a person can have sex with or whom a person may live
with. We don't want the court to take the role of an old-fashioned father who
needs to approve his daughter's suitors.

The courts here are on the horns of a dilemma. Looking at the issue of
capacity to consent to sex, Ralph Sandland[17] has written about the construction of sexuality of those with intellectual impairment. Historically, he argues
that the sexuality of those with intellectual impairments was seen as a danger,
a result of animal instinct, something 'monstrous'. He is concerned that the
courts too readily accept this understanding as a justification for restricting the
sexual liberty of those with mental conditions. However, there is the opposing
view that recognises the widespread sexual abuse of those with mental impairments. Striking the balance between protection and autonomy is difficult in
this area. The more strict we are about what information we require people to
have in order to have capacity, the more people are found to be lacking capacity. But the looser we are about how much information a person needs to
understand to have capacity, the greater the risk that a person is not protected
from harm due to a decision they have made based on little information.

WISDOM AND CAPACITY

Section 1(4) of the MCA states that '[a] person is not to be treated as unable
to make a decision merely because he makes an unwise decision'. Doctors must
not assume that because they disagree with a decision, the patient lacked capacity. Peter Jackson J in *Heart of England NHS Foundation Trust v JB* emphasised:

> The temptation to base a judgment of a person's capacity upon whether they
> seem to have made a good or bad decision, and in particular on whether they
> have accepted or rejected medical advice, is absolutely to be avoided. That would
> be to put the cart before the horse or, expressed another way, to allow the tail of
> welfare to wag the dog of capacity. Any tendency in this direction risks infringing
> the rights of that group of persons who, though vulnerable, are capable of making
> their own decisions. Many who suffer from mental illness are well able to make
> decisions about their medical treatment, and it is important not to make unjusti-
> fied assumptions to the contrary.[18]

---

[17] R. Sandland, 'Sex and capacity: the management of monsters?' (2013) 76 *Modern Law Review* 981.
[18] *Heart of England NHS Foundation Trust v JB* [2014] EWHC 342 (COP), at para. 7.

That said, it is important to notice the word 'merely' in section 1(4) of the MCA. This indicates that the lack of wisdom in the decision can be taken into account along with other evidence to decide that the person lacked capacity. So, a doctor is entitled to assume that someone who has severe learning difficulties who makes a bizarre choice is lacking capacity. There is little doubt that in practice the wisdom of the decision affects assessment. If a patient is agreeing with what is proposed by the doctor, little is done to assess capacity; whereas if there is disagreement, there is likely to be a thorough assessment.[19, 20]

One question that may be asked about a person making an apparently unwise decision is why they are doing so. It may be, for example, that their religious or personal beliefs mean they reach a conclusion others find hard to understand. A Jehovah's Witness refusing a blood transfusion would be a well-known example. If there is such an explanation for their decision, they cannot be found to lack capacity.

Even if there is no apparent reason for the unwise decision, there is a need to exercise care. Hedley J, in *A NHS Trust v P*,[21] observed that 'the intention of the Act is not to dress an incapacitous person in forensic cotton wool but to allow them as far as possible to make the same mistakes that all other human beings are at liberty to make and not infrequently do'.

There is a problem here if a person understands the facts and reaches a conclusion that seems illogical on the facts: it is hard not to conclude that there is a defect in the reasoning caused by the mental condition. Indeed, it is difficult to know how else an assessment could be made, bar relying on the lack of rational connection between the facts and conclusion.[22]

WEIGHING THE INFORMATION

To be competent the patient must also be able to use the information, weigh it, and be able to make a decision.[23] This means that even though a patient may fully understand the issues involved, if they are in such a panic that they are unable to process the knowledge to reach a decision then they will lack capacity to make the decision.[24]

A Local Authority v E[25] demonstrates the difficulty well. The case concerned a 32-year-old woman who suffered from anorexia nervosa and other

---

[19] P. Brown, A. Tulloch, C. Mackenzie, G. Owen, G. Szmukler and M. Hotopf, 'Assessments of mental capacity in psychiatric inpatients: a retrospective cohort study' (2013) 13 *BMC Psychiatry* 115.

[20] N. Banner and G. Szmukler, '"Radical interpretation" and the assessment of decision-making capacity' (2013) 30 *Journal of Applied Philosophy* 379.

[21] *A NHS Trust v P* [2013] EWHC 50 (COP).

[22] T. Thornton, 'Capacity, mental mechanisms, and unwise decisions' (2011) 18 *Philosophy, Psychiatry and Psychology* 127.

[23] See M. Donnelly, 'Capacity assessment under the Mental Capacity Act 2005: delivering on the function approach' (2009) 29 *Legal Studies* 464.

[24] *Bolton Hospitals NHS Trust v O* [2003] 1 FLR 824.

[25] *A Local Authority v E* [2012] EWHC 1639 (COP).

health conditions, including alcohol dependence and a personality disorder. She refused to eat and the doctors recommended forced feeding, to which she objected. Jackson J concluded that E lacked capacity to refuse treatment in relation to forcible feeding:

> [T]here is strong evidence that E's obsessive fear of weight gain makes her incapable of weighing the advantages and disadvantages of eating in any meaningful way. For E, the compulsion to prevent calories entering her system has become the card that trumps all others. The need not to gain weight overpowers all other thoughts.

Jackson J went on to determine that it was in E's best interests to receive the treatment. From one point of view the decision is readily justifiable. As a result of her condition, E was so obsessed with avoiding calorie intake that she was unable to weigh up different factors to make a decision.

A similar point was made in assessing the capacity of a vegan 15-year-old girl who refused the MMR vaccine because it contained animal products.[26] She was found to lack capacity because she did not consider the competing arguments and simply refused on the basis of her moral objection to taking animal products.

The problem with both these cases is that perfectly competent people have absolute moral principles, which they apply regardless of the consequences. For example, some people believe abortion is always wrong. There is no weighing up of competing arguments to be done because they simply follow that rule. We might disagree with the absolute principles such people have adopted, but sticking to an absolute moral principle and so not weighing up competing arguments is not necessarily indicative of a lack of capacity.

One way of analysing *A Local Authority v E*[27] is to say that the disease of anorexia had changed E's reasoning process. The 'real' E would want to live, and we should take that into account.[28] A similar approach has sometimes been used when considering a person with 'needle phobia' who agrees to an injection when calm but refuses when they see the needle. We might argue that the 'real them' wants the injection. The difficulty with that kind of argument is that it might make it too easy to determine that a person making an unwise choice is acting out of character. It is always tempting, when seeing a friend making a bad decision, to say that it is not the 'real them'. On the other hand, that approach has an appeal when a condition such as anorexia changes a person's values and perceptions.

---

[26] *F v F* [2013] EWHC 2783 (Fam).

[27] [2012] EWHC 1639 (COP).

[28] T. Hope, J. Tan, A. Stewart and J. McMillan, 'Agency, ambivalence and authenticity: the many ways in which anorexia nervosa can affect autonomy' (2013) 17 *International Journal of Law in Context* 20.

VULNERABLE ADULTS

The orthodox view is that if a patient is deemed to have capacity, but only just, that patient must be treated in the same way as those who undoubtedly have capacity.[29] However, the courts in the last few years have been developing the inherent jurisdiction to deal with 'vulnerable adults': adults who are found officially to have capacity, but who are nevertheless thought to need protection.[30] Munby J has defined this group in this way:

> [T]he inherent jurisdiction can be exercised in relation to a vulnerable adult who, even if not incapacitated by mental disorder or mental illness, is, or is reasonably believed to be, either: (i) under constraint; or (ii) subject to coercion or undue influence; or (iii) for some other reason deprived of the capacity to make the relevant decision, or disabled from making a free choice, or incapacitated or disabled from giving or expressing a real and genuine consent.[31]

The courts will make the decision based on what is in the best interests of the individual. The Court of Appeal approved of the jurisdiction in *DL v A Local Authority*.[32] In *A NHS Trust v Dr A*,[33] it was held that it could be used to authorise forced feeding on a competent, but deluded, man.

The case law has been criticised as a clear infringement of the principle of autonomy.[34] However, the use of the jurisdiction could be justified once it is appreciated that there is a difference between having capacity and being autonomous. A person may have mental capacity but be unable to exercise it because they are in an abusive relationship, as in *DL v A Local Authority*. Protection of autonomy requires the courts to protect people being robbed of their autonomy by being pressurised or forced by others (or delusions) into acting against their genuine wishes. In other words, the definition of 'capacity' in the MCA is narrow and leaves some of those who lack autonomy to be judged to have capacity. For example, a person may lack understanding but not due to a mental disorder, or a person may be in an abusive relationship and utterly in thrall to their abuser; in both these cases the person would not fall under the MCA but would nevertheless lack the ability to exercise autonomy.

CONCLUSION

The definition of 'capacity' is problematic. If we set the bar too low, there is a danger that people's choices will be respected in the name of autonomy even though their decisions are not a product of their own free choice or are not

---

[29] J. Herring, 'Losing it? Losing what? The law and dementia' (2009) 21 *Child and Family Law Quarterly* 3.

[30] See J. Herring, *Vulnerable Adults and the Law* (Oxford University Press, 2016).

[31] *Re SA (Vulnerable Adult With Capacity: Marriage)* [2005] EWHC 2942 (Fam), para. 77.

[32] *DL v A Local Authority* [2012] EWCA Civ 253.

[33] *A NHS Trust v Dr A* [2013] EWHC 2442 (COP).

[34] B. Hewson, '"Neither midwives nor rainmakers" – why DL is wrong' (2013) *Public Law* 451.

informed decisions. Where they suffer serious harm as a result, it may be questioned whether relying on a flawed decision-making process is a sufficient justification for allowing the harm.

On the other hand, if the bar for capacity is set too high, people who are perfectly able to make decisions about their lives are deprived of their freedom to exercise autonomy, and decisions are made paternalistically on their behalf. One solution to the dilemma is to be more flexible in cases on the borderline of capacity, and so attach considerable weight to the views of those who are found to lack capacity in making a best interests assessment, especially in cases where no great harm will come from abiding by their decision, and to use the vulnerable adult jurisdiction to protect those who are found to just have capacity but are making a decision which will cause them serious harm.

Debate 2
How should the law respond to advance decisions?

INTRODUCTION

Some people are worried about how they may be treated if they lose capacity. They may want to ensure that even if they do lose capacity, they are treated in line with their religious or other values. That will be particularly true for those who are unhappy about the idea of others making an assessment of what is in their best interests. They may be interested in issuing an 'advance decision', which seeks to set out how they would like to be treated if they lose capacity.

ADVANCE DECISIONS: LAW

Section 24(1) of the MCA defines an advance decision:

> 'Advance Decision' means a decision made by a person ('P'), after he has reached 18 and when he has capacity to do so, that if –
>
> (a) at a later time and in such circumstances as he may specify, a specified treatment is proposed to be carried out or continued by a person providing health care for him, and
> (b) at that time he lacks capacity to consent to the carrying out or continuation of the treatment,
>   the specified treatment is not to be carried out or continued.

It is important to realise that the advance decision only comes into effect when a person has lost capacity. So, for example, if a Jehovah's Witness signs an advance decision so that she will never ever receive a blood transfusion, it will not be effective if she later loses her faith and consents to receiving a blood transfusion.

Another important limitation is that under the MCA advance decisions only apply to 'refusals'. So a person cannot use an advance decision to demand that they be treated in a particular way, only that they will not be treated in a particular way. So an advance decision requiring that they be given a particular drug if they lose capacity will not be effective. However, an advance decision stating they should not be given a particular drug if they lose capacity will be. An advance decision can cover refusals of life-saving treatment, although then the advance decision needs to be in writing, signed and witnessed by a third party.[35] Strikingly, in any refusal the advance decisions does not need to be in writing nor does the person making it need to have received specialist advice.[36]

There is one obvious concern with advance decisions. A person may have made an advance decision many years ago but it may no longer represent their views. This is dealt with by section 25 of the MCA, which sets out four ways in which an advance decision may be ineffective:

- P, with capacity, has withdrawn the advance decision. This does not need to be in writing.
- P has created a lasting power of attorney (LPA) after making the advance decision and given the LPA the power to make the decision in question.
- P has done anything else which is clearly inconsistent with the directive in the advance decision.
- '[T]here are reasonable grounds for believing that circumstances exist which P did not anticipate at the time of the advance decision, and which would have affected his decision had he anticipated them.'[37]

A good example of why these provisions are important is *HE v A Hospital NHS Trust*,[38] where there was evidence that a woman who had signed an advance decision refusing blood transfusions was no longer a practising Jehovah's Witness.[39] It is also important to emphasise that the advance decision is only relevant if it specifies the treatment in question.

Critics claim that these provisions make it easy for a doctor or a legal adviser to a trust who does not want to follow an advance decision to find a way around it. For example, in many cases it would not take much imagination to argue that the particular situation of the patient was not covered by the directive. Similarly, it would not be difficult to make a case that the circumstances had not been foreseen by the patient: a novel treatment is now available; P's family is desperate for P to receive treatment; P's family situation has changed since they issued the advance decision. All of these reasons could be used to claim that the advance decision is no longer binding. In one of the few cases to

---

[35] MCA, s. 25(6).
[36] *Briggs v Briggs* [2016] EWCOP 53. See C. Auckland, 'Protecting me from my directive: Ensuring appropriate safeguards for advance directives in dementia' (2017) *Medical Law Review*, Advance access online at https://academic.oup.com/medlaw/advance-article-abstract/doi/10.1093/medlaw/fwx037/4083527?redirectedFrom=fulltext
[37] MCA, s. 25(4).
[38] *HE v A Hospital NHS Trust* [2003] EWHC 1017 (Fam).
[39] See also *A Local Authority v E* [2012] EWHC 1639 (COP).

uphold an advance decision, *X Primary Care Trust v XB*,[40] it was notable that the patient had drafted it in careful consultation with his doctor and shortly before he lost capacity. However, recently, in *Briggs v Briggs*[41] Charles J stated that the Mental Capacity Act regimes for advance decisions had been created specifically to enable people to make decisions for their future care and courts should be reluctant to find an advance decision ineffective.

There is extensive protection for those who act against an advance decision. Under section 26(2) of the MCA:

> A person does not incur liability for carrying out or continuing the treatment unless, at the time, he is satisfied that an advance decision exists which is valid and applicable to the treatment.

Section 26(3), in similar terms, provides a defence to someone who withdraws or withholds treatment believing (incorrectly) that there is a valid advance decision requiring this. These provisions mean that it will be very difficult for a doctor to be legally liable for not following, or incorrectly following, an advance decision.[42]

Academic opinion on these provisions differs. To some we should not deprive patients of beneficial treatment unless we are absolutely clear they would not have wanted it. Relying on imprecise documents or vaguely remembered comments is insufficient to justify withholding necessary medical treatment. To others these provisions mean that advance decisions are effectively unenforceable.[43] There are too many ways in which a doctor can easily determine that the advance decision is inapplicable.

ETHICAL ISSUES SURROUNDING ADVANCE DECISIONS

Should we follow advance decisions? It should be noted that many people decide not to make advance decisions. They are happy to allow doctors and families to make decisions on their behalf. However, there are some who want to control what happens if they lose capacity. As Dworkin has put it, 'they want their deaths, if possible, to express and in that way vividly to confirm the values they believe most important'.[44] If someone has gone to the effort of making an advance decision, why not follow it? After all, if there is a dispute over how a patient should be treated, is it not more appropriate to listen to the patient's own views (made when competent) than the views the doctors have at the moment? As we shall see, the issue is not quite as straightforward as that question suggests.

[40] *X Primary Care Trust v XB* [2012] EWHC 1390 (Fam).
[41] *Briggs v Briggs* [2016] EWCOP 53.
[42] A. Maclean, 'Advance directives and the rocky waters of anticipatory decision-making' (2008) 17 *Medical Law Review* 1.
[43] C. Johnston, 'Advance decision making – rhetoric or reality?' (2014) 34 *Legal Studies* 497.
[44] R. Dworkin, *Life's Dominion* (HarperCollins, 1993).

Different person

Some opponents of advance decisions claim that when a person loses capacity, they become a different person from the person they were when they issued the directive. This view is most commonly taken by those who take a psychological understanding of the self. We are, it is said, a collection and continuity of memories and life stories.[45] In the case of an Alzheimer's patient, although their body remains the same, the loss of memory or connection with relatives or friends means that, with the onset of Alzheimer's, a new person has come into being. The values and principles that were important to the competent person have no relevance and meaning to the new person without capacity.[46]

This view can be challenged from two perspectives. First, Ronald Dworkin has replied to such arguments that even if there is some validity in the claim that the person has changed since developing Alzheimer's, their 'critical interests' remain. He distinguishes critical interests, which are fundamental to our life story and help define who we are (important relationships, career goals, etc.), and experiential interests, which are particular experiences that we enjoy at a particular time (types of food we enjoy; whether we like watching trashy TV and the like). He argues these critical interests stay with us even if capacity is lost. Rebecca Dresser responds by saying that if a person has lost the capacity to understand their critical interests, those interests should not be given weight.[47]

A second line of challenge to the 'change in personality argument' is to reject the psychological understanding of the self. One way of doing this is to support a relational understanding and argue that to their friends and family the Alzheimer's patient has not changed their identity. Although a person may cease to understand their values, they will still be a treasured part of their family or community. Ensuring they can live as a member of that community recognises the value of communal relationships to our selves.

Scenario to ponder

Margo is described as a 54-year-old woman, suffering from dementia but extraordinarily happy. Each of her days is virtually the same. She rereads pages of a book she never finishes; eats the same food (peanut butter and jelly); and paints the same picture. Earlier in her life she foresaw that she would fall into this condition and wrote an advance decision, saying that she should not be given life-saving treatment if she became demented. She falls ill with pneumonia. Without treatment she may well die. Should she be treated?

---

[45] This is developed from the theories of D. Parfit, *Reasons and Persons* (Oxford University Press, 1984).

[46] J. Robertson, 'Second thoughts on living wills' (1991) 21 *Hastings Center Report* 6, 7.

[47] R. Dresser, 'Missing persons: legal perceptions of incompetent patients' (1994) 46 *Rutgers Law Review* 609; R. Dresser, 'Dworkin on dementia: elegant theory, questionable policy' (1995) 25 *Hastings Center Report* 32; R. Dresser, 'Precommitment: a misguided strategy for securing death with dignity' (2013) 81 *Texas Law Review* 1823.

For Ronald Dworkin the advance decision should be followed in Margo's case. When Margo had capacity she wanted to avoid living the life of a person with dementia, and found such a life lacking in value and indeed positively degrading. For Dresser, however, much as Margo may have felt these things earlier, the current Margo is happy and enjoying life. The sense of degradation she feared in the past has no meaning for her now.

Impossibility of foresight

A second set of arguments against advance decisions claims that it is in fact impossible to know what having a lack of capacity will feel like. We cannot, therefore, make any kind of informed decision about how we would like to be treated if we lose capacity. People tend to imagine that suffering from dementia is a terrifying experience, yet some sufferers seem very happy.[48] We imagine that being rendered paraplegic would make our life worthless, yet studies show that paralysed people are able to find considerable joy in their lives. It is one thing to think now about how you would feel if a terrible medical condition fell upon you, but it is another to actually be in that situation. It seems humans are significantly over-pessimistic when predicting how they will cope with a misfortune.[49] Further, it is difficult to imagine all the possible scenarios one might find oneself in. You might decide that you would rather die quickly if suffering from a prolonged illness, but would that be your view if, by intervention, you could be kept alive long enough to see your first grandchild?

The current person's best interests

Other commentators argue that we should focus on the best interests of the person as they are now. Agnieszka Jaworska[50] puts the point this way:

> [T]he caregiver … is faced with a person – or if not a fully constituted person, at least a conscious being capable of pleasure and pain – who, here and now, makes a claim on the caregiver to fulfil her needs and desires; why ignore these needs and desires in the name of values that are now extinct?

John Robertson[51] takes a similar line, arguing:

> The values and interests of the competent person no longer are relevant to someone who has lost the rational structure on which those values and interests rested. Unless we are to view competently held values and interests as extending

---

[48] S. Behuniak, 'The living dead? The construction of people with Alzheimer's disease as zombies' (2011) 31 *Ageing and Society* 70.
[49] P. Menzel and B. Steinbock, 'Advance directives, dementia, and physician-assisted death' (2013) 41 *Journal of Law, Medicine and Ethics* 484.
[50] A. Jaworska, 'Respecting the margins of agency: Alzheimer's patients and the capacity to value' (1999) 28 *Philosophy and Public Affairs* 105, 120.
[51] J. Robertson, 'Second thoughts on living wills' (1991) 21 *Hastings Center Report* 6, 7.

even into situations in which, because of incompetency, they can no longer have meaning, it matters not that as a competent person the individual would not wish to be maintained in a debilitated or disabled state. If the person is no longer competent enough to appreciate the degree of divergence from her previous activity that produced the choice against treatment, the prior directive does not represent her current interests merely because a competent directive was issued.

The merits of these views will depend on the extent to which you are confident that the doctor can assess the best interests of a current person. If you take the view that doctors, in fact, have no special expertise on the nature of human well-being, or at least no better than anyone else, then you might question whether, even if we focus on the person as they are now, the views of the doctor should count for any more than the views of the person the patient once was.

Compromise views

In weighing up these competing arguments, it might be suggested that a middle path be promoted. The compromise view might avoid the extremes of the argument. It seems that failing to pay any attention to a past directive can be harsh. For example, in one case a devout Muslim woman lost capacity and an issue arose whether she should be cared for in a way which complied with Muslim tradition. Hegarty J was clear that she should:

> I do not think for one moment that a reasonable member of the public would consider that the religious beliefs of an individual and her family should simply be disregarded in deciding how she should be cared for in the unhappy event of supervening mental capacity. On the contrary, I would have thought that most reasonable people would expect, in the event of some catastrophe of that kind, that they would be cared for, as far as practicable, in such a way as to ensure that they were treated with due regard for their personal dignity and with proper respect for their religious beliefs.[52]

Where someone has issued an advance decision or has clear prior views, and following these will not harm the current patient, it seems there needs to be a good reason to ignore that. However, the view that we should always follow an advance decision, whatever its impact on the current person, seems to operate too harshly too.

Advance decisions on this view should carry some weight but not overriding weight. They should be followed unless they cause the current individual harm[53] or significant harm.[54] One might argue that in relation to the 'different person' argument, the correct answer is that there are senses in which the

---

[52] *Ahsan v University Hospitals Leicester NHS Trust* [2007] PIQR 19.

[53] J. Herring, 'Losing it? Losing what? The law and dementia' (2009) 21 *Child and Family Law Quarterly* 3.

[54] A. Maclean, 'Advance directives and the rocky waters of anticipatory decision-making' (2008) 17 *Medical Law Review* 1.

person without capacity is a different person, but also senses in which they are the same. Further, one might argue that even if a person has lost capacity, their current wishes and feelings still deserve respect.

CONCLUSION

As we have seen in this debate, three broad views emerge on advance decisions. For some people, advance decisions should be given full effect so that we are given maximum control over our lives and are able to determine what happens to us when we lose capacity. Others argue that when a person loses capacity and has no connection with the values that led to their issuing the advance decision, we should ignore that advance decision. We should, instead, focus on their current interests, wishes and values, and seek to promote their current best interests as best we can determine them. Finally there is a compromise view which seeks to acknowledge that we should place some weight on advance decisions, but also place weight on the current interests of the individual.

Debate 3

Are the interests of others relevant to best interests?

INTRODUCTION AND THE LAW

In an assessment of the best interests of a patient who lacks capacity (P), are the interests of others relevant? At first sight it seems the answer to that question is obvious: No. The court must focus simply on what is best for P. The MCA appears to make it clear that the focus should be on P's best interests, not the interests of others. Munby J in *Re MM* summarised well the approach that should be adopted in determining a person's best interests:

> MM's welfare is the paramount consideration. The focus must be on MM's best interests, and this involves a welfare appraisal in the widest sense, taking into account, where appropriate, a wide range of ethical, social, moral, emotional and welfare considerations. Where, as will often be the case, the various factors engaged pull in opposite directions, the task of ascertaining where the individual's best interests truly lie will be assisted by preparation of a 'balance sheet' of the kind suggested by Thorpe LJ in *Re A (Male Sterilisation)*.[55] This will enable the judge, at the end of the day, to strike what Thorpe LJ referred to as 'a balance between the sum of the certain and possible gains against the sum of the certain and possible losses'.[56]

Section 4 of the MCA states that included within the factors to be taken into account in determining best interests are the views of:

(a) anyone named by the person as someone to be consulted on the matter in question or on matters of that kind,

---

[55] *Re A (Male Sterilisation)* [2000] 1 FLR 549, 560.
[56] *Re MM (An Adult)* [2007] EWHC 2003 (Fam), para. 99.

(b) anyone engaged in caring for the person or interested in his welfare,

(c) any donee of a lasting power of attorney granted by the person, and

(d) any deputy appointed for the person by the court, as to what would be in the patient's best interests.

However, these people are consulted in a limited way: they are to advise on what is in P's best interests. The views of family members are to be taken into account only in so far as they assist in determining P's best interests.[57] They can never be used to justify making an order which would be against P's best interests.[58] Only P's own interests, what is good for them, are to be taken into account.

Many commentators feel this approach is appropriate. Those lacking capacity are vulnerable, and it is not difficult to find examples of cases where those lacking capacity have been taken advantage of. For their protection we must insist that the sole focus of the court should be on the interests of the person lacking capacity. However, this straightforward view has been challenged in a number of ways.

Human rights

It might be argued that the right to respect for family life of the family of the person lacking capacity would be relevant. In *A Local Authority v E*,[59] it was held that although there is no presumption that a person lacking capacity is better off cared for by their family than in an institution, 'nevertheless the normal assumption [is] that mentally incapacitated adults who have been looked after within their family will be better off if they continue to be looked after within the family rather than by the state'.[60]

Where P is to be removed from their family then the right to respect for private and family life under Article 8 ECHR will be involved. Thorpe LJ, in *K v LBX*,[61] has given definitive guidance on such cases:

> I conclude that the safe approach of the trial judge in Mental Capacity Act cases is to ascertain the best interests of the incapacitated adult on the application of the section 4 checklist. The judge should then ask whether the resulting conclusion amounts to a violation of Article 8 rights and whether that violation is nonetheless necessary and proportionate.

This suggests that some weight is attached to the family life rights, but these should be generally subsumed within a 'best interests' test. That said, Thorpe LJ's approach does seem to imply that the court should rethink the outcome of the 'best interests' test if it cannot be justified on a human rights analysis.

---

[57] *Re MM (An Adult)* [2007] EWHC 2003 (Fam), [108].

[58] *A Primary Care Trust v P, AH, A Local Authority* [2008] EWHC 1403 (Fam).

[59] *A Local Authority v E* [2012] EWHC 1639 (COP).

[60] Ibid, para. 66.

[61] *K v LBX* [2012] EWCA Civ 79, para. 35.

Assisting another indirectly benefits P

It can be said to be in a patient's best interests to act in a way which is primarily designed to help another, if there is also a benefit to P. The best known example is the following:

Leading case

Re Y (Adult Patient) (Transplant: Bone Marrow) [1997] Fam 110

This case involved a 25-year-old woman (Y) who had severe mental and physical disabilities. Her sister needed a bone marrow transplant, without which the sister would die. Y was the only suitable match the doctors could find. It was held that the transplant would benefit Y, because if the sister were to die this would cause severe distress to Y's mother. The mother visited Y very regularly, and if her visits were to be limited, that would be harmful to Y. It was held that Y would benefit in emotional, social and psychological ways from the procedure.

This case has received criticism.[62] Opponents will argue that it opens the door to misuse and P being used by others for their own benefit. Supporters will claim the case can be justified in terms of relational interests, which we shall explore next.

Relational interests

Some commentators have warned against seeing the concept of 'best interests' in too individualistic a way.[63] Inevitably we all live in relationships, and we cannot understand our own interests separately from others. To harm our families is to harm us. Further, it has been argued that it is not in a patient's interest to live in a relationship in which no account is taken of the interests of their carer, especially where that carer is a member of their family.[64] Few people would be happy with the idea that if they were to lose capacity a decision would have to be made which benefited them a little bit, even if that caused grave harm to the person caring for them.[65] Indeed no carer could take every

---

[62] P. Lewis, 'Procedures that are against the medical interests of the incompetent person' (2002) 12 *Oxford Journal of Legal Studies* 575.

[63] J. Herring, *Caring and the Law* (Hart Publishing, 2013).

[64] J. Herring and C. Foster, 'Welfare means relationality, virtue and altruism' (2012) 32 *Legal Studies* 480; C. Foster and J. Herring, *Altruism, Welfare and the Law* (Springer, 2016).

[65] J. Herring, 'The place of carers' in M. Freeman (ed.), *Law and Bioethics* (Oxford University Press, 2008).

decision for a person who had lost capacity based solely on what is in that person's best interests.[66] This view suggests that we need to consider whether the decision is a reasonable one as part of a relationship which benefits P.

Some support for such a line of reasoning can be found in *Re G (TJ)*. A woman had lost capacity, and the question arose whether payments she had been making to her adult daughter, of whom she was fond and who was in financial need, should continue. Morgan J held:

> [T]he word 'interest' in the best interests test does not confine the court to considering the self-interest of P. The actual wishes of P, which are altruistic and not in any way, directly or indirectly self-interested, can be a relevant factor. Further, the wishes which P would have formed, if P had capacity, which may be altruistic wishes, can be a relevant factor.[67]

As this case demonstrates, 'best interests' need not be interpreted in a selfish way. They can include acting altruistically to one's friends and family.

A rather different example is *A NHS Trust v DE*.[68] The court ordered that DE, a young man who lacked mental capacity to make the decision, should be given a vasectomy. Although the procedure was not going to benefit him directly, it would mean that he could have a relationship with his girlfriend (who would have found pregnancy confusing and distressing). The court took into account that, without it, his parents would be worried. That was something that DE would not want. Here, the relational values played a major part in justifying the procedure.

Less straightforward was *Re N (Deprivation of Liberty Challenge)*[69] where a man with paedophilic tendencies (but who had never committed an offence) wanted to be free to walk around wherever he wanted. The local authority sought authorisation to restrict his liberty, fearing that he would (as he had done in the past) attempt to find children who would engage in sexual relations with him. The authorisation was granted on the basis that it was in his best interests to be prevented from committing offences against children.

Opponents of these kinds of arguments are deeply wary of using incapacitous people as a means of assisting another person. We would not force a competent person to act altruistically without their consent, nor should we so force an incapacitous person.[70] Indeed, a study by Roy Gilbar[71] suggests that although patients want relatives and carers involved in the decision-making process, they want to keep the final say over what should happen to them.

---

[66] See further J. Herring, *Caring and the Law* (Hart Publishing, 2013).

[67] *Re G (TJ)* [2010] EWHC 3005 (COP), para. 56.

[68] *A NHS Trust v DE* [2013] EWHC 2562 (Fam).

[69] *Re N (Deprivation of Liberty Challenge)* [2016] EWCOP 47.

[70] P. Lewis, 'Procedures that are against the medical interests of the incompetent person' (2002) 12 *Oxford Journal of Legal Studies* 575.

[71] R. Gilbar, 'Family involvement, independence, and patient autonomy in practice' (2011) 19 *Medical Law Review* 192.

THE NATURE OF BEST INTERESTS

Lurking behind these debates is a larger one about what we mean by 'best interests'. One view may be that we are simply wanting the result that will create the most happiness for P. However, this approach (hedonism) has problems. Not many people live their lives solely in order to give themselves pleasure. Most people deliberately take decisions that they know will not promote their own immediate happiness, in order to achieve a longer-term goal, or for the good of others. And even if there are people who live solely for pleasure, few would promote it as the best way to live a life. No parent would raise a child by seeking simply to promote their happiness.

An alternative view may be that a good life is one marked by virtue.[72] The idea can be seen in the writing of Socrates, Plato and especially Aristotle.[73] There are two problems with this approach. The first is what exactly virtue is. Is bravery a virtue? Is hard work? If we cannot agree on what the virtues are, it will be difficult for a court to determine which virtues to seek to promote in a person.

A second, more fundamental problem is whether one can promote virtue in a person who lacks capacity. If the court decides to give all the money of a person with dementia to good causes, is it right to say the person is being generous? If you have no control over what you are doing or cannot understand it, in what sense can you be virtuous? Many people believe that unchosen acts cannot be virtuous. Others disagree. Hursthouse writes:

> A virtue is an excellent trait of character. It is a disposition, well entrenched in its possessor – something that, as we say, goes all the way down, unlike a habit such as being a tea-drinker – to notice, expect, value, feel, desire, choose, act, and react in certain characteristic ways. To possess a virtue is to be a certain sort of person with a certain complex mindset. A significant aspect of this mindset is the wholehearted acceptance of a distinctive range of considerations as reasons for action.[74]

This 'all the way down' understanding of virtue does not define itself purely by reference to choices. It seems to allow for desires, attitudes and sensibilities to be virtues. These can certainly be found in those lacking capacity. Anyone dealing with those lacking mental capacity knows they can be capable of love, comfort, pity and courage, even if not as the result of a conscious decision.

A central part of a good life for many people is found in their relationships with others. Indeed, it is through our relationships with others that we come to an understanding of ourselves. Our sense of self is a mixture of interlocking and

---

[72] R. Hursthouse, *On Virtue Ethics* (Oxford University Press, 1999).

[73] Aristotle, *Nicomachean Ethics*, ed. R. Crisp (Cambridge University Press, 2000 [C4 BCE]).

[74] R. Hursthouse, 'Virtue Ethics', *Stanford Encyclopedia of Philosophy*, available at http://plato.stanford.edu/entries/ethics-virtue/.

sometimes conflicting social identities.[75] Herring and Foster argue in favour of a more relational understanding of welfare:

> A judge who seeks to assess the best interests of X by taking her out of her social context and examining her in isolation in a forensic petri dish will come to a wrong conclusion. Essentially this is because it is meaningless to continue to talk about 'X' once she has been removed from her context. She will have ceased to exist. The judge will be determining the best interests of a non-entity.[76]

There are certainly dangers in Herring and Foster's approach. It is easy to find examples of where those lacking capacity have faced appalling abuse. Moving away from the starting point that their interests must be our primary concern poses great dangers. However, what relational supporters claim is that we need a better understanding of what welfare or best interests means – one that takes into account the relational nature of our lives and the altruism which is an important part of human flourishing.

Conclusion

The relatively small question of whether it is appropriate to consider the interests of others in determining the best interests of a person lacking capacity turns out to raise some very big questions. The claim to focus simply on the interests of P has appeal because too often the interests of those lacking capacity are downgraded and their human rights ignored. However, doing so ignores the relational interests that we all have, and the fact that few of us want to have decisions made simply on the basis of what is good for us. For many, the relational approach can only be supported if it provides sufficient protection for P's individual interests and rights.

Further Reading

Debate 1

N. Banner and G. Szmukler, '"Radical interpretation" and the assessment of decision-making capacity' (2013) 30 *Journal of Applied Philosophy* 379.

P. Bartlett, 'The United Nations Convention on the Rights of Persons with Disabilities and mental health law' (2012) 75 *Modern Law Review* 752.

R. Fyson and J. Cromby, 'Human rights and intellectual disabilities in an era of "choice"' (2013) 57 *Journal of Disability Research* 1164.

J. Herring, *Vulnerable Adults and the Law* (Oxford University Press, 2016).

---

[75] A. Donchin, 'Autonomy, interdependence, and assisted suicide: Respecting boundaries/crossing lines' (2000) 14 *Bioethics* 187.

[76] J. Herring and C. Foster, 'Welfare means relationality, virtue and altruism' (2012) 32 *Legal Studies* 480.

T. Hope, J. Tan, A. Stewart and J. McMillan, 'Agency, ambivalence and authenticity: the many ways in which anorexia nervosa can affect autonomy' (2013) 17 *International Journal of Law in Context* 20.

J. Wall and J. Herring, 'Capacity to cohabit: hoping "everything turns out well in the end"' (2013) 27 *Child and Family Law Quarterly* 417.

Debate 2

C. Auckland, 'Protecting me from my directive: ensuring appropriate safeguards for advance directives in dementia' (2017) *Medical Law Review*, Advance access online at https://academic.oup.com/medlaw/advance-article-abstract/doi/10.1093/medlaw/fwx037/4083527?redirectedFrom=fulltext

R. Dresser, 'Dworkin on dementia: elegant theory, questionable policy' (1995) 25 *Hastings Center Report* 32.

R. Dresser, 'Precommitment: a misguided strategy for securing death with dignity' (2013) 81 *Texas Law Review* 1823.

R. Dworkin, *Life's Dominion* (HarperCollins, 1993).

J. Herring, 'Losing it? Losing what? The law and dementia' (2009) 21 *Child and Family Law Quarterly* 3.

R. Heywood, 'Revisiting advance decision making under the Mental Capacity Act 2005: a tale of mixed messages' (2015) 23 *Medical Law Review* 81.

A. Jaworska, 'Respecting the margins of agency: Alzheimer's patients and the capacity to value' (1999) 28 *Philosophy and Public Affairs* 105.

C. Johnston, 'Advance decision making – rhetoric or reality?' (2014) 34 *Legal Studies* 497.

A. Maclean, 'Advance directives and the rocky waters of anticipatory decision-making' (2008) 17 *Medical Law Review* 1.

P. Menzel and B. Steinbock, 'Advance directives, dementia, and physician-assisted death' (2013) 41 *Journal of Law, Medicine and Ethics* 484.

Debate 3

C. Foster and J. Herring, *Altruism, Welfare and the Law* (Springer, 2016).

R. Gilbar, 'Family involvement, independence, and patient autonomy in practice' (2011) 19 *Medical Law Review* 192.

J. Herring and C. Foster, 'Welfare means relationality, virtue and altruism' (2012) 32 *Legal Studies* 480.

J. Samanta, 'Lasting powers of attorney for healthcare under the Mental Capacity Act 2005: enhanced prospective self-determination for future incapacity or a simulacrum?' (2009) 17 *Medical Law Review* 377.

P. Lewis, 'Procedures that are against the medical interests of the incompetent person' (2002) 12 *Oxford Journal of Legal Studies* 575.

CHAPTER 4

Medical Negligence

Introduction

Medical negligence is one of the main areas of litigation in relation to medical practitioners' actions. Every day, doctors, surgeons and other healthcare professionals work to cure the sick and injured. Inevitably, mistakes are made and people are harmed. Where such mistakes were foreseeable and could have been avoided, the medical professional may be held responsible and will be required to compensate the patient for the harm suffered. The law in this area is complex and much is contested. Here, we focus on three of the most hotly debated questions in medical negligence:

- to what standard of care should doctors be held;
- should a lost chance of a better medical outcome be compensated; and
- should parents be compensated for the cost of raising unwanted children.

Debate 1
To what standard of care should doctors be held?

The Law

When a doctor accepts a patient into their care, and attends that patient in their professional capacity, the doctor comes under a duty of care towards the patient. This can also arise when the patient is accepted for treatment at a hospital. Once this duty has been assumed, the doctor must act in accordance with the accepted practices of a responsible body of medical practitioners.[1] This is the 'standard of care', and it requires the practitioner to both do, and refrain from doing, certain things to protect their patients' interests.[2] Usually English law does not find a person liable in negligence simply for omitting to act, as

---

[1] *Bolam v Friern Hospital Management Committee* [1957] 1 WLR 582.
[2] See further E. Jackson, *Medical Law: Text, Cases and Materials*, 2nd edn (Oxford University Press, 2010), 103–04.

'the common law does not impose liability for pure omissions'.[3] However, a medical practitioner's duty means that the practitioner is required to do things as well as not do them, and not doing them would constitute a negligent omission. The duty also requires that the doctor not exacerbate a patient's condition, but a doctor defendant will generally not be liable if the patient claimant is left no worse off than they would otherwise have been.[4]

How do we determine what is required by a standard of care? Normally, the standard is that of the reasonable person, and the courts will weigh a range of factors in working out how someone should act in the face of a risk. These include the magnitude and seriousness of the risk, the cost and ease of precautions, and the usefulness of the defendant's conduct.[5] But in the case of medical practitioners, the approach is different. The standard is that of a responsible doctor, skilled in the particular speciality. Therefore, a surgeon must act as a responsible, skilled surgeon would, and a general practitioner (GP) must act as a responsible GP would. An inexperienced doctor will be held to the same general standard, although this approach assumes that the junior doctor will have access to (and will seek) advice from senior colleagues.[6] In an emergency, some account of the pressures of the situation will be taken into account in determining the standard.[7]

Crucially, it is not the *courts* that determine what this reasonable doctor would do, but instead the *medical profession* determines the content of the standard. The test for a doctor's standard of care has become known as the '*Bolam* test', arising from McNair J's direction to the jury in *Bolam v Friern Hospital Management Committee*, and it directs medical practitioners to act 'in accordance with a practice accepted as proper by a responsible body of medical [persons] skilled in that particular art'.[8] This test has been confirmed in numerous decisions by many courts, including the House of Lords and, since its inception in 2009, the Supreme Court of the United Kingdom.[9] However, in Chapter 3 in *Montgomery v Lanarkshire Health Board*[10] the Supreme Court departed from *Bolam* in relation to the standard of care expected when disclosing risks to patients.

What is the Appropriate Standard of Care for Doctors?

The fundamental debate in the context of standard of care is whether the *Bolam* test places medical practitioners under the appropriate standard. We should first ask why doctors are subject to a different standard of care. A key reason

---

[3] *Smith v Littlewoods* [1987] AC 241, 271, per Lord Goff. See also *Stovin v Wise* [1996] AC 923, 943–44, per Lord Hoffman.
[4] *East Suffolk Rivers Catchment Board v Kent* [1941] AC 74.
[5] See, e.g., *Bolton v Stone* [1951] AC 850.
[6] *Wilsher v Essex Area Health Authority* [1987] 1 QB 730, per Glidewell LJ.
[7] Ibid., per Lord Mustill.
[8] *Bolam v Friern Hospital Management Committee* [1957] 1 WLR 582, 587 (McNair J).
[9] *Whitehouse v Jordan* [1981] 1 WLR 246; *Maynard v West Midlands* [1984] 1 WLR 634.
[10] *Montgomery v Lanarkshire Health Board* [2015] UKSC 11.

is that medical knowledge is highly complex and specialised, and therefore a judge could not be expected to work out what would be a reasonable (that is, non-negligent) course of treatment. For example, Lord Scarman in *Maynard v West Midlands RHA*[11] stated that a judge's view of which course of treatment was preferable could not in and of itself establish negligence.

It is also important to notice that the test evolved in the 1950s, when deference to the medical profession was high and the maxim of 'doctor knows best' was still influential. Emily Jackson suggests that the test is also explained by a 'sense of professional solidarity', that judges might have trusted the medical profession as best placed, due to its professional status, to make decisions, just as judges themselves have professional skills to make legal judgments.[12]

But should the medical profession be left to determine the standard of care required of its members? One objection to the *Bolam* test is that it makes it extremely difficult for a patient to succeed in a claim for medical negligence. Less than 20 per cent of actions are successful, and part of the reason is that it is very difficult to prove that a doctor fell below the standard of care. As long as a doctor can find other medical professionals to say that they would have acted similarly, that doctor will not be found negligent. According to the *Bolam* test this is all that is necessary, and the court is not expected to scrutinise the *content* of the expert testimony. It need only satisfy itself that the witnesses are expressing their honest beliefs and are credible. To win, the claimant would have to show that no body of responsible medical opinion supported the defendant's behaviour. Given the variance in opinion within the medical profession, it will generally be very difficult to do this, as all the defendant must do is find an expert who agrees that their behaviour was reasonable.

In some ways, this might be a good thing, as it allows for different views on treatment, which reflects the reality of medical practice, which necessarily entails weighing the risks and benefits of different treatments, and the evaluation of many factors that will affect their success. However, the downside is that really requires doctors to only meet the *minimum responsible* standard of care, not a *reasonable* standard, nor even a *gold standard*. We might think that we should ask more of doctors, and that like everyone else they should have to do what is reasonable. We might even think they should be aiming for best practice. But then this might be asking too much if we recognise that doctors are under many pressures, and we should set our expectations at a fair level. This might be compelling, particularly if we assume that doctors are likely to be trying their best to help their patient. On the other hand, this means that doctors are effectively told they will not be liable if they only do the responsible minimum; we might want them to aim higher.

For example, in one case doctors were not found to be negligent for using a widely accepted, but quite toxic anti-fungal treatment for an eye infection,

---

[11] *Maynard v West Midlands RHA* [1984] 1 WLR 634, 644.
[12] E. Jackson, *Medical Law: Text, Cases and Materials*, 2nd edn (Oxford University Press, 2010), 116.

despite the availability of other drugs that were effective treatments but had lower toxicity.[13] The treatment they chose was within the range of accepted treatments, and so following *Bolam* that was not negligent, but there was clear evidence in that case that there were better treatments on offer. Similarly, in *Whitehouse v Jordan*, Lord Edmund-Davies suggested that 'some ... errors may be completely consistent with the due exercise of professional skill' and so are not negligent, while noting that 'other acts or omissions in the course of exercising "clinical judgment" may be so glaringly below proper standards as to make a finding of negligence inevitable'.[14] Therefore, it seems that even a doctor who makes a mistake will not necessarily be liable for the implications for the patient. Clearly, then, doctors need not give the best care, only the minimum responsible care, and this can in some cases be potentially quite a low standard.

This may seem harsh, but it might be unfair to make doctors liable for the full cost of harm if they do the minimum expected of a responsible doctor, and even responsible doctors make mistakes or choose only a good but not best treatment, despite their best efforts to do otherwise. It seems unreasonable to say that doing what a responsible doctor would do is not enough if, by definition, they have done what a responsible doctor would do. It would be unreasonable to expect perfection, and as Lord Denning stated in *Whitehouse v Jordan*:

> If [doctors] are to be found liable [sc. for negligence] whenever they do not effect a cure, or whenever anything untoward happens, it would do a great disservice to the profession itself.[15]

This suggests then that much depends on whether we think leaving it to doctors to determine what is responsible treatment is appropriate. Are we right to think that the medical profession is sufficiently trustworthy that it can be left to effectively self-regulate? The specialised and complex nature of medical decisions is a good reason to leave determinations about the right course of action to knowledgeable experts. If judges were called upon to make such determinations, it is likely that they would be unable in many cases to understand and apply the necessary information. This would be particularly difficult in cases where there is a difference of medical opinion about the best course of treatment, and without medical training it would be very difficult, if not impossible, for a judge to decide whose view was preferable and whether any course of action was so poor that it must be considered negligent.[16]

But there are reasons to think that we should not leave the medical profession to self-regulate entirely, as Lord Woolf has pointed out in explaining the shift away from *Bolam* that started in the late twentieth century. Writing extra-judicially, he commented that 'the "automatic presumption" of beneficence' of the medical profession has been 'dented by a series of well-publicised

---

[13] *Bellarby v Worthing & Southlands Hospitals NHS Trust* [2005] EWHC 2089.

[14] *Whitehouse v Jordan* [1981] 1 WLR 246 (HL), 257–58.

[15] *Whitehouse v Jordan* [1980] 1 All ER 650 (CA), 658.

[16] See further *Maynard v West Midlands RHA* [1984] 1 WLR 634.

scandals'.[17] Certainly, events like the Alder Hey organ retention scand
the revelations of falsified research into the relationship between autism and
the MMR vaccination, to name but two, have suggested that there is a need
for scrutiny of the medical profession. We should not immediately assume that
because a number of doctors agree on a course of action it is a reasonable one.

This problematic aspect of the *Bolam* approach is exacerbated by the fact
that it does not require a large body of medical opinion in favour of the defendant doctor's approach to be found. For example, in *Defreitas v O'Brien*,[18] it was
sufficient that only five specialists would have endorsed the defendant's choice
of treatment. This means that even if there is a very large body of opinion that
holds that one treatment is better, the doctor will not be negligent if they preferred a less popular approach. This cuts both ways: it may be that the doctor
preferred a more old-fashioned treatment. This might be good if the treatment has been tested over many years, because it might be less effective but
the side-effects might be more well-known. But alternatively, the doctor might
be clinging to what they know best, and should instead be more open-minded
about new techniques or treatments. However, in doing so the doctor might
take an unknown risk. It is difficult to know which approach is best, and in part
this is why assessment is left to doctors. But the doctor simply needs to find similarly minded colleagues who would support the approach taken. Their views
will not necessarily identify the best approach, or even a reasonable approach
based on all the evidence.

A better approach might be that a defendant doctor should have to do more
than find some like-minded colleagues. Perhaps reference should have to be
made to the growing body of professional standards and guidance released by
the Royal Colleges of Medicine in support. This might bolster a doctor's case
by demonstrating that they are operating within the range of best practice. If
this cannot be shown, but other doctors still support the doctor's approach,
then perhaps the test should ask for more than just their support; it should ask
for evidence of why they have diverged from best practice if one has been put
forward by the appropriate professional body such as the National Institute of
Health and Care Excellence or the relevant Royal College. Indeed, in recent
times the courts have made reference to such guidance to help them determine
what a responsible body of medical professionals would (and should) do.[19]

BOLITHO: A STEP IN THE RIGHT DIRECTION?

Of late, the courts have taken a less deferential approach to the medical profession in determining the standard of care. Lord Woolf has attributed this
to a number of factors, including recent scandals, but also to the growing

---

[17] Lord Woolf, 'Are the courts excessively deferential to the medical profession?' (2001) 9
Medical Law Review 1, 12.
[18] *Defreitas v O'Brien* [1993] 4 Med LR 281.
[19] See, e.g., *Richards v Swansea NHS Trust* [2007] EWHC 487, per Field J.

availability of medical information that is intelligible to lay people, and also the problems faced by claimants in bringing successful claims.[20] The biggest shift came in 1998. Since that time the *Bolam* test has been subject to what is often called the '*Bolitho* gloss', as the decision in *Bolitho v City and Hackney Health Authority* means that the assessment of the standard of care is no longer determined solely by a body of medical practitioners. Instead, the court must now be 'satisfied that, in forming their views, the experts have directed their minds to the questions of *comparative risks and benefits* and have reached a *defensible conclusion* on the matter' (emphasis added).[21] *Bolitho* picked up on an approach suggested as early as the 1960s when Sachs LJ in *Hucks v Cole* stated that the fact that other doctors would have done the same as the defendant should not, in and of itself, excuse him of negligence.[22]

The *Bolitho* gloss means that a medical practitioner's actions (or omissions) may still be negligent even if they were in accord with a body of medical opinion, if those actions or omissions lacked a logical or reasonable basis. As Rachel Mulheron has put it:

[I]f the risk of an adverse outcome for the patient could have been easily and inexpensively avoided by an alternative course of medical treatment or diagnosis, then the doctor's conduct will be held to be negligent, even if a body of medical opinion did endorse that conduct.[23]

This new approach had the potential to bring about a huge shift in the way medical negligence was determined, but in the sixteen years since *Bolitho* was decided, this has not been the case. In part, this is because a court may not be able to detect logical flaws in a doctor's approach. Beatson J suggested in *French v Thames Valley Strategic Health Authority* that a judge is most likely to invoke the *Bolitho* qualification to *Bolam*:

where a case does not involve difficult or uncertain questions of medical treatment or complex, scientific or highly technical matters, but turns on failure to take a simple precaution the need for which is obvious to the ordinary person considering the matter.[24]

Also, the nature of the gloss means it will not be invoked often, as it will not usually be the case that a doctor's approach lacks a logical basis.[25] In the years since *Bolitho*, the gloss has been applied to question a doctor's behaviour in

---

[20] Lord Woolf, 'Are the courts excessively deferential to the medical profession?' (2001) 9 *Medical Law Review* 1.

[21] *Bolitho v City and Hackney Health Authority* [1998] AC 232, 242 (HL) (Lord Browne-Wilkinson).

[22] *Hucks v Cole* [1993] 4 Med LR 393 (the case was heard in 1968 but not reported until 1994).

[23] R. Mulheron, 'Trumping Bolam: a critical legal analysis of Bolitho's "gloss"' (2010) 69 *Cambridge Law Journal* 609, 620.

[24] *French v Thames Valley Strategic Health Authority* [2005] EWHC 459, para. 112.

[25] *Wisniewski v Central Manchester Health Authority* [1998] Lloyd's Rep Med 223 per Brooke J.

only a few decisions. In *Marriott v West Midlands RHA*,[26] the Court of A[
held that there was no logical basis to support a doctor's decision not to `....`
to hospital a man who had been knocked unconscious for twenty minutes and
then suffered numerous symptoms indicative of problems over the ensuing
days. Similarly, *Bolitho* was invoked to allow the court to disregard expert witnesses who supported what the court called the 'untenable' decision not to
conduct a vaginal exam on a woman in labour upon her admission to hospital
purely due to concerns about 'infection'. Such a decision was 'not defensible
and lacked a logical basis', and those in support of it could not have 'properly
directed their minds to the comparative risks and benefits' of the practice.[27]

It is a rare doctor who has no logical basis for their approach, but this does
not mean that that approach might not have been careless or could have been
done better. This, in fact, is the fundamental failure of *Bolitho* as an improvement
on *Bolam*. It does not change the fact that a doctor can escape liability for negligence if that carelessness was constituted only by a failure to take the most *reasonable* approach. As long as other doctors would do as that doctor did, and they
did not entirely lack a logical basis for doing so, then the patient has no recourse
even if a more effective, easily deployed treatment could have been chosen.

That said, Margaret Brazier and José Miola have argued that *Bolitho* is still
a step in the right direction, and may yet mean that the courts question more
doctors' actions and so aid claimants in medical negligence actions. They argue
that with the increasing availability of medical information that can be understood
by lay people there will be more reference to this in litigation. This will enable
judges to question doctors better. They further point out that doctors themselves
are the ones preparing such materials, as they work to better articulate and dissem-
inate information about best practices.[28] Self-regulation can work as a means to
determine the standard of care if doctors and professional bodies assist in outlining what should be expected from a responsible medical practitioner.[29] This, combined with the courts' willingness to question those standards and the evidence
of experts, may help claimants in the future, as long as the courts are prepared to
continue moving away from excessive deference to the medical profession.

BOLAM AFTER MONTGOMERY

We discussed *Montgomery v Lanarkshire Health Board*[30] in Chapter 2. The
Supreme Court held that a doctor had to disclose all material risks to a patient
and offer the choice between reasonable alternative forms of treatment.

---

[26] *Marriott v West Midlands RHA* [1999] Lloyd's Rep Med 23.

[27] *Reynolds v North Tyneside Health Authority* [2002] Lloyd's Rep Med 459, 463. See also
Burne v A [2006] EWCA Civ 24.

[28] M. Brazier and J. Miola, 'Bye-Bye Bolam: a medical litigation revolution?' (2000) 8 *Medical
Law Review* 85.

[29] However, cf. A. Samanta et al., 'The role of clinical guidelines in medical negligence litigation: a shift from the Bolam standard' (2006) *Medical Law Review* 321, in which the authors
argue that some clinical guidelines may be informed by economic and other concerns, render-
ing them a less appropriate means to determine the negligence standard.

[30] *Montgomery v Lanarkshire Health Board* [2015] UKSC 11.

In reaching this decision it decided that the *Bolam* test (what disclosure and discussion was practised by a responsible body of medical opinion) was not the test to be used. Instead it was for the law to determine the extent of disclosure required. The reason for this was:

> The doctor's advisory role cannot be regarded as solely an exercise of medical skill without leaving out of account the patient's entitlement to decide on the risks to her health which she is willing to run (a decision which may be influenced by non-medical considerations). Responsibility for determining the nature and extent of a person's rights rests with the courts, not with the medical professions.[31]

But that immediately raises a couple of questions. The first is whether there might be other areas of medical practice which are not seen as a matter of 'medical skill' and so fall outside the *Bolam* test. Indeed, in *Muller v King's College Hospital*[32] Kerr J appeared to accept an argument that *Bolam* did not apply in a case where a doctor misdiagnosed a biopsy on the basis there was no special medical skill involved. Instead he thought the question should be whether a reasonable professional would have detected the cancer in the biopsy. If that decision is developed in later cases it may well be that *Bolam* becomes restricted to where a doctor is exercising specialist discretion or perhaps is abandoned altogether.

A second question is: if the law now focuses on the rights of the patient, why is the right to be told of risks seen as a more important right than the right to receive the best medical treatment? Arguably, it is the latter which is the more important right. Yet currently the law of tort seems to hold doctors to a higher standard of care when discussing matters with their patients than when they are wielding their scalpel. Is there a good reason for that?

Scenario to ponder

Abdul is diagnosed with a skin condition. In the past he has had bad experiences with doctors, and he has often turned to alternative medicine when ill. He goes to a practitioner of traditional Chinese herbal medicine, Mr Situ, who treats his skin condition with a herbal remedy. He takes the remedy nine times, and suffers acute liver failure and dies. The evidence establishes that the remedy was, on the balance of probabilities, the cause of his death. Should Mr Situ be held liable for Abdul's death?[33]

---

[31] Para. 83.

[32] *Muller v King's College Hospital* [2017] EWHC 128 (QB).

[33] These are the facts of the only case so far to consider the standard of care to be applied to alternative medicine practitioners. Mr Situ was found to be not liable as he acted in accordance with the standards of practice accepted within traditional Chinese herbal medicine in the UK. It was also noted in the decision that Abdul had himself chosen to reject orthodox medicine and pursue alternative treatment: *Shakoor v Situ* [2001] 1 WLR 410.

CONCLUSION

For a long time, the courts deferred to the expertise of medical profession-als. In many ways this 'doctor knows best' approach was appropriate; on many technical matters, this is true. But this approach also allowed the medical pro-fession to protect its own, and for some claimants this may well have made the difference between obtaining compensation and otherwise. While there is much to be said for deferring to those with the relevant expertise, it will always be problematic to leave a group to self-regulate. The courts need to take an active role in scrutinising the actions of medical professionals, and the *Bolitho* gloss is a welcome step towards ensuring this is undertaken. Medical profes-sionals should be expected to do more than simply defer to other colleagues to support them in their course of action; they must be able to justify their choices objectively as well. That said, the testimony of experts and their opinions will always remain valuable, as a court cannot be expected to fully appreciate the complex evidence in front of it in some medical negligence cases. Giving judges the discretion to call for a logical basis for the medical professional's choice to be offered is a step in the right direction.

We might also think that the adversarial approach to evidence is perhaps not the most effective way to determine what a doctor ought to do. Perhaps there is space for a better way of doing this, using impartial witnesses and drawing on the expertise and guidance of the professional bodies that regulate doctors. We might also wonder whether merely doing what a responsible doctor would do is enough, when best practice standards are in place. A further step forward, then, might be to import reference to these into the standard, to ensure that doctors should do the best that can be expected of them, not merely that which at least one other responsible doctor would do.

Debate 2

Should a lost chance of a better medical outcome be compensated?

INTRODUCTION

One of the most vexed debates in medical negligence is whether a patient should be able to claim for a 'lost chance'. Academic debate has swirled around the questions raised by lost chance cases for nearly thirty years, in large part because the arguments and issues in relation to lost chances are extremely complex. We can only touch upon them in quite a simple way in this chapter, but we will explain the core questions that form the basis of the debate and present some of the positions people have taken in response to them.

There are two ways in which a patient might be said to have lost a chance as a result of a doctor's breach of duty. They might have lost the chance of receiving a treatment that could have successfully cured or reduced the impact of their con-dition. This might occur if a doctor fails to offer a treatment that a responsible doctor would have offered when presented with a condition like the claimant's. Alternatively, the doctor's breach might have diminished the patient's chance of recovering from the illness. This might occur when the doctor fails to diagnose or treat a condition in a timely manner, and the condition worsens during the period of delay, and this decreases the patient's chances of recovering. Failing to diagnose a cancer that will spread if left untreated is a good example.

Some argue that patients who lose a chance should be able to recover for this loss. Others, including the courts, take the position that such recovery should not be permitted. To understand this debate, we first need to understand some of the basic aspects of medical negligence. Put simply, for someone to be liable for medical negligence under the common law it must be shown that they were under a duty of care, that they breached this duty (fell below the standard of care), that there was actionable damage, that this was caused by the breach, and that the damage that occurred was not too remote (that is, it was foreseeable).[34] The aim of applying these requirements is to determine who, if anyone, is liable to the claimant for the harm suffered.[35]

Of these factors, causation is considered important to establishing liability on the grounds that a person should be culpable for the consequences of their actions. The courts take a fairly unscientific approach to causation, which is to be 'understood as the man in the street, and not as the scientist or the metaphysician, would understand it'.[36] The courts use the seemingly simple 'but for' test to determine whether a breach caused or materially contributed to the harm, which requires the court to ask: 'But for the breach, would the damage have occurred?' For example, if someone went to hospital and did not receive proper treatment (a breach of the doctor's duty), but the treatment would have made no difference to whether they would recover, then the doctor who breached their duty will not be liable in negligence. It could not be said that 'but for' the breach, the damage would not have occurred.[37]

The test must be satisfied 'on the balance of probabilities'. This means that it must be more likely than not that the breach caused or materially contributed to the loss. Put another way, the court must be satisfied that there is a 51 per cent likelihood or greater that the breach caused the loss. If this is the case then the defendant will be considered the cause of the loss as a matter of certainty. They will be liable for the full amount of the loss. It is important to remember that this creates a clear separation between determining causation and working out the amount of the loss. The level of certainty about whether the defendant caused the loss is not relevant to the proportion of that loss for which they will be liable. As long as it is more than 50 per cent likely that the defendant's breach was the cause of the loss, they will be liable for the full amount.

---

[34] Causation is often referred to as 'factual causation', and the remoteness requirement as 'legal causation'. This can be confused, therefore we will use 'causation' to mean 'factual causation', and 'remoteness' to refer to foreseeability of damage (avoiding the term 'legal causation').

[35] See, e.g., *Lamb v Camden LBC* [1981] QB 625, per Lord Denning.

[36] *Yorkshire Dale Steamship Co. v Minister of War Transport* [1942] AC 691, 701, per Lord Wright.

[37] See, e.g., *Barnett v Chelsea Hospital* [1969] 1 QB 428.

Explaining the Lost Chances Problem

We can now examine what is happening in a lost chance claim. In these cases, the claimant reformulates what constituted the damage claimed. The claimant recasts the harm as the lost chance itself. The loss is the loss of an opportunity to be treated, or the loss of a chance of recovery, not the physical injury that results from this loss. This is done because it is not possible to prove that it is more than 50 per cent likely that the doctor's breach caused the physical harm (such as a failure to recover from cancer). This may be necessary if there is a lost opportunity for treatment, where there is less than a 50 per cent chance that the treatment would have worked. In such cases, it could not be said that it is more likely than not that but for the failure to treat, the patient would have recovered: it was more likely than not that the patient would have died even if treated. In diminished chances cases this recasting is necessary because it cannot otherwise be shown that the doctor (rather than the underlying disease) was the cause of the physical injury, unless the patient's chances of recovery were reduced from being very substantial to very low. By recasting the loss, the claimant attempts to 'jump' an evidentiary gap as they avoid having to prove that it is more likely than not that the doctor's breach caused the physical injury (for which they want compensation). Instead, they try to argue that they need only prove that the doctor's breach caused the loss of the chance, and that it is this that must be proved on the balance of probabilities.

Why the Problem Arises in the Context of Medicine

Lost chance cases arise in the context of medicine because in the medical context the claimant will often have already been suffering from a condition that might cause them loss when they come to the doctor. That is, there is already an underlying causal factor, and the doctor is expected to prevent or reduce its impact, and so avoid harm happening to the patient. In many lost chance cases, the doctor fails to take the action that would have avoided the harm (this is the breach) and so the harm occurs. This might mean the disease takes its course when it could have been avoided, or that the patient's chance of recovering is reduced. The doctor's breach has reduced or destroyed the chance to recover.

Two Key Cases

The arguments around lost chance cases are complicated, and it is important first to have a clear understanding of the sort of fact situations to which they relate. Therefore, we will begin by outlining the two major cases that have shaped the law on the question of recovery for the loss of a chance. We will explore the reasoning behind these decisions as we consider the arguments for and against allowing claims for lost chances.

Hotson v East Berkshire Health Authority

The first decision, *Hotson v East Berkshire Health Authority*,[38] was appealed all the way to the House of Lords. In *Hotson*, the claimant was a 13-year-old boy who fell while climbing a tree. The fall caused a fracture to the upper part of his femur bone, the epiphysis. The boy suffered permanent damage to his hip joint, and as a consequence was irreversibly disabled. It was almost certain that he would later suffer painful osteoarthritis. Despite being taken to hospital, he was not correctly diagnosed or treated for five days. The damage to his femur caused some of his blood vessels to rupture and bleed into the joint. This in turn compressed the remaining blood vessels, cutting off the blood supply to the bone tissue comprising the epiphysis, which in turn caused that tissue to die (necrosis). It was possible that sufficient blood vessels were still intact post-fall and that these could have been enough to supply sufficient blood to keep the epiphysis alive. If this had been the case, which the judge thought was 25 per cent likely, then the failure to treat had caused them to be compressed, and hence the negligence was the cause of the injury. However, on the evidence it was 75 per cent likely that even if the boy had received treatment, sufficient damage had already occurred such that treatment would not have made any difference to the outcome. He would have been disabled regardless.

Hotson argued that because of the doctor's negligence he had denied him the chance of a recovery. He might well have been disabled regardless, but he might not have been. The negligence turned the probability that he would be disabled into a certainty. The trial judge agreed and awarded him 25 per cent of the value of his physical injury as damages. The Court of Appeal concurred, supporting this award. It agreed that the hospital's negligence had on the balance of probabilities caused him to lose the opportunity of treatment that might have saved his hip. The House of Lords overturned the decision on appeal, and Hotson's claim for damages failed.

Gregg v Scott[39]

In this case, a doctor failed to diagnose that Malcolm Gregg had lymphoma (cancer) as early as he ought to have done. Had the doctor diagnosed it and sent Gregg to a specialist, his chances of survival would have been 42 per cent. Due to the delay, those chances were reduced to 25 per cent. 'Survival' in the context of cancers means living for ten years. The change in Gregg's chances was 17 per cent. Mr Gregg tried to claim for this drop in his chances, but his claim was rejected by the House of Lords. Part of the reason, as we shall see, was that he could not show that it was more likely than not that the doctor's delay made a difference to his outcome. Ken Mason and Graeme Laurie encapsulate

---

[38] *Hotson v East Berkshire Health Authority* [1987] 2 All ER 908.
[39] *Gregg v Scott* [2005] UKHL 2.

the point well when they say, 'even without negligence, there would have been a 58% chance that the patient would not survive the decade'.[40]

It should be noted that there is an important difference between *Hotson* and *Gregg*, namely that at the time each case was decided, only in *Hotson* had the injury manifested that the doctor should have acted to prevent.

WHY SHOULD LOST CHANCES BE COMPENSATED?

Lost chances are compensated in other contexts

One argument sometimes put forward in favour of compensating lost chances in medical negligence cases is that the law already compensates lost chances in other contexts. The classic case raised in support of the view is *Chaplin v Hicks*,[41] in which a woman entered a competition to win a place in the chorus line of a musical show. Six thousand women entered, and the plaintiff made the final shortlist of fifty, from whom would be chosen the final twelve to whom a place on the chorus line would be offered. To have a chance at selection, the plaintiff needed to attend an appointment in person. Due to the defendant's negligence, she did not learn of the appointment in time to attend, and consequently was not present and lost her chance to be selected. The jury found that she had lost something of value and awarded her substantial damages of £100.[42] If the chance of winning a competition can be compensated, why not a chance at a better outcome when one is ill?

One distinction that should be made between these cases and medical negligence cases is the nature of the evidence about chances. While in *Chaplin* the plaintiff had a seemingly simple 1:4 chance of being chosen (although this takes no account of her attributes, upon which the decision would have been made),[43] the 'chances' in a case like *Gregg v Scott* are based on epidemiological data. Such data do not tell us what a particular person's chance of recovery would be; we are not currently capable of such predictions in most, if not all, medical prognoses. Rather, they tell us the rates of recovery following treatment of classes of people sharing what are thought to be salient similar characteristics. Chief Justice Spigelman drew out this distinction in the Australian case of *Seltsam Pty Ltd v McGuiness*, in which he explained that there is a difference between the 'general causation' referred to in epidemiological data, which suggests that a particular factor (such as exposure to a carcinogen) may be capable of causing a disease, and 'specific causation', which refers to whether that factor caused the disease in an individual case.[44]

---

[40] K. Mason and G. Laurie, *Mason and McCall Smith's Law and Medical Ethics* (Oxford University Press, 2010), 338.

[41] *Chaplin v Hicks* [1911] 2 KB 786 (CA).

[42] The jury's view was approved on appeal: [1911] 2 KB 786. See also *Allied Maples Group Ltd v Simmons & Simmons* [1995] 1 WLR 1602.

[43] The amount awarded by the jury was roughly 25 per cent of what she would have been paid had she been selected for the chorus line.

[44] See *Seltsam Pty Ltd v McGuiness* (2000) 49 NSWLR 262, [60]–[101]. See also A. Sullivan, 'What is a loss of a chance claim?', *Medico-Legal Society of NSW*, available at www.medicolegal. org.au/resources/publications-archive/p2008/loss-of-chance-of-a-better-outcome/sullivan.

Another distinction, pointed out by Jane Stapleton, is that in economic loss cases of this kind, the lost chance is the 'gist' of the action. It is not a pure chance in the sense used in *Gregg*, but a real opportunity to make a financial gain that the claimant would have had (as in *Chaplin*) but which they have been denied.[45] Economic opportunities are themselves things of value, and this is the damage the loss of *that* value (hence it is the 'gist' of the action). Tony Weir distinguishes the cases thus:

> Losing a chance of [a monetary] gain is a loss like the loss of the gain itself, alike in quality, just less in quantity: losing a chance of not losing a leg is not at all the same kind of thing as losing the leg.[46]

Something real has been lost

Lord Nicholls in *Gregg* made a different argument. In his view a chance is not nothing, even a chance of less than 50 per cent:

> The patient could recover damages if his initial prospects of recovery had been more than 50%. But because they were less than 50% he can recover nothing. This surely cannot be the state of the law today. It would be irrational and indefensible. The loss of a 45% prospect of recovery is just as much a real loss for a patient as the loss of a 55% prospect of recovery. In both cases the doctor was in breach of his duty to his patient. In both cases the patient was worse off. He lost something of importance and value. But, it is said, in one case the patient has a remedy, and in the other he does not.[47]

Lord Nicholls' view appears compelling, as it seems unfair to draw a line of this kind between the cases. But there are problems with his view. He speaks of a 'chance' as something one has, and which can be lost in the way one might lose a book, but this is misleading. Chances are not things one has; they are probabilities about what might happen in the future. Talking of 'having a chance' obscures the real question, which is how certain can we be about the implications of the doctor's failure to treat or diagnose? When the chance is less than 50 per cent originally, we cannot say it is more likely than not that a complete obliteration of that chance was the reason the patient did not recover, because it is more likely that in fact he would never have recovered anyway the other causal factor in the situation, namely his original injury or disease would have caused him not to recover regardless.

If we looked at this even more carefully, we would see that whether a patient responds to treatment or not is not a matter of 'chance', it is determined by his genetics, his past history, whatever environmental factors he has been exposed to and so on. These all have an impact on how well a treatment works for a particular person. It is not magic, but it is something that we don't yet fully

---

[45] J. Stapleton, 'Loss of chance of cure from cancer' (2005) 68 *Modern Law Review* 996, 1005.

[46] T. Weir, *An Introduction to Tort Law*, 2nd edn (Clarendon Press, 2006), 80.

[47] *Gregg v Scott* [2005] UKHL 2, para. 3, per Lord Nicholls.

understand in some cases. So we know for sure that everyone will respond to being fully decapitated by dying, because we know (from all the evidence to date) that human beings cannot survive in this state. But we do not know enough about most other diseases to know how treatments will play out for each particular person, hence we talk in probabilities.

Regarding these as 'personal chances', however, obscures what medical statistics are really trying to express. Timothy Hill writes that to do so confuses statistical chances about what happens in similar situations (the sort of statistics used in *Hotson*) with personal chances.[48] Applied to the sort of situation that arose in *Gregg*, this means that Gregg did not have a 42 per cent personal chance of surviving, he had a 42 per cent statistical chance of doing so; 42 out of 100 people with a tumour like his in the past had survived for ten years. Whether he would be one of them could not be determined until the time had run out. When his chance dropped to 25 per cent, he did not lose a personal chance, but rather only 25 per cent of people before him diagnosed at that stage had survived. He might have been one of the people who would survive, he might not, but if we had to guess, the more likely scenario, given what we knew of past similar cases, would be that he would not survive.

This is in fact how some of the judges involved in the *Hotson* case reasoned. Lord Justice Croom-Johnson in the Court of Appeal stated:

> If it is proved statistically that 25% of the population have a chance of recovery from a certain injury and 75% do not, it does not mean that someone who suffers from that injury and does not recover from it has lost a 25% chance. He may have lost nothing at all. What he has to do is prove that he was one of the 25% and that the loss was caused by the defendant's negligence. ... If the plaintiff succeeds in proving that he was one of the 25% and that the defendant took away that chance, the logical result would be to award him 100% of his damages and not only a quarter.[49]

We rarely have data about personalised chances. The courts must, as doctors do, rely on evidence of what has happened in similar cases in the past and make predictions about the future. And, in fact, Marc Stauch argues that this is what courts already do when they reason about causation generally.[50]

The doctor has done the wrong thing

Given this, why might it be argued that Hotson should have recovered damages to compensate him for his lost opportunity? Part of the reason is that we know the hospital failed in its treatment of him. They had done

---

[48] T. Hill, 'A lost chance for compensation in the tort of negligence by the House of Lords' (1991) 54 *Modern Law Review* 511, 512.

[49] *Hotson v East Berkshire Health Authority* [1987] 1 All ER 210 (CA), 223, per Croom-Johnson LJ.

[50] M. Stauch, 'Causation, risk, and loss of chance in medical negligence' (1997) 17 *Oxford Journal of Legal Studies* 201.

something wrong. Perhaps, given the nature of the doctors' duty, when they have done something in breach of it that *might* have had an impact, compensation should be awarded. Lord Nicholls put it slightly differently in *Gregg*:

> The doctor's negligence diminished the patient's prospects of recovery. And this analysis of a patient's loss accords with the purpose of the legal duty of which the doctor was in breach. In short, the purpose of the duty of care is to promote the patient's *prospects* of recovery by exercising due skill and care in diagnosing and treating the patient's condition.[51]

According to this argument, the doctor failed to do as he ought to have done, and this, combined with the possibility that it made a difference, should in such cases be sufficient for an award to be made. But tort law does not compensate a claimant simply because the defendant did something wrong; that wrong must be the reason the claimant has suffered loss.

We might try to salvage this argument by thinking about what it would be like if doctors ignored patients with less than even chances, knowing that they could not be found liable if they did so. Imagine that there is always a 45 per cent chance that a patient with Condition A will recover if given Treatment B. This means if one hundred patients present to the doctor with Condition A, we can expect forty-five to be cured if treated by the doctor, and fifty-five of them would die anyway. But if the doctor simply didn't bother to treat anyone, one hundred would die. Yet because each person could never prove that it was more likely than not that the doctor caused their death, that doctor could never be found negligent despite having taken a course of action that seems clearly wrong, given their position as a doctor. We know that some people will die who would otherwise recover if treated; it simply cannot be proved which those will be, due to the state of medical knowledge. Those in favour of recovery for lost chances might argue that this lack of ability to prove their case, when they can show statistics about the *likelihood* that the doctor made all the difference in their cases, should not bar their claims entirely. This argument is, however, susceptible to the challenges made in the next section of this debate.

We might also bolster the argument in this section by saying this is not merely a case in which there is a wrong but no causation. As Lord Nicholls argued in *Gregg*, it cannot be right that someone who comes to a doctor with a less than even chance of surviving can never claim if that doctor is negligent and reduces or destroys that chance.[52] In cases where the statistical chance of recovery is quite high, such as 42 per cent, the possibility that the doctor had an impact on the possible outcomes in such a case would be substantial. In

---

[51] *Gregg v Scott* [2005] UKHL 2, para. 20, per Lord Nicholls.
[52] Ibid. para. 22, per Lord Nicholls.

Lord Nicholls' view, this point is all the more compelling when we view a doctor's duty to promote a person's chance of survival:

> A patient should have an appropriate remedy when he loses the very thing it was the doctor's duty to protect. To this end the law should recognise the existence and loss of poor and indifferent prospects as well as those more favourable.[53]

WHY SHOULD LOSS OF CHANCE CLAIMS BE REJECTED?

They are just cases in which there is a lack of evidence

We have seen above that there is a difference between statistical and personal chances. Hotson did not himself have a 25 per cent chance.[54] Rather, 25 per cent of people with an injury like his would respond to treatment and recover, while 75 per cent would not.[55] If Hotson could have shown he was in the 25 per cent group then he would have shown that the failure to treat was the *entire* reason he was disabled; he would have been fine and recovered had the hospital done as it should, but its breach meant his opportunity to recover was lost. But he lacked the proof to manage this, and so all that could be said was that it was 25 per cent likely that he was someone who could recover, and so it could never be said that the hospital's breach was more likely than not the reason he did not recover.

This was the view taken in the House of Lords in *Hotson*. According to Lord Bridge:

> Unless the plaintiff proved on a balance of probabilities that the delayed treatment was at least a material contributory cause of the avascular necrosis he failed on the issue of causation and no question of quantification could arise.[56]

What mattered was the state in which he arrived, and this was a matter of past fact.[57] But there was no way to know the actual state of Hotson's blood vessels when he arrived; it was only possible to know the *probability* that enough remained based on data about past similar injuries. Therefore, these numbers went only to whether the breach could be proved to be a cause, and as it was more likely that someone with an injury like his would not have sufficient blood vessels remaining, then the evidence as it stood couldn't show that it was more likely that the breach made any difference to the outcome.

The same could be said of *Gregg*. Mr Gregg simply could not show that he was someone who would have survived had he been treated promptly but

---

[53] Ibid., para. 24, per Lord Nicholls.
[54] See *Hotson v East Berkshire Health Authority* [1987] 2 All ER 908, 909 per Lord Mackay.
[55] See, e.g., ibid., per Lord Bridge.
[56] Ibid., 924, per Lord Bridge. Lord Ackner took a similar view.
[57] T. Hill, 'A lost chance for compensation in the tort of negligence by the House of Lords' (1991) 54 *Modern Law Review* 511, 515.

now would not due to the delay. All that we can know is that fifty-eight out of one hundred people in Gregg's position before the delay would have died, no matter what the doctor did. For them, the doctor's actions would have made no difference. Twenty-five of those one hundred people could withstand a delay and would have survived even if diagnosed late. Again, for them, the doctor's actions made no difference. But for seventeen of the one hundred patients, the delay was crucial. They could have been saved if their cancers had been caught early, but they could not withstand a delay. What we cannot know is into which group Gregg fell. But we can know that it is only 17 per cent likely that he was someone for whom the delay would have made all the difference. It could not be said that it was more likely than not that the doctor's action was determinative with any certainty. On this view, both claimants faced an evidentiary problem that they could not surmount, and so necessarily failed in their claims.

To allow loss of chance claims would undermine the rules on causation

It might be that we think the courts should respond to these evidentiary problems by applying different causation rules. However, both Lords Hoffman and Phillips openly resisted changing the basis of causation proof from one of probability to one of possibility in *Gregg*. It would undermine the admittedly rough-and-ready justice that the 'but for' test achieves in most cases, and would produce similar problems of inconsistence and definition created by the exception made in the earlier case of *Fairchild v Glenhaven Funeral Services*[58] to 'treat an increase in risk as equivalent to the making of a material contribution where a single noxious agent is involved'. Lord Hoffman refused to generalise the exception on the grounds that to do so would:

> involve abandoning a good deal of authority.... Furthermore the House would be dismantling all the qualifications and restrictions with which it so recently hedged the Fairchild exception ... [A] wholesale adoption of possible rather than probable causation as the criterion of liability would be so radical a change in our law as to amount to a legislative act.[59]

Lord Phillips agreed, pointing out:

> There is a danger, if special tests of causation are developed piecemeal to deal with perceived injustices in particular factual situations, that the coherence of our common law will be destroyed.[60]

However, the evidentiary problem in lost chance cases is not the same as that in other situations. We are faced with something unknowable – what someone's

---

[58] [2002] UKHL 22.

[59] *Gregg v Scott* [2005] UKHL 2, paras 85 and 90, per Lord Hoffman.

[60] Ibid., per Lord Phillips.

personal chance of responding to treatment was – but we have data about other people's experiences that give us a fair chance of guessing what might have happened. On Timothy Hill's view this is the same for many cases, and he argues that:

> [t]he emotive speech and obvious feelings of sympathy for a 'loss of chance' plaintiff must not let us colour or obscure the real issue the existence of an 'evidentiary gap'. Proof of causation should not be accepted on anything less than the balance of probabilities, as is common with all civil actions.[61]

But these situations arise where a medical practitioner has failed to do what they ought to do when faced with an ill or injured person. Perhaps this might lead us to take a different line that allows for partial recovery, to get around the evidentiary problems that will beset such cases, particularly if we think that for a doctor to be negligent is especially problematic.

Further, diminished chances cases are not merely cases in which there is an evidentiary gap about the implications of a prior event that caused the damage, and the doctor's influence on that situation. They are instead cases of real medical uncertainty about how a patient in a particular position will progress. This kind of uncertainty, rather than merely lack of evidence, is perhaps not a sufficient reason for the court to refuse to allow any compensation, especially where the doctor's action is entirely negligent and the reduction in chance is substantial. We might see such cases as unfair in a way that is similar to those addressed in *Fairchild*, and hence consider them also cases in which causation rules should be modified. Jane Stapleton points out that in *Fairchild* the courts were prepared to aid claimants who also faced an evidentiary gap in proving liability on the part of employers who had exposed them to asbestos. She notes that this raises the question of why, in *Hotson*:

> [w]here stable statistics were available [about past events], the Lords unanimously refused radical doctrinal assistance to the claimant, yet in [*Fairchild*] where stable statistics were not available the Lords unanimously gave such assistance ... When one compares the two responses it looks as if the House of Lords will refuse to help claimants who face *quantifiable* evidentiary gaps but will help other claimants to jump much more extreme *unquantifiable* evidentiary gaps.[62]

Conflates causation and determination of quantum

One of the problems with recasting damage as a lost opportunity or reduced chance is determining the value of that damage. What is a chance worth? One approach is to value the damage as the cost of the physical injury multiplied

---

[61] T. Hill, 'A lost chance for compensation in the tort of negligence by the House of Lords' (1991) 54 *Modern Law Review* 511, 523.

[62] J. Stapleton, 'Loss of chance of cure from cancer' (2005) 68 *Modern Law Review* 996, 1004.

by the percentage chance. For example, Lord Phillips in *Gregg* felt there might be an argument for '[p]ermitting a recovery of damages that is proportionate to the increase in the chance of the adverse outcome'.[63] So, if someone had a 20 per cent chance of recovering from an injury, and the injury itself would be valued at £100,000, the damages should be 20 per cent of this, namely, £20,000. But this creates a problem, because this approach would blur the distinction between causation and determining quantum of damage, as the percentage chance that the doctor caused the harm would be used to determine the amount of loss (if the damages sought are based on a percentage of the cost of the physical injury that resulted). In *Hotson*, their Lordships were resistant to adopting this approach. Lord Ackner put it in direct terms:

> Once liability is established, on the balance of probabilities, the loss which the plaintiff has sustained is payable in full. It is not discounted by reducing his claim by the extent to which he has failed to prove his case with 100% certainty.[64]

If such an approach were taken, it would also undermine the law's approach to causation and quantum for those who *can* prove causation on the balance of probabilities. As Lady Hale explained in *Gregg v Scott*, almost any personal injury case could be recast in this manner, and unless it could be shown with 100 per cent certainty that the defendant's action caused the loss, the claimant's damages should be reduced accordingly. One could not have two approaches operating in tandem, with a percentage chance approach working when causation cannot be established on the balance of probabilities but full recovery for those cases where it can. To do so, argued Lady Hale, would '[s]urely be a case of two steps forward three steps back for the great majority of straightforward personal injury cases'.[65] Were we to use the chance *always* to determine quantum and avoid this problem then very few (if any) claimants would ever be fully compensated. As soon as any doubt could be raised, their award would be reduced.

Tying quantum to the question of the chance lost would also see cases in which great argument would be had over each percentage point, as this could mean hundreds or perhaps thousands of pounds' difference in the award. In cases of medical negligence this would be particularly problematic, as there are often two interacting causal factors: the underlying medical problem that the doctor was expected to treat, and the negligent acts or failures on the doctor's part. Sometimes, the doctor might do nothing, and the underlying condition simply takes its course in a way it wouldn't have done if the doctor had acted responsibly. Sometimes, however, the doctor might act in a way that changes the progress of the condition but does not fix it. Depending on the factual matrix, it could be very difficult to determine in many cases what the

---

[63] *Gregg v Scott* [2005] UKHL 2, para. 34, per Lord Phillips.

[64] *Hotson v East Berkshire Health Authority* [1987] 2 All ER 908, 928 per Lord Ackner.

[65] *Gregg v Scott* [2005] UKHL 2, para. 225, per Lady Hale.

doctor's percentage contribution to the outcome actually was. If quantum was determined by the percentage chance of proving the causal relationship, then in many cases it would be very difficult to work out how much the claimant should recover.

Another problem related to quantum is: what should the court do if the doctor does reduce the claimant's chances, but the claimant eventually recovers and the possible physical harm does not materialise? If we had said that it is the *chance* or *opportunity* lost that is the actual loss to be compensated, how can we value this if the value was determined by reference to the physical loss sustained? Further, why should we compensate such lost chances if the patient actually suffers no physical injury?

Despite these concerns, a number of academic commentators have argued in favour of proportionate recovery. We could, as Marc Stauch argues, make more use of statistical evidence when we have access to it. Where we know the statistical likelihood of something being the case (as in *Hotson*), we could decrease damages by that percentage likelihood. We would then share the burden of the loss between the claimant and the defendant, and this sharing would reflect our uncertainty about whether the defendant was in fact the cause. This, in his view, is preferable to allowing the loss to fall entirely on the claimant, when there is too much evidentiary uncertainty of the kind that arises in lost chance cases.[66] As Walter Scott argues:

> In cases where causation falls anywhere near the 50 per cent borderline, justice to both parties is much better served by adopting a proportionate approach.[67]

Scott goes on to argue that we could avoid the problems of wrangling over percentage points by using 'bands' of liability:

> If the objection is that litigation would tend to be intensified by arguments about a percentage point one way or the other, this could be avoided by allowing arbitrary 'bands' at say, 10 per cent, 25 per cent, 33 per cent and so on.[68]

If, then, the percentage chance was not entirely accurate, this would just mean that the claimant's award fell into the next band, rather than over the 50 per cent line (which would on the current approach result in there being no recovery).

However, there would be significant hurdles to overcome if we were to put in place a proportionate recovery approach. It would mean any patient with even a slight chance that was affected would have a claim, which would lead to significant increases in litigation and heated debates over small changes in

---

[66] M. Stauch, 'Causation, risk, and loss of chance in medical negligence' (1997) 17 *Oxford Journal of Legal Studies* 201.

[67] W. Scott, 'Causation in medico-legal practice: a doctor's approach to the "lost opportunity" cases' (1992) 55 *Modern Law Review* 522, 525.

[68] Ibid., 523.

probability of outcome. As Scott, a doctor, writes, '[n]o one with any proper understanding of medical matters would pretend that a precise estimation of likelihoods is at all easy',[69] and it would therefore further increase the complexity of evidence in medical cases.

Further, we would either have to have proportionate recovery for all claims, meaning very few people would ever be fully compensated, even if we were all but certain the doctor had caused the harm, or we could try to ameliorate the problems by only invoking the proportionate approach below the 50 per cent line. Lady Hale summed up the problems with both approaches aptly in *Gregg*:

> It would in practice always be tempting to conclude that the doctor's negligence had affected … [the claimant's] chances to some extent, the claimant would almost always get something. It would be a 'heads you lose everything, tails I win something' situation.[70]

However, as Stauch argues, we could address concerns about increased litigation if lost chance cases were allowed if we limited these to the loss of a substantial chance.[71] This does, of course, raise the problem of what constitutes a substantial chance. We might just be closing one can of worms to open another.

A final problem with proportionate recovery based on chances is: what should we do if the chance was lost but the claimant suffered no damage? For example, in *Gregg*, even though the claimant's 'chance' of recovery was reduced, by the time the case was decided by the House of Lords eight years after the delayed diagnosis, it was beginning to look like he would survive the full ten years. He might have suffered no harm (in terms of dying of cancer) at all. Should he still be compensated? We could resolve this problem by limiting claims to those where the injury in fact occurs. Therefore, if Mr Gregg had survived for ten years (that is, not suffered the injury), his reduction in survival chances would not be compensable as he had not actually suffered a loss. We would conceptualise the lost chance as valuable, contingent on the actual physical outcome to which the chance referred. This does suggest that chances themselves are worth nothing, but then that is part of the fundamental problem with such claims. A contingent valuation would have its own problems, but might still be preferable.

PERHAPS OUR APPROACH TO CAUSATION IS WRONG

Many academic commentators have argued that the 'but for' test is in itself problematic. It cannot deal with multiple cause cases effectively, and takes a simplistic approach to any causation problem by requiring us to run a binary

---

[69] Ibid., 523.

[70] *Gregg v Scott* [2005] UKHL 2, para. 28, per Lady Hale.

[71] M. Stauch, 'Causation, risk, and loss of chance in medical negligence' (1997) 17 *Oxford Journal of Legal Studies* 201.

hypothetical where we compare only two possible cases. But there might well be many alternative explanations, comprised of many different sets of causes. One of the main critics of the way the courts have dealt with causation, including loss of chance cases, is Jane Stapleton. She argues that the courts should take a wider view of what may constitute a cause, and add to 'but for' causes those causes that can be said to 'make a positive contribution to the relevant mechanism by which the phenomenon came about'.[72]

She explains a case like *Hotson* as one in which there was a causal threshold; that there needed to be sufficient causal forces, of whatever source, to bring about a harm. In that case, this threshold was the amount of blood vessels damaged. This happened in part due to the fall, and in part due to the delay (as a delay would mean continued bleeding into the joint, compressing the remaining vessels and damaging them as well). In 75 per cent of cases the fall would have done enough damage for the necrosis (which led to the eventual harm, the disability) to occur. In 25 per cent of cases it would not, and the necrosis could have been avoided as this extra causal force would not have been added. However, the delay would have 'topped up' the causal forces to reach the threshold, and the necrosis would have followed.

The delay on this analysis is a tortious cause, the fall a non-tortious cause. When there is a delay, in 25 per cent of cases the tortious cause makes all the difference; in 75 per cent it does not – the threshold is 'over-subscribed'. So the delay was unnecessary to reach it (hence the title of Stapleton's paper, 'Unnecessary Causes') but *was* a positive contribution to the forces causing the harm. This perhaps chimes with Lord Nicholls' intuition that the doctor had done something wrong in *Gregg*, and with those who think there should be proportionate recovery.' Just because the doctor's failure is not a 'but for' cause does not mean it is necessarily irrelevant. It will depend on the particular factual matrix. In future cases that are cast as losses of chance, Stapleton's analysis may be valuable.

CONCLUSION

Lost chance cases are problematic because they involve a number of difficult elements: multiple causal factors; a doctor's duty and our expectations of what a breach of that should mean; and evidentiary uncertainty of a number of kinds. While the law needs to remain coherent, and therefore should depart from the rules of causation only with very good reason, these might be just such sufficient reasons. The rules of causation deal well with simple cases but, as many academic commentators have pointed out, they lack the capacity to adequately cope with complex, multifactorial situations and ones involving numerous possible causal sets.

Causation in law is not a science, it is a policy choice. In cases where there were compelling reasons to find the defendant liable, the courts have been

---

[72] J. Stapleton, 'Unnecessary causes' (2013) 129 *Law Quarterly Review* 39, 39.

prepared to take a modified approach to causation. The exceptional approach in *Fairchild*, in cases of exposure to asbestos, is one such example. The decision in *Chester v Afshar* is another.[73] In that case, a doctor was held liable for failing to warn a patient of the risks associated with an operation, although the patient gave evidence that she would have had the operation even if she had been told of them (although at a different time). This should have meant that she failed the causation requirement, as the failure to warn did not affect her decision, but the court held that this would make the doctor's duty to warn close to meaningless, and so decided that he should be liable regardless.

In the face of these challenges, and the fact that in some lost chance cases there is a very real (if not better than even) chance that the doctor's failure made all the difference to a patient's outcome, perhaps the courts should rethink their commitment to the standard rules and consider again some of the alternatives that are available.

Debate 3

Should parents be compensated for the cost of raising unwanted children?

INTRODUCTION

When something goes wrong before conception or during pregnancy, this can give rise to a number of harmful outcomes for which someone might seek compensation. These can be broken down into harms for which the child might claim, and those for which the mother or parents might claim. Some claims will be successful, others will not. The key debate in this area of law is the question of which harms should be compensated. We look first at the basis of the various claims that might arise, and then turn to the compensation debate.

THE LAW AND SOME TERMINOLOGY

A child might want to claim if they have suffered injuries as a result of negligence prior to their birth. This might be negligence by one or both parents (such as exposure to a harmful chemical before conception), or by a medical practitioner (perhaps an error made during the IVF process). Negligence that occurs while the child is *in utero* may also cause injury. An example would be negligent exposure to a drug that causes birth defects. In such cases, the child will want compensation for the cost of those injuries, and could claim in negligence, or more usually under the Congenital Disabilities (Civil Liability) Act 1976, which covers most claims of this kind.

---

[73] *Chester v Afshar* [2004] UKHL 41. In *Crossman v St George's Healthcare NHS Trust* [2016] EWHC 2878 (QB) the approach to causation in *Chester* was said to be 'exceptional and limited' and only to apply to cases where there was a failure to disclose a material risk. See also Chapter 2.

A common law claim on the part of the child would only arise once the child was born alive[74] as, according to *Paton v BPAS*, a foetus *in utero* is not a legal person and 'cannot … have any right of its own at least until it is born and has a separate existence from the mother'.[75] The Congenital Disabilities (Civil Liability) Act takes the same approach, allowing claims on behalf of children only once they have been born alive.[76] The child may claim against any person (apart from their mother) who owed a duty of care to one of the child's parents, and where the breach of this duty caused the complained-of harm.[77] In all but cases of harm due to negligent driving, a child cannot claim against their own mother for injuries suffered due to the mother's actions.[78]

Sometimes, however, a child born with a disability will want to claim not for the cost of their injuries, but for the harm of being born at all. Such claims are referred to as 'wrongful life' claims. These have been consistently rejected by the court on the basis that being alive cannot be worse than being dead.[79]

In other cases, the mother or parents may wish to claim compensation for the costs associated with an unwanted pregnancy or birth. 'Wrongful conception' claims arise when a woman has become pregnant against her wishes. This might occur following a negligently performed sterilisation of either the man or the woman, or the failure to provide accurate information about the success or reliability of a sterilisation.[80] The duty in such cases is owed to both the person sterilised and foreseeable, proximate partners.[81] As long as the claimant has had sexual intercourse without realising that the sterilisation procedure was negligently performed, or is unaware of the risks of imperfect protection against pregnancy, then the negligent breach will be the cause of the resulting pregnancy.[82] Compensation in such cases usually includes the pain and suffering associated with the pregnancy and birth, post-birth costs and the cost of raising the child.

'Wrongful birth' claims made by the parents arise when a pregnancy has resulted in a birth due to the negligence of the defendant. This generally occurs when the woman would have terminated the pregnancy, but does not due to the negligence of the defendant. A good example would be a doctor giving misleading information about the results of a pre-natal test, which the woman relies upon and then loses the chance to terminate the pregnancy. Wrongful

---

[74] *Burton v Islington Health Authority* [1993] QB 204.

[75] *Paton v British Pregnancy Advisory Service* [1979] QB 276, 279.

[76] Congenital Disabilities (Civil Liability) Act 1976, s. 4(3).

[77] Congenital Disabilities (Civil Liability) Act 1976, s. 1.

[78] Congenital Disabilities (Civil Liability) Act 1976, s. 1.

[79] Most recently in *Criminal Injuries Compensation v First Tier Tribunal* [2017] EWCA Civ 139.

[80] See, e.g., *Thake v Maurice* [1986] QB 644; *McFarlane v Tayside Health Board* [2000] 2 AC 59 (both cases concerning advice about whether a sterilisation operation was guaranteed to prevent future pregnancy).

[81] *Goodwill v British Pregnancy Advisory Service* [1996] 1 WLR 1397.

[82] Where the patient *is* aware that there is a risk of pregnancy then the decision to have sex will constitute an intervening act and this, rather than the negligent breach, will be the cause of the resulting pregnancy. In such cases, the negligent sterilisation or failure to warn will not attract liability: *Sabri-Tabrizi v Lothian Health Board* [1998] BMLR 190.

birth claims often arise out of the same facts as wrongful life claims, but in the first the mother or parents are claiming for their damage (similar to those in wrongful pregnancy claims), while in the latter the children themselves are claiming compensation for their existence.

A series of cases have confirmed that in wrongful conception and birth cases (collectively 'wrongful pregnancy' cases), the woman will be entitled to compensation for the pain and inconvenience associated with being pregnant and giving birth.[83] Costs associated with the state of being pregnant and giving birth will also be compensated. This includes the cost of special maternity clothing and lost wages.[84]

Prior to 2000, the courts had also been prepared to compensate the costs of raising an unwanted child, as in cases such as *Emeh v Kensington and Chelsea and Westminster Area Health Authority*.[85] Brooke J confirmed in *Allen v Bloomsbury Health Authority*[86] that the foreseeable and compensable costs of raising an unwanted child would include the financial losses suffered by the parents 'to feed, clothe, house, educate and care for until the child becomes an adult', and also earnings lost in taking time to care for the child and child-minding expenses.[87] Such costs could even include the expense of future private education for the unwanted child where, because the family into which the child was born had provided private education for their other children, this was an expected cost in raising any other child who came into their family.[88] In 2000, in the case of *McFarlane v Tayside Health Board*, the House of Lords decided that compensation for the costs of raising an unwanted child would no longer be allowed.[89] In that case, Mr McFarlane was negligently informed that his vasectomy operation had rendered him completely sterile. He failed to use contraception with his wife, and she became pregnant with what would be their fifth child. The parents claimed for maintenance costs, but were eventually denied. The legal position on maintenance was reversed, such that compensation would no longer be allowed.

Despite this seemingly firm position, later cases have held that the *additional* cost of raising an unwanted *disabled* child over and above the normal costs of raising a child will be compensated. Any extra costs arising from the

---

[83] *Walkin v South Manchester Health Authority* [1995] 1 WLR 1543 (Lord Auld); *McFarlane v Tayside Health Board* [2000] 2 AC 59 (Lord Steyn and Lord Clyde).

[84] See variously *Udale v Bloomsbury Area Health Authority* [1983] 1 WLR 1098; *Thake v Maurice* [1986] QB 644; *Benarr v Ketting Health Authority* (1988) 138 NLJ 179; *Allen v Bloomsbury Health Authority* [1993] 1 All ER 651; *McFarlane v Tayside Health Board* [2000] 2 AC 59.

[85] *Emeh v Kensington and Chelsea and Westminster Area Health Authority* [1985] QB 1012 (*Emeh*), esp. at 1022, per Waller J.

[86] *Allen v Bloomsbury Health Authority* [1993] 1 All ER 651, 662.

[87] This position was supported in *Crouchman v Burke* (1997) 40 BMLR 163; *Allan v Greater Glasgow Health Board* 1998 SLT 580.

[88] *Benarr v Ketting Health Authority* (1988) 138 NLJ 179.

[89] *McFarlane v Tayside Health Board* [2000] 2 AC 59 (*McFarlane*).

parent's disability will not be compensable, but a 'conventional award' to reflect the infringement of autonomy will be made in wrongful pregnancy cases. This award is currently £15,000.

Over the past thirty years the question of compensation has been debated back and forth in the courts. The best flavour of that debate is gained by letting the judges speak for themselves. We will explore their reasoning, and also some responses that can be made to it, below. We will first examine the debate over compensation for maintenance costs, and then consider the approach to disability in later cases.

Why Should the Parents be Compensated?

In the years before the decision in *McFarlane v Tayside Health Board*,[90] a number of judges had expressed reservations about awarding compensation for the cost of maintaining a child. But for the most part, throughout the 1980s and 1990s, damages for the cost of maintaining the unwanted child until they reached adulthood were awarded.

The harm was foreseeable and caused by the careless act

One of the fundamental legal issues in this area is the ambit of what are considered 'foreseeable losses'. Tort compensation is generally limited to foreseeable losses, and in some cases there are special rules about how to determine what the bounds of such a loss are. If we already accept that the pain and discomfort of the pregnancy and delivery of the child are foreseeable and compensable on this basis, then the costs associated with bringing up that child must be foreseeable on the same basis. Lord Justice Slade took this view in *Emeh*.[91] It is clear from the case law that a woman is not expected to have an abortion, and a failure to do so cannot constitute an intervening act that would become the cause of the harm.[92]

In *McFarlane*, however, Lord Slynn pointed out that 'it is not enough to say that the loss is foreseeable … if foreseeability is the only test there is no reason why a claim should necessarily stop at the date when a statutory duty to maintain a child comes to an end'.[93] Such compensation claims were about the scope of liability, not just the quantum of damages. He argued that for claims of (pure) economic loss, 'there may have to be a closer link between the act and the damage than foreseeability' to create liability. There must also be

---

[90] Ibid.

[91] See, e.g., the reasoning of Slade LJ in *Emeh v Kensington and Chelsea and Westminster Area Health Authority* [1985] QB 1012, 1023. Where such harm flowed from a breach of damage, compensation was recoverable, see *Sciuriaga v Powell* (1979) 123 SJ 406, per Watkins J.

[92] See, e.g., *Emeh v Kensington and Chelsea and Westminster Area Health Authority* [1985] QB 1012, 1024, per Slade LJ.

[93] *McFarlane*, 75, per Lord Slynn.

sufficient proximity, and it should be fair, just and reasonable to impose a duty on someone in the claimant's position.[94]

Given this, one argument against compensation is that even though a doctor can foresee the costs associated with having an unwanted child if the doctor is negligent, it would not be fair, just and reasonable to make them liable for those costs because the doctor has not assumed responsibility for them. When someone by their negligence causes someone else *pure* economic loss (that is, loss not consequential on property damage or personal injury), that person will usually only be liable if they have in some way assumed responsibility for the consequences, and it was this area of law to which Lord Slynn was referring.[95] Had the parents wanted to ensure such responsibility was taken, they could have made a contract with the doctor before seeking advice or treatment.

However, there are some serious objections to be made. For one, if the pregnancy *is* regarded as a personal injury (which it seemingly is if compensation is available for the physical effects of pregnancy and birth), the economic loss is arguably *consequential* on that injury and so should be recoverable to the extent that it is foreseeable. In support of this view, Laura Hoyano has described the law pre-*McFarlane* as:

> 15 years of consistent English appellate authority which had applied the conventional professional negligence template to find liability for maintenance costs, the claim being categorised as a consequential economic loss directly flowing from the failed sterilisation which was not only objectively foreseeable but directly contemplated by the parents and the surgeon.[96]

Lady Hale, in the post-*McFarlane* case of *Parkinson*,[97] also (rightly) questioned how it could be said that the doctor could not have assumed responsibility for the costs of maintaining a child when he had been expressly engaged to perform a procedure designed to prevent further children being born.

The High Court of Australia has also been critical of the divergence in the UK from normal principles of tort recovery in unwanted pregnancy cases. In a case concerning facts very similar to those in *McFarlane*, Justice Callinan stated:

---

[94] Ibid., referring to *Caparo Industries Plc v Dickman* [1990] 2 AC 605. Lord Hope agreed: *McFarlane*, 95, per Lord Hope. We do not go into the technicalities of recovery for pure economic loss here, but Lord Hope provides an exploration in the judgment.

[95] See the line of cases commencing with *Hedley Byrne & Co Ltd v Heller & Partners* [1964] AC 465, which in this case were applicable as the 'extended' *Hedley Byrne* principle as per Lord Steyn's judgment (*McFarlane*, 77).

[96] L. Hoyano, 'Misconceptions about wrongful conception' (2002) 65 *Modern Law Review* 883, 884. See also *Parkinson v St James and Seacroft University Hospital NHS Trust* [2002] QB 266 (*Parkinson*) [56]–[80], per Lady Hale.

[97] *Parkinson*, paras 78–80.

All the various touchstones for, and none of the relevant disqualifying conditions against, an award of damages for economic loss are present here.[98]

Justice Kirby was scathing about the importation of 'moral' assessments to reject compensating, holding that courts should not depart from ordinary tort principles:

> [O]n the footing of their personal religious beliefs, or 'moral' assessments concealed in an inarticulate premise dressed up, and described, as legal principle or policy ... neither the invocation of scripture nor the invention of a fictitious oracle on the Underground ... authorises a court of law to depart from the ordinary principles governing the recovery of damages for the tort of negligence.[99]

Alastair Mullis has pointed out that many of the reasons courts resist compensation, particularly in economic loss cases, are not present in wrongful pregnancy cases. There is no 'floodgates' argument to be made, as the situations in which claims can be made are not numerous and the class of claimants is neither wide nor difficult to ascertain.[100]

The unwanted child places parents under a financial burden

In many of the cases before the courts, the financial burden of the unwanted child on the parents was great, and that they had taken steps to avoid it made it clear that they were trying not to incur such a burden. It is understandable and reasonable that a person who has sought to avoid having a child they do not want should be unhappy about the financial burden this places on them, in addition to any other personal reasons they may have had for wanting to avoid having a child. The very fact that they sought sterilisation is evidence that they wanted to avoid having a child, and also had behaved as responsibly as they could in trying to do so. For some, the financial burden will be significant. For example, in *Udale v Bloomsbury Area Health Authority*,[101] the family concerned already had four children, and the addition of a fifth, unwanted child created great difficulties. As the judge noted, they had very little space in which to house the new child:

> The house had three bedrooms. Mr and Mrs Udale slept in the front bedroom; the two elder girls in the back bedroom; the two younger girls had bunk-beds in the third bedroom. This was really only a box-room, 9' x 9'. The baby has had to go in there to make a third. It is obviously a squash.[102]

---

[98] *Cattanach v Melchior* [2003] HCA 38, para. 299, per Callinan J.

[99] Ibid., 53, per Kirby J. Here, Kirby J is referring to statements made in UK cases that are discussed later in this chapter.

[100] A. Mullis, 'Wrongful conception unravelled' (1993) 1 *Medical Law Review* 320.

[101] *Udale v Bloomsbury Area Health Authority* [1983] 1 WLR 1098.

[102] Ibid., 1104.

Similarly, in the *Thake v Maurice*, the claimants had five children already, all living with them in a three-bedroom council house. Indeed, their situation was sufficiently difficult that Mr Thake opted to have his vasectomy performed under local anaesthesia, as this was the cheapest way in which it could be done.[103]

WHY SHOULDN'T THE PARENTS BE COMPENSATED?

A number of reasons have been offered by the courts to support their refusal to award maintenance costs for healthy, but unwanted, children.

It would be wrong to characterise a child as a financial burden

A strong sense that it would be wrong to characterise a child as a financial liability and nothing else pervades the English courts' thinking on claims for the maintenance of unwanted children. Many judges have found this objectionable, but a distinction should be made between the birth of a child and the costs associated with it. One can celebrate the one while lamenting the other. Kirby ACJ made this point in *CES v Superclinics (Australia)*,[104] an Australian case cited by Lord Millett in *McFarlane*:

> [I]t was not the child as revealed which was unwanted. Nor is the child's existence the *damage* in the action. The birth of the child is simply the occasion by which the negligence of the respondents manifests itself in the economic injury to the parents. It is the economic damage which is the principal unwanted element.[105]

However, this did not resolve the matter in Lord Millett's view, for despite all arguments otherwise, he felt that the law must take the birth of a healthy child to be a blessing, not a detriment, and it would be 'morally offensive to regard a normal, healthy baby as more trouble and expense than it is worth'.[106]

The costs of raising a child are offset by the benefits

Given this sense that a child should be seen solely as a joyful benefit, it is not surprising that some of the judges argued that the financial and other hardships of having a child were offset by the joy of the child's birth, which is in our society 'a blessing and an occasion for rejoicing'.[107] It was, for Lord Steyn in *McFarlane*, repugnant to the sanctity and value of human life to evaluate the costs and benefits of a child.[108] A feeling of repugnance about the idea of weighing benefits versus costs ran through a number of the judgments, and

---

[103] *Thake v Maurice* [1986] QB 644, 654.
[104] *CES v Superclinics (Australia)* (1995) 38 NSWLR 47.
[105] Ibid., 75, per Kirby ACJ.
[106] *McFarlane*, 114, per Lord Millett.
[107] *Udale v Bloomsbury Area Health Authority* [1983] 1 WLR 1098, 1109.
[108] *McFarlane*, 82, per Lord Steyn.

it could be argued that it is wrong to even engage in such an exercise. But as Lord Millett pointed out, this observation is no solution, for it means the court should either not engage in it and award nothing, or not engage in it and award all costs.[109] Justice Peter Pain put the matter well in *Thake*:

> A healthy baby is so lovely a creature that I can well understand the reaction of one who asks: how could its birth possibly give rise to an action for damages? But every baby has a belly to be filled and a body to be clothed. The law relating to damages is concerned with reparation in money terms and this is what is needed for the maintenance of a baby.[110]

The benefits of a child are incommensurate with the costs

A related reason not to award compensation is that the benefits of a child are speculative and incalculable, and therefore *incommensurate* with the costs of raising that child. Given this, no offset calculation can be made, and it is considered better to simply say that the benefits and burdens are in equilibrium, and so no award is needed. The judges in *McFarlane* were influenced by what they saw as the inherent difficulty in determining how much should be awarded, with many considering that the amount should be reduced by the benefits the parents accrued by having a child, albeit an unwanted one. As Lord Slynn put it:

> Of course there should be joy at the birth of a healthy baby, at the baby's smile and the teenager's enthusiasms but how can these be put in money terms and trimmed to allow for sleepless nights and teenage disobedience?[111]

Lord Hope emphasised that there are:

> benefits in the arrangement as well as costs. In the short term there is the pleasure which a child gives in return for the love and care which she received during infancy. In the longer term there is mutual relationship of support and affection which will continue well beyond the ending of the period of her childhood.[112]

For their Lordships in *McFarlane*, it was not 'fair, just and reasonable to leave these benefits out, and to do so would mean that the parents were overpaid'.[113] According to Lord Hope, the costs could be estimated, but these benefits were 'incalculable', and therefore 'the logical conclusion, as a matter of law, is that the costs ... are not recoverable as damages'.[114] He reasoned that

---

[109] *McFarlane*, 111, per Lord Millett.

[110] *Thake v Maurice* [1986] QB 644, 666, per Peter Pain J. The court in *Emeh* agreed.

[111] *McFarlane*, 75, per Lord Slynn.

[112] *McFarlane*, 97, per Lord Hope.

[113] *McFarlane*, 97, per Lord Hope. This was how Lord Hope brought the set off approach within the legal analysis.

[114] *McFarlane*, 97, per Lord Hope.

it could be determined that the costs would not exceed the value of these benefits in the long run, and so they should not be compensated at all for fear of over-compensation.

However, this is not the law's approach to benefits of this kind. Lord Clyde pointed out:

> It may be that the benefit which a child represents to his or her parent is open to quantification, but there is no principle under which the law recognises such a set off.[115]

Imagine that a woman's leg is very badly broken in an accident caused by a negligent driver. She spends weeks in hospital, and in the course of her treatment falls in love with her doctor, and he in turn falls in love with her. They find great joy in their relationship, but no court would suggest that her compensation be reduced to account for these benefits. Lord Clyde made a similar argument, stating that 'the loss sustained by a mineworker who is rendered no longer fit for work underground [is not] offset by the pleasure and benefit he may enjoy in the open air of a public park'.[116] The same approach should be taken to the benefits of having children.

Such balancing is also speculative and focuses on one aspect of these benefits. We might also say that the strain the child's financial burden places on the parents affects their relationship, which in turn affects their children, and hence this intangible loss ought also to be in the calculus. The law rightly does not engage in such speculations in cases like the woman with the broken leg, and it arguably should not have done so in the case of children's expenses either.

Wealthier claimants would get higher compensatory awards

A related argument is that the quantum of damages would be affected by the wealth or otherwise of the parents, as the award would need to take account of the actual expenses incurred, and if the child were born into a wealthier family that already had children, the expectation would be that this child would be maintained to the same standard. Effectively, rich parents would receive a *higher* compensatory award than those less well off. As Lord Steyn pointed out, this would be 'unseemly' to commuters on the London Underground.[117] Exactly such an award was made in *Benarr v Kettering Health Authority*[118] for the costs of private schooling, and it was this kind of award that concerned their Lordships in *McFarlane*.[119]

However, these concerns could be met by using tariffs for awards, or basing the amounts on the average cost of raising a child. There are measures

---

[115] *McFarlane*, 103, per Lord Clyde.
[116] *McFarlane*, 103, per Lord Clyde.
[117] *McFarlane*, 82, per Lord Steyn.
[118] *Benarr v Kettering Health Authority* (1988) NLJ 179.
[119] *McFarlane*, 91, per Lord Hope.

of these costs calculated as minimum costs, produced by various agencies. For example, the Centre of Economic and Business Research produces the *Cost of a Child* report, and uses various datasets and information about the price of food to produce a costing. In 2013, this was £227,266 to raise a child to the age of 18.[120] Such measures could be used to address concerns about determining quantum, and also to avoid the 'unseemliness' of awarding wealthy parents more. The courts already use tariffs in other contexts, and such an approach could be justified by the problems other measures pose.

It may be harming for a child to learn that their parents wanted to be compensated for their existence

One of the big concerns raised against compensation was the worry, expressed for example by Jupp J in *Udale*, that making such an award would have problematic social implications, and it would be harming to a child to learn that they had been unwanted:

> It is highly undesirable that any child should learn that a court has publicly declared his life or birth to be a mistake, a disaster even, and that he or she is unwanted or rejected. Such pronouncements would disrupt families and weaken the structure of society.[121]

However, as Peter Pain J stated in *Thake*, decided after *Udale*, he did not agree that the child would be harmed by knowing they were the subject of a claim for unwanted birth or pregnancy. In *Thake*, the girl in question was undoubtedly much loved, but was still a significant financial burden on her parents. Additionally, unwanted pregnancies are not rare, and it is evident that many of these accidental conceptions produce children who are much-loved members of their families.[122]

The parents in these cases were not seeking compensation because they had a child for which they felt no love, but because they were as a result of its unwanted birth now placed under a considerable financial burden (one, indeed, they had sought to avoid). Further, as Waller LJ pointed out in *Emeh*, compensation for maintenance costs 'may in some cases be an encouragement and help to bring up an unplanned child'.[123] Being given the resources to deal with the burden would, in fact, improve the relationship between the parents and child, rather than undermine it.

---

[120] H. Osborne, 'Cost of raising a child surges past £225,000', *The Guardian*, 23 January 2014, available at www.theguardian.com/money/2014/jan/23/cost-raising-child-surges.

[121] *Udale v Bloomsbury Area Health Authority* [1983] 1 WLR 1098, 1109.

[122] *McFarlane*, 75, per Lord Slynn.

[123] *Emeh*, 1021, per Walker LJ.

It is inappropriate for scarce NHS resources to be used to pay for healthy children

The position is also informed by the view that it would be unacceptable to take funds from a cash-strapped NHS to pay the costs of a healthy child. Tony Weir has made the point that it is problematic to take resources from the NHS, which is already under-resourced, and divert these from helping the sick to paying for the upkeep of healthy children.[124] Jonathan Herring rightly responds that 'this kind of argument could be used to deny nearly any claim against the NHS' by a patient injured by a staff member's negligence.[125] Emily Jackson argues that if we are concerned to reduce the burden on the NHS of paying out for negligence claims, this should be done via Parliament.[126]

Also, such money, though from the NHS, is ultimately from the Government, and so when this money is used, it spreads the cost of such children over the whole of the community. From this perspective, it is arguably more just that we all shoulder the burden of an unwanted child and ensure its parents can adequately care for it than place the whole of the burden on the parents who had already acted responsibly in trying not to come under such a burden.

An intriguing question is whether the outcome of these cases would be different if the patients were receiving private treatment. A technical legal reason why it might is that a private patient has a contract with their hospital and so could bring a contractual claim, which would not be possible for an NHS patient, who can only sue in tort. It may also be argued that the public policy arguments based on the cost to the NHS would not apply in the case of private treatment. However, *obiter*, in *ARB v IVF Hammersmith Ltd*,[127] Jay J thought the outcome of such cases would be the same whether bought in contract or in tort. You can understand that the law would look very unfair if private patients were given a remedy when NHS patients were not.

The harm done was disproportionate to the wrong

Lord Clyde argued in *McFarlane* that the losses sustained were disproportionate to the wrong done. On this view, the doctor's action was negligent, but the harm it caused was so wildly disproportionate to the loss suffered that she should not be liable, although he felt that the doctor ought to be liable for limited damages.[128] This approach has many merits, as it recognises the wrong done but takes account of the fact that the cost it brings is very high relative to the error. However, Lord Millett found this argument unconvincing, rightly pointing out that in other cases of small medical errors that led to large harms

---

[124] T. Weir, 'The unwanted child' (2000) 59 *Cambridge Law Journal* 238, 238.

[125] J. Herring, *Medical Law and Ethics*, 6th edn (Oxford University Press, 2016), 298.

[126] E. Jackson, *Medical Law* (Oxford University Press, 2010), 748.

[127] *ARB v IVF Hammersmith Ltd* [2017] EWHC 1428 (QB).

[128] *McFarlane*, 106, per Lord Clyde.

this approach was not taken.[129] Emily Jackson has made the point similarly, explaining that damages are meant not to reflect the degree of fault, but to put the claimant in the position she would have been but for the negligence.[130]

Doctors might have an incentive to encourage abortions

There is also the concern that if large financial awards are made in compensation for maintenance costs, then the medical practitioners who might be liable to pay these will have an incentive to encourage women to terminate unwanted pregnancies.[131] Physicians should not be put in a position of conflict of this kind, nor should we set up a situation in which women might be subject to pressure in making the decision to continue with a pregnancy or not. Arguably, it is unlikely that many (if any) physicians would press a woman to terminate her pregnancy, as they are bound by their profession's code of ethics, and, further, the award is likely to be paid by an insurance company on their behalf, rather than from their own pockets.

Distributive justice arguments

Objections to compensation are also raised on the basis of distributive justice. On this view, we should aim for a just distribution of costs and benefits across society, rather than corrective justice (which requires the person who causes harm to compensate the person who suffers it). In Lord Steyn's view, a distributive justice approach would mean that the losses should be borne by the parents rather than falling on the medical practitioner. He considered that lay people would find this view correct, as they would 'instinctively' feel that 'the law of tort has no business to provide legal remedies consequent on the birth of a healthy child, which all of us regard as a valuable and good thing'.[132]

While it might be that some would find it morally problematic to compensate in such cases, this is not, with respect, a strong argument. Many academic commentators have criticised the Lords' references to the thinking of people on the Underground on the basis that we cannot know what such people are thinking, and even if we did survey them, the views of a sample of people are not determinative of the right moral position to take on an issue.[133]

We also might just as easily say that the law of tort has every business compensating people for costs they had sought to avoid, and have incurred only due to the negligence of someone else. Indeed, in these kinds of cases we are talking about people who have taken active, responsible steps to avoid these

---

[129] *McFarlane*, 109, per Lord Millett.

[130] E. Jackson, *Medical Law* (Oxford University Press, 2010), 736.

[131] E.g. *Udale v Bloomsbury Area Health Authority* [1983] 1 WLR 1098, 1109, per Jupp J.

[132] *McFarlane*, 82, per Lord Steyn.

[133] R. Oppenheim, 'The "mosaic" of tort law: the duty of care question' (2003) *Journal of Personal Injury Law* 152.

costs, not merely innocent victims who have had hardship befall them. They placed their trust in a medical professional who failed them. It seems extremely just that they should be compensated. They might very well love their child deeply, as many in the cases gave evidence they did, but this says nothing about whether they could bear (or should bear) the very real financial implications of an unwanted birth.[134]

SHOULD IT MAKE A DIFFERENCE IF THE CHILD IS DISABLED?

Later cases put the *McFarlane* approach to the test when the question arose of whether parents might be compensated for the *additional* cost of raising a disabled child. In *Parkinson v St James and Seacroft University Hospital NHS Trust*, the Court of Appeal found that such additional costs *could* be compensated.[135] This raises the question of why disability should matter, given that much of the reasoning in *McFarlane* rested on the view that a child was a blessing and its benefits outweighed any costs it brought with it.

In *Parkinson*, the claimant, Angela Parkinson, had four children already, and underwent a sterilisation operation to avoid having a fifth child as she did not believe she could raise another child. The sterilisation was performed negligently and she conceived her fifth child. The family were placed under terrible strain by the news that they were expecting another child, and the Parkinsons separated prior to Scott's birth. Mrs Parkinson also had to give up paid employment to care for him, as Scott suffered from autism spectrum disorder which caused him to be very difficult to control and violent towards other children. The Court of Appeal awarded Mrs Parkinson the extra costs of caring for Scott.

If, as in *McFarlane*, a child was to be seen as a blessing worth the cost, how was it that Mrs Parkinson was awarded the extra costs associated with Scott's disability? One reason was that it was *foreseeable* that a failed sterilisation might result in the birth of *a child with congenital disabilities* because it is always possible that a child will be born with disabilities.[136] Therefore, Scott's special needs were a foreseeable loss. It could also be said that a doctor performing a sterilisation had assumed responsibility for such consequences, and sufficient proximity could be found between the doctor and the parents who were claiming for these losses. That is, the ordinary requirements for the recovery of economic loss were present.[137] In this case, it was found that Scott's disabilities flowed from his conception, not from some other intervening cause.

But this reasoning did not lead to a full award, as Brooke LJ then held that the distributive justice argument applied, finding that 'ordinary people would

---

[134] Lady Hale, in the post-*McFarlane* case of *Parkinson*, made the point that it is far from clear what the traveller on the London Underground might think. Speculation about the traveller's views did little, in her view, to provide a solution (at 290).

[135] *Parkinson v St James and Seacroft University Hospital NHS Trust* [2002] QB 266.

[136] Ibid., Brooke LJ, para. 50, following the reasoning of Waller LJ in *Emeh*.

[137] Ibid.

consider that it would be fair for the law to make an award in such a case'.[138] Lady Hale emphasised in *Parkinson* that the costs of care of a child flowed 'inexorably' from the 'invasion of bodily integrity and personal autonomy involved in every pregnancy'.[139] But she conceded that she was bound by the decision in *McFarlane* that the benefits of a healthy child were at least equal to the costs, what she called the 'deemed equilibrium'. This also, she argued, treated 'a disabled child as having the same worth as a non-disabled child. It affords him the same dignity and status. It simply acknowledges that he costs more'.[140]

Looked at in this way, the distinction can be justified. It rests on a view that all children bring equal blessings, are all equally valuable, but some cost more than the norm. Therefore, if we accept that the normal costs of a child are offset by their blessings, then it can still be reasonable to provide extra for extra costs. In reality, according to Lady Hale, it is 'much less likely' that a disabled child 'brings as much pleasure and as many advantages as does a normal healthy child',[141] but we do not need to engage in this kind of unpleasant evaluation on her approach, because we simply accord all children the same value and do not make any calculations about the actual 'value' or otherwise of a particular child.

Alasdair McLean argues that this approach is flawed. If the original reason we could not balance the benefits of a child against the costs was that those benefits were incalculable and hence incommensurable, then the offset calculation remains just as impossible. If we then also see the costs of disability as merely additional maintenance costs, then we face exactly the same problem, and so the same argument against any award should apply.[142]

A concern about the law in this area is that it conceptualises a disabled child as a harm. Lady Hale tried to manoeuvre around this by saying disabled children simply cost more. However, Stephen Todd has suggested we should 'grasp the nettle'[143] and recognise that 'the birth of a handicapped child is surely a matter for condolence, whereas that of a healthy child is (despite the expense) a reason for congratulation'.[144] This attitude is deeply problematic. It sits uncomfortably with the view in many of the decisions that a child is to be seen as a blessing, and so the parents should be happy to have it even if it is something they tried to avoid and cannot afford. If a child is a blessing, and so cannot be compensated, the moral foundation of this must be that parents should love what they receive in the form of children, and not see them as

---

[138] Ibid.

[139] *Parkinson*, para. 73, per Lady Hale.

[140] Ibid., para. 90, per Lady Hale.

[141] Ibid.

[142] A. Maclean, 'An Alexandrian approach to the knotty problem of wrongful pregnancy: *Rees v Darlington Memorial Hospital NHS Trust* in the House of Lords', *Web Journal of Current Legal Issues*, vol. 3, 2004, available at www.bailii.org/uk/other/journals/WebJCLI/2004/issue3/maclean3.html.

[143] S. Todd, 'Wrongful conception, wrongful birth and wrongful life' (2005) 27 *Sydney Law Review* 525, 535.

[144] Ibid., 535.

a burden. But this is not true on the view given here if the child is disabled; such children *are* being conceptualised as a burden. Lady Hale's view navigates some of this problem by arguing that the child simply costs more than normal, and so costs beyond the norm should be compensable, and she was of course bound by *McFarlane*. If we were really to grasp the nettle, what we should conclude is that *any* child who is not wanted and who is a financial burden, is a burden and should be compensated if they exist due to someone else's negligence. We cannot logically have it both ways, and the nettle is really grasped when we accept that no matter how much the parents come to love their child, this is irrelevant as to whether or not they can bear the financial costs they were trying (rightly) to avoid.

SHOULD IT MAKE A DIFFERENCE IF THE MOTHER IS DISABLED?

Following *Parkinson* came the case of *Rees v Darlington Memorial Hospital NHS Trust*,[145] in which it was made clear that the added costs of the *parent's* being disabled will not be recoverable. In that case, Katrina Rees had sought sterilisation to avoid having a child, as she felt that her blindness would made it very difficult for her to provide adequate care. The Court of Appeal awarded her the extra costs, but this decision was overturned by the House of Lords.

In the Court of Appeal, Waller LJ (dissenting) felt the situation was no different to that in *McFarlane*, as a healthy baby had been born. He argued that it was wrong to allow the mother's disability to make all the difference, when other things that made caring for a child hard (such as the financial status of the parents) had not been relevant in *McFarlane*. Here, then, disability was not to make a difference, even though disability causing higher costs had made *all the difference* in *Parkinson*. Because the child in *Rees* was healthy, the *McFarlane* principle applied.

The House of Lords declined in *Rees* to revisit its thinking in *McFarlane*, concurring with the reasons given in the case. However, one important step back from the harshness of the decision was made. The House of Lords recognised, as previous judges had, that a woman's autonomy had been undermined, and she had consequently suffered a wrong in not being able to decide to limit her family as she wished. The House therefore agreed to a 'conventional award' of £15,000 in recognition of this wrong. The award was not meant as compensation, nor subject to calculation; it would simply 'afford some measure of recognition of the wrong done'.[146] Lords Hope and Steyn, who had decided *McFarlane*, dissented on the conventional award in *Rees*, both considering it something for Parliament to implement after much consideration and study.

Nicky Priaulx has criticised the 'nexus drawn between disability and incapacity' in *Rees*, noting Waller LJ's comments in the Court of Appeal that many

---

[145] *Rees v Darlington Memorial Hospital NHS Trust* [2003] UKHL 52.
[146] Ibid., para. 42, per Lord Bingham.

parents face hardship and there was something uncomfortable about distinguishing on the basis of disability.[147]

Stephen Todd has argued that the decision in *Rees* on compensation is coherent and right, because the costs of raising a child are infinitely variable according to the needs of the child and the circumstances of the parents. A parent's disability is simply one of these many factors, one that increases the costs of caring for the child but which still falls within the kinds of costs excluded in *McFarlane*, and cannot be disentangled form the costs of the birth.[148] But there are many problems with this. For one, we could disentangle the extra costs of managing a disability from the normal costs of parenting if that disability meant the parent could not do something that is regarded as a normal and needed part of parenting, such as driving a child to places they need to be. For another, we can (as noted earlier) determine the basic cost of raising a child that is generalised and sets aside differences in circumstances, and then added costs due to the disability in particular could be disentangled from this.

CONCLUSION

The decision in *Rees*, which encapsulates the current state of the law, has both benefits and problems, and the law in this area remains rather a mess. One benefit of the *Rees* approach is that it goes some way to providing money to a woman who has been harmed, while avoiding making the NHS burdened by large awards. But this is inconsistent with the law's approach to any other negligence on the part of NHS staff. It also is simply a choice between who bears the loss. It does not make the loss go away. While the NHS might not be able to afford those costs, nor could many of the people who have brought claims for unwanted children. Indeed, the very people who brought them were people who had had sterilisations to avoid these costs because they could not bear them. Probably many people have had unwanted children as the result of unsuccessful sterilisations, but they have not claimed because the costs were outweighed by the benefits for them. Exactly the people least able to bear those costs are the ones hit hardest by the *McFarlane* rule. Samantha Singer has also rightly pointed out that in some cases, most people would think compensation was justified given the difficulties having an unwanted child brings. She argues that this was particularly so in *Rees*, where Karina Rees had very good reasons for trying to avoid having a child because of the burden under which it would place her.[149]

---

[147] N. Priaulx, 'That's one heck of an "Unruly horse"! Riding roughshod over autonomy in wrongful conception' (2014) 12 *Feminist Legal Studies* 317, 321.

[148] S. Todd, 'Wrongful conception, wrongful birth and wrongful life' (2005) 27 *Sydney Law Review* 525, 534.

[149] S. Singer, 'Casenote: Rees v Darlingon' (2004) 26 *Journal of Social Welfare and Family Law* 403.

The real issue with *Rees*, and the state of the law as it stands, is, as Priaulx points out, that *Rees* 'destabilises the most criticised aspect of the House of Lords' decision [in *McFarlane*]: the assumption that an "unwanted" healthy child is a source of unbridled joy'.[150] Having departed from the normal principles of tort recovery, and attempting also to bring in moral concerns, the courts have created an incoherent area of law that punishes those who are unreasonably burdened due to the mistakes of others. As Alasdair Maclean comments, while the strength of the conventional award is that it 'makes no arbitrary distinction between claimants', the award will probably please no one, 'except perhaps the NHS', because it under-compensates actual losses and fails to do corrective justice.[151] Perhaps this is an area of law in which the courts would have done better to stay with the established principles of recovery, rather than dabble in moral arguments that have emerged as unconvincing and have left the innocent victims bearing the high financial burden caused by someone else's carelessness.

FURTHER READING

Debate 1

M. Brazier and J. Miola, 'Bye-bye Bolam: a medical litigation revolution?' (2000) 8 *Medical Law Review* 85.

R. Mulheron, 'Trumping Bolam: a critical legal analysis of Bolitho's "gloss"' (2010) 69(3) *Cambridge Law Journal* 609.

A. Samanta et al., 'The role of clinical guidelines in medical negligence litigation: a shift from the Bolam standard' (2006) 14(3) *Medical Law Review* 321.

Lord Woolf, 'Are the courts excessively deferential to the medical profession?' (2001) 9 *Medical Law Review* 1.

Debate 2

T. Hill, 'A lost chance for compensation in the tort of negligence by the House of Lords' (1991) 54 *Modern Law Review* 511.

W. Scott, 'Causation in medico-legal practice: a doctor's approach to the "lost opportunity" cases' (1992) 55 *Modern Law Review* 522.

J. Stapleton, 'Loss of chance of cure from cancer' (2005) 68 *Modern Law Review* 996.

J. Stapleton, 'Unnecessary causes' (2013) *Law Quarterly Review* 39.

M. Stauch, 'Causation, risk, and loss of chance in medical negligence' (1997) 17 *Oxford Journal of Legal Studies* 201.

---

[150] N. Priaulx, 'That's one heck of an "Unruly horse"! Riding roughshod over autonomy in wrongful conception' (2014) 12 *Feminist Legal Studies* 317, 322.

[151] A. Maclean, 'An Alexandrian approach to the knotty problem of wrongful pregnancy: *Rees v Darlington Memorial Hospital NHS Trust* in the House of Lords', *Web Journal of Current Legal Issues*, vol. 3, 2004, available at www.bailii.org/uk/other/journals/WebJCLI/2004/issue3/maclean3.html.

Debate 3

L. Hoyano, 'Misconceptions about wrongful conception' (2002) 65 *Modern Law Review* 883.

L. Hoyano, 'McFarlane v Tayside health board' in J. Herring and J. Wall (eds), *Landmark Cases in Medical Law* (Hart, 2015).

A. Maclean, 'An Alexandrian approach to the knotty problem of wrongful pregnancy: *Rees v Darlington Memorial Hospital NHS Trust* in the House of Lords', *Web Journal of Current Legal Issues*, vol. 3, 2004, available at www.bailii.org/uk/other/journals/WebJCLI/2004/issue3/maclean3.html.

N. Priaulx, 'That's one heck of an "Unruly horse"! Riding roughshod over autonomy in wrongful conception' (2014) 12 *Feminist Legal Studies* 317.

CHAPTER 5

Reproduction

INTRODUCTION

Reproduction involves decisions relating to an aspect of human experience that deeply affects an individual's identity, body and future life experience. As Allen Buchanan et al. suggest, 'the capacity to be ... self-determining is a central condition of personhood'.[1] It is important that we respect and protect these choices to enable people to live the best lives they can. Reproduction is important for many people, and so it might be particularly important to respect their autonomy in this sphere of experience.

As John Robertson argues:

> reproductive choices have such a major impact on a person's life – on one's identity, one's body, and one's sense of meaning – that we are committed to assigning discretion over them to the individuals directly involved, unless great harm to others from the choice would ensue.[2]

Having children is a clearly vitally important facet of life, something which is evidenced both by the fact most people do have children, and by the anguish suffered by those who cannot.[3] Raising children is an enriching experience, while reproduction, including pregnancy and birth, is a very personal and emotionally important aspect of human self-expression. Reproductive choices are therefore important in people's lives because having the ability to make choices in this context enables them to choose about issues that clearly affect their well-being.[4]

Some, such as Julian Savulescu, have suggested that the only reason to restrict reproductive rights would be that harm will be suffered by others if people are

---

[1] A. Buchanan et al., *From Chance to Choice: Genetics and Justice* (Cambridge University Press, 2000), 215–16.

[2] J. Robertson, 'Liberalism and the limits of procreative liberty: a response to my critics' (1995) 52 *Washington and Lee Law Review* 233, 234.

[3] As quoted in P. Spallone, *Beyond Conception: The New Politics of Reproduction* (Bergin & Garvey, 1989), 69.

[4] See A. Buchanan et al., *From Chance to Choice: Genetics and Justice* (Cambridge University Press, 2000), 214, 219.

free to make any choices they wish.[5] A second reason to restrict reproductive rights is to ensure that the rights (and possibly interests) of others are not unduly infringed. This issue applies to autonomy in all contexts, but is particularly relevant in relation to reproductive decisions because, as Onora O'Neill argues, reproduction is not simply self-expression; it brings a third party – the child – into existence, who may have interests that will be infringed by the reproductive decisions we make.[6] Finally, principlist approaches require that we balance the principles of beneficence, non-maleficence and justice against respecting autonomy. In some instances this will place restrictions on rights to make free choices. In the case of reproductive decision making, we need to consider the good of the resulting child, the good of the parents and the good of the wider community.

In this chapter we look at two debates that arise in the regulation of reproduction where people's choices about reproduction are currently restricted: the use of pre-natal genetic diagnosis techniques, and surrogacy. We examine the two key debates that arise as a consequence of these restrictions: whether we should be permitted to select our children's traits, and whether surrogacy should be permitted.

Debate 1

Should parents be allowed to choose their children's genetic traits?

INTRODUCTION

As the science of human genetics has advanced, we have become increasingly able to identify the traits an embryo or foetus will have when it develops into a person. There is range of ways in which this can be done. Embryos can be created outside the womb using assisted reproductive techniques (ART), and then a few cells extracted for examination. The embryo with the desirable trait can then be implanted, or conversely the embryo carrying an unwanted trait can be discarded. This technique is called 'pre-implantation genetic diagnosis' (PGD). Once implanted and developing, we can use blood tests, ultrasound and invasive tests, such as amniocentesis, to predict, and in some cases detect, the traits of the developing foetus. If an unwanted trait is detected, the pregnancy can be terminated. In the future, it may also be possible to alter traits before and perhaps even after implantation.

While parents can effectively select their child's traits to a degree via terminating pregnancies, selecting embryos for implantation is the most direct method, and is obviously more appealing as it does not involve multiple pregnancies and terminations. PGD also allows selection *for* as well as against traits.

---

[5] See, e.g., J. Savulescu, 'Deaf lesbians, "designer disability", and the future of medicine' (2002) 325 *British Medical Journal* 771, 773. See also M. Ryan, 'The argument for unlimited procreative liberty: a feminist critique' (1990) 20 *Hastings Center Report* 6, 7.

[6] O. O'Neill, *Autonomy and Trust in Bioethics* (Cambridge University Press, 2000), 61–63.

Therefore, in this chapter we focus on PGD in considering whether parents should be allowed to select their children's traits.

There are numerous reasons why a parent might wish to select for or against traits. The primary reason is to avoid disability. Where a genetic disorder runs in a family, the potential parents might want to use PGD to select against embryos carrying the disease-related genetic mutation. Where that disease is caused by a mutation on one of the sex chromosomes, the parents might want to test for the sex of the embryo to help them choose which to select. In some cases, parents may wish to select in favour of a trait some would regard as a disability, as in the high-profile case of two deaf lesbians who sought to increase their chances of producing a deaf child.[7] More often, however, parents might want to select embryos with traits they think are likely to promote a good life for them, such as intelligence or sporting ability. We can currently detect many diseases, but tests for traits such as intelligence cannot yet be detected via PGD, and such tests may be a way off as many such traits involve a complex interaction between many genetic factors.

PGD is also sometimes used to produce what are known as 'saviour siblings'. In these cases, the parents already have a child, one who is suffering from a condition that could be treated using closely matched tissue. If such tissue is not available, they may want to have another child in the hope that this new child will be a match. PGD is used to ensure this by examining the embryos pre-implantation and selecting the one that will have the needed tissue type.

The key debate in relation to PGD, then, is when it will be appropriate, if at all, to select the traits of our offspring. Here, we will examine some general views on the question, as well as some of the specific arguments for and against selection for particular reasons.

THE LAW

As PGD involves embryo selection, it necessarily entails the creation of embryos using in vitro fertilisation (IVF). This brings it under the ambit of the Human Fertilisation and Embryology Act 1990 (the Act) and the extensive amendments made to the Act in 2008. PGD is subject to the licensing scheme under the Act, and clinics are not permitted to perform PGD without such a licence. The Human Fertilisation and Embryology Authority (HFEA) places limits on how PGD may be done, which traits can be tested for and the reasons for which it can be done. Given the concerns this practice raises, it is not surprising that the legislation puts in place tight controls on the use of PGD.

Under the 1990 Act (as amended by the Human Fertilisation and Embryology Act 2008), PGD is only permitted to establish whether the embryo has an abnormality:

---

[7] *BBC News*, 'Couple "choose" to have deaf baby', 8 April 2002, available at http://news.bbc. co.uk/1/hi/health/1916462.stm.

- that may affect its capacity to result in a live birth; or
- that is associated with a significant risk that the person with the abnormality will have or develop a serious physical or mental disability, a serious illness or any other serious medical condition.[8]

Testing for the sex of the embryo is only allowed where there is a particular risk that any resulting child will have or develop a gender-related serious physical or mental disability, a gender-related serious illness, or any other gender-related serious medical condition.[9] PGD can be used to produce a saviour sibling where the existing child 'suffers from a serious medical condition which could be treated by umbilical cord blood stem cells, bone marrow or other tissue of any resulting child'.[10]

It is thus clear that at present, selection is permitted only on very limited grounds. We now consider whether this is the appropriate place to draw the line, exploring first whether parents should be allowed to choose their child's traits at all, and then turning to the four main areas of current debate: selecting against disability, sex selection, the creation of saviour siblings, and selecting for disability.

SELECTING TRAITS

Commodifying children and the impact of selection on the parent/child relationship

The predominant argument against allowing parents to choose their children's traits is that this risks the development of a culture in which 'designer babies' are created, where the child is a commodity. On this view, the child is treated as an object and created for the parents' purposes, not for its own sake, which some consider harming. For example, David King writes:

> Selecting the 'best' amongst multiple embryos sets up a new relationship between parents and offspring … They are no longer a gift from God, or the random forces of nature, but selected products, expressing in part their parents' aspirations, desires and whims.[11]

Writing in the context of selecting against disability, Erik Parens and Adrienne Asch explain that some consider that selection of traits 'signals an intolerance of diversity not merely in the society but in the family, and ultimately it could harm parental attitudes toward all children'.[12]

---

[8] Human Fertilisation and Embryology Act 1990 Sch 2, para. 1ZA(1), (2).

[9] Human Fertilisation and Embryology Act 1990 Sch 2, para. 1ZA(1), (3).

[10] Human Fertilisation and Embryology Act 1990 Sch 2, para. 1ZA(1)(d).

[11] D. King, 'Preimplantation genetic diagnosis and the "new" eugenics' (1999) 25 *Journal of Medical Ethics* 176, 182.

[12] E. Parens and A. Asch, 'Disability rights critique of prenatal genetic testing: reflections and recommendations' (2003) 9 *Mental Retardation and Developmental Disabilities Research Reviews* 40, 42.

One of the truly valuable things about the parent–child relationship is that it is built on unconditional love. Parents generally love their children regardless of their traits, and this is beneficial to both. It promotes a parent's emotional maturity, while unconditional love provides a child with emotional and psychological security of a unique and lasting kind. Such unconditional love stems in part from the bonding that occurs even before a child is born, and some is likely to be linked to hormonal effects, but it is also a dimension of the human experience that parents almost invariably love their children. Becoming a parent is necessarily a self-regarding choice. It must have a dimension of self-interest, as until the child is created there can be no child for whom that choice is being made. But once the child arrives, this basis shifts and the child becomes the object of that love, which is given usually without condition.

If we were able to choose our children's traits, however, this might well be undermined. Having chosen the child's traits, we might no longer love it unconditionally, but love it in part contingently – for the traits we hoped it had (and which we chose based only on our own preferences) rather than solely for itself. This could undermine part of the fundamental nature of the parent–child relationship, and cause harm to both. Further, as Herring argues, the error of a parent seeking to engineer their child to be a particular way is:

> the error of failing to be open to change as an adult; failing to learn from children; failing to see that the things you thought were important are, in fact, not. It is failing to find the wonder, fear, loneliness, anxiety, spontaneity, and joy of childhood and to re-find them for oneself.[13]

The right to an open future

In addition, if children are created in the manner of their parents' choosing, those children may experience harms if they do not behave as the parents had hoped or expected. Arguably, children have a 'right to an open future', where they have the right to develop to the point where they have the capacity to make choices about their own lives.[14] When children are selected on the basis of traits, this suggests that the parents have hopes for how those children will live their lives. Each child is born under a raft of expectations based on their potential (chosen) capacities, and this may shape the choices they feel they can make. If they do not, for example, choose to pursue the career to which they are suited by their chosen traits, they may suffer if their parents are disappointed.

---

[13] J. Herring, 'Parental responsibility, hyper-parenting and the role of technology' in R. Brownsword, E. Scotford and K. Yeung (eds), *The Oxford Handbook of Law, Regulation and Technology* (Oxford University Press, 2017), 418.

[14] A. Buchanan et al., *From Chance to Choice: Genetics and Justice* (Cambridge University Press, 2000), 164.

Preference for some traits over others

If parents could choose their children's traits, it is also likely that some traits would be more popular than others, such as height or intelligence. The process of selection would eventually increase the instance of some traits, while decreasing that of others, creating stigmatised minorities. David King suggests that parents would tend to choose traits that 'conform to social norms', and this is likely to increase the likelihood that children not in possession of those traits would be potentially disadvantaged, placing further pressure on parents to choose traits to avoid this.[15] Parents would feel this pressure if social tolerance for difference decreased as selective forces reduced the range of traits in the community. Further, for some traits, the advantage comes from having an ability others do not possess; selection processes would undermine this, which might be a good thing by reducing disparity in opportunity.

Some suggest that most traits are actually trivial, such as eye colour, and that therefore it does not matter if people choose them or not. John Harris, for one, makes such an argument, suggesting, then, that if a trait is not trivial, its selection should not be left to chance.[16] But this simplistic view sets aside the generalised impact of people collectively choosing particular traits. If everyone chooses the same trait then all children will have this trait and the comparative advantage of having it will be lost. But if only most parents choose it, the others leaving it to chance, those children without the trait will be comparatively disadvantaged. Collective choices also send a much more stark message about how people ought to be. We need only look at the impact of perfect women's bodies, regularly presented in advertising and fashion, on women's sense of how they should be to imagine how negative such a message can be. Allowing selection of traits would also foster an attitude towards people that reduces them to their desirable traits, rather than the whole of their person, their choices and their beliefs. Emily Jackson argues in response to some of these concerns that even if we did use PGD in this way, the genetic traits we choose would not be completely determinative of the person's qualities, so some of these harms might be overstated.[17]

SELECTING AGAINST DISABILITY

Many of these concerns already arise in the context of PGD and pre-natal testing, as there is a cluster of traits that we already select against – those that cause disability. The law already allows for this via PGD, as does the law on abortion. The debate around whether we should try to avoid creating disabled children via PGD is emotive and complex. Here, we will try to focus on a few areas of debate to get a sense of the key issues.

---

[15] D. King, 'Preimplantation genetic diagnosis and the "new" eugenics' (1999) 25 *Journal of Medical Ethics* 176.

[16] Cited in J. Herring, *Medical Law and Ethics*, 6th edn (Oxford University Press, 2016), 402.

[17] E. Jackson, *Medical Law: Text, Cases and Materials* (Oxford University Press, 2010), 806.

Avoiding harm to the potential child

When determining whether to offer PGD for a genetic condition, the HFEA Code of Practice requires the clinic to have regard to, amongst other things, the likely degree of suffering associated with the condition, the availability of effective therapy, now and in the future, the speed of degeneration in progressive disorders, the extent of any intellectual impairment, the social support available, and the family circumstances of the people seeking treatment.[18] These criteria are directed at limiting testing to serious disabilities that are expected to have a negative impact on the child's quality of life.

In many ways, we already work to eliminate disability, particularly by trying to alleviate its effects or cure those that can be cured. Much medical research is devoted to this task. It would seem, then, that we regard disability as something to be avoided, and so it might seem obviously the right thing to test embryos and select against disability when we can. This seems particularly consistent given that abortion is permitted on the grounds of serious disability, and testing for numerous conditions via ultrasound screening and blood tests is commonplace during pregnancy. The aim here is to avoid a child's coming into the world to suffer from the difficulties, pain and decreased opportunities that are said to come with disability.

One argument made in support of this position is that it prevents harm to the potential child produced, as it avoids the creation of a child who will suffer from a disability. Many take the view, which is supported by the legal position, that we should have the option to select against disability on this basis. A major proponent of this view is Julian Savulescu, who maintains that when all other things are equal, we should select against the embryo that will be disabled.[19] He calls this the Principle of Procreative Beneficence, which he argues holds us *morally obligated* to select the embryo with the traits most likely to produce the best life: 'Reproduction should be about having children who have the best prospects.'[20] John Harris argues that selecting against disability reduces the incidence of harm in the world, and is therefore the right thing to do.[21]

There are many problems with this view.[22] One is that it misconceives what is important about parenting, which, as we saw above, is unconditional love. When we choose a child based on its traits, this unconditionality might be

---

[18] Human Fertilisation and Embryology Authority Code of Practice 2011, para. 10.7.

[19] J. Savulescu, 'Procreative beneficence: why we should select the best children' (2001) 15 *Bioethics* 413.

[20] J. Savulescu, 'Deaf lesbians, "designer disability", and the future of medicine' (2002) 325 *British Medical Journal* 771.

[21] J. Harris, 'Is there a coherent social conception of disability?' (2000) 26 *Journal of Medical Ethics* 95.

[22] It has been the subject of considerable criticism in the ethics literature: see, e.g., R. Bennett, 'When intuition is not enough. Why the principle of procreative beneficence must work much harder to justify its eugenic vision' (2014) 28 *Bioethics* 447; R. Bennett, 'The fallacy of procreative beneficence' (2009) 23 *Bioethics* 265; P. Herissone-Kelly, 'Wrongs, preferences and the selection of children: a critique of Rebecca Bennett's argument against the principle of

undermined. Savulescu's view also does not clearly determine what is meant by the 'best' life. He argues that it is for parents to determine this, thereby making the rather confused overall argument that parents are obliged to choose the embryo with the best prospects, but retain their reproductive autonomy to determine what this might be. If we leave that question entirely to the parents' opinion, the moral obligation becomes rather hollow. For example, Rob Sparrow has commented that Savulescu's libertarianism 'can be maintained only at the cost of [his] theoretical commitment to maximizing welfare – the commitment that generates the obligation to pursue non-person-affecting enhancements in the first place'.[23]

It is also very difficult to determine what constitutes 'harm'. The HFEA Code gives some guidance, stressing that the disability should be serious and that the suffering it causes should be taken into account. However, in practice it will be difficult to know what is sufficient suffering. It may be that some disabilities do not cause particular suffering to those who have them, but may place significant burdens on those around them. A good example is Down's Syndrome, a genetic condition associated with some physical and health problems in some cases, but most particularly in almost all cases the person with Down's will have mental impairment. Generally, people with Down's Syndrome will have an IQ of around 50, with very few testing above 70, and some as low as 20. Most have the mental age of a pre-teen. But studies show that people with Down's Syndrome are generally happy and sociable. While they face some difficulties, arguably they do not suffer greatly. As one father of a Down's child said:

> You're led to believe that it's the worst thing that could possibly ever happen to you. And then you realise it's just another human being who happens to be a little bit different. She just takes a bit more effort and she is a bit slower to pick up on things.[24]

Yet Down's Syndrome is one of the conditions tested for in almost all pregnancies in the UK at the 12-week stage, and more than 90 per cent of women choose to terminate if they receive a diagnosis of Down's Syndrome.[25] We can speculate as to why this might be the case, but it is likely that for many women it is in part because they feel that caring for a child with Down's will

---

procreative beneficence' (2012) 26 *Bioethics* 447; A. Hotke, 'The principle of procreative beneficence: old arguments and a new challenge' (2014) 28 *Bioethics* 255; S. Stoller, 'Why we are not morally required to select the best children: a response to Savulescu' (2008) 22 *Bioethics* 365; I. de Melo-Martin, 'On our obligation to select the best children: a reply to Savulescu' (2004) 18 *Bioethics* 79.

[23] R. Sparrow, 'A not-so-new genetics: Harris and Savulescu on human enhancement' (2011) 41 *Hastings Centre Report* 36, 37.

[24] *BBC News*, 'Steep Rise in Down's Pregnancies' 27 October 2009, available at http://news.bbc.co.uk/1/hi/health/8327228.stm.

[25] NHS, 'Down's Syndrome Q&A', available at www.nhs.uk/news/2008/11November/Pages/DownssyndromeQA.aspx.

be very large burden for many decades. Some may wish to avoid this burden, and perhaps this is reasonable, as it can be argued that one person should not have to subsume their life to that of someone else by committing themselves to providing lifelong care and support. We are not morally obliged to do so, and hence the reasons that support termination for disability on these grounds might also support PGD. However, we might question whether it is reasonable to deny a potential life on the grounds of other another person's autonomy. On the other hand, where a potential parent will suffer considerable harm in having to care for a disabled child, especially where they lack resources, then this might be grounds for at least putting that harm into the balance.

We might also question whether PGD should be permissible in cases where a disability is also associated with traits that make someone's life go well. Asperger Syndrome is often raised as an example of such a disorder, which has problematic implications for sufferers in terms of social interactions, but is also often associated with 'high levels of ability in areas such as maths, science, engineering and music'.[26]

Finally, it is important to remember that selecting against disability via PGD does not avoid harm to a child as such; it avoids the creation of a particular child, one of whose traits was that they would have been disabled in some way. When we make this choice, we are choosing to not create a particular person on the basis of a trait that they have. We use this trait rather than any of their other qualities to determine whether they should exist in preference to someone else. We set aside all their other qualities and focus on this one. This raises the question: what does selecting against disability say about our attitudes to disabled people?

Sending a message to the disabled community

One concern about using PGD to avoid creating disabled children is that it sends a message to the disabled community that their lives are less valuable that those of non-disabled people. As Erik Parens and Adrienne Asch explain, this is called the 'Expressivist' argument, and its central claim is that 'prenatal tests to select against disabling traits express a hurtful attitude about and send a hurtful message to people who live with those same traits'.[27] Further, as Jonathan Herring asks, 'does it not perpetuate the promotion of the myth of idealism as to human nature: that any child which is not perfect can be rejected by a parent?'[28]

Julian Savulescu responds to this concern by pointing out that there is a difference between selecting against disability when choosing embryos,

---

[26] P. Walsh, 'Asperger syndrome and the supposed obligation not to bring disabled lives into the world' (2010) 36 *Journal of Medical Ethics* 521, 522.

[27] E. Parens and A. Asch, 'Disability rights critique of prenatal genetic testing: reflections and recommendations' (2003) 9 *Mental Retardation and Developmental Disabilities Research Reviews* 40, 42.

[28] J. Herring, *Medical Law and Ethics*, 6th edn (Oxford University Press, 2016), 403.

and believing that disabled lives are less valuable. Selecting against disability, he writes:

> does not necessarily imply that the lives of those who now live with disability are less deserving of respect and are less valuable. To attempt to prevent accidents which cause paraplegia is not to say that paraplegics are less deserving of respect. It is important to distinguish between disability and persons with disability. Selection reduces the former, but is silent on the value of the latter.[29]

Others, such as Alan Buchanan, point out that to avoid sending this message, we need to create people who will come into the world in a state of disability, which is harming. Buchanan also agrees with Savulescu that we can distinguish between valuing (or otherwise) a disability, and the value we accord to a disabled person.[30] Bonnier Steinbock comments:

> However, there is no reason why society cannot both attempt to prevent disability and to provide for the needs of those who are disabled. As a matter of fact, the rise of prenatal screening has coincided with more progressive attitudes toward the inclusion of people with disabilities.[31]

Colin Gavaghan argues that we would send a less discriminatory message if parents were free to choose embryos on any basis. This would allow:

> [p]rospective parents to utilize [PGD] to implement their own values and preferences. In doing so, we might avoid the imposition by the state of a single, simplistic view of what constitutes 'normality' and 'disability', a view that is not universally shared.[32]

But as we saw earlier, there are good reasons to suspect that most parents would select particular traits and reject others, disability included. Therefore, even if the state was not sending the message to the disabled, the collective impact of the parents' choices would do so.

Reducing disability may also free up resources to provide help and assistance to disabled people who do come into existence, whether through birth or by accident. But then it might be that as the numbers of disabled people decrease, they become such a minority that they have less voice in seeking support from

---

[29] J. Savulescu, 'Procreative beneficence: why we should select the best children' (2001) 15 *Bioethics* 413, 423.

[30] A. Buchanan et al., *From Chance to Choice: Genetics and Justice* (Cambridge University Press, 2000). See also J. Hammond, 'Genetic engineering to avoid genetic neglect: from chance to responsibility' (2010) 24 *Bioethics* 160.

[31] B. Steinbock, 'Disability, prenatal testing, and selective abortion', in E. Parens and A. Asch (eds), *Prenatal Testing and Disability Rights* (Georgetown University Press, 2000), 121.

[32] C. Gavaghan, 'Right problem, wrong solution: a pro-choice response to "Expressivist" concerns about preimplantation genetic diagnosis' (2007) 16 *Cambridge Quarterly of Healthcare Ethics* 20, 26.

the state. It may be that there is a need for 'critical mass', that is, sufficient disabled people to attract attention and resources. This is probably unlikely, however. We divert resources to caring for those who cannot help themselves in many ways; we are not likely to forget their plight, and any reduction in the draw on resources frees up more aid for those who need it.

Discrimination

We could also argue that in choosing embryos, we discriminate against those we do not select, if that selection is made purely on the basis of their disability. This argument holds for all cases of selection. By not choosing an embryo, we fail to give it a chance at life. If we make this choice purely on the basis of a trait, we are discriminating on the basis of that trait. But this argument rests in part on the embryo having rights, or at least interests. If the embryo is considered not to have rights or interests, that is, that it has no moral status, then we cannot have harmed it. However, one problem with this approach is that it assumes that a disabled life is less worth having than a non-disabled life.

SELECTING SEX

The HFEA allows sex selection on a limited basis to avoid disease, but beyond this the practice is not permitted. Why would a potential parent want to select a child's sex? For many, there is a desire for family balancing. They already have one or more children of one sex, and it is seen as good to have children of both sexes in a family. This might be because the parents want the experience of bringing up a child of the opposite sex, or because it is considered good for children to grow up with siblings of both sexes. These are positive reasons, but there are also negative reasons, such as the desire to have a replacement child if one has been lost.[33]

One of the key arguments against permitting sex selection is that one sex would be preferred over another, leading to a shift in the ratio of males to females in the population. This has been evidenced in India and China, despite their efforts to prevent sex selection. But the reasons for the shift in those countries do not apply in the UK to any great degree. In China, parents have historically preferred boys because they are more able to take on heavy labouring work on family farms, and also because bloodlines pass through the male line, while girls move into the families of the men they marry. Girls will therefore not stay with their own family to take on work in support of it, nor will they be there to care for their parents in old age. Having a boy, then, is considered more likely to support a family's prosperity.[34] With the introduction of the one-child policy in China, the pressure to ensure the birth of a male child

---

[33] J. Herring, *Medical Law and Ethics*, 6th edn (Oxford University Press, 2016), 403.

[34] T. Branigan, 'China's great gender crisis', *Guardian*, 2 November 2011, available at www. theguardian.com/world/2011/nov/02/chinas-great-gender-crisis.

was exacerbated, resulting in sex-selective abortions and infanticide. But in the UK there is no such entrenched preference for boys, nor do social conditions promote the desirability of boys. Also, unlike in China until very recently, parents are free to have as many children as they like in the UK, and hence there is no need to use sex-selective practices to ensure that a boy is born. Therefore, there is no reason to suppose that the sex ratio would be adversely affected by allowing parents to practice sex-selective PGD.

There are, however, other reasons to restrict the use of PGD. Jonathan Herring comments that, without restrictions, the UK might not then be well placed to criticise the practice in other countries.[35] There is the further concern that the UK will become a destination for reproductive tourism, with couples from countries where the practice is not permitted coming to the UK to access sex-selective PGD. This would then mean the UK would be contributing to the harmful implications of sex preference elsewhere, even if it is not a problem here.

We might also question the impact on the child produced, just as we have done where the child's traits have been selected. It is just as discriminatory to allow parents to choose the sex of their child as it is to choose any other trait. Sex selection will also occur in the context of ongoing inequality between the sexes even in this country, where women do still endure sexist attitudes and discriminatory treatment in many contexts. Interestingly, the HFEA found that there is little public support for sex selection, with 80 per cent of respondents to one survey reportedly against the practice.

SAVIOUR SIBLINGS

The arguments around using PGD to select traits in the creation of a saviour sibling are rather different from those discussed earlier. In such cases, the selection of traits is not made to benefit the person being produced, but someone else. The child produced will be used as a donor for the already living child, and is created with the intention of taking tissue from the saviour sibling at an age when it is not capable of consenting. Such creation falls foul of Immanuel Kant's imperative that we do not use people merely as a means to an end. They should, he argued, be treated as an end in themselves, if we are to treat them with appropriate respect as moral agents.

But whether this will be harming depends on how the child will actually be treated once born. Given that it is being born to parents who love their existing child so much that they are prepared to go through the expense and difficulty of creating a new child to help save the one they already have, it is unlikely that they will be uncaring, thoughtless parents. The experience of bearing a child usually creates a bond between child and mother, and the parents will also be presented with a living baby that needs their care as much as any other. It is profoundly unlikely that the parents will look upon it as simply a source of tissue when confronted with the reality of defenceless baby born of their own

---

[35] J. Herring, *Medical Law and Ethics*, 6th edn (Oxford University Press, 2016), 404.

gametes. That said, this does not remove the risk that the child itself will perceive itself as created merely for another's sake, and this might have damaging
psychological impacts. The risk of this occurring is exacerbated by the fact that
the sibling it was born to save may continue to be unhealthy, and consequently
take up much of the parents' time and attention.

It may be, alternatively, that the child feels a sense of altruism and fulfilment
at being able to help a sibling to recover from illness. As Merle Spriggs points
out, it may be beneficial to the saviour sibling to act as a donor.[36] Indeed, the
courts have taken a similar line of thinking in cases of tissue donations from
people who are unable to consent, reasoning that it is in their best interests to
help, and we might take a similar approach here. The great problem here, then,
is that much of this is speculation, and it will also depend very much on the
particular situation, the disorder and the personalities of those involved.

SELECTING FOR DISABILITY

Perhaps even more divisive and complex than the debate around using PGD
to avoid disability is that around its use to *select for disability*. The issues in
this area hit the headlines in 2002, when lesbian couple Sharon Duchesneau
and Candy McCullough made headlines with their decision to choose a family
friend who suffered from hereditary deafness to be their sperm donor.[37] Both
women were themselves deaf, and their goal was to increase their chances of
producing a deaf child. For the couple, deafness was not a disability but instead
a cultural identity which is the basis of a strong, tight-knit community.

On one hand, we could accept that some conditions are not disabilities, and
that a condition like deafness is merely a difference. But critics of the couple
have argued that deafness is clearly a disability. John Harris argues that this is
so because the person misses out on worthwhile experiences.[38] Julian Savulescu
points out that deafness is a disability because 'deaf people are denied the world
of sound, music, and the most fundamental form of human communication',
and argues further that 'people who claim that deafness represents a unique
culture that can be fostered only by being deaf are mistaken' because a hearing
child can participate by learning to sign.[39]

Whether either point is true is partly a matter of opinion about what is
important in life, although Savulescu is at least partly right, because one aspect
of what is good about deafness – community – can be achieved in other ways,
while hearing music and other pleasurable sounds cannot. We could say that

---

[36] M. Spriggs, 'Is conceiving a child to benefit another against the interests of the new child?'
(2005) 31 *Journal of Medical Ethics* 341.

[37] *BBC News*, 'Couple "choose" to have deaf baby', 8 April 2002, available at http://news.
bbc.co.uk/1/hi/health/1916462.stm.

[38] J. Harris, 'Is there a coherent social conception of disability?' (2000) 26 *Journal of Medical
Ethics* 95, 98.

[39] J. Savulescu, 'Deaf lesbians, "designer disability," and the future of medicine' (2002) 325
British Medical Journal 771, 772.

disability is a lack of something that is within the ordinary range of human capacities, and that without that capacity, someone will miss out on important aspects of life. Unless this is forgone for something at least as good, then it is probably wrong to select for such a trait.

In other situations, parents might wish to select for disability because it will be easier to care for a child affected by the same condition as themselves, rather than because they consider the condition one which is to be preferred for its own sake. Such situations are rare, but for couples who are both affected by dwarfism, having a child of a normal size would make providing care very difficult as the child will grow too large to carry despite being an infant. As many such people live in homes specially adapted for their shorter height, a child of normal height would soon have difficulties. For Duchesneau and McCullough, communication with a deaf child would also have been easier. In such cases, it might be said that if any child is to be born to such a couple, then the disabled child will be subject to benefits that a non-disabled child would not. However, this is only true to the extent that the child is interacting with the parents; as the rest of the world is not adapted to the child, it will face the same difficulties the parents faced. If the disability reduces the child's capacities, that child may have fewer options in life or lack experiences (as in the case of deafness), and this might be considered a harm.

This leads us to an oft-made argument against selecting for disability (which is also often made in support of selecting against disability). When people want to select for disability, it could be said again that they are harming the child – the converse of the harm of failing to select against that disability discussed above. But this argument comes up against what is known as the 'non-identity problem', a problem made famous in the work of philosopher Derek Parfit.[40] In this context, the problem suggests that if the parents are selecting between embryos, then the disabled child cannot be harmed by being brought into existence unless existence is worse than non-existence. For example, John Harris argues that a disabled child cannot complain about being brought into existence 'because for them the alternative was non-existence',[41] but he does consider that they have been wronged.

How, if the non-identity problem holds, can it be wrong to select for disability? One way to approach this is to reconceptualise the problem. The non-identity problem sets up a binary choice between existence and non-existence. If existence is worse than non-existence, then bringing someone into that existence is wrong and we have committed a person-affecting wrong. Otherwise, we have done nothing wrong, yet this seems strongly counter-intuitive, and indeed Parfit himself shared the feeling of unease about the conclusion that flowed from the problem he identified.[42]

---

[40] D. Parfit, *Reasons and Persons* (Clarendon Press, 1987).

[41] J. Harris, 'Is there a coherent social conception of disability?' (2000) 26 *Journal of Medical Ethics* 95, 97.

[42] D. Parfit, *Reasons and Persons* (Clarendon Press, 1987), 371.

The non-identity problem has resisted solution, but many have raised responses that have some merit and explain some aspects of our intuitions. In the context of PGD, one is that there are harms to society and to those who will have to take on the burden of care for the disabled person.[43] Others reject the idea that we should only be concerned about 'person-affecting' actions.[44] Still others argue that the fundamental claim in the non-identity problem – that the only harm is creating a life not worth living – is flawed, and that there are other ways we can be said to be harming or wronging the person whom we create.[45]

We can here add some texture to the problem by considering the situation in which someone who is brought into a badly disabled existence finds themselves. Once created, they cannot easily choose to end their life, partly because human beings tend to resist this except in all but the worst situations, and also because they will lose some things that are precious to them, such as their relationships. They also know that they will harm those who love them by absenting themselves from the world. It is not a neutral choice, nor is it easy for people to conceptualise non-existence and choose it. Generally, people seem to choose it only in the worst situations, but this does not mean someone who is faced with these difficulties and unpleasant choices might not prefer never to have been put in that position in the first place. Creating the situation where they are faced with only these two difficult options might be a problematic thing to do in and of itself. Doing so has produced circumstances in which someone has only bad options, and perhaps this is what renders it a harmful thing to do. The third option would be for them never to know what existence is like, and if we consider this the best option, this might explain why the non-identity problem leads to a conclusion we find intuitively hard to accept.

Parfit himself proposed a partial solution by conceptualising the wrong as something other than a person-affecting harm, and has offered the 'Impersonal Total Principle' which says that '[i]f other things are equal, the best outcome is the one in which there would be the greatest quantity of whatever makes life worth living'.[46] No one person is less well-off, but the net total of good life in the world is less if we select disabled embryos. But as Rebecca Bennett argues, this notion of 'free-floating' impersonal harm is 'a very difficult concept to take seriously', precisely because it does not rest on any harm to persons as such.[47] Both Bennett and Parfit also recognise that solving the non-identity problem via a notion of impersonal harm, where we should increase the level of net flourishing in the world by excluding disabled lives, leads to a 'Repugnant

---

[43] Noted in R. Bennett, 'When intuition is not enough. Why the principle of procreative beneficence must work much harder to justify its eugenic vision' (2014) 28 *Bioethics* 447, 452.

[44] D. Parfit, *Reasons and Persons* (Clarendon Press, 1987).

[45] See, e.g., D. Benatar, *Better Never to Have Been: The Harm of Coming into Existence* (Oxford University Press, 2006).

[46] D. Parfit, *Reasons and Persons* (Clarendon Press, 1987), 378.

[47] R. Bennett, 'When intuition is not enough. Why the principle of procreative beneficence must work much harder to justify its eugenic vision' (2014) 27 *Bioethics* 447, 453.

Conclusion'.[48] We would be compelled to bring into existence as many good lives as possible, leading to over-population and eventually numerous lives of low quality, rather than fewer lives but of good quality. The actual quality of those lives would no longer be the most relevant element, which is precisely what is repugnant about the conclusion if (as it should be) our focus was originally on the welfare of persons.

But that said, we allow parents considerable freedom in how they raise their children, including choices about treatment. Where that treatment is within the acceptable range, even if it is not the best course of action, parents are permitted to choose it for their children. However, we do not permit parents to create a life of suffering for a child. Parents are expected to provide appropriate treatment for their children, and where they fail to do so or refuse on grounds that are not considered sufficient, the courts will step in to ensure children receive the care they need.

CONCLUSION

There are compelling arguments on either side of the debate about whether parents should be allowed to choose their children's traits. The 1990 Act has struck a balance that is directed at avoiding serious harms, while allowing parents some choices. At present, the choices a parent could make via PGD are fairly limited, and we cannot yet enable the selection of traits like intelligence. This is not, however, an implausible future development, albeit one which is some way off. Therefore, we must continue to consider all the arguments, and constantly re-evaluate as the science develops, and as we learn more from experience about the real impacts of designing our children. We should ensure that we pay attention to both the obvious harms of choosing (or not choosing) to select traits and the more subtle implications it may have for our relationships and society.

Debate 2
Should surrogacy be permissible?

INTRODUCTION

Surrogacy is a complex and divisive area of law because it involves both a woman's choices about her body and the sometimes conflicting interests of other parties – the potential child and the commissioning couple. Surrogacy also raises difficult questions about women's reproductive freedom, and about the effect of legal regulation on defining cultural and social roles for women. There is also the worry that those involved will be harmed – the child, the surrogate and the commissioning couple. In this debate, we consider these arguments, and also whether surrogacy arrangements should be enforced by the law and surrogacy on a commercial basis should be permitted.

---

[48] Ibid., 454.

WHAT IS SURROGACY?

Surrogate motherhood can take a number of forms, each of which raises particular concerns in addition to general concerns about surrogacy per se. Surrogacy arrangements can be made between close friends or relatives, who have established personal relationships. When no payment is made, such surrogacy is usually called 'altruistic surrogacy'. Alternatively, surrogacy can be arranged between strangers, either privately or through a 'broker'. 'Commercial surrogacy' generally refers to arrangements when money passes from the commissioning couple to the surrogate as payment for undertaking the surrogate pregnancy. Often such arrangements will be between strangers and may be governed by a contract. A partially commercial arrangement might involve the couple paying only for the surrogate's expenses, not her actual 'services'.

In addition, the exact nature of the surrogate pregnancy may differ. 'Partial surrogacy' (also known as 'traditional surrogacy') involves artificial insemination of the surrogate with the commissioning man's sperm – the surrogate is therefore also donating one of her eggs. 'Gestational surrogacy' occurs when an egg from the commissioning woman is fertilised with sperm from the commissioning man using IVF and implanted in the surrogate's uterus.[49] Embryos can also be created using both donor sperm and a donor egg. The surrogate brings the embryo to term, and it is then adopted by the commissioning couple.

Famous surrogacy arrangements

Elton John and David Furnish: a homosexual male couple who had previously been barred from adopting a Ukranian orphan on the basis of their age.

Nicole Kidman and Keith Urban: Kidman explained that she had 'tried and failed and failed and failed. Not to be too detailed, but I've had an ectopic pregnancy, miscarriages and I've had fertility treatments. I've done all the stuff you can possibly do to try to get pregnant.'[50]

Ricky Martin: single homosexual man, who explained his path to fatherhood: 'OK, what are my options? Am I going to adopt? I just sat in front of the computer, doing research, until I found surrogacy, and I was like: "Woah! This looks really interesting" ... I interviewed so many people that were part of this beautiful world, and I decided this was going to be my way.'[51]

(Continued)

---

[49] See, e.g., T. Frame, 'The perils of surrogate motherhood' (2003) June *Quadrant* 30, 37.
[50] E. Murphy, 'Nicole Kidman on marriage to Cruise, pregnancy struggles', *ABC News*, 4 October 2012, at http://abcnews.go.com/blogs/entertainment/2012/10/nicole-kidman-on-marriage-to-cruise-pregnancy-struggles/.
[51] Celebrity Baby Scoop, '10 celebrities who used surrogates', available at www.pnmag.com/baby-buzz/10-celebrities-who-used-surrogates/.

Famous surrogacy arrangements (*Continued*)

Neil Patrick Harris and David Burtka: homosexual male couple, who had twins via a surrogate, using sperm from each man: 'two eggs, two embryos, one of mine, one of his'.[52]

Other celebrities who have used surrogates to have children:

- Michael Jackson
- Cristiano Ronaldo
- George Lucas and Mellody Hobson
- Sarah Jessica Parker and Matthew Broderick

THE LAW

Surrogacy in the UK is governed by the Surrogacy Arrangements Act 1985. The Act was passed following recommendations made in 1984 by the Committee of Inquiry into Human Fertilisation and Embryology (known as the 'Warnock Committee' after its chair, Dame Mary Warnock). The Act defines a surrogate mother as:

> a woman who carries a child in accordance with an arrangement ... made before she began to carry the child, and ... made with a view to any child carried in pursuance of it being handed over to, and parental responsibility being met (so far as practicable) by, another person or other persons.[53]

One of the major concerns about surrogacy, as we will see, is who has custody of any child produced if there is a dispute. The UK approach is clear that the gestating mother is the legal mother with all parental rights, regardless of whether the child was conceived using her eggs, donor eggs or those of the commissioning woman.[54] The father is the man who provided the sperm, unless donor sperm from a licensed clinic was used. As a result, for the commissioning parents to become the child's legal parents, the woman (and sometimes the man) will need to obtain a parental order under the Human Fertilisation and Embryology Act, or officially adopt the child. For a parental order to be made, the surrogate's consent is required, and the commissioning couple must also be living together in an enduring relationship. The order must also be in the best interests of the child.[55]

---

[52] Ibid.

[53] Surrogacy Arrangements Act 1985, s. 1(2).

[54] Human Fertilisation and Embryology Act 1990, s. 33.

[55] Human Fertilisation and Embryology Act 1990, s. 54. In a series of cases the courts have emphasised the importance of the welfare of the child and been willing to make a parental order, even where the formal requirements of s. 54 are not met, providing the making of the order promotes the welfare of the child; e.g. *AB and CD v CT (Parental Order: Consent of Surrogate Mother)* [2015] EWFC 12 (Fam); *Re A and B (Children) (Surrogacy: Parental Orders: Time Limits)* [2015] EWHC 911. See K. Horsey, 'Fraying at the edges' (2016) 24 *Medical Law Review* 608.

If the commissioning couple are not eligible for a parental order, they may attempt to adopt the child. In many cases, the surrogate simply gives the child to the commissioning parents and no legal steps are taken.[56]

If no application for a parental order or adoption is made, the surrogate will be the child's legal mother.[57] Therefore, if the commissioning parents do not wish to take over parenting of the child, the child will remain the birth mother's legal responsibility. If the surrogate refuses to give up the child, the court will be guided by what is in the best interests of that child. For example, in *Re TT*, Baker J reasoned, in response to a claim for custody by the commissioning couple where the surrogate had refused to give up the child:

> I have reached the clear conclusion that T's welfare requires her to remain with her mother. In my judgment, there is a clear attachment between mother and daughter. To remove her from her mother's care would cause a measure of harm. It is the mother who, I find, is better able to meet T's needs, in particular her emotional needs.[58]

The courts clearly take the view that the bond that develops between the surrogate and child is important, and that it would be harming to the child if this were broken.[59] Consequently, as she is the legal mother, the surrogate is often in a strong position, and the court will usually not take the child from her to give to the commissioning parents unless there is a strong risk that the child will be harmed. In *A v C*, F and his wife could not have children, and made an agreement with a 19-year-old girl that she would be inseminated with F's sperm and carry a child for them as a surrogate. The girl agreed, but then changed her mind once pregnant and refused to give up the child when he was born. The court refused to give custody to F and his wife, and they were also later refused access to the boy because it was likely to be harmful to him.[60]

However, in some cases, if the welfare of the child points to it, custody will be given to the commissioning parents. This is particularly likely if the child has been living with them since birth and the surrogate has later changed her mind about giving the child up.[61] The commissioning parents may also gain custody if the surrogate has acted deceitfully and appears not to be best able to promote the child's welfare.[62]

If, as is often the case, the surrogacy entails the use of Assisted Reproductive Technology (ART), then the practice is further controlled via the Human

---

[56] M. Brazier, A. Campbell and S. Golombok, *Surrogacy: Review for Health Ministers of Current Arrangements for Payments and Regulation, Report of the Review Team*, Cm 4068 (HMSO, 1998) [5.7].

[57] Human Fertilisation and Embryology Act 2008, s. 33.

[58] *Re TT* [2011] EWHC 33 (Fam), [73]. The court will follow the welfare checklist laid down in the Children Act 1989, s. 1.

[59] *Re TT* [2011] EWHC 33 (Fam).

[60] *A v C* [1984] Fam Law 241.

[61] *Re ME* [1995] 2 FLR 789.

[62] *Re N* [2007] EWCA Civ 1053.

Fertilisation and Embryology Act 1990 and the HFEA Code of Practice. As with any other use of ART, the clinic providing IVF or other services will be required to have regard to the welfare of any child created. Specifically in relation to surrogacy, the clinic must:

> take into account the possibility of a breakdown in the surrogacy arrangement and whether this is likely to cause a risk of significant harm or neglect to any child who may be born or any existing children in the surrogate's family.[63]

Therefore, any clinician providing services to enable a surrogate pregnancy must consider the welfare of the child to be born and that of any other children who may be affected by the birth.[64] Clinics may also impose their own restrictions or guidance, and these usually include requirements that the potential surrogate is under 36 years old, has been pregnant before and has completed her own family.[65]

While surrogacy itself is not illegal in the UK, some practices associated with it are. It is an offence to arrange, negotiate or even offer to negotiate the making of a surrogacy arrangement on a commercial basis.[66] However, neither the commissioning parents nor the surrogate can be guilty of this offence.[67] The legislation also prohibits payment in exchange for surrogacy services except to cover the surrogate's expenses.[68] Anything more than this is illegal, as is advertising surrogacy services.[69] The effect of these provisions is to allow for altruistic surrogacy and to enable the surrogate to be compensated for her costs, but commercial surrogacy is prohibited. Organisations that help commissioning parents contact surrogates on a non-commercial basis are allowed. Where a payment beyond compensation for expenses has been made, the court has grounds to refuse a parental order to transfer parentage.[70] Despite this, the courts have granted orders in such cases regardless.[71] The prohibitions on commercial surrogacy also mean that commercial brokering services are not permitted, but unpaid, altruistic matching services are.

In addition to banning commercial surrogacy, the Act also explicitly states that any contract for surrogacy will be unenforceable. This means that people are free to make surrogacy contracts to outline their obligations, but the court will not hold either party to these obligations in any way.[72]

---

[63] Human Fertilisation and Embryology Authority, *HFEA Code of Practice*, para. 8.12.
[64] Human Fertilisation and Embryology Act 1990, s. 13(5).
[65] Bourn Hall Clinic, 'Surrogacy', available at www.bourn-hall-clinic.co.uk/treatments/surrogacy.
[66] Surrogacy Arrangements Act 1985, s. 2(1).
[67] Surrogacy Arrangements Act 1985, s. 2(2).
[68] *Re C (Application by Mr and Mrs X)* [2002] EWHC 157 (Fam).
[69] Surrogacy Arrangements Act 1985, s. 3.
[70] Human Fertilisation and Embryology Act 2008, s. 54(8).
[71] *Re L* [2010] EWHC 3146 (Fam).
[72] Surrogacy Arrangements Act 1985, s. 1A.

Arguments For and Against Surrogacy

One of the key arguments against surrogacy is that it may be harming to the child, and this would justify prohibiting surrogacy arrangements. There are a number of ways this can happen. It is possible that the child may experience confusion about their origins,[73] or be the subject of a distressing custody battle if the surrogate refuses to give them up (particularly problematic if the child has lived with the surrogate for some time). There is, however, little evidence either way to show whether these children suffer harm; and as it is likely that many of these children will be taken into a loving family where they are wanted if the surrogacy arrangement is successful, there may be insufficient evidence to justify prohibiting surrogacy on this basis.

Further, one thing to bear in mind is that those who currently seek surrogacy do so because they deeply want a child, and hence many of the children created in this way are likely to be wanted children brought up by people who wish to love and provide for them. The same cannot always be said of 'naturally' conceived children.[74] Despite this, some, such as George Annas, have refuted the idea that surrogacy is 'family building', suggesting that such a view is:

> deceptive, and that reproduction by this means helps one family but at the expense of another: 'the "surrogate mother" arrangement creates a family bond only by destroying a family bond'.[75]

This criticism assumes that such a bond develops between surrogate and child, which may or may not be true. Many surrogates use coping techniques from the start of the surrogacy to help them avoid bonding with the child, and so this breaking of a bond may not be as serious as Annas suggests.

Further, the creation of a loving family and the happiness of those who can become parents might outweigh this risk. As Jonathan Herring has pointed out, surrogacy also 'widens the variety of family forms' by allowing gay couples and single men to have children.[76] Some will consider this a good thing, while others who believe that children should grow up in a nuclear family with a father and a mother perhaps will be less keen.

Another argument in favour of surrogacy is that this kind of work has significant benefits for the surrogate. Some report feelings of satisfaction and altruism that come from having helped the childless couple to experience parenthood. One has said:

---

[73] E.g., Minister of Government Services Canada, *Proceed with Care: Final Report of the Royal Commission on New Reproductive Technologies* (1993), 689.

[74] National Bioethics Consultative Committee, 'Discussion of options', *Surrogacy Report* 1 (1990).

[75] G. Annas, 'Death without dignity for commercial surrogacy: the case of Baby M' (1988) 18 *Hastings Center Report* 21, 21.

[76] J. Herring, *Medical Law and Ethics*, 6th edn (Oxford University Press, 2016), 401.

Surrogacy is a way we can give back to the world in a significant way. We're not rich people. We would never be able to donate a large sum of money for something like funding a wing of a hospital.

We don't have the monetary resources to change the world. But I am able to grow big, beautiful, healthy surrogate babies. This is a way that my family can do something to change our little corner of the world, by helping another family in a way they cannot help themselves. That's what being a surrogate is about to me.[77]

Another has said: 'For us, giving someone a baby is as noble as giving a kidney to someone who needs it.'[78]

However, while some surrogates may benefit, others may not. Some definitely have negative experiences of surrogacy. There are a great many things that may go wrong in a surrogacy arrangement. The surrogate may change her mind and refuse to give up the child, or may wish to abort the pregnancy.[79] In some cases, the relationship between surrogate and commissioning couple deteriorates, and may lead to some parties refusing to follow the terms of the arrangement. A surrogate carrying the commissioning party's biological child might resort to blackmail to extort more money (if payment is permitted) as she has a powerful lever. If the child is born with a disability, there may be a situation where both the commissioning couple and the surrogate reject responsibility for its care.[80] All of these are potentially harming situations that are set in motion by the surrogacy arrangement, and would be prevented by prohibiting the practice.

In response, there is a strong argument in favour of surrogacy in that it respects women's autonomy and their ability to decide what to do with their bodies. Throughout this book we have seen arguments in support of allowing people the freedom to do as they wish about personal matters, as long as they do not harm others. If a woman wants to enter a surrogacy arrangement, this would suggest we should permit her to do so. Indeed, many surrogates resist the suggestion that they are harmed or being used by others:

I am here in order to help. ... I don't even call it a womb for rent. I call myself an oven. ... An oven that bakes the bread for hungry people. I just help them. ... Like if my friend needed a loan, I would save from my own food, and I would give her a loan. Would they then say that I am being used? What idiocy that is.[81]

---

[77] Information on Surrogacy, 'Being a Surrogate Mother – How Surros View Surrogacy', available at www.information-on-surrogacy.com/being-a-surrogate.html.

[78] G. Annas, 'Death without dignity for commercial surrogacy: the case of Baby M' (1988) 18 *Hastings Center Report* 21, 23. See also R. Blackford, 'Surrogate motherhood and public policy' (2003) March *Quadrant* 30, 31.

[79] This will be particularly problematic in gestational surrogacy where the child is not genetically related to the gestating mother.

[80] T. Frame, 'The perils of surrogate motherhood' (2003) June *Quadrant* 30, 39–40.

[81] E. Tehman, *Birthing a Mother: The Surrogate Body and the Pregnant Self* (University of California Press, 2010), 31.

We might further argue that the negative experiences of some surrogates are not sufficient reason to prevent all women from making the choice to bear children for others.[82]

However, we might also argue that it is the law's role to protect people as well as promote liberty, and where the woman might suffer harm, this might support a prohibition, or at a minimum some protective regulation. If the harms to the surrogate are sufficiently great and likely, this would be a reason to prevent women entering into such arrangements. As this would be an infringement of their reproductive liberty, we would need good reasons to do so. How might a surrogate be harmed? It may be emotionally and psychologically traumatic to give up a child she has carried. There are also the physical harms associated with pregnancy and birth.

Given that we do not restrict other women from conceiving because of the harms associated with pregnancy, it would be unreasonable to do it for surrogates who are acting voluntarily. However, concerns about the psychological harms might be a sufficient reason, as these might be harms that a surrogate cannot fully appreciate until she experiences them. But this is in fact the very reason not to use this as a basis, because if she cannot know (she who knows herself best), how can anyone else know better for her? Prohibiting surrogacy on this basis is particularly unjustified given the absence of clear evidence that surrogacy psychologically harms surrogates.[83]

It is important for the debate around surrogacy to be informed about the realities of surrogacy. Research suggests that despite our intuitions, surrogates generally do not find it difficult to give up the child. Elly Tehman's study of surrogates' experiences and self-conception demonstrates that surrogates use techniques to help them cope with the impending separation from the child they have carried. One said:

> I am only carrying the issue, I don't have any part in the issue. ... I mean, I gave them life, because without me they would not have life. Because [the intended mother] couldn't carry them. Only someone with a womb, a good womb, could hold the children for her. So I am the one. ... I just held them in my belly, like an incubator. I was their incubator for nine months! ... And the second that they were born, I finished the job and that was it.[84]

While this may be the case for many, it is not so for all, and therefore concerns about harm to the surrogate will be more acute in the context of enforcing surrogacy agreements, which will be discussed later.

---

[82] See, contra, J. Raymond, 'Reproductive gifts and gift giving: the altruistic woman' (1990) 20 *Hastings Center Report* 7.

[83] This was a finding of the Brazier Committee on surrogacy: M. Brazier, A. Campbell and S. Golombok, *Surrogacy: Review for Health Ministers of Current Arrangements for Payments and Regulation, Report of the Review Team*, Cm 4068 (HMSO, 1998), [4.26]. The Committee's report stated: 'there is not strong enough evidence to warrant attempts to ban surrogacy because of its effect on surrogate mothers' but 'there is sufficient cause for concern to make regulation essential'.

[84] E. Tehman, *Birthing a Mother: The Surrogate Body and the Pregnant Self* (University of California Press, 2010), 32.

There are valid concerns that women might be coerced into surrogacy, whether overtly or through more subtle pressure such as familial pressure, feelings of guilt and emotional manipulation by surrogacy brokers and others. This is at least a good reason to *regulate* surrogacy, and perhaps bring the practice into the open with designated structures to manage it, rather than allow it to occur in an ad hoc manner behind a veil of secrecy. However, regulation rather than prohibition might be the appropriate response to such a concern, given the benefits of surrogacy. The law could take note of the potential harms of surrogacy to the surrogate and commissioning parents by putting controls in place, such as the provision of compulsory counselling before and after the pregnancy and the provision of access to psychological aid. Concerns for the surrogate could also be factored into custody arrangements by allowing her access to the child (if given to the couple) where appropriate and where undue harm to the child will not result.

Some object to surrogacy arrangements because they argue that such arrangements reinforce the ideological view that a woman's role is as child-bearer and domestic labourer.[85] For example, Janice Raymond argues that surrogacy 'reinforces the perception and use of women as a breeder class ... This is not symbolic or intangible but strikes at the core of what a society allows women to be and become'.[86] But in the absence of clear harms, this is probably quite a weak reason to constrain women's choices about their bodies. While there may be legitimate arguments for the state to intervene in, or prevent, surrogacy arrangements on the basis of social harms from the practice of surrogacy, these are not sufficiently convincing to justify prohibition. It may be that some women's choices are culturally constrained, but this is not a case for paternalistically preventing them from making these choices for their own good. Rather, it demonstrates the need for surrogacy to occur in a legally controlled way.

Indeed, it might be argued that permitting surrogacy may actually *reduce* gender inequalities by reinforcing the separation between child-bearing and child-rearing, continuing a shift away from the view that being the gestational mother entails being the primary caretaker. In doing so, we may move further away from the assumption that in bearing a child, a woman is expected to stay in the home to care for it.[87] As Marjorie Shultz argues, this separation allows for plurality of parenting models, based on parental commitment to the child rather than a gendered basis for determining who will care for the child.[88]

---

[85] This argument is outlined, but not supported, in R.J. Arneson, 'Commodification and commercial surrogacy' (1992) 21 *Philosophy and Public Affairs* 132, 162–63.

[86] J. Raymond, 'Reproductive gifts and gift giving: The altruistic woman' (1990) 20 *Hastings Center Report* 7, 11.

[87] M.L. Shanley, '"Surrogate mothering" and women's freedom: a critique of contracts for human reproduction' (1993) 18 *Signs: Journal of Women in Culture and Society* 618, 620.

[88] M. Shultz, 'Reproductive technology and intention-based parenthood: an opportunity for gender neutrality' (1990) 2 *Wisconsin Law Review* 297, 344.

Accepting that some forms of surrogacy should be legally permitted does not mean we must accept entirely unregulated surrogacy – regulation may address many of the concerns about surrogacy discussed. Regulation could include assessment of potential surrogates and commissioning couples to determine whether there has been coercion; to assess the psychological fitness of each party to undertake such an arrangement; to clarify each party's understanding of the nature of the arrangement and ensure they are fully informed of its complexities.[89] Regulation could also be used to limit or prevent particular types of surrogacy arrangements – for example, commercial arrangements – and lay down requirements for permitted surrogacy, such as the rights of each party in particular circumstances. Regulatory mechanisms could further be used to deal with problems that may arise, for example by developing systems for dealing with complaints if the surrogate refuses to give up the child, if the child is disabled in some way or, alternatively, if the commissioning couple no longer wish to take the child. The state could further develop arrangements for promoting the interests of the child in each of these, and other, cases.

ENFORCING SURROGACY ARRANGEMENTS

The heart of the debate here is whether surrogacy agreements should be enforceable in the way contracts are. On one side of the debate, enforcing contracts for surrogacy against surrogates may be a way to respect female autonomy. Such an argument can be made from a feminist perspective, that enforcing women's voluntarily taken obligations is in a way respecting those decisions, rather than releasing them from them on the basis that they did not perceive the risks.[90] However, a response is that surrogacy contracts are not like other contracts because of the complex and intimate nature of the work. In particular, it is arguably very difficult for a woman to conceive of what it will be like to give up a child she has carried, so her consent cannot be fully informed. For example, as Susan Dodds and Karen Jones state:

> No two women experience pregnancy in quite the same way and the same woman can experience different pregnancies differently … Thus, how can a woman give fully informed consent to part with a child she will have felt growing and developing inside her, that she will have given form to through her body, before she knows the feelings these experiences will have produced?[91]

This view suggests that surrogates are unable to foresee the risks of surrogacy, and hence they make their choice to become surrogates without fully

---

[89] See, e.g., National Bioethics Consultative Committee, 'Discussion of options', *Surrogacy Report* 1 (1990), 45.
[90] See M.L. Shanley, '"Surrogate mothering" and women's freedom: a critique of contracts for human reproduction' (1993) 18 *Signs: Journal of Women in Culture and Society* 618, 622.
[91] S. Dodds and K. Jones, 'Surrogacy and autonomy' (1989) 8 *Bioethics News* 6, 6.

understanding the nature or implications of that choice – i.e. they are not competent and therefore the state can justifiably override their choice (in prohibiting surrogacy) or not hold them to it (by not enforcing the agreement). If we did otherwise, we would be holding the surrogate to a non-voluntary obligation.[92] But this rests on an empirical claim about the nature of women's knowledge and understanding of the pregnancy experience, and their ability to accurately predict how they will feel both about the pregnancy and about giving up the child. For some, it may be true that they think they can cope with surrogacy but cannot. For others, they may be right about their capacity to cope. This will be particularly so for women who have already experienced pregnancy; they may be well aware of how they are affected by it.

Additionally, the idea that women cannot give informed consent to agree to something they have never experienced is at odds with many other areas in which we bind people to their decisions and promises. The same is true each time someone takes on a mortgage for the first time, or agrees to sell something valuable. But is there something so different about surrogacy that we should take a different approach? Perhaps so, because of the intensity of the psychological experience of pregnancy, the emotion of birth, and the nature of the bond that develops between mother and child. Also, while the experience is subjective for the individual, the state has the capacity to gather evidence of many women's experiences of surrogacy and draw some general conclusions about trends in the effect it may have on these women. From these we might make quite good guesses about how others will react. Therefore, there is some cause to doubt women's capacity to competently choose surrogacy. Further, we do not enforce employment contracts because of the implications this has for autonomy, and surrogacy contracts are in some ways very similar.

On balance, then, perhaps there are sufficient reasons not to enforce surrogacy arrangements. In doing so, the law allows women to make their choices, but takes account of the unpredictability and potentially great emotional and psychological distress involved in forcing a surrogate to give up a child she may have.

COMMERCIALISING REPRODUCTION

Even if we supported enforcing surrogacy arrangements, there is another strand of objection to some forms of surrogacy, specifically those involving payment to the surrogate. It is argued that commercialising surrogacy affects women's consent, and may lead to exploitation.[93] As the Brazier Committee

---

[92] M.L. Shanley, '"Surrogate mothering" and women's freedom: a critique of contracts for human reproduction' (1993) 18 *Signs: Journal of Women in Culture and Society* 618, 626. See also M. Brazier, A. Campbell and S. Golombok, *Surrogacy: Review for Health Ministers of Current Arrangements for Payments and Regulation, Report of the Review Team*, Cm 4068 (HMSO, 1998), para. 4.25.

[93] See S. Wilkinson, 'Exploitation in international paid surrogacy' (2016) 33 *Journal of Applied Philosophy* 125.

stated, 'payment increases the risk of exploitation if it constitutes an induce-ment to participate in an activity whose degree of risk the surrogate cannot ... fully understand or predict'.[94] It is probably true that surrogates are motivated by money, but it is not entirely clear that this is problematic.[95] We already allow people to do many jobs they probably would not do if they were not being paid, so there needs to be something different about surrogacy for this to be a real concern. On one view, a woman who agrees to be a paid surrogate is making the decision about the risks and benefits of a job as any other; it is simply that the risks are different.

One concern often raised is the idea that commercial surrogacy commodi-fies children. The argument is that commercial surrogacy equates to children being 'bought and sold', which is considered objectionable because it dimin-ishes the children's inherent value as beings with moral standing, it is degrad-ing and reduces them to the same level as goods that can be traded.[96] Where the child is born with an unanticipated disability, this concern might be even more severe if the couple decides to reject that child.

While these might be valid worries, commodification arguments obscure what is actually happening in a surrogacy arrangement. Rather than selling a child, it is more accurate to say that the gestating mother is being paid for her labour in gestating the child. Further, if we think about what is happening in a surrogacy arrangement, it is less certain that the child is treated like a commod-ity. The harm of commodification (and objectification) is that we treat people like things, and ignore their human agency; we fail to respect their autonomy. But is this harm arising in a surrogacy arrangement? Probably not, because far from the child's interests not being considered, in fact the commissioning couple seek to welcome the child into a loving family and nurture it just as they would if they had given birth to it themselves. The child's interests and desires are given great value by the couple who so badly want to bring a child into their lives. There is nothing to suggest that the commissioning couple will view the child as their 'possession' any more than other parents will, and so the treatment of the child does not resemble how we treat objects or commodities, because we treat those like possessions – a surrogate child is not treated like a possession but just like any other child.

---

[94] M. Brazier, A. Campbell and S. Golombok, *Surrogacy: Review for Health Ministers of Current Arrangements for Payments and Regulation, Report of the Review Team*, Cm 4068 (HMSO, 1998), para. 4.25.

[95] This finding emerged from the Brazier Committee inquiry: ibid., para. 5.14. The Committee found that many surrogates are 'primarily motivated by payment'.

[96] See, e.g., M. Warnock, *A Question of Life: The Warnock Report on Human Fertilization and Embryology* (Blackwell, 1985), para. 8.11; G. Annas, 'Death without dignity for commer-cial surrogacy: the case of Baby M' (1988) 18 *Hastings Center Report* 21, 22. George Annas argues that the commodification of children 'devalues them (and all children) by treating them like products or pets for our own pleasure'.

That said, there is the concern that commercial surrogacy (and perhaps all surrogacy) treats the child as a 'means to an end' – a version of Kant's view that people, as beings with moral standing, should never be used *solely* as a means to another's end. The objection is that because the child is sought through an arrangement, rather than produced naturally as part of a couple, it is sought for the commissioning couple's ends, not its own. This may be true to a degree. Couples seeking children through surrogacy do want the child to fulfil their own desires to be parents, to give love to another person and to have the valuable emotional returns that come from parenthood. But this is true of all decisions to become a parent. The method of obtaining the child does not alter or exacerbate this. Also it is not true that the child will be used once it arrives, any more than any other children are.

However, the concern gains a little more bite when the child produced is born disabled, or is otherwise not as expected (perhaps a mix-up with embryos so that it is not biologically related to the commissioning couple). Imagine that the surrogate gives birth to a boy with Duchenne muscular dystrophy, who will require significant levels of care throughout childhood and will not live to be an adult. As Tom Frame rightly points out, there may be instances where both the surrogate and the commissioning couple reject the child.[97] Where this occurs, we might reasonably consider that the couple have rejected the child because they were seeking a perfect child, and hence only want the 'right' one that meets their desires. This does assume that a commissioning parent or couple will act in this way, and that may not be true, but it is certainly possible. It does suggest that in some cases the concerns around commodification may have some weight.

An alternative concern about commercial surrogacy is the commercialisation of women's reproduction. For some, such as Carole Pateman, surrogacy would be 'another provision in the sexual contract, as a new form of access to and use of women's bodies by men'.[98] Similarly, Debra Satz argues that contract pregnancy 'gives increased access to and control over women's bodies and sexuality'. This reinforces the traditional inequality of the subordination of women's interests to those of men.[99]

This argument can be challenged on the grounds that women who take on commercial surrogacy are in control of their labour, and are in fact being

---

[97] T. Frame, 'The perils of surrogate motherhood' (2003) June *Quadrant* 30.

[98] As cited in R. Arneson, 'Commodification and commercial surrogacy' (1992) 21 *Philosophy and Public Affairs* 132, 161. See also R. Rowland, 'Surrogacy – a feminist perspective on ethics' in M. Meggitt (ed.), *Surrogacy – In Whose Interest?* (Mission of St James and St John, Proceedings of National Conference on Surrogacy, 1991).

[99] D. Satz, 'Markets in women's reproductive labor' (1992) 21 *Philosophy and Public Affairs* 107, 124–25. Carole Pateman makes a similar argument: C. Pateman, *The Sexual Contract* (Polity Press, 1988), 209. See also R. Rowland, 'Surrogacy – a feminist perspective on ethics' in M. Meggitt (ed.), *Surrogacy – In Whose Interest?* (Mission of St James and St John, Proceedings of National Conference on Surrogacy 1991); M. Radin, 'Market-inalienability' (1987) 100 *Harvard Law Review* 1849, 1930–31.

appropriately paid for their voluntary work. It is, in fact, a better position than labouring unpaid, as women have for centuries. If surrogacy is voluntary then it is not true that the woman is being controlled by a man.[100] We might actually argue that allowing women to sell their reproductive labour is a way for some women to earn money and remove themselves from the conditions – like poverty – that actually oppress them. Giving women the option of commercial surrogacy gives them more options to earn money, and is in fact a means of earning that can be easier than going out of the home. It also means they do not need to put their own children in care while they work, so it may be a preferable form of labour for some.

CONCLUSION

Surrogacy is clearly a vexed area of the law on reproduction, and one not easily solved by legal mechanisms. While on balance it seems that enforcing surrogacy arrangements would leave the courts too little discretion to protect the interests of the most vulnerable person involved – the child – there are good reasons to hold people to at least some of their obligations where possible. It is particularly important that all three parties are considered in any approach taken by the law, for while the potential harms to the child and the surrogate are evident, we ought not to forget that the commissioning couple are vulnerable themselves. They will usually be people who have been through the agonising experience of trying and failing to conceive a child, and if they are resorting to surrogacy, they probably want a child very much. When they do not gain custody of the child, they will experience disappointment, as well as seeing their genetic offspring cared for by another. For some, this will be very difficult to bear, but then of course the potential harms to the surrogate and the child are far from small. A delicate balancing is required, and this is best done when the court has the widest discretion. Introducing money into the equation may be fair, but it may also create more problems than it solves, and we must tread carefully before moving in that direction.

FURTHER READING

Debate 1

R. Bennett, 'When intuition is not enough. Why the principle of procreative beneficence must work much harder to justify its eugenic vision' (2014) 28 *Bioethics* 447.

A. Buchanan et al., *From Chance to Choice: Genetics and Justice* (Cambridge University Press, 2000).

J. Harris, 'Is there a coherent social conception of disability?' (2000) 26 *Journal of Medical Ethics* 95.

---

[100] See, e.g., R.J. Arneson, 'Commodification and commercial surrogacy' (1992) 21 *Philosophy and Public Affairs* 132, 161.

J. Harris, *How to be Good. The Possibility of Moral Enhancement* (Oxford University Press, 2016).

J. Herring, 'Parental responsibility, hyper-parenting and the role of technology' in R. Brownsword, E. Scotford and K. Yeung (eds), *The Oxford Handbook of Law, Regulation and Technology* (Oxford University Press, 2017).

B. Hofmann, '"You are inferior!" Revisiting the expressivist argument' (2017) 31 *Bioethics* 1.

E. Parens and A. Asch, 'Disability rights critique of prenatal genetic testing: reflections and recommendations' (2003) 9 *Mental Retardation and Developmental Disabilities Research Reviews* 40.

J. Savulescu, 'Procreative beneficence: why we should select the best children' (2001) 15 *Bioethics* 413.

J. Savulescu, 'Deaf lesbians, "designer disability," and the future of medicine' (2002) 325 *British Medical Journal* 771.

S. Stoller, 'Why we are not morally required to select the best children: a response to Savulescu' (2008) 22 *Bioethics* 365.

Debate 2

M. Brazier, A. Campbell and S. Golombok, *Surrogacy: Review for Health Ministers of Current Arrangements for Payments and Regulation, Report of the Review Team*, Cm 4068 (HMSO, 1998).

T. Frame, 'The perils of surrogate motherhood' (2003) June *Quadrant* 30.

P. Gerber and K. O'Byrne, *Surrogacy, Law and Human Rights* (Routledge, 2015).

K. Horsey, 'Fraying at the edges' (2016) 24 *Medical Law Review* 608.

D. Satz, 'Markets in women's reproductive labor' (1992) 21 *Philosophy and Public Affairs* 107.

M. Shultz, 'Reproductive technology and intention-based parenthood: an opportunity for gender neutrality' (1990) 2 *Wisconsin Law Review* 297.

E. Tehman, *Birthing a Mother: The Surrogate Body and the Pregnant Self* (University of California Press, 2010).

S. Wilkinson, 'Exploitation in international paid surrogacy' (2016) 33 *Journal of Applied Philosophy* 125.

CHAPTER 6

Abortion

Debate 1

The legal status of the foetus

INTRODUCTION

The status of the foetus is one of the most fiercely debated issues in medical law and ethics. This is because it raises some profound questions about what it means to be a person and what is valuable about life. People's feelings can run high. To some the embryo is a person from the moment of conception and abortion is akin to murder. To others life does not begin until birth and claiming 'foetal rights' undermines the rights women have. It is commonly believed that the view you take about foetal status will determine what you think about abortion. However, as we shall see in Debate 2, a coherent case can be made for claiming a foetus is a person but that abortion should still be legally permitted. For this first debate, however, we will focus on the arguments over the status of the foetus.

THE LAW

The courts, perhaps understandably, have sought to avoid the controversial issue of the status of the foetus. They seem happier to discuss what a foetus is not than what a foetus is. It is clear that under English law a foetus is not a person until it is born.[1] That does not mean that a foetus is 'a nothing'. Perhaps the most authoritative statement can be found in *Attorney-General's Reference (No. 3 of 1994)*,[2] where the House of Lords rejected an argument, proposed by the Court of Appeal, that a foetus should be regarded as part of the mother, equivalent to a leg or an arm. It also rejected the view that a foetus was a person. Lord Mustill explained that a foetus is a 'unique organism'. That suggests that

---

[1] A. Alghrani and M. Brazier, 'What is it? Whose is it? Repositioning the fetus in the context of research?' (2011) 70 *Cambridge Law Journal* 51.
[2] *Attorney-General's Reference (No. 3 of 1994)* [1998] AC 245.

it is something deserving of protection and respect, even if it is short of being a person. Hence, the foetus is protected to some extent under the criminal law, through the procuring a miscarriage offences[3] and the Abortion Act 1967, which restricts when it is lawful to have an abortion. However, it is not possible to bring proceedings 'in the name of the foetus'.[4] Further, simply injuring a foetus is not an offence, unless the foetus is born alive and then becomes a person.

The issue of foetal status came before the Grand Chamber of the European Court of Human Rights in *A, B, C v Ireland*. The Court avoided making a clear statement about the status of the foetus, stating:

> A broad margin was specifically accorded to determining what persons were protected by Article 2 of the Convention [right to life]: the Court had conclusively answered in its judgments in *Vo v. France* and in *Evans v. The United Kingdom* that there was no European scientific or legal definition of the beginning of life so that the question of the legal protection of the right to life fell within the States' margin of appreciation.[5]

The European Court in effect 'passed the buck' and said it was for each country to determine for itself the status of the foetus, and the European Court would not take a particular line on that thorny question.

We will now consider some of the views as to the status of the foetus. We will not seek to cover them all but focus on those which seem to have most support in the current literature.

THE FOETUS IS A PERSON FROM THE MOMENT OF CONCEPTION

Many of those who oppose abortion take the view that a foetus is a person from the moment of conception. It is in line with many religious traditions, although the view is adopted by those of no faith and is rejected by some religious commentators. We will not explore the specifically religious reasons for (or against) treating the foetus as a person,[6] because we assume that they would not be relied upon in a debate over what the law should be in a secular democracy.

Those who take the view that the foetus is a person from the moment of conception might rely on three kinds of argument. First, it might be argued the foetus is a person by virtue of its nature or substance at the point of conception. Second, it might be argued a foetus is a person at conception by virtue of its potential to become a person. Third, it might be argued that we don't know when a foetus becomes a person, so to be safe we should take it to be at the moment of conception. These three arguments need to be considered separately.

---

[3] Offences Against the Person Act 1861, ss 58 and 59.
[4] *Paton v BPAS* [1979] QB 276.
[5] *A, B, C v Ireland*, Application no. 25579/05, para. 185.
[6] See, for one view, D.A. Jones, *The Soul of the Embryo* (Bloomsbury Academic, 2004).

The foetus is a person by virtue of its nature

The argument is that from the moment of conception, a foetus is a person deserving of full human rights by virtue of its nature or substance. How might such a claim be made? One claim is that the moment of conception is when the entire genetic make-up of the person is established.[7] Our genetic composition is central to who we are. It is our biological essence. You can in biological terms be traced back to the embryo you were at conception.[8] Francis Beckwith writes:

> At conception, a whole human being, with its own genome, comes into existence, needing only food, water, shelter, and oxygen, and a congenial environment in which to interact, in order to grow and develop itself to maturity in accordance with her own intrinsically ordered nature. It is a unified organism with its own intrinsic purpose and basic capacities, whose parts work in concert for the perfection and perpetuation of its existence as a whole.[9]

Christopher Kaczor argues that 'each human being has inherent moral worth simply by virtue of the kind of being it is'.[10] He goes on to argue:

> A human embryo is properly classified as an individual human being rather than a collection of human cells, a member of the kind *Homo sapiens* rather than simply a 'heap' of cells of human origin. A shaving of your skin may contain living human cells, but the skin shavings as a group are just an uncoordinated heap, whereas you are a self-developing and self-integrated whole whose various parts (skin, eyes, arms, blood) serve the whole. Skin cells are merely parts of a human being without a dynamic, intrinsic orientation to develop towards maturity in the human species. By contrast, the human embryo is a whole, complete organism, a living individual human being whose cells work together in a coordinated effort of self-development towards maturity. If all human beings are persons, then the human embryo is a person.[11]

Opponents of this view will reject the idea that it is our genetic structure or our biological essence which makes us people of moral worth. When we relate to other humans, we do so on the basis of their intellect, their emotions and/ or their appearance. It is argued that we cannot relate to the embryo at the moment of conception. It has none of the characteristics we value in other people. Even if, in a biological sense, we might be traced back to the foetus we once were, we have no memory of or psychological link to that time.

[7] F. Beckwith, *Defending Life: A Moral and Legal Case Against Abortion Choice* (Cambridge University Press, 2007).

[8] C. Wolf-Devine and P. Devine (2009), 'Abortion: a communitarian pro-life perspective' in M. Tooley, C. Wolf-Devine and P. Devine (eds), *Abortion: Three Perspectives* (Oxford University Press, 2009), 86.

[9] F. Beckwith, 'Defending abortion philosophically: a review of David Boonin's *A Defense of Abortion*' (2006) 31 *Journal of Medicine and Philosophy* 177.

[10] C. Kaczor, *The Ethics of Abortion* (Routledge, 2011), 105.

[11] Ibid., 105.

Those who disagree with the argument that personhood begins at conception might also note that 'it is striking that the usual fate of the fertilized human egg is to die'.[12] Estimates suggest that fewer than 15 per cent of fertilised eggs will result in a birth.[13] Setting personhood at conception means that the vast majority of people die within a few days. That seems so odd, it suggests that life cannot begin at conception. However, in reply to such points, it has been asked, 'Would we say that in an impoverished country, where there was an infant mortality rate of 90 per cent, the children born were of lower moral status than those born where there was a much lower rate?'[14] Does the likelihood of death affect moral status?

The foetus should be treated as a person at conception to play safe

It might be argued that because we cannot know when a foetus becomes a person, we should play safe and choose the moment of conception. Margaret Brazier has written:

> Perception of the status of the embryo derives in many cases from the presence or absence of religious belief ... The dispute reaches stalemate ... The humanity of the embryo is unproven and unprovable. But that acts both ways. Just as I cannot prove that humanity was divinely created and that each and every one of us possesses an immortal soul, so it cannot be proved that it is not so.[15]

The premise of this argument is that there must be a particular moment in time when a foetus becomes a person. If so, it is clearly important that we do not put this too late in the timescale or else a moral person may be harmed. Given that, and the difficulty in identifying any other clear dramatic moment in the development of the foetus, conception is the safest time to determine personhood begins.

One way of understanding the argument is to claim that we should accept there is a risk that a foetus could be a person. Beckwith[16] argues that we would not allow a shooting range to operate if it was close to a school and there was a small chance a child would be killed, and therefore we should not allow abortion if there is a small chance that a foetus is a person. His analogy is not, however, exact, because those who are prevented from being allowed to shoot are not suffering a severe lack of liberty as a result, while denying a woman access to an abortion would restrict her bodily integrity and her

---

[12] The words of Professor Brown reported in *Smeaton* [2002] 2 FCR 193, para. 129.

[13] J. Harris, '(ARTBs) Assisted reproductive technological blunders' (2003) 29 *Journal of Medical Ethics* 205.

[14] F. Beckwith, 'Of souls, selves, and cerebrums' (2005) 31 *Journal of Medical Ethics* 56, 58.

[15] M. Brazier, 'Embryo's "rights": abortion and research' in M. Freeman (ed.), *Medicine, Ethics and Law* (Stevens, 1988), 134.

[16] F. Beckwith, *Defending Life: A Moral and Legal Case Against Abortion Choice* (Cambridge University Press, 2007), 60.

liberty. A closer comparison might be forbidding the driving of cars because of the small risk of death.[17]

The argument assumes that there should be a clear point in time at which a foetus becomes a person. One response is that this is an error, and there are plenty of concepts where a distinction is drawn, even though there are borderline cases where it is difficult to tell what side of the line a case falls on. Everyone agrees there is a difference between night and day, even though the exact point at dawn when day starts is hard to identify. So too we might say we are clear that a born baby is a person and a conceptus is not, even if we have problems identifying borderline cases. Another criticism that could be used is that, in fact, conception is not the 'bright line' event that it is sometimes portrayed to be. Conception and fertilisation take place over a period of time (normally about twenty-two hours). It is therefore as difficult to pinpoint the moment during the conception process at which personhood begins as it is for other theories to pinpoint when life begins.[18]

The foetus has moral claims based on its potential

A different kind of argument is that in killing a foetus we are depriving it of a potential life. It often is made in this way. If we think about what is the harm done when a person is killed, a popular answer is that they are deprived of the life they would have enjoyed if they had not been killed. That is why it is generally seen as a greater tragedy when a 9 year old is killed than when a 90 year old is killed. If we recognise this as the central wrong in killing, it provides us with a reason why it is wrong to kill the foetus. It will be deprived of its future life. Notably this argument does not rest on an argument that the foetus is a person from conception, but rather that the wrong done to it (the deprivation of life) is the central wrong in the killing of a person.

One difficulty with this argument is that we do not normally treat someone with the potential to be X as having the same rights as X. I might have the potential to be a police officer, but that does not mean you should treat me as a police officer. It also seems in danger of claiming too much. If someone refrains from sexual intercourse, are they depriving someone of a future?

THE FOETUS BECOMES A PERSON AT VIABILITY

Some commentators have relied on viability as the mark of the start of personhood. That is the time when the foetus can live apart from the mother, with appropriate medical care. It involves asking whether the foetus would survive if prematurely born at that point. With current medical technology, that would be around twenty-two weeks.

---

[17] D. Stretton, 'Critical notice – defending life: a moral and legal case against abortion choice by Francis J. Beckwith' (2008) 34 *Journal of Medical Ethics* 793.
[18] G. Williams, 'The foetus and the right to life' (1994) 53 *Cambridge Law Journal* 71.

Why might viability be relied upon as a marker of personhood? It indicates that the foetus has developed to such a stage that its organs are capable of being self-supporting. Elizabeth Wicks[19] argues it is the point at which the foetus has 'integrative function of a human organism'.

For some, a problem with viability is that it produces uncertainty. Any premature baby is in a precarious state, and it can be touch and go whether it will survive. Another concern is that whether a foetus is viable depends on where in the world you live and what medical resources there are. Is there something uncomfortable about saying that a 25-week foetus is a person in Britain but not in a remote part of a developing country? Further investigation may be made of what viable means. A foetus might be kept alive with highly specialist equipment from an early age, but to what extent is that self-sufficiency?

THE FOETUS BECOMES A PERSON AT SENTIENCE

A popular approach is to argue that a foetus becomes a person when it develops sentience, or is capable of brain activity or self-awareness.[20] This may be at around twenty to twenty-four weeks, although that is debated.[21] One way of justifying this claim is to argue that we should base our approach to the question 'When does life begin?' on the question 'When does life end?'. There is much support for the view that brain death (the cessation of brain activity) should be the mark of death (see Chapter 9). If so, it is arguable that life should therefore be said to begin at the point when brain activity starts. John Harris has put the argument this way:

> I argue that the moral status of the embryo and indeed of any individual is determined by its possession of those features which make normal adult human individuals morally more important than sheep or goats or embryos.[22]

As we shall see, such an approach could, in fact, also lead to the view that life does not begin until sometime after birth. What makes someone a person is not merely sensation or sentience (an animal can experience these), but rather being a 'rational self-conscious being', and that does not start until months or even years after birth. We will discuss this view below. From Kaczor's perspective (mentioned on p. 151), a person's life should be valued not for what they do or think, but for what they are: a living person.

---

[19] E. Wicks, *The Right to Life and Conflicting Interests* (Oxford University Press, 2010).

[20] B. Steinbock, *Life Before Birth* (Oxford University Press, 1992), 5

[21] D. Boonin, *A Defense of Abortion* (Cambridge University Press, 2002).

[22] J. Harris, 'Rights and reproductive choice' in J. Harris and S. Holm (eds), *The Future of Human Reproduction: Choice and Regulation* (Oxford University Press, 1998), 79.

THE FOETUS BECOMES A PERSON AT BIRTH

This is the view that best reflects the current law, namely, that it is not until birth that the foetus acquires full legal personhood. At birth the child becomes entirely separate from the mother and is capable of existing independently from her. The child has a biologically independent existence. Only then are they able effectively to interact with others and become a member of the wider community.

Some see birth as an arbitrary moment to allocate responsibility. It is a dramatic moment for the mother, but the foetus does not change its nature a few minutes before or after. It has the same capabilities as it did a few minutes earlier. Why does a 30-week-old foetus who has been born prematurely have a different moral status from a 30-week-old foetus which has yet to be born? Should the geography of where they are living affect their status? As Charles Foster has asked, should a journey of a few centimetres down the birth canal make a huge difference to the moral status of the foetus?[23]

POST-BIRTH

One view which appears to have growing support is Harris's view that someone is not a person until they are 'a rational and self-conscious being'. This means that a foetus is not a person. Nor indeed is a newborn infant.[24] Peter Singer has written:

> If the fetus does not have the same claim to life as a person, it appears that the newborn baby does not either, and the life of a new born baby is less value to it than the life of a pig, a dog, or a chimpanzee is to the nonhuman animal.[25]

The shocking conclusion is that infanticide (the killing of babies) is permissible.

In a highly controversial article, Alberto Giubilini and Francesca Minerva[26] suggest precisely that.[27] As a newborn baby has not acquired sufficient attributes to become a person, 'post-birth abortion' (i.e. infanticide) should be permitted. As the baby cannot value life, they cannot be harmed by its being taken away.

This argument clarifies the key question in this debate: 'What is it that gives life its moral value?' Clearly for Singer and others it is mental capacity and the ability to reason and be self-aware that generate value. It is these things that make us different from other animals, and they are what we value in each other. But not everyone will accept that. Others argue that it is being

---

[23] C. Foster, *Choosing Life, Choosing Death: The Tyranny of Autonomy in Medical Ethics and Law* (Hart Publishing, 2009).

[24] M. Tooley, *Abortion and Infanticide* (Oxford University Press, 1983).

[25] P. Singer, *Writings on an Ethical Life* (Ecco Press, 2000), 160.

[26] A. Giubilini and F. Minerva, 'After-birth abortion: why should the baby live?' (2013) 39 *Journal of Medical Ethics* 261.

[27] Although similar views have been suggested for many years.

in caring relationships that generates moral value.[28] Yet others find value in the fact of being similar members of the same species. Jacqueline Laing somewhat acerbically comments:

> Whether or not we are exercising our capacities or abilities, are in pain or desirable to third parties are insufficient grounds on which to judge human moral value. So too are qualities like evincing rationality, capacity for self-reflection or moral sensibility, characteristics that exclude many professors of moral philosophy for a lifetime. Even human dignity does not fluctuate and should not be regarded as fluctuating.[29]

Andrew McGee also points to the powerful instinct to love one's offspring, which helps form the basis of our moral codes:

> Our lives are defined in large part in terms of our relationships with our loved ones and, especially, our offspring. The value we afford to human life therefore stems from the central role our loved ones play in our lives, and the meaning they give to them.[30]

McGee's comments perhaps help make sense of the claims of the prominent ethicist Robert George, that the arguments in favour of infanticide are simply 'moral madness'.[31] Indeed, he does not see the issue as worthy of discussion, because 'anyone should immediately be able to see that killing infants because they are unwanted is unacceptable'.[32] But critics will reply that gut instinct reactions will not do, and we need to provide a coherent argument as to why babies are morally different from foetuses.[33]

GRADUALIST VIEW

Arguably the most popular answer among academic commentators to the status of the foetus question is to promote the gradualist view. This rejects the view that there is a particular point in time when a foetus becomes a person. Rather, there is a process during which the foetus acquires increasing moral and legal interests until, in time, it becomes a person. Kate Greasley claims:

> there is no sharp borderline between the absence of moral personhood and its attainment ... since there is no good reason to think that personhood is the kind

---

[28] J. Herring, *Caring and the Law* (Hart Publishing, 2013), Chapter 7.

[29] J. Laing, 'Infanticide: a reply to Giubilini and Minerva' (2013) 39 *Journal of Medical Ethics* 336.

[30] A. McGee, 'The moral significance of babies' (2013) 39 *Journal of Medical Ethics* 345, 345.

[31] R. George, 'Response to: Is the pro-choice position for infanticide "madness"?' (2013) 39 *Journal of Medical Ethics* 302.

[32] Ibid., 303. See also J. Finnis, 'Capacity, harm and experience in the life of persons as equals' (2013) 39 *Journal of Medical Ethics* 281.

[33] J. McMahan, 'Infanticide and moral consistency' (2013) 39 *Journal of Medical Ethics* 273.

of property that emerges wholly and instantaneously ... The coming-to-be of persons is incremental and vague at the margins of life.[34]

The argument is that we value a range of things about people, and it is the combination of characteristics that generates value in human life. In the early stages only a few of these characteristics are present. Gradually, as the foetus gets older, it acquires more and more characteristics, and so greater respect is due to it. Typically, proponents of the view suggest that birth marks the point at which there is a sufficient number of the relevant characteristics so that the foetus has now acquired personhood.[35] That may accord with the experiences of pregnant women.[36] Another attraction of this view is that it accords with the widely held intuition that an abortion at an early stage requires less justification (if any) than a later abortion.

One major difficulty for the gradualist view is that once a person is born, we do not normally accept the idea that people are more or less human. The idea, for example, that a person with a mental disorder is less human than someone else is repugnant. We treat all born people as people, full stop. So why are we willing to accept that foetuses can have degrees of personhood, if we are not willing to take this view with born people? This argument is that we must reject any suggestion that there are degrees of personhood, because that is a dangerous argument, and instead locate a clear point at which personhood begins.

THE RELATIONSHIP VIEW

Some commentators reject the basis of much of this debate. They argue that we cannot sensibly discuss the status of the foetus in isolation from the woman.[37] She is not simply a foetal container.[38] Rather, our discussion should focus on the relationship between the mother and foetus: they are both two and one.[39] It makes no sense to talk of the interests of the foetus without considering its relationship with the mother. John Seymour explains that the key feature of the relationship approach is 'its emphases on the shared needs and interdependence of the woman and her foetus, whose relationship is seen as characterized by "[c]onnectedness, mutuality, and reciprocity"'.[40]

---

[34] K. Greasley, *Arguments About Abortion* (Oxford University Press, 2017), 147.

[35] See the discussion in A. Sanger, *Beyond Choice* (Public Affairs, 2004).

[36] C. Mackenzie, 'Abortion and embodiment' (1992) 70 *Australasian Journal of Philosophy* 136.

[37] J. Herring, 'The loneliness of status: the legal and moral significance of birth' in F. Ebtehaj, J. Herring, M. Johnson and M. Richards (eds), *Birth Rites and Rights* (Hart Publishing, 2011).

[38] G. Annas, 'Pregnant women as fetal containers' (1986) 16 *Hastings Centre Report* 13.

[39] J. Seymour, *Childbirth and the Law* (Oxford University Press, 2000).

[40] Ibid., 190.

Jonathan Herring argues that the relational approach provides a way of looking at pregnancy issues in the way women do:

> The abstracted weighing of the interests of the fetus/baby and woman pays no account of the complex interactions between them; and between them and those who are in relationship with them; not to mention the broader social context which has such an impact on the actual and perceived moral and legal obligations that are imposed. We need to move from an idealised analysis and listen to voices of women faced with pregnancy decisions and decisions concerning birth and children. There we usually find not the language of status, rights, viability or choice: but the language of despair; ecstasy; interconnection and guilt. The language is that of relationships: seeking to do the right thing 'for everyone'. It is there we need to start the legal and moral analysis of pregnancy and find the significance of birth.[41]

Under the relational approach, what the law should protect is not an individual's capacities, but rather good relationships between people. This opens up the possibility of the law having a different response to a case where the pregnant woman wants to terminate the pregnancy and one where she wants the pregnancy to continue.

Opponents of the relationship approach argue that we cannot discuss the maternal–foetal relationship in any meaningful way without deciding whether a foetus should be regarded as equivalent to a strand of her hair[42] or as having the same status as an adult person. Another concern is that emphasis on the relationship rather than the interests of those involved might too easily lead to an overriding of the woman's rights, especially given the strong image that motherhood holds in our society. Or the argument might go the other way, that a focus on regarding the foetus and woman 'as one' gives the woman a say in how the relationship should progress, thereby downplaying the protection of the foetus.

CONCLUSION

It is probably a fair observation that all of the theories promoted have their difficulties. Some of the approaches would lead to what many would regard as undesirable outcomes: the legality of infanticide or the outlawing of contraception. There is added complication that the way we determine when life begins may impact on the interests of severely disabled people. At the heart of the debate is a question about what makes life morally valuable: is it the ability to think and reason? Is it self-awareness or the ability to feel pain? Is it being

---

[41] J. Herring, 'The loneliness of status: the legal and moral significance of birth' in F. Ebtehaj, J. Herring, M. Johnson and M. Richards (eds), *Birth Rites and Rights* (Hart Publishing, 2011), 109–10.

[42] M. Warren, 'On the moral and legal status of abortion' in L. Schwartz (ed.), *Arguing About Abortion* (Wadsworth, 1992).

a member of the human species or having human DNA? Or is its value found in relationships?[43] Because people give different answers to these questions, they disagree on the moral status of the foetus. These somewhat theoretical issues have become the focus of a political debate. Abortion is currently seen as a criminal offence, although lawful if the terms of the Abortion Act 1967 are complied with. Some campaigners want to decriminalise abortion to help reduce its stigma. Opponents argue that criminalisation is appropriate because it recognises that something worthy of legal protection is harmed in the abortion process.[44]

Debate   2

How should we balance the interests of the pregnant woman and foetus?

INTRODUCTION

The abortion debates can easily become polarised between those who emphasise a woman's right to choose whether or not to terminate the pregnancy and those who argue that a foetus is a person with a right to life. In popular writing this is presented as the debate between the 'pro-choicers' and the 'pro-lifers'. In this debate we will explore how we might balance the claims resting in the foetus with those resting in the pregnant woman.

Before doing so, it is worth noting that for some perspectives this kind of balancing between the interests of the foetus and woman is unnecessary. Those who believe the foetus has no interests of its own[45] will find there is no real balancing to undertake, because the interests of the foetus are so low that the woman's interests will easily win out. A balancing approach is only needed for those who believe the foetus is a person or, if not a person, has some significant interests. The relationship-based approach might also argue that it is not a matter of weighing up their interests, as their interests are intertwined and cannot be separated.

This issue is one where it is particularly important to separate the question of morality and law. It is one thing, for example, to ask 'What morally is the most ideal thing to do?', but a different thing to ask 'What should the law require people to do?'. You might believe the most moral thing to do would be to sell all (or most) of what you have and give the proceeds to the poor, but even if you did, you would not think the law should require that. It is, therefore,

---

[43] C. Foster and J. Herring, *Identity, Personhood and the Law* (Springer, 2017).

[44] S. Sheldon, 'The decriminalisation of abortion: an argument for modernisation' (2016) 36 *Oxford Journal of Legal Studies* 334.

[45] M. Warren, 'On the moral and legal status of abortion' in L. Schwartz (ed.), *Arguing About Abortion* (Wadsworth, 1992).

a perfectly respectable view to believe that abortion is (or nearly always is) immoral but that the law should leave the choice up to the individual.[46]

Many commentators have found a scenario produced by Judith Jarvis Thomson a useful starting point for discussion of how to balance the competing interests in an abortion case.

JARVIS THOMSON'S VIOLINIST

Judith Jarvis Thomson's article poses the following hypothetical example:

> **Scenario to ponder**
>
> You wake up in the morning and find yourself back to back in bed with an unconscious violinist. A famous unconscious violinist. He has been found to have a fatal kidney ailment, and the Society of Music Lovers has canvassed all the available medical records and found that you alone have the right blood type to help. They have therefore kidnapped you, and last night the violinist's circulatory system was plugged into yours, so that your kidneys can be used to extract poisons from his blood as well as your own. The director of the hospital now tells you: 'Look, we're sorry the Society of Music Lovers did this to you – we would never have permitted it if we had known. But still, they did it, and the violinist is now plugged into you. To unplug you would be to kill him. But never mind, it's only for nine months. By then he will have recovered from his ailment, and can safely be unplugged from you.'[47]

Jarvis Thomson assumes that you will say that you are entitled to unplug yourself. Note that she is not claiming that is the most virtuous thing to do. Maybe an extremely virtuous person, with no other competing obligations, would remain plugged in, but she is assuming that you would agree that the law should not compel you to be plugged in.

It may be that you disagree with Jarvis Thomson's assumption and in fact believe that the law should require you to remain hooked up to the violinist. If that is your response then her analogy has failed in its aim. However, you might then consider whether you think the law should generally require people to undergo invasive procedures to keep others alive. For example, should there be compulsory organ donation, blood donation and the like?

---

[46] D. Boonin, *A Defense of Abortion* (Cambridge University Press, 2002), 5.

[47] J. Jarvis Thomson, 'A defense of abortion' (1971) 1 *Philosophy and Public Affairs* 47, 62.

Most people, it seems, accept that the person should not be required to be hooked up to the violinist. Jarvis Thompson would then say the scenario is identical to abortion, and if you accept that the person should not remained hooked up to the violinist, you should agree that abortion should be lawful. In brief, the reason why many people are instinctively drawn to the conclusion that you should be able to release yourself from the violinist is that our society puts much weight on the right to bodily integrity. You should not be required to have your body touched or invaded without your consent. There are severe limits on the extent to which one person should be able to use another person's body for their own gain without that person's consent.

While most commentators have accepted that the person should be able to unhook themselves from the violinist, they have rejected the argument that this leads to support for the legalisation of abortion. An analysis of these arguments is helpful in thinking through the broader issues on balancing the claims of the foetus and the woman.

FORCE AND RESPONSIBILITY

Jarvis Thomson's analogy involves a person who is forced into being linked up to the violinist. Opponents of her analogy argue that this means it is only analogous to pregnancy following rape.[48] The difference between the violinist and abortion is that (outside the context of rape) the woman has chosen to engage in sex and so assumes responsibilities to the foetus. Jarvis Thomson responds with a different analogy:

Scenario to ponder

'Suppose it were like this: people-seeds drift about in the air like pollen, and if you open your windows, one may drift in and take root in your carpets or upholstery. You don't want children, so you fix up your windows with fine mesh screens, the very best you can buy. As can happen, however, and on very, very rare occasions does happen, one of the screens is defective; and a seed drifts in and takes root. Does the person-plant who now develops have a right to the use of your house? Surely not – despite the fact that you voluntarily opened your windows, you knowingly kept carpets and upholstered furniture, and you knew that screens were sometimes defective.'[49]

---

[48] M. Tooley, *Abortion and Infanticide* (Oxford University Press, 1983), 45.

[49] J. Jarvis Thomson, 'A defense of abortion' (1971) 1 *Philosophy and Public Affairs* 47, 59.

The essence of Jarvis Thomson's argument here is that women should not be regarded as responsible for the foetus's vulnerable position. This argument seems strongest where the pregnancy has resulted from contraceptive failure and the couple may be taken to have used reasonable efforts to ensure that a foetus was not created. Using a different analogy, Thomson[50] argues that the fact a householder has left their windows open does not give a burglar the right to enter and remain in the house. Her point here is to argue that a woman who has sex cannot thereby be taken to have accepted being pregnant, any more than a householder who leaves a window open gives a burglar the right to enter. She argues that a foetus has no right to use a woman's body without her consent.[51]

Some commentators do not find this seed or burglar analogy very convincing. Meilaender argues that the womb is the natural place for a foetus to be, so it cannot be seen as similar to an invader or intruder.[52] Marquis[53] argues that a burglar is responsible for entering a house and can be removed by force, while a foetus is not blameworthy for being in a womb. Others reply that the fact a woman has known that using contraception is not 100 per cent reliable means that she has undertaken the risk of pregnancy and so is responsible for the foetus if the risk materialises.[54]

An alternative line of argument is to set the responsibility question to one side. A person's right to bodily integrity is not lost even if they are responsible for another person's need for their body. A parent who had a child, knowing the child would have a genetic condition, would not be required to donate an organ to cure the child, even if they had knowingly created the child with the particular vulnerability. A person can use self-defence against an attack, even if they were being attacked because they had taunted the attacker.[55] Boonin[56] suggests that in the end, these debates come down to a key question: do we as a society agree that a woman who engages in sexual intercourse thereby takes on the responsibility for any foetus created? If sex creates the risk of a foetus being created, is it right that the costs of that risk should fall only on women?

POSITIONING OF THE ARGUMENT

Kaczor[57] raises another point. He argues that we would regard the violinist scenario very differently if it was the violinist who wanted to unplug himself,

---

[50] Ibid., 58.

[51] Ibid., 138.

[52] G. Meilaender, *Bioethics: A Primer for Christians* (Eerdmans, 1998).

[53] D. Marquis, 'Manninen's defense of abortion rights is unsuccessful' (2010) 10 *American Journal of Bioethics* 56.

[54] See the discussion at B. Steinbock, *Life Before Birth* (Oxford University Press, 1992), 78.

[55] *R v Keane* [2010] EWCA Crim 2514, although that would not be true if the defendant had taunted the victim deliberately with the hope they would react with violence in response to which the defendant could kill in self-defence.

[56] D. Boonin, *A Defense of Abortion* (Cambridge University Press, 2002), 164.

[57] C. Kaczor, *The Ethics of Abortion* (Routledge, 2011).

thereby killing us. Jarvis Thomson, he argues, skews our perception by positioning us as the one doing the unplugging.

However, there may be a difference based on the original position of the parties. Kamm has argued that unplugging the violinist simply returns him to the position he would have been in before he came into contact with you. By unplugging him you are not harming him but returning him to the position he was initially.[58] Similarly, in relation to abortion, no wrong is done to the foetus through abortion: the foetus is simply returned to the position it would have been in without the woman's sustenance. In Kaczor's argument, if the violinist were to unplug himself and that were to kill you, he would not be returning you to where you were before you met but rather putting you in a worse position, and so he would be harming you.

Killing/Letting Die

Another distinction between Thomson's violinist analogy and abortion is that in the case of the violinist, by unplugging yourself you are letting the violinist die, which is an omission (in that it is a withdrawal of support), while in some methods of abortion the foetus is killed by a positive act (e.g. by cutting it up).[59] If, rather than unplugging the violinist, you shot him dead, would that not lead to a different response?

The validity of this argument depends in part on whether you think there is a difference between an act and an omission. Many philosophers find the distinction one of little or no moral significance. However, it does play an important role in the law. You may not be required to donate a kidney to your sick child, who dies as a result, but you may not shoot them dead.

Self-Defence

If abortion, at least in some contexts, is seen as an act that kills a person, it becomes harder to justify than if it is seen as withdrawal of support. If it is an act, the most likely justification, if any, is found in self-defence. The essence of the claim is that in abortion the woman is defending herself against the pain, injuries, indignities and bodily intrusion which can accompany a pregnancy. McDonagh writes:

> A woman's bodily integrity and liberty is just as violated by preborn life that implants itself, using and transforming her body for nine long months without consent, as she is when a born person massively imposes on her body and liberty without consent, as in rape, kidnapping, slavery, and battery.[60]

---

[58] F. Kamm, *Creation and Abortion* (Oxford University Press, 1992).

[59] Some forms of abortion would seem to operate as a withdrawal of support.

[60] E. McDonagh, *Breaking the Abortion Deadlock* (Oxford University Press, 1996), 169.

The self-defence argument raises several issues. First, self-defence is only justified to avoid a threat of death or very serious injury, and it may be questioned whether the effects of a normal pregnancy are sufficiently grave to justify a killing. This will depend on how grave you regard the physical invasions of unwanted pregnancy. Second, self-defence normally involves defence against a blameworthy aggressor, which a foetus is not. However, self-defence in the criminal law is available to those who are being attacked, even if the attacker is blameless (e.g. they are sleepwalking or a child). That response still leaves the question of whether the foetus can be regarded as an 'aggressor'. In the criminal law a distinction is drawn between killing a person who poses an unjust threat to you (where self-defence may be available) and killing a person to avoid an unpleasant consequence caused by someone else (where self-defence cannot be used). So self-defence is available if someone is trying to push you off a boat into a stormy sea. However, if the boat has capsized and your only way of survival is to push someone else off a floatation device so you can use it, you cannot use self-defence because they are not threatening you. So the key question is then whether the foetus can be seen to be posing an unjustified threat to the woman. Does the foetus have a right to use the woman's body for support?

INTENT

Some commentators have distinguished the violinist scenario based on the concept of intention. In the case of the violinist, when you unplug yourself, you do not intend to kill the violinist.[61] You would be delighted if somehow he managed to survive, although you realise that is unlikely. However, in the case of abortion, most procedures are done with the purpose of killing the foetus. If the foetus survives *in utero*, the abortion will be regarded as a failure. Even if the woman does not want the foetus to die, she is consenting to a process which will inevitably result in its death. Such an argument relies on the doctrine of double effect and the controversial distinction between foresight and intention. As we will see in Chapter 10, the significance between the two is fiercely debated.

CONCLUSION

The Jarvis Thomson analogy helpfully brings out the key issues in the debate. Does the woman's right to bodily integrity give her the right to remove the foetus? To what extent is the woman responsible for the foetus being inside her, and how does that impact on her right of bodily integrity? Does the foetus have a right to be protected by the pregnant woman? It is the answers to these questions which will impact on how you respond to the question of balancing the rights and interests of the pregnant woman and the foetus.

---

[61] J. Finnis, 'The rights and wrongs of abortion' (1973) 2 *Philosophy and Public Affairs* 117.

Debate 3

Should counselling before abortion be mandatory?

INTRODUCTION

The counselling of women seeking an abortion has become a major political issue in recent years. In Britain, and to an extent in the US, the 'pro-life' activists have accepted the reality that the law is not going to be changed to prohibit abortion. They have instead focused their efforts on attempting to reduce the number of abortions. In the US a number of states have introduced legislation creating certain requirements before a woman can have an abortion: for example, that she be given certain information; be required to wait a set period of time; that she attend counselling; and/or view a sonogram of the foetus.[62] To give one example, in Idaho a woman seeking an abortion must be given materials that describe and give photographs of foetuses from the fourth to the twenty-fourth week of gestation. She must also be given a description of all procedures used for abortion and told of any foreseeable risks to the woman caused by abortion.[63] This is regardless of the length of her pregnancy or the method of abortion which is to be used. It is clear that these measures were introduced with the hope that, as a result, some women will decide not to proceed with an abortion. However, they are often justified as ensuring that the abortion decision is the result of an informed decision. In some ways this is a politically astute tactic. The 'pro-choice' camp emphasises the importance of choice for women, and the 'pro-life' groups are able to say that by providing women with more information and counselling, they are simply ensuring that women are able to make the informed choice the 'pro-choice' camp have called for.

LAW

In the UK, a woman seeking an abortion must consult her doctor, and two doctors must confirm the grounds made out in the Abortion Act 1967. There is no explicit requirement for counselling. However, the general law of negligence and consent will apply. So the doctor must ensure that the woman understands the procedure in broad terms and must ensure she is aware of any relevant risks. There is a report of a woman suing the NHS for not warning her of the psychological complications following an abortion, nor offering her counselling after it.[64] There is probably a variety of practice in how much doctors

---

[62] D. Mollen, 'Reproductive rights and informed consent: toward a more inclusive discourse' (2013) *Analyses of Social Issues and Public Policy* 1.

[63] I. Vandewalker, 'Abortion and informed consent' (2012) 19 *Michigan Journal of Gender and Law* 1.

[64] S. Boseley, 'Woman to sue NHS for post-abortion trauma', *The Guardian*, 13 June 2002, available at https://www.theguardian.com/society/2002/jun/13/NHS.uknews.

talk through the issues with patients. One report looking at young women's experiences with abortion services found that generally the professionals they encountered were non-judgemental and respectful of their choice. However, a minority complained about being 'over-counselled' about the pros and cons of the abortion decision, although others complained that there was not enough time to talk about their decision.[65] The BMA policy is that there should be 'timely and impartial counselling and advice for women requesting abortion, should they wish to receive it'.[66] Pro-life groups offer 'impartial counselling', which some people claim provides inaccurate advice,[67] although their supporters would argue they tell women facts about the disadvantages of abortion that the pro-choice camp do not want discussed.

In 2011, Nadine Dorries MP attempted to introduce an amendment to the Health and Social Care Bill which would have required women seeking abortions to receive 'independent' counselling. Although the proposal was rejected, the Health Minister did agree to review the counselling received by women seeking an abortion. At the time of writing no changes in the law have been proposed. In this debate we will consider whether the law should be changed to be more explicit about what information women seeking a termination should be given.

INFORMATION AND CHOICE

At the heart of the debate is whether offering people more information and requiring them to think through the issues will give them a better opportunity to make more autonomous choices. Given the gravity of the issue and the complexity of the moral debates, some commentators believe that the more information and counselling the better. After all, how can giving more information be a bad thing?

Supporters of requiring information or counselling emphasise that the information should be unbiased. Only 'facts' should be presented, and women should be allowed to make their own decision. The difficulty is that, particularly in an area like abortion, there is no real agreement over what the relevant 'facts' are. A pro-lifer might argue that the foetus's capacity for sentience and ability to feel pain are important facts to take into account. A pro-choicer might argue these are not relevant because the woman's right to choose trumps any claims of the foetus. In short, even if the parties to the debate can agree that relevant information should be given, they cannot agree what information is relevant.

Scott Woodcock[68] argues that compulsory information provision in the US involves 'providing information about the procedure that tends to create

---

[65] E. Lee, 'We still need abortion as early as possible, as late as necessary', *Spiked*, 9 July 2004.

[66] BMA, *MP Misrepresents BMA Abortion Policy* (BMA, 2012).

[67] E. Barnett, 'Abortion scandal: inside Britain's unregulated "pro-life" clinics', *The Daily Telegraph*, 11 February 2014.

[68] S. Woodcock, 'Abortion counselling and the informed consent dilemma' (2011) 59 *Bioethics* 495, 496.

feelings of guilt, anxiety and strong emotional reactions to the recognizable form of a human foetus'. He argues that the 'information' is selected to produce a certain outcome (a decision not to terminate the pregnancy). Further, that in fact the 'information' does not inform but works at an emotional level. We will return to this point when looking at sonograms. Woodcock acknowledges there is a difficulty here. What some women may regard as useful information, others will not. He sees the solution as leaving the issue to doctors and patients. The doctor should be responsive to the needs of the particular woman and cultivate a trusting relationship with patients.[69] To some that is idealistic given the controversial nature of the procedure, and it would be preferable to produce clear guidelines to protect women from doctors who hold strong views on the topic.

UNWANTED INFORMATION

To critics, it is wrong to provide people with information that they don't want. Of course, if a woman wants to see a sonogram of her foetus, or to be given information on her foetus's capacity to feel pain, or wants to discuss the moral aspects of the issue, she should be able to. However, such information should not be forced upon her. She has, if you like, a right not to know information.[70]

Hila Spear disagrees and argues that information should be provided, regardless of whether the woman wishes to hear it:

> Consider the reality that for other invasive medical procedures, women and men are often provided with more information than they want to know in order to make sure they have truly been informed. Newly diagnosed cancer patients are thoroughly informed of their treatment options. Before this, the unpleasant and most often distressing and disturbing facts about their disease and prognosis are given ... How paternalistic to decide that some information is too upsetting and stressful for the patient. If every woman who contemplated abortion was properly informed about the possible negative consequences, ... her right to choose would be protected.[71]

One response to this claim is that there is a difference between information which is upsetting and information which is harmful. Woodcock[72] argues:

> In the case of abortion ... certain kinds of information can lead to emotional harm in the form of guilt, shame and other negative feelings that are reliably associated with women being presented with the fine details of fetal development or

---

[69] P. Laufer-Ukeles, 'Reproductive choices and informed consent: fetal interests, women's identity and relational autonomy' (2011) 37 *American Journal of Law and Medicine* 567.

[70] J. Herring and C. Foster, '"Please don't tell me": the right not to know' (2011) 21 *Cambridge Quarterly of Healthcare Ethics* 12.

[71] H. Spear, 'Regarding abortion: informed consent or selective disclosure?' (2004) 39 *Nursing Forum* 31, 32.

[72] S. Woodcock, 'Abortion counselling and the informed consent dilemma' (2011) 59 *Bioethics* 495, 499.

surgical abortion methods, and these feelings tend to exert powerful influences on women considering the termination of a pregnancy whether they reflectively endorse the feelings or not.

A separate claim is that certain kinds of information are not autonomy enhancing but rather autonomy undermining. That might be so if they manipulate a person. Imagine, for example, that you have been asked by a school to judge an art competition. Your best friend's daughter is one of the entrants. You might ask not to be told the names of the artists because that information would hinder your decision. A person may be aware that they have prejudices or biases in certain ways, and may try to make sure they do not know certain kinds of information so that they can make a better choice. The fact that the judges in the TV show *The Voice* cannot see the contestants is an example of that. These examples demonstrate that more information does not necessarily equate to better information. So a woman should decide what information she wants to know about so that she can make the best decision for her life, and this may involve deciding not to receive some information.

The attraction of the view that the woman should decide what information she wishes to be given is that it bypasses the arguments over which bits of information should be taken into account. Of course, that will leave some to claim that abortion decisions will be made without women knowing an essential piece of information. However, that may be questioned. Generally, in medical law a person can consent if they understand the proposed procedure in broad terms.[73] It is extremely unlikely that any woman seeking an abortion will not understand 'in broad terms' the nature of the procedure. Even if one were to include moral issues, it is hard to believe that in broad terms the outline views are not known. In short, it seems that the information requirements that proponents seek require far more information to be given than is required in other procedures.[74]

SONOGRAM AND ABORTION

One particular issue which has proved especially controversial in the US is whether a woman seeking an abortion should be required to have and/or view a sonogram of her foetus. Supporters of such a requirement claim that it means the woman has to face up to the decision she is making. Carol Sanger[75] has argued that the image of the foetus in our society has come to take on powerful connotations well beyond its actual informational value, and the image raises a host of emotions which are not entirely logical. This may be reinforced when

---

[73] See Chapter 2.

[74] M. Manian, 'The irrational woman: informed consent and abortion decision-making' (2009) 16 *Duke Journal of Gender Law & Policy* 223.

[75] C. Sanger, 'Seeing and believing: mandatory ultrasound and the path to a protected choice' (2008) 56 *UCLA Law Review* 351.

put in the context of a broader patriarchal system which disadvantages women in the burdens of reproduction and care, and creates an image of motherhood which makes it hard for women to act against. Hence, Sanger argues that by showing the ultrasound, the image is designed to 'promote' the woman into the category of a mother. She argues that it is not really information (everyone knows what a foetus looks like) but rather is about manipulation.

REGRET AND ABORTION

A common argument in this context is that many women regret their abortion decisions, and that if only they were given better information they would be able to make a better choice. The data behind this claim are hotly disputed, with different surveys finding different levels of reported regret.[76]

One problem is with the meaning of 'regret'. While a study may show that some women regret the abortion, it may be unclear whether they are regretting becoming pregnant rather than regretting the abortion. Further, there is strong cultural conditioning that abortion is a sad event that is to be regretted. It would not be socially acceptable for a woman to say she found the abortion a positive experience. So the response to surveys may reflect what women think they are expected to say, rather than what they feel.[77]

Kate Greasley[78] has helpfully identified three different ways the 'regret' argument can be used:

1. It might be said that a woman should be warned she is likely to feel regret, and be given counselling and information to ensure her decision is informed.
2. The fact there are levels of regret indicates that women come to realise that they have made a morally bad choice. Although in theory a majority of women may think abortion is a morally neutral choice, among those who have undertaken the procedure high levels of regret indicate that many realise it is wrong.
3. The high levels of regret show that abortion is bad for women. The long-term feelings of guilt and remorse outweigh any short-term benefits.

Greasley rejects these arguments. She points out that it is wrong to assume that something that is regretted is an indication that a person felt something was immoral. Someone may regret a divorce without thinking the divorce was morally wrong. Often people are faced with two wrongs and may make the morally correct decision in choosing the lesser wrong, but quite properly regret

---

[76] D. Fergusson, J. Horwood and J. Boden, 'Reactions to abortion and subsequent mental health' (2009) 195 *British Journal of Psychology, General Section* 420.

[77] E. Dadlez and W. Andrews, 'Post-abortion syndrome: creating an affliction' (2010) 24 *Bioethics* 445.

[78] K. Greasley, 'Abortion and regret' (2012) 38 *Journal of Medical Ethics* 705.

they were in that dilemma. A police officer shooting dead an offender who was about to kill someone might regret the killing, without thinking they did the wrong thing. Further, a person may be harmed by something but not regret the decision. For example, Greasley claims, a woman may be psychologically scarred by giving birth, but not wish she had not given birth. She also points out that talking of regret about abortion does not consider the impact on the woman if she had proceeded to give birth. That might produce even higher levels of regret or mental ill-health than the abortion.[79]

CONCLUSION

Women with an unwanted pregnancy will have a wide range of wishes and needs in respect of what information they need and what level of counselling (if any). The dangers in setting down what information must be given is that women will be given information they do not need or want. Further, for some, the provision of 'information' may operate as emotional pressure, rather than actually providing knowledge. There is, therefore, much to be said in favour of allowing women to choose how much information, advice and counselling they need, rather than mandating that through the law.

FURTHER READING

Debate 1

A. Alghrani and B. Brazier, 'What is it? Whose is it? Repositioning the foetus in the context of research?' (2011) 70 *Cambridge Law Journal* 51.

F. Beckwith, *Defending Life: A Moral and Legal Case Against Abortion Choice* (Cambridge University Press, 2007).

D. Boonin, *A Defense of Abortion* (Cambridge University Press, 2002).

M. Fox and S. McGuinness, 'The science of muddling through: categorising embryos' in A. Mullock et al. (eds), *Pioneering Healthcare Law: Essays in Honour of Margaret Brazier* (Routledge, 2016).

A. Giubilini and F. Minerva, 'After-birth abortion: why should the baby live?' (2013) 39 *Journal of Medical Ethics* 261.

K. Greasley, *Arguments about Abortion* (Oxford University Press, 2017).

J. Herring, 'The loneliness of status: the legal and moral significance of birth' in F. Ebtehaj, J. Herring, M. Johnson and M. Richards (eds), *Birth Rites and Rights* (Hart Publishing, 2011).

C. Kaczor, *The Ethics of Abortion* (Routledge, 2011).

C. Mackenzie, 'Abortion and embodiment' (1992) 70 *Australasian Journal of Philosophy* 136.

M. Tooley, *Abortion and Infanticide* (Oxford University Press, 1983).

H. Watt, *The Ethics of Pregnancy, Abortion and Childbirth: Exploring Moral Choices in Childbearing* (Routledge, 2016).

---

[79] T. Kendall, V. Bird, R. Cantwell and C. Taylor, 'To meta-analyse or not to meta-analyse: abortion, birth and mental health' (2012) 200 *British Journal of Psychology* 12.

Debate 2

D. Boonin, *A Defense of Abortion* (Cambridge University Press, 2002).

R. Dworkin, *Life's Dominion* (HarperCollins, 1993).

J. Finnis, 'The rights and wrongs of abortion' (1973) 2 *Philosophy and Public Affairs* 117.

K. Greasley, 'Is sex-selective abortion against the law?' (2016) 36 *Oxford Journal of Legal Studies* 535.

K. Greasley and C. Kaczor, *Abortion Rights: For and Against* (Cambridge University Press, 2017).

J. Jarvis Thomson, 'A defense of abortion' (1971) 1 *Philosophy and Public Affairs* 47.

C. Kaczor, *The Ethics of Abortion* (Routledge, 2011).

B. Manninen, 'The value of choice and the choice to value: expanding the discussion about fetal life within prochoice advocacy' (2013) 28 *Hypatia* 663.

N. Priaulx, 'The social life of abortion law: on personal and political pedagogy' (2017) 25 *Medical Law Review* 73.

S. Sheldon, 'The decriminalisation of abortion: an argument for modernisation' (2016) 36 *Oxford Journal of Legal Studies* 334.

Debate 3

K. Greasley, 'Abortion and regret' (2012) 38 *Journal of Medical Ethics* 705.

M. Manian, 'The irrational woman: informed consent and abortion decision-making' (2009) 16 *Duke Journal of Gender Law & Policy* 223.

D. Mollen, 'Reproductive rights and informed consent: toward a more inclusive discourse' (2013) *Analyses of Social Issues and Public Policy* 1.

C. Sanger, 'Seeing and believing: mandatory ultrasound and the path to a protected choice' (2008) 56 *UCLA Law Review* 351.

S. Woodcock, 'Abortion counselling and the informed consent dilemma' (2011) 59 *Bioethics* 495.

CHAPTER 7

Organ Donation

The Current Law

Before some of the key issues in the debates over organ donation are examined, we will outline the law on organ donation in brief. Section 1 of the Human Tissue Act 2004 permits the removal, storage and use of organs for transplantation from a deceased person as long as there is 'appropriate consent'. The consent can be oral or in writing. If the deceased consented (most typically by signing up to the organ donation register) then that decision must be respected, so a family does not have the right to overrule the refusal of a patient to donate or a desire to donate. That does not mean that the doctors must use the organs of a person who has signed on the register. There may be good reasons why their organs are inappropriate. Or indeed the doctors are entitled to decide not to use the organs given the strong opposition of relatives.

If the deceased has not expressed a view on donation then the doctors should ascertain whether the deceased has nominated a representative to make decisions about the deceased's organs on death. If no view has been expressed and no one has been nominated as a representative, the person who stood in the closest 'qualifying relationship' to the deceased immediately before death can make the decision.[1] Section 27(4) of the 2004 Act ranks the qualifying relationships in the following order:

(a) spouse or partner;
(b) parent or child;
(c) brother or sister;
(d) grandparent or grandchild;
(e) child of a person falling within paragraph (c);
(f) stepfather or stepmother;
(g) half-brother or half-sister;
(h) friend of long standing.

The person who is highest up the list immediately before the death of the deceased can make the decision. It will be a criminal offence attracting a

---

[1] Human Tissue Act 2004 (HTAct 2004), s. 3(6).

maximum prison sentence of three years if a surgeon performs an organ trans-plant from a deceased person without the necessary consent.[2] However, it will be a defence if the surgeon concerned reasonably believed that the appropriate consent had been given.[3]

Debate 1
The interests of the dead

INTRODUCTION

What interests do you have once you have died? To some that might seem an odd question: surely, once you are dead you no longer exist and can have no interests. However, as we shall see, the issue is more complex than that. The question is relevant to a wide range of issues, from burial law to the retention of organs for research. However, for now our particular focus is on whether the person who is now dead can claim any particular inter-ests over their organs which could be used for transplantation. Why should their wishes not to donate, or to donate, have any weight now they are dead?

Notably, in the debates over organ donation it is nearly always assumed that the views of the deceased carry some weight. Even those in favour of compul-sory removal of organs on death feel the need to put forward arguments to justify this, implying there are some interests of the deceased involved which need to be outweighed, even if they are not substantial.

THE VIEW THAT A DEAD PERSON CANNOT BE HARMED

As already mentioned, a popular view is that once a person is dead they are no more, and so they cannot be harmed or wronged.[4] The argument is that interests can only be held by living things. Some people would limit that to humans, and others include animals. However, it would be generally agreed that hitting your friend is to seriously wrong them; to hit your computer is not to wrong the computer. That is because we do not (although who knows, maybe we will in the future!) believe computers have interests that are worthy of respect. They lack the capacity to experience things we think important, such as pain, pleasure and the like. Similarly, the argument goes, once a person is dead, their body falls into the category of inanimate things that cannot hold interests.

---

[2] HTAct 2004, s. 5(1) and (7).
[3] HTAct 2004, s. 5(1)(b).
[4] J. Callahan, 'On harming the dead' (1987) 97 *Ethics* 341; J. Harris, 'Law and regulation of retained organs: The ethical issues' (2002) 22 *Legal Studies* 237.

The View that a Dead Person can be Harmed

One argument is that people do have interests when alive which continue after they have died.[5] One way of showing that is to argue that we simply do care about what happens to us after we die and how we will be remembered. It is not uncommon for people to refer to their 'legacy'. Politicians are concerned how they will be regarded in history, philanthropists give large sums of money to have buildings named after them, parents pass on the family photograph album – all in an attempt to prolong and preserve their memories. However, the fact that people might believe they can be benefited or harmed after their death does not per se make their assessment correct. So, how can we give substance to the widespread assumption?

Narrative Theory

One view is that we should understand our lives as a story. Our lives are made up of a narrative, partly constructed by our own understandings, but also of others' interactions with and understandings of ourselves. These stories are central to our understandings of ourselves. The story of the self continues after death, and we are legitimately concerned with how the story ends. Masterton, Hansson and Höglund explain:[6]

> We understand ourselves in relation to others and to the outside world, the stories we tell ourselves, the stories we tell others about ourselves and the stories others tell about us. By telling our story, our identity is created and re-created and we look at ourselves through the other. Since personal identity is fragmented and is to be found in other people's narratives as well as one's own, no one can have complete access to their own narrative. Due to this entanglement of narratives, the creation and maintenance of one's identity is not something one can carry out in isolation. Upon death, much of the narrative is lost, but not all. Part of the person's narrative can be found in others and traces of their life can continue to link their story to the present.

Although, therefore, the body is dead, the narrative about the self continues, and hence the self can be harmed where the narrative is harmful. It is not necessary to buy into the whole 'narrative self' approach to be persuaded by this argument. Even if you separate the 'narrative self' from the 'real self', you can argue we have interests in the well-being both of our real self and of our narrative self. That is one reason why many people feel particularly strongly if they have been misunderstood or misrepresented. It could be claimed that even though the 'real self' ends at death, the 'narrative self' continues. Critics might

---

[5] W. Glannon, 'Persons, lives and posthumous harms' (2001) 32 *Journal of Social Philosophy* 127.

[6] M. Masterton, M. Hansson and A. Höglund, 'In search of the missing subject: narrative identity and posthumous wronging' (2010) 41 *Studies in History and Philosophy of Biological and Biomedical Sciences* 340, 346.

be willing to accept that we have an interest in the narrative identity while we are alive, but once we are dead there is no 'us' to be harmed. So the viability of the narrative line of argument is the extent to which the narrative self is sufficiently person-like to be capable of being wronged.[7]

Relational theory

According to relational theorists, the self is constituted through relationships with others.[8] What creates our identity and self-understanding is not to be understood in terms of us alone but by and through our relationships. People commonly define themselves by their relationships with others, be that as aunt, Arsenal Football Club supporter or anthropologist. From such a perspective, the self can continue though the practices and memories of those remaining. The treatment by a community of a deceased member is the ongoing aspect of the self. The person may have died, but the relationships of others to the corpse and the deceased have not.

To be clear, this view is not saying just that relatives have interests in how a body is treated. Rather, it is arguing that the separation of the interests of the deceased and of the relatives may be inappropriate. We have a community of individuals who have a collective interest in seeing that their dead are buried in accordance with the rituals and traditions of that community. Bob Brecher[9] writes, 'although dead, we do not cease entirely to be members of a particular community; and it is on that account that the dead can be said to have interests'. In a similar vein, Simona Giordano argues that:

> We experience some others (the significant others) as a part of ourselves. Even once the loved person is dead, she or he continues to be, in some important way 'my daughter' or 'my father'. This person belongs in some sense to the significant others.[10]

If this kind of argument were put in terms of the law, it might be expressed in terms of Article 8 rights.[11] Margaret Brazier explains:

> The image of the newly dead person remains fixed in the minds of most bereaved families. Mutilation of the body becomes a mutilation of that image. Reason may tell the family that a dead child could not suffer when organs were removed. Grief coupled with imagination may overpower reason. Families grieve differently just as they live their lives differently. Respect for family life requires respect for such differences.[12]

---

[7] M. Masterton, *Duties to Past Persons: Moral Standing and Posthumous Interests of Old Human Remains* (Uppsala University, 2010).

[8] K. Gergen, *Relational Being* (Oxford University Press, 2009).

[9] B. Brecher, 'Our obligations to the dead' (2002) 19 *Journal of Applied Philosophy* 109, 113.

[10] S. Giordano, 'Is the body a republic?' (2005) 31 *Journal of Medical Ethics* 470, 471.

[11] European Convention on Human Rights, Art. 8 (Right to respect for private and family life).

[12] M. Brazier, 'Retained organs: ethics and humanity' (2002) 22 *Legal Studies* 550, 566.

Religious rights

Many of those who have concerns about how their body will be treated after death have religious faith. They may argue that they believe in an afterlife and that a person's soul or essence continues, and so believe that a person can be harmed after death. That is a matter of faith because no one can prove that there is an afterlife. That creates a difficulty for the law, because it would not want to be seen taking sides in such a dispute. What might justify a response of the law that the dead have no interests, however, is that *if* there is an afterlife, it is beyond our imagining and the law cannot engage with those existing in its jurisdiction. In other words, any afterlife must be outside the remit of the law. So, in so far as there may be souls or other post-death forms of existence, they are outside the scope of the law. The law can therefore assume that, for the purposes for which the law operates, there is no 'person' once they are dead, while being neutral on the question of an afterlife.

Other arguments based on religious rights might be made. As Brazier also points out, a number of religions, especially Judaism and Islam, require respect for the integrity of the dead body.[13] To ignore those wishes is to infringe the rights to respect for religious belief under Article 9 of the European Convention on Human Rights.[14] Brazier explains the seriousness of the issue:

> Relatives of people whose organs were removed without consent have expressed to me fears that at the Resurrection their beloved husband or father will not be resurrected because he was not buried whole. Or he will endure eternity disfigured and disabled. It is easy to mock such beliefs from an atheist, agnostic or 'liberal' viewpoint. The pain such a belief must produce is acute and life-destroying.[15]

John Harris forcefully rejects attaching weight to such beliefs:

> [T]he complaints of those who object to actions that violate the physical integrity of the corpse are scarcely rational. Illusions are fine, but whether the State and the Courts should give judicial or official support to these illusions is more doubtful, particularly when to do so might deprive others of life saving therapies.[16]

Brazier and McGuiness of course accept Harris's right to consider such religious views as 'illusions' and irrational; however, they argue that the state must respect religious difference. They explain:[17]

> Freedom of conscience and freedom of religion are considered important features of most liberal democracies. They are important because they allow us to be the

---

[13] S. McGuiness and M. Brazier, 'Respecting the living means respecting the dead too' (2008) 28 *Oxford Journal of Legal Studies* 297.

[14] European Convention on Human Rights, Art. 9 (Freedom of thought, conscience and religion).

[15] M. Brazier, 'Retained organs: ethics and humanity' (2002) 22 *Legal Studies* 550, 561.

[16] J. Harris, 'Law and regulation of retained organs: the ethical issues' (2002) 22 *Legal Studies* 237, 238.

[17] S. McGuiness and M. Brazier, 'Respecting the living means respecting the dead too' (2008) 28 *Oxford Journal of Legal Studies* 297, 304.

authors of our own lives … If we want to take steps to curtail individual freedoms, we must move cautiously, even if we believe that the overall benefit will be large.

Harris was probably overstating his case. It seems implausible that we would pay no attention to a person's beliefs when they were deceased. As Brazier and McGuiness point out, no one would suggest that we use human bodies as dog meat. A more plausible case is that the interests of others (e.g. those needing organs) may trump the weight attached to protection of religious belief. Harris argues:

> If we can save or prolong the lives of living people and can only do so at the expense of the sensibilities of others, it seems clear to me that we should. For the alternative involves the equivalent of sacrificing people's lives so that others will simply *feel* better or not feel so bad, and this seems nothing short of outrageous.[18]

There is a further issue, and that is whether religious beliefs should be accorded more weight than other beliefs about organ donation. So should the beliefs of a person that organ donation is 'yucky' carry weight, or are they to be ignored? That raises larger issues over the appropriate protection for religious belief than we can discuss here.

The interests of living people

Perhaps the most popular way of putting the argument that it is possible to harm people who have died is to argue that we should respect the wishes deceased people had while they were alive. What happens to us when we die can therefore harm the interest we have while alive in how our dead bodies are to be treated. Joel Feinberg puts it this way:

> All interests are the interest of some person or other, and a person's surviving interests are simply the ones that we identify by naming *him*, the person whose interests they were. He is of course at this moment dead, but that does not prevent us from referring now, in the present tense, to his interests, if they are still capable of being blocked or fulfilled, just as we refer to his outstanding debts or claims, if they are still capable of being paid. The final tally book on a person's life is not closed until some time after his death.[19]

Feinberg indicates the kind of interests that are most likely to be infringed as 'the desire to maintain a good reputation, … the desire that some social or political cause triumph, or the desire that one's loved ones flourish'.[20] So when a person is 'wronged' after death, this is not a wrong to the corpse or some

---

[18] J. Harris, *Wonderwoman and Superman. The Ethics of Human Biotechnology* (Oxford University Press, 1992), 1.

[19] J. Feinberg, *The Moral Limits of the Criminal Law. Harm to Others* (Oxford University Press, 1984), 83.

[20] Ibid.

ongoing nature of the self, as the narrative or relational understandings would have it, but a wrong to the living person they once were. Ronald Dworkin states:

> It makes sense to say that people who are now dead or permanently unconscious still have interests. We mean that their lives will have been more successful if the interests they formed while alive and conscious flourish when they are unconscious or dead.[21]

One way to think about this is that we can be harmed by things of which we are unaware. A person who is sexually assaulted while they are asleep and a person who is unaware that they have been defrauded are harmed, even if they are not conscious of what has happened.[22] A person who wanted to write a book that changed the way people thought about a certain issue would have their interests advanced even if they died before the book was published and acclaimed. George Pitcher argues that a person is harmed if their interests or desires are severely set back.[23] For those whose interests and desires relate to things that happen after their death, they can be harmed if those interests and desires are subsequently ignored.[24] So the author writing the book then has interests that the book is a success. If after the author's death the publishers refuse to publish the book, the interests the author had when alive and writing the book have been set back. Critics[25] suggest this is backwards causation: an event post-death cannot cause a setback of interests the person had while alive. As you can imagine, the philosophical debates continue, with little consensus emerging.[26]

It may help in this debate to consider the distinction made by Josie Fisher[27] between transcendent and personal interests. Some interests we have depend on our experiencing them; these are personal interests. I might hope to cook a delicious meal for myself. That plan can only succeed if I am there to experience it. If I fell ill and could not eat the meal, I would have failed. However, other interests, for example that my children thrive or that more people recognise the merits of feminism, might be independent of my experiencing them. I want my children and feminism to thrive whether I am there to see them or not. These are transcendent interests. On this approach, while a person's death will mean their personal interests can no longer be harmed, their transcendent interests may be.

---

[21] R. Dworkin, *Life's Dominion* (Vintage, 1990), 33.

[22] T. Wilkinson, 'Respect for the dead and the ethics of anatomy' (2014) 27 *Clinical Anatomy* 286.

[23] G. Pitcher, 'The misfortunes of the dead' in J. Fischer (ed.), *The Metaphysics of Death* (Stanford University Press, 1993).

[24] J. Stacey Taylor, 'Harming the dead' (2008) 33 *Journal of Philosophical Research* 185.

[25] J. Callahan, 'On harming the dead' (1987) 97 *Ethics* 97.

[26] D. Sperling, *Posthumous Interests: Legal and Ethical Perspectives* (Cambridge University Press, 2008).

[27] J. Fisher, 'Harming and benefiting the dead' (2001) 25 *Death Studies* 557.

Scenario to ponder

Tom was born into an orthodox Jewish family. Although he loves his family very much, he does not practise his faith. He tells his friends that he hopes when he dies, his body can be used for research. When he dies his family want to bury the body in line with Jewish tradition. They say they will be distraught if they cannot do that, and that Tom would never have wanted to cause his family pain. What should be done to his body when he dies?

CONCLUSION

While there is a widespread intuition that we should respect the wishes of the deceased about what happens to their body, it has been hard to explain precisely why that is so. Although there are problems with each of the arguments in favour of doing so, it may be that taken together they form a powerful case to give weight to the views of the deceased in deciding what to do with their organs.

Debate 2
Consent and organ donation

As we have seen in Debate 1, most people accept that the views of the deceased person play an important role in deciding what should happen to their organs on their death. The current law reflects this by requiring would-be donors to explicitly opt in. They must sign up to the donor transplant list. However, there have been many calls for the law to be reformed. Many of these are motivated by concerns that insufficient organs become available to meet the number of people who need transplants. Official figures suggest that, by March 2013, there were 7,332 patients on the 'waiting list' for organ transplants. Unfortunately, in 2012–13, 466 died and 766 people were removed from the list, usually because they had become too ill to receive a transplant. Others will have died without even reaching the waiting list.[28] There has been a 20 per cent increase in the waiting time for a new donated kidney since 2010, despite increasing rates of donation. To be blunt, many people die because of the shortage of organs. This has been described as a 'terrible and unnecessary tragedy'.[29] It raises a fierce debate over the extent to which we should presume consent, or even dispense with a requirement that donors consent.

We will now consider some of the ways that we might deal with the consent of the deceased.

---

[28] NHS Blood and Transplant, *Organ Donation: Statistics* (NHS, 2013).

[29] J. Harris, 'Organ procurement: dead interests, living needs' (2003) 31 *Journal of Medical Ethics* 242, 242.

Opt In

This is the current system. The individual has the burden of registering their wish to donate organs. Without their consent (or consent of their families), a donation is not possible. This is similar to the general rule in medical law. A doctor cannot touch a patient without consent or other legal authorisation.

Supporters of the current approach might share concerns over the shortage of organs but would see the solution in making it easier for people to register their organs and finding ways of encouraging them to do so.[30] Certainly in the UK, much has been done to make it easier for people to register their wish to donate their organs. For example, there is an easy-to-use website to register your wishes.[31] Some might argue in favour of incentives to register. This could include giving priority to those who need organs, and even tax advantages. These would be controversial and might not be effective in increasing the number of organs.

Opt In: Mandated Choice

One version of the opt-in approach which appeals to some is 'mandated choice'. This requires people to indicate whether or not they wish to donate. This deals with one of the concerns about the opt-in method, namely, that some people who have not opted in might, if they had got round to it, have wished to donate. Indeed, if you think we should attach significant weight to the views of the deceased, it is the best way of knowing what they wanted, rather than having to guess.

There would be some practical difficulties. How could we make sure that everyone had registered their choice? This might not be as difficult as imagined. We might, for example, require all people registering with their doctor to state their preference as regards organ donation. Currently all those applying for a driving licence must answer a question about organ donation. So we are already quite close to a mandated choice system anyway. A rather different concern is that the costs of administrating the system will exceed any benefits that might come from it.

There are two practical issues which are tricky. The first is to what extent we should give people choice beyond the simple 'yes' or 'no' to donation. Should we have an 'undecided' box? Or 'I leave it up to my family?'. The latter in particular seems a reasonable choice that some people might wish to make. The point is that if the organ donation issue is to place significant weight on autonomy and the right of people to choose what happens to their body, these choices may not be readily reduced to a 'yes' or 'no' answer. Perhaps the answer for supporters of mandated donation is simply to provide a 'yes' or

---

[30] A. Vincent and L. Logan, 'Consent for organ donation' (2013) 108 *British Journal of Anaesthesia* 80.

[31] NHS Blood and Transplant, *Organ Donation*, available at www.organdonation.nhs.uk.

'no' choice, or a box for people to respond otherwise. No doubt most will use either 'yes' or 'no'.

A second question is what to do about people who change their mind after they have made their choice. Arrangements could easily be made for those who wish to change their option once registered. Harder may be cases where a person made their choice many years ago but their current lifestyle indicates that they have changed their views (e.g. they recently joined a religious group which opposes organ donations, although they had previously registered no objection). One response is that the burden is on people to correct their choices if they change their mind, or we might have a procedure where clear evidence of a change of heart could override the stated wish. It does not seem that these difficulties are sufficient to oppose the mandated choice proposal.

A final, principled objection is that people should not be forced to make a choice if they do not want to. Respect for autonomy should include allowing a person not to choose. Again, we might be able to get round this by giving people a third blank box in which to enter their comments. Alternatively, it might be said that being compelled to tick one box or another is a very minor infringement of personal liberty and that the good results of the system justify this.

OPT OUT

Another proposal is to move to an opt-out system. It has received much support, including from the British Medical Association (BMA).[32] In Wales, the Human Transplant (Wales) Act 2013 created an opt-out system. In October 2017 Prime Minister Theresa May indicated she supported a presumption in favour of consent. But what arguments are there to support a presumption of consent to organ donation?

Presumed consent

Some support an opt-out system on the basis that it is a reasonable guess that people who do not express a view wish to donate their organs. The argument is most commonly made by reference to a number of surveys of public opinion which indicate that, while a majority of people would want to donate organs on their death, only a minority get round to it.[33] In other words, the current opt-in system often defeats people's wishes and in fact undermines their autonomy. If we moved to an opt-out system, there might be some whose wishes would also be defeated (those who would not wish to donate but had not got round to opting out) but they would be smaller in number. So it is claimed that an opt-out system has the benefit of ensuring that more people's wishes are met and that more organs are available for donation.

---

[32] BMA, *Organ Donation* (BMA, 2009).
[33] See J. Herring, *Medical Law and Ethics* (Oxford University Press, 2013), Chapter 8, for a summary of these.

Critics may reply that 'presumed' consent is a nonsense. Normally, in medical law, consent requires a positive assent from the patient and silence will not do. However, it might be noted that silence can be taken as consent in other contexts. It is not unusual at a business meeting for the chair to say, 'We will take the proposal as supported unless anyone objects'; or when taking a vote to ask those who object to raise their hands, those who do not being taken to support the proposal. Opponents will reply that when we are dealing with an issue as important as organ donation, we should be strict about what is taken as consent, and it is too dangerous to allow inactivity to indicate consent.

Govert den Hartogh[34] argues that as long as consenters are informed of the meaning of their silence and that the costs of registering dissent are insignificant, an opt-out system is justifiable. Notably, in his view consent should be seen not as a state of mind but as a public act. So seen, as long as the meaning of the act is well publicised, a person cannot complain if it does not meet their genuine consent, any more than a person who gets into a taxi and asks to be taken somewhere cannot complain that they did not intend to promise to pay for the ride and did not realise how taxis work.

Opponents of an opt-out scheme may raise this question: 'Which is worse: the harm to those who, under the opt-in system, wish to donate and fail to register, or the harm to those who, under an opt-out system, would wish to object to donation but have failed to do so?' Both systems have the potential for an 'error' (i.e. a person whose assumed wishes do not accord with their actual wishes).[35] Some argue that both cases are equally bad because they have both involved someone's wishes not being met.[36] But we would not necessarily say the same about a living person. Consider the difference between wanting a nose piercing but not being able to find anyone who will pierce your nose, and not wanting a nose piercing but it being forced upon you. Both interfere in your autonomy in the sense of not allowing you to do what you want with your body, but most agree the second scenario is worse. That is because many people feel that a breach of autonomy accompanied by an interference in their bodies is worse than just a breach of autonomy on its own.

Moral obligation

A different argument is that we should assume that people consent because that is the morally correct thing to do. A range of arguments might be drawn on to make such a moral claim, but many will centre on the argument that for a minimal cost to yourself, you can save a person's life, and so that is a good

---

[34] G. den Hartogh, 'Tacitly consenting to donate one's organs' (2011) 37 *Journal of Medical Ethics* 344.

[35] A.-M. Jacob, 'Another look at the presumed-versus-informed consent dichotomy in post-mortem organ procurement' (2006) 20 *Bioethics* 293.

[36] D. Wilkinson and J. Savulescu, 'Should we allow organ donation euthanasia? Alternatives for maximizing the number and quality of organs for transplantation' (2012) 26 *Bioethics* 32.

thing to do. The argument may then be that if you wish to act 'immorally', the burden should be on you to make this clear. The difficulty with this is that we do not normally assume that people consent to something just because that is the right thing to do. It is morally good to give money to help the starving in developing countries, but we do not have a system where people's money is taken from them and given to good causes without their consent. Indeed, there might be a broader concern with such an approach. If people are forced or pressurised into doing good, we deprive people of the chance of being virtuous.

The interests of the dead and the living

Another way to support an opt-out system would be to question whether much weight should attach to the interests of the dead. We have looked at some of the arguments on this in Debate 1. You might conclude that once someone has died, they have no interests, in which case you would probably support a system allowing donation, regardless of the view of the deceased. However, you might take the view that on death a person has interests but these are very limited, and only rarely would using someone's organs without their consent be a serious wrong. So if a person's fundamental beliefs were involved, that might justify attaching sufficient weight to their views to mean their organs could not be used; but if it was just a casual preference or indifference, this would be insufficient. If that was your view, you might then argue that if a person has a strong belief of the kind you would regard sufficient to mean their organs should not be used, they would register their objection. You might accept that some who do not register would oppose the use of their organs, but reasonably assume that their views could not be strongly held.

Practical considerations

Most supporters of the opt-out scheme would accept there would need to be extensive publicity and education so that people would understand the scheme. They accept we would want to reduce the number of people who did not consent, but did not register, to as small a number as possible. Otherwise there is a danger that the scheme would fall into disrepute. Indeed, the Organ Donation Taskforce was concerned that an opt-out scheme might create mistrust between patients and clinical staff,[37] and expressed the concern that if patients ceased to trust the system, this would lead to large numbers opting out, and even reducing the number of organs available.[38]

---

[37] Organ Donation Taskforce, *The Potential Impact of an Opt Out System for Organ Donation in the UK* (TSO, 2008).

[38] See R. Rieu, 'The potential impact of an opt-out system for organ donation in the UK' (2010) 36 *Journal of Medical Ethics* 534, for criticism of the Taskforce's report.

Belgium, Italy and Greece have all moved to an opt-out scheme, and this has increased the number of organs available for transplant.[39] However, the link between an opt-out scheme and increasing organ donation rates is not as straightforward as might at first appear. It is true that in some countries the increase has been dramatic.[40] But when Austria moved to an opt-out scheme, this had little impact on the number of donations.[41] A move to an opt-out scheme may therefore only have a noticeable impact on donation rates if it has the support of medical professionals and the general public. Noticeably, Spain has dramatically increased its rate of organ donors without moving to an opt-out scheme, through education and publicity about the importance of organ donation.[42]

MANDATORY DONATION

The most radical option for reform would be to argue that we should take the organs of the deceased if appropriate for transplantation, regardless of their views. This proposal has been called 'cadaveric conscription'.[43] This would appeal to those who believe that once a person is dead, their wishes count for nothing. Antonia Cronin and John Harris reject claims that consent from the deceased is required for organ donation:

> When I am dead I have lost the capacity that it is the point of autonomy and the law to protect. I am no longer able to think critically about preferences, desires or wishes. I am no longer able to make choices. 'I' no longer exist.[44]

However, as we have seen (see Debate 1), that may be a little extreme. Most people would feel that if a person died asking to be buried at a particular place or in line with certain religious traditions, we would need some kind of reason not to comply with their wishes. So a more moderate version can be made, namely that the wishes of the deceased carry a little weight, but not much. If their organs will save a life, the claims of those needing the transplantation will readily outweigh the interests we would place on the views of the deceased.

Harris notes that we are already willing to override the wishes of the deceased about what happens to their bodies in some contexts. For example,

---

[39] Z. Hawley, D. Li and K. Schnier, 'Increasing organ donation via changes in the default choice or allocation rule' (2013) 32 *Journal of Health Economics* 1117.

[40] P. Chouhan and H. Draper, 'Modified mandated consent for organ procurement' (2003) 29 *Journal of Medical Ethics* 157.

[41] B. New, M. Solomon and R. Dingwall, *A Question of Give and Take* (King's Fund Institute, 1994).

[42] V. English and A. Sommerville, 'Presumed consent for transplantation: a dead issue after Alder Hey' (2003) 29 *Journal of Medical Ethics* 147.

[43] A. Spital, 'Conscription of cadaveric organs for transplantation: a stimulating idea whose time has not yet come' (2005) 14 *Cambridge Quarterly of Healthcare Ethics* 107.

[44] A. Cronin and J. Harris, 'Authorisation, altruism and compulsion in the organ donation debate' (2010) 36 *Journal of Medical Ethics* 627, 628.

post-mortems can be carried out on a cadaver, whatever the views of the person when they were alive. Harris questions whether the public interest in post-mortems being performed is necessarily greater than having organs available for transplant. He emphasises that if an organ can be used to save life, we need a very strong reason not to use it:

> [T]here is almost universal agreement that death is usually the worst harm that can befall a human person who wants to live. … [R]ights or interests would have to be extremely powerful to warrant upholding such rights or interests at the cost of the lives of others. … [T]he interests involved after death are simply nowhere near strong enough [to justify doing this].[45]

We looked at the arguments over the interests of the deceased in Debate 1 and will not repeat them all here. One objection raised there was religious rights, and it is interesting that even some supporters of compulsory conscription of cadaveric organs accept the need for an exception where there are strong religious objections.[46] That might blur the line between a conscription system and an opt-out one. It would require a case to be made for why objections based on religious views were given more weight than non-religious objections, and would give rise to difficult questions over the definition of a religion.

Most of the writing in favour of mandatory donation has based its support on the fact that the deceased has no interest in the organ. But a stronger argument may be made, that society has a positive claim on the organ.

It may be argued that simply asserting that the deceased has no claim to the organs is not enough to make the case for allowing the organs to be removed by the state. Robert Truog argues that human organs of a deceased should be regarded as a societal resource.[47] Giordano,[48] likewise, claims that a useable cadaveric organ should be seen as a 'public thing'. Neither writer puts forward a particular set of arguments as to why that should be so regarded, beyond the fact that they are needed by the NHS to treat patients. Jonathan Herring and P-L. Chau[49] point to the interdependency between bodies and the wider environment, to make a case for there being a communal nature between bodies, and that line of argument might be developed to explain why wider society should have a claim to an organ. Cécile Fabre[50] relies on the principle

---

[45] J. Harris, 'Organ procurement: dead interests, living needs' (2003) 29 *Journal of Medical Ethics* 130, 132.

[46] A. Spital, 'Conscription of cadaveric organs for transplantation: a stimulating idea whose time has not yet come' (2005) 14 *Cambridge Quarterly of Healthcare Ethics* 107.

[47] R. Truog, 'Are organs personal property or a societal resource?' (2005) 5 *American Journal of Bioethics* 14.

[48] S. Giordano, 'Is the body a republic?' (2005) 31 *Journal of Medical Ethics* 470.

[49] J. Herring and P-L. Chau, 'My body, your body, our bodies' (2007) 15 *Medical Law Review* 34.

[50] C. Fabre, *Whose Body is it Anyway?: Justice and the Integrity of the Person* (Clarendon Press, 2006).

of sufficiency, which means that people who lack the requirements for a minimally flourishing life have a claim to resources owned by those who have more than they need for a minimally flourishing life. So the deceased has no need for their organs, while the person in need does.[51]

A further benefit of the mandatory donation model would be cost and ease of use. There would be no need to create and monitor a register, or to have procedures to deal with problematic cases.

CONCLUSION

This controversial debate raises some major issues. These include the weight that should be attached to the wishes of a person once they are dead; the extent to which the law should encourage, presume or even enforce altruism; and the nature and strength of the claims of those who need organs. Those who emphasise the importance of individual control over their bodies and rights of self-determination are likely to support an opt-in system. Those who emphasise the importance of responsibilities to fellow citizens and the communal good will prefer an opt-out or even mandatory donation model.

Debate 3

Directed donation

If you donate an organ in England and Wales, the NHS will arrange for it to be transplanted into the person at the top of the waiting list (provided it is compatible). While there might be arguments about how we decide the priorities of the waiting list, its use is generally taken for granted. But should we allow donors to decide who should get an organ? Maybe they would rather their organ go to a member of their family than to the person who is on top of the list? Maybe they would rather the organ go to a member of their religious faith or to someone who lives in their town? How should we treat the wishes of such a donor? Does it matter whether the donor is living or deceased? These are some of the questions examined in this section.

THE CURRENT LAW

All donations of organs must take place under the auspices of the NHS in England and Wales. Making arrangements for a private donation is forbidden.[52] There is a major distinction between donation from the deceased and donation from a person who is alive.

---

[51] W. Glannon, 'The case against conscription of cadaveric organs for transplantation' (2006) 17 *Cambridge Quarterly of Healthcare Ethics* 330.
[52] Human Tissue Act 2004.

Directed donation and the deceased

The current approach of the NHS is clear. In its question and answer sheet on organ and tissue donation, its response to the question 'Can I agree to donate to some people and not to others?'[53] is:

> No. Organs and tissue cannot be accepted unless they are freely donated. No absolute conditions can be attached in terms of potential recipients. The only restriction allowed is which organs or tissue are to be donated.

The Human Tissue Authority guidance is less straightforward and states:

> No organ should be transplanted under a form of consent which seeks to impose restrictions on the class of recipient of the organ, including any restriction based on a recipient's gender, race, colour, language, religion, political or other opinion, national or social origin, association with a national minority, property, birth or other status (including characteristics protected under the Equality Act 2010).[54]

Notably, this seems to permit, or at least not forbid, conditions which are not dependent on a 'status'. Would it be possible to, for example, leave an organ only for those who are members of the Benedict Cumberbatch fan club?

Organs are only distributed according to a set of criteria which create a waiting list. The NHS explains on which grounds it is decided where organs from the deceased should be placed:

> Many things need to match or be very close to ensure a successful organ transplant. Blood group, age and weight are all taken into account. For kidneys another important factor is tissue type which is much more complex than blood grouping. The best results can be achieved if a perfect match is found.
>
> There is a national, computerised list of patients waiting for an organ transplant. The computer will identify the best matched patient for an organ or the transplant unit to which the organ is to be offered. Normally, priority is given to patients who most urgently need a transplant. NHSBT[55] operates the transplant list and donor organ allocation system. It works round the clock, every day of the year and covers the whole of the UK.
>
> The aim of the system is to ensure that the allocation of organs is carried out in a fair and unbiased way.[56]

---

[53] NHS, *Organ and Tissue Donation – Your Questions Answered* (NHS, 2012).

[54] Human Tissue Authority (2017) *Donation of Solid Organs and Tissue for Transplantation* (HTA), 8. The reference to the Equality Act would include conditions based on age and sexuality.

[55] NHSBT stands for the organisation NHS Blood and Transplant.

[56] NHS, *Patient Selection and Organ Donation* (NHS, 2010).

Despite the apparently clear policy against directed donation, the views of the deceased can be taken into account, as long as they are not imposed as strict conditions. The NHS explains:[57]

> The fundamental principle of all deceased organ donation is that donation must be unconditional and free of financial reward. However, there are circumstances where a deceased organ donor has a relative or friend of long standing who is in need of an organ to whom they would have wished to allocate their organ. In these cases, it is possible for the family to request allocation of an organ to a named individual although the consent for organ donation must be unconditional.

In deciding whether to take the donor's views into account, the following factors are considered:[58]

- that there is appropriate consent/authorisation to deceased donor organ donation;
- that the consent or authorisation for organ donation is not conditional on the request for the allocation of a donor organ to the specified relative or friend of long standing going ahead;
- that there are no others in desperately urgent clinical need of the organ … who may be harmed by the organ being allocated to a named individual;
- that in life the deceased had indicated a wish to donate to a specific named relative or friend of long standing in need of an organ; or, in the absence of that indication, the family of the deceased expresses such a wish;
- that the specific named relative or friend of long standing is on the transplant waiting list or could be considered to be placed on the waiting list in line with 2005 Directions to NHS Blood and Transplant as amended or subsequent directions;
- that the need for a transplant is clinically indicated for the intended recipient.

So, while a person cannot require that their organs be given to a particular person, they can express a preference as to whom they would like to receive the organ; and if that person is high up the list and closely associated with the donor, then the donor's preference might be taken into account and mean that that person will receive the organ.

Directed donation and the living

In the case of living donors, it is common for donations to be directed. Indeed, we have almost the flip-side position of the approach to deceased donors. Where, as a living donor, you wish to donate to a person in a special relationship with you, the process is relatively straightforward, as long as: the donation is clinically appropriate; there is full consent; there is no reward; and there is approval from the Human Tissue Authority (HTA). Where, however, the

---

[57] Ibid.
[58] NHS, *Patient Selection and Organ Donation* (NHS, 2010).

donation is to a stranger, or for the use of anyone, there appears a degree of mistrust surrounding the donation. A full mental health assessment is required, something not needed if the donation is to a family member. Counselling and referral to a committee of the HTA is required before the donation can be accepted.[59]

What the law requires

Although we have set out the position as stated by the NHS, Antonia Cronin and James Douglas have mounted a spirited attack on its legal basis. First, as they argue, the Human Tissue Act 2004 itself does not rule out conditional donations. This is clearly correct. The NHS rejection of conditional donation is not, therefore, a legal requirement but rather a policy-based or ethical approach.

Second, they argue that if a condition has been attached to an organ, to use the organ without regard to that consent may be unlawful. The Guidance to the Human Tissue Act 2004 is somewhat opaque on whether an organ can be used if a person attempts to make a directed donation.[60] One reading is that the attempted direction should be treated as a preference, rather than as a direction. Cronin and Douglas argue that the Human Tissue Act requires consent, which in the case of a deceased person means 'a decision of his to consent to the activity, or a decision of his not to consent to it' in force immediately before he died. This definition does not prohibit conditional donations. Indeed the authors note that in paragraph 105, the Human Tissue Authority Code on consent states:

Consent can be:

- General, i.e. if someone consents to the use of tissue for research, it need not be limited to a particular object
- Specific, i.e. a person limits their consent – a sample can only be used for research into a particular condition
- Both general and specific, i.e. a general consent subject to specific exceptions.[61]

Cronin and Douglas argue:

The conclusion from this interpretation of consent is clear but disconcerting. If a donor's consent has been limited to specific situations, it follows that any allocation of organs contrary to such limitations vitiates that consent and amounts to dealing with the organs without consent.[62]

---

[59] A. Cronin and J. Douglas, 'Directed and conditional deceased donor organ donations: law and misconceptions' (2010) 18 *Medical Law Review* 275.

[60] NHS, *Requested Allocation of A Deceased Donor Organ* (NHS, 2010), 2.

[61] Human Tissue Authority, *Consent* (2009).

[62] A. Cronin and J. Douglas, 'Directed and conditional deceased donor organ donations: law and misconceptions' (2010) 18 *Medical Law Review* 275, 285.

One possible way around this conclusion might be to distinguish between a condition precedent (this organ is a gift to these people only) and a condition subsequent (I want to donate my organs; I would like to donate to X but if that is not possible then anyone can use them). The difficulty is that in many cases it will be difficult to know which of these two views the deceased will have. If the medical team is acting unlawfully unless there is effective consent, it will want to ensure there is proper consent. It is not surprising, however, given the shortage of organs, that if there is a donation, even one that seeks to impose a condition, those involved may try to find a way to use the organ. Cronin and Douglas's point is that doing so may breach the law. Whether it does requires a careful analysis of what it was the donor would want. If they had been aware that their directed donation was not permitted, would they be willing for their donation to be treated as an unrestricted donation, with a preference, or would they rather have had the donation rejected? It is likely that most people would prefer their wish to be treated as a preference, so at least there would be a chance that their request would be met. Key, perhaps, is whether this is a case where the person's primary wish is that a particular person receive their organ, in which case they may prefer their wish to be treated as a preference, or whether their primary motivation is that certain people should *not* receive an organ, for example the racist condition. In such a case, it seems more plausible that the donor would rather the organ went to no one if their condition might not be met.

ETHICAL PRINCIPLES

In the ethical debates over directed donation a number of themes emerge.

Altruism

The NHS explains the reason against conditional donation in this way:

> It is a fundamental principle of the UK donation programme that organs are freely and unconditionally given. Consent or authorisation for organ donation must not be conditional on their request for the allocation of a donor organ to the donor's specified relative or friend going ahead. Conditionality offends against the fundamental principle that organs are donated altruistically and should go to patients according to the agreed criteria.[63]

Much of this reasoning is circular. Telling us that unconditional donation is required because there is a principle that organs should be given unconditionally is merely restating the argument and does not provide a justification for it. The primary argument of substance is that organs should be given altruistically.

---

[63] NHS, *Requested Allocation of A Deceased Donor Organ* (NHS, 2010), 2.

This argument could also be challenged in a number of ways. First, we might question why the altruism is important, or at least sufficiently important to restrict directed donation. Generally, if someone is doing something good, we would not normally stop them because their motivation is bad. So a person saving a drowning child should not be prevented from doing so because they are motivated by a wish to claim a reward. Similarly, if a person wishes to donate an organ which will save a life, should it matter whether we approve of their motivation or not? Even if we might think it better that people donate organs altruistically, it is not clear that we should *prohibit* those who do not.

Second, the argument rests on the questionable assumption that someone giving an organ to someone other than a friend or family is not acting altruistically. Many people make sacrifices for friends or families in many ways, or give charitable donations to particular groups. It is not clear that they are more or less altruistic than a person who gives money to the government, asking that it be spent in a good cause.[64] Indeed, it might be argued that donating to those with whom we are in a close relationship reflects the value and importance of those relationships to recipients. It reflects our personal and social identity.[65]

Even if you were persuaded that those donating to 'the person in greatest need' were more altruistic than a person donating to their cousin who needed a transplant, is there is a sufficient difference in the degree of altruism to make a significant moral difference? Or to bar the donation altogether?

Impartial justice

One principle that is relied upon to justify the NHS policy is that organs should be distributed by the state in a way which is fair.[66] The argument is that donated organs are a very valuable resource, and we should provide them on an impartial basis to the person at the top of the waiting list. There would, quite rightly, be an outcry if the committee determining the allocation of organs decided to give the organ to a relative of one of its members rather than to the person most in need. That would be seen as manifestly unfair. Is it any different if the donor is seeking to determine who gets the organs? People should not 'jump the queue' because they know the right people.[67]

There was, for example, an outcry in the US when it was believed that a celebrity baseball player, Mickey Mantle, was moved up the list because of his fame.[68]

---

[64] J. Blustein, *Care and Commitment: Taking the Personal Point of View* (Oxford University Press, 1991).

[65] M. Hilhorst, 'Directed altruistic living organ donation: partial, but not unfair' (2004) 8 *Ethical Theory and Moral Practice* 197.

[66] T. Wilkinson, 'Impartiality, acquisition, and allocation' in T. Wilkinson (ed.), *Ethics and the Acquisition of Organs* (Oxford University Press, 2011).

[67] A. Caplan, S. Zink and S. Wertlieb, 'Jumping to the front of the line for an organ transplant is unfair' *Chicago Tribune*, 1 September 2004.

[68] D. Hanto, 'Ethical challenges posed by the solicitation of deceased and living organ donors' (2007) 356 *New England Journal of Medicine* 1062.

One way to question the justice argument is to ask whether the person who would receive the organ if the direction was ignored has any kind of right or interest in the organ. Were they deprived of something to which they should have been entitled?

Imagine a case, clearly simplified, where there were five people on the list ranked in this way: A, B, C, D, E. If a person died who had made a conditional donation for person E, would A (or indeed any of the others above E) be able to complain that they had been treated unfairly? Do those above E have a specific claim to the organ?[69]

Guido Pennings offers this analysis:

> All persons ranked higher on the list than the person who receives the organ after conditional donation are harmed compared to the situation they would be in if no conditions had been attached to the donation. The first person on the list is harmed most since he or she would normally have received the organ. Those following would have moved up one place. The interests of the people higher up are thwarted or impeded without actually being set back.[70]

The difficulty in making this argument is that it needs to be shown that A has a claim to the organ. Yet that seems hard to make out. A cannot claim a right to a particular organ. At most the claim would have to be that the state put in place a reasonable system for allocating organs and that it is followed. So the claim is not so much that directed donation deprives a particular person of an organ to which they had a claim, but rather that the state failed to deal fairly with those in need of organs by allowing directed donation.

Shaun Pattinson argues:

> A directed donation changes the position of the specified recipient in the sense of removing any opposition based on the rights or interests of the donor or representatives, by virtue of their waiver. Directed donation does not, however, bolster the claims of those others who could benefit from transplantation of the organ; their claims remain overridden and they are therefore not potential beneficiaries of the organ at the point of allocation.[71]

His argument is that where there is a directed donation, the requested recipient's claim on the organ is strengthened because they now have a stronger claim than anyone else to be given the organ. Indeed one might go further and suggest, at least in some cases (e.g. the racist donor), that the interests of the person on top of the list have been reduced because the donor has specifically indicated they do not want the organ to go to the person at the top of the

---

[69] C. Robertson, 'Who is really hurt anyway? The problem of soliciting designated organ donations' (2005) 5 *American Journal of Bioethics* 13.

[70] G. Pennings, 'Directed organ donation: discrimination or autonomy?' (2007) 24 *Journal of Applied Philosophy* 41, 46.

[71] S. Pattinson, 'Directed donation and ownership of human organs' (2011) 31 *Legal Studies* 392, 406.

list if they belong to the specified race. That provides a further reason against giving the organ to that person. This then returns, however, to the argument about whether the wishes of the deceased should carry weight. Those who don't think they should carry much weight would not be convinced. Is the importance of an impartial system greater than the weight of the wishes of the deceased?

Practical problems

To some, the debates over directed donation should focus on utilitarian concerns. We should ask: 'What approach to directed donation will produce the best outcomes?' A central question would then become: 'Will allowing directed donations mean that more or fewer lives will be saved?' It might be thought that allowing directed donations will save more lives because there will be some people who will only donate if they can direct the organ. However, it may be that if directed organ donation means that people have less confidence in the organ donation system, others will be put off donating.[72] It might also be that although the numbers of donated organs are increased, they are not given to the most appropriate people and so their effectiveness is diminished.

A second practical concern is whether allowing directed organ donation will lead to people offering to pay would-be donors to name them as their preferred recipient. Of course, the Human Tissue Act 2004 makes payment for organs illegal, and we could include payment to be listed as a preferred recipient in this embargo. This problem may not be as large as might be imagined. Paying to be listed as a preferred recipient is a far more risky proposition than buying an organ. You would not know when a person might die and whether their organ would be useable. Anyone seeking to obtain an organ in this way would need to pay a large number of people.

A third concern is that it might simply put people in a difficult position. If you could direct your organ, how could you choose if you had several family members or friends who might benefit? This argument is at its strongest if we imagine a world in which conditional organ donation was possible. We would see individuals pressuring relatives to name them as preferred organ recipients; we would see heart-rending advertisements from individuals, asking that they be named; there would be the danger of money being paid to encourage donation. We might be worried that organs would be donated on the basis of one's ability to look good on a YouTube video or in a Facebook entry, rather than on clinical need.[73] The argument is, then, that while one can sympathise with an individual case, say where a dying uncle wants on his death his organ to be

---

[72] L. Boulware, M. Troll, N. Wang et al., 'Perceived transparency and fairness of the organ allocation system and willingness to donate organs: a national study' (2007) 7 *American Journal of Transplantation* 1778.

[73] A. Glazier and S. Sasjack, 'Should it be illicit to solicit? A legal analysis of policy options to regulate solicitation of organs for transplant' (2007) 17 *Health Matrix* 63.

used for his ill niece, the broader picture which would emerge if conditional donations were allowed would be highly unattractive.

There is a website (www.MatchingDonors.com) which seeks to assist in matching donors and recipients. This might be said to increase donations, because a person may have a particularly strong incentive to give if there is an identified recipient, rather than a nameless person, 'on the top of the list'.[74] Charities working in developing countries have recognised this by enabling people to 'sponsor' a particular child or family, so they will feel they are giving to an identified person rather than 'the poor'.

LIVING ORGANS

One issue we have already highlighted is the difference between living and deceased donors. Living donors are able to make conditional gifts and, provided the donation is approved by the HTA, that condition will be respected. As we have seen, deceased donors' conditions will not be taken into account. Douglas and Cronin claim that this distinction is anomalous. They give the example of the case of Laura Ashworth:

Scenario to ponder

Laura Ashworth, aged 21, wished to donate a kidney to her mother, Rachel Leake, who had end-stage renal failure. However, Laura died before being a living donor. Her wish to donate to her mother would have been followed had she donated as a living donor. However, as a deceased donor, it was not a binding condition. The HTA ruled that:

> The central principle of matching and allocating organs from the deceased is that they are allocated to the person on the waiting list who is most in need and who is the best matched with the donor. This is regardless of gender, race, religion or any other factor.[75]

If one were to justify the distinction between living and deceased donors, two arguments might be used. The first is that one might predict that people will be reluctant to make a living donation unless they are able to direct who receives it. The cost in terms of time, effort and pain is such that we might expect that only a tiny number of people will donate to the general good. The donation on death is less costly. Indeed, unless one has particular religious or other objections to the removal of organs, it might be seen as costless. We might therefore expect that denying conditional donations would dramatically reduce the

---

[74] R. Epstein, 'The human and economic dimensions of altruism: the case of organ transplantation' (2001) 30 *Journal of Legal Studies* 459.
[75] Human Tissue Authority, *Statement on Directed Donation of Organs* (HTA, 2008).

number of organs available in the case of live donors, but have only a small impact on deceased organ donations. Such a utilitarian assessment might justify a distinction in treatment. In response it might be said that this is largely guess-work, and calculating how people will respond to changes in organ donation is not straightforward.

A second argument is this. One objection to conditional organ donations is that people with a seriously ill friend or relative will feel under considera-ble pressure to donate conditionally. This is reflected in the various procedural requirements that ensure that a live donation is fully consented to. If you are worried by this issue, you might take the view that we can be confident after a lengthy discussion with live donors that there was genuine consent, but we cannot do that with a deceased person. It is better, therefore, not to allow these donations. However, it might be questioned whether it is more important to protect people from coerced choices by not giving effect to a conditional dona-tion, even though that way some people will not be able to exercise their choice to conditionally donate, or more important to allow people to donate, even though some people will not have been exercising a free choice.

OWNERSHIP

Lurking only somewhat in the background of this debate are the arguments about ownership of bodily material. A key issue is, as Robert Truog has put it: 'Are organs personal property or a societal resource?'[76] If I own my body parts, surely I can determine who should receive them, just as I can with any other property?[77] If I do not own my organs, it becomes more plausible to see them as a public resource and so not subject to conditional donation. It is worth remembering that people are free to use their property in any way they wish. If they give their money to charities that primarily work for the benefit of white people, or only buy presents for their friends of a certain race, we might think less of them, but they are free to dispose of their property in whatever arbitrary way they choose.

Shaun Pattinson[78] argues that the principle of proprietary control underpins the 2004 Act. He argues that the guidance issued by the HTA and NHS on organ donation should reflect that principle and permit conditional donation. However, his reading of the Act has not been universally accepted.[79] The Act can be seen as a compromise between competing claims, and is certainly not a straightforward reflection of a property approach. Indeed, the only instance

---

[76] R. Truog, 'Are organs personal property or a societal resource?' (2005) 5 *American Journal of Bioethics* 14.

[77] E. Colleran, 'My body, his property? Prescribing a framework to determine ownership inter-ests in directly donated human organs' (2007) 80 *Temple Law Review* 1203.

[78] S. Pattinson, 'Directed donation and ownership of human organs' (2011) 31 *Legal Studies* 392.

[79] J. Herring and P-L. Chau, 'My body, your body, our bodies' (2007) 15 *Medical Law Review* 34, 39.

where the 2004 Act refers to property in body parts is in the exclusion from the prohibition on commercial dealings of material 'which is the subject of property because of an application of human skill'.[80] The reference to its being property because of an application of skill suggests that the Act does not generally regard body parts as property, otherwise it would not require a reason to make the material property.

Pattinson[81] raises the case of a deceased man in 1998, whose relatives had agreed to donate his organs on condition they were given to white recipients. His liver and kidneys were accepted and transplanted. However, subsequently, after a review, the HTA made it clear that no conditions should be attached to the donation or organs.[82] Many people's initial reaction would be to be so horrified by the condition as to agree that it should be ignored. However, the issue is difficult. Should the organ not be used at all? In that case, we might have to face the fact that our principles have led to someone's death. Or should the condition be ignored and the organ given to the person at the top of the list? In that case, can we justify overruling the wishes of the deceased, while respecting the wishes of those who do not wish to donate full stop?

Those who reject the ownership argument may simply deny that people own their organs in the way suggested (see Chapter 8, where we explore this further). However, there are other points they may make. First, as Eike-Henner Kluge points out, organ donation is not simply a personal action but a social one:

> It is a social act not solely because it is embedded in a social context – most gift transactions have that nature – but because it requires society's direct and immediate participation. Society itself becomes a participant giver, and the organ, which as tissue was merely a private good, becomes a social good when it is an organ-as-donated.[83]

While a person is free to give their money to others, that does not require the involvement of others. Organ transplantation, however, involves considerable time, effort and money from the NHS and its staff. In a sense, organ donation is a community practice, not a personal one. It is far from clear why considerable community resources should be granted to enable the meeting of one person's preference.

Second, as Guido Pennings notes, there are limits on autonomy. He explains:

> We allow people to decide what to do with their time and money but we do not allow people to decide who will live and who will die. That decision is, like decisions regarding the spending of health care resources, a choice that has to be negotiated within society.[84]

---

[80] HTAct 2004, s. 32(9)(c).

[81] S. Pattinson, 'Directed donation and ownership of human organs' (2011) 31 *Legal Studies* 392.

[82] Human Tissue Authority, *Statement on Directed Donation of Organs After Death* (HTA, 2008).

[83] E.-H. Kluge, 'Designated organ donation: private choice in social context' (1989) 19 *The Hastings Center Report* 10, 12.

[84] G. Pennings, 'Directed organ donation: discrimination or autonomy?' (2007) 24 *Journal of Applied Philosophy* 41, 44.

As Truog notes, we might draw links between the treatment of the bodies of the dead and the treatment of their property.[85] In the case of wills, if inadequate provision is made for those to whom the testator owes moral obligations, these obligations can be enforced, even though the testator has left property to others. An autopsy may be required, even if that is not wanted and whatever objections the deceased may have had. These examples show that the public good and an acknowledgement of moral obligation can take precedence over the wishes of the deceased in a way unimaginable in the case of a living person.

CONCLUSION

This debate provides a practical example of how it might matter whether you are said to own your own body (see Chapter 8). As with the second debate, there is a clash between the importance of promoting individual control and the promotion of the social good. Given we have a National Health Service, which is designed to promote the health of all, it is more in the spirit of the institution that individuals cannot direct how health resources are used.

FURTHER READING

Debate 1

M. Brazier, 'Retained organs: ethics and humanity' (2002) 22 *Legal Studies* 550.

M. Brazier, 'The body in time' (2015) 7 *Law, Innovation and Technology* 161.

B. Brecher, 'Our obligations to the dead' (2002) 19 *Journal of Applied Philosophy* 109.

J. Callahan, 'On harming the dead' (1987) 97 *Ethics* 341.

W. Glannon, 'Persons, lives and posthumous harms' (2001) 32 *Journal of Social Philosophy* 127.

J. Harris, 'Law and regulation of retained organs: the ethical issues' (2002) 22 *Legal Studies* 237.

S. McGuiness and M. Brazier, 'Respecting the living means respecting the dead too' (2008) 28 *Oxford Journal of Legal Studies* 297.

D. Sperling, *Posthumous Interests: Legal and Ethical Perspectives* (Cambridge University Press, 2008).

Debate 2

G. den Hartogh, 'Tacitly consenting to donate one's organs' (2011) 37 *Journal of Medical Ethics* 344.

A.-M. Farrell, D. Price and M. Quigley (eds), *Organ Shortage: Ethics, Law and Pragmatism* (Cambridge University Press, 2011).

---

[85] R. Truog, 'Are organs personal property or a societal resource?' (2005) 5 *American Journal of Bioethics* 14.

S. Giordano, 'Is the body a republic?' (2005) 31 *Journal of Medical Ethics* 470.

W. Glannon, 'The case against conscription of cadaveric organs for transplantation' (2008) 17 *Cambridge Quarterly of Healthcare Ethics* 330.

J. Harris, 'Organ procurement: dead interests, living needs' (2003) 29 *Journal of Medical Ethics* 130.

A. Spital, 'Conscription of cadaveric organs for transplantation: a stimulating idea whose time has not yet come' (2005) 14 *Cambridge Quarterly of Healthcare Ethics* 107.

R. Truog, 'Are organs personal property or a societal resource?' (2005) 5 *American Journal of Bioethics* 14.

Debate 3

E.-H. Kluge, 'Designated organ donation: private choice in social context' (1989) 19 *The Hastings Center Report* 10.

S. Pattinson, 'Directed donation and ownership of human organs' (2011) 31 *Legal Studies* 392.

G. Pennings, 'Directed organ donation: discrimination or autonomy?' (2007) 24 *Journal of Applied Philosophy* 41.

CHAPTER 8

Selling and Owning Human Body Parts

Introduction

In the last chapter, we looked at the specific debates around organ donation and how the law provides people with a say in what is done with their organs. In this chapter, we look at two further debates about the sorts of control people should have over their body parts.

It is often suggested in the organ donation debate that there would be more organs available for transplant if we gave people a monetary incentive to provide them. In the first debate in this chapter we consider whether people should be allowed to sell their organs. A wider debate into which this question sometimes fits is whether people should own their body parts. Cutting across both debates is the tension we have seen in many of the debates in this book between respecting people's autonomy and protecting them from harm.

Debate 1

Should people be allowed to sell their organs?

As long as the supply of organs for transplant falls short of demand, there will be debate about how to increase that supply. One option is to permit a market in organs.

The Law

The sale of human organs and most human tissue is prohibited. Under section 32 of the Human Tissue Act 2004, it is an offence if a person:

(a)   gives or receives a reward for the supply of, or for an offer to supply, any controlled material;

(b)   seeks to find a person willing to supply any controlled material for reward; or

(c)   offers to supply any controlled material for reward.

It is also an offence to initiate, negotiate or arrange such exchanges.[1] Any advertising to enable such exchanges to be made is also prohibited according to section 32(2) of the Act.

There are some notable exceptions. It is permissible for the donor's expenses to be compensated,[2] although it is not yet clear how widely this will be interpreted. We know from some of the cases on surrogacy that the prohibitions on commercial exchanges have been interpreted widely (see Chapter 5). It may be that the same concerns about exploitation or fairness are influential if cases of payment for organs arise, but as yet the law is untested. Gametes and embryos also are excluded from the ambit of section 32.[3]

The Act also allows for the sale of 'material which is the subject of property because of an application of human skill'.[4] This provision mirrors the common law work and skill exception (see Debate 2 below) and, as we shall see, is rather ambiguous. It is intended to account for the sales of preserved tissue samples that are created by commercial firms to supply the medical research industry. Such companies create cell lines and specific tissue cultures, which can be ordered by medical researchers.[5] This exception also probably allows for sales such as hair for wigs and extensions,[6] and for unusual instances such as artworks created from human tissue (see Debate 2) or the trade in antique human remains.[7]

ARGUMENTS FOR AND AGAINST ORGAN SALES

Those in favour of a market argue that offering a monetary incentive could encourage people to give, increasing the number of organs available for transplant. For example, Benjamin Hippen argues:

> The current system of organ procurement which relies on donation is inadequate to the current and future need for transplantable kidneys. The growing disparity between demand and supply is accompanied by a steep human cost. I argue that a regulated market in organs from living vendors is the only plausible solution.[8]

Those in favour of a market approach have argued that the clear need for organs means:

---

[1] Human Tissue Act 2004, s. 32(1).

[2] Ibid., s. 32(7)

[3] Ibid., s. 32(9).

[4] Ibid., s. 32(9)(c).

[5] ATCC, 'Cell Lines', available at https://www.lgcstandards-atcc.org/Products/Cells_and_Microorganisms/Cell_Lines.aspx?geo_country=gb.

[6] C.C. Izundu, 'Who would sell their hair for cash?', *BBC News*, 22 March 2012, available at www.bbc.co.uk/news/magazine-17043055.

[7] Doe & Hope, 'A Late 19thC Osteological Human Part Skeleton & Skull in Pine Box, Supplied by Millikin & Lawley, London', available at www.doeandhope.com/products/a-late-19thc-osteological-human-part-skeleton-skull-in-pine-box-supplied-by-millikin-lawley-london-alv23.

[8] B. Hippen, 'In defense of a regulated market in kidneys from living vendors' (2005) 30 *Journal of Medicine and Philosophy* 593, 600.

The burden of proof rests with those who oppose such sales to show that they are immoral. Like Alice at the Knave's trial, then, we should hold that the default position should be that markets in human organs are 'innocent until proven guilty'.[9]

This view assumes that the demand for organs justifies taking steps to meet that demand by increasing supply. Some question this assumption. For example, Ruth Richardson has suggested that there is a 'fearful symmetry' between dissection and organ harvesting that 'once the need was recognized, a supply was obtained; and once a supply was obtained, it always fell short of demand'.[10] Similarly, Nancy Scheper-Hughes argues that the current demand for organs is, with 'the expansion of new patient populations', creating 'invented needs and artificial scarcities'.[11] The main riposte to this view is that if we can save lives without harming others, then we should do so.

Market supporters often make arguments based on individual autonomy. They argue that markets allow people, particularly those in poverty, to choose to sell an organ if they need or wish to, hence respecting their autonomy. This benefits them both by respecting their decisions as moral agents, and in the form of the monetary benefits they gain. For example, Julian Savulescu argues:

> People have a right to make a decision to sell a body part ... If we should be allowed to risk damaging our body for pleasure (by smoking or skiing), why not for money which we will use to realise other goods in life? ... To prevent [people] making these decisions is ... paternalism in its worst form.[12]

On this view, people in poverty should be given the opportunity to make the decision to sell a body part, as they may consider this a good option to raise money and be prepared to accept the risks. One response to this is that the sale of organs would be exploitative of the poor. But what does it mean to exploit people? Janet Radcliffe-Richards explains:

> What is bad about exploitation, and makes it different from the offering of inducements that is a normal part of buying and hiring, is that the exploiter seeks out people who are so badly off that even a tiny inducement can improve on their best option, and in that way can get away with paying less than would be necessary to someone who had more options available.[13]

---

[9] J. Taylor, 'A "Queen of Hearts" trial of organ markets: why Scheper-Hughes's objections to markets in human organs fail' (2007) 33 *Journal of Medical Ethics* 201, 204.

[10] R. Richardson, *Death, Dissection and the Destitute*, 2nd edn (Phoenix, 2001), 421.

[11] N. Scheper-Hughes, 'Bodies for sale – Whole or in parts' (2001) 7 *Body and Society* 1, 3–4. Renée Fox and Judith Swazey have argued that the lack of organs for transplantation came to be conceptualised as a problem of supply and demand in the late 1980s as the procedure became more routine. This shift came with a concomitant reduction in focus on the special gift aspect of donation: R. Fox and J. Swazey, *Spare Parts: Organ Replacement in American Society* (Oxford University Press, 1992), Chapter 3.

[12] J. Savulescu, 'Is the sale of body parts wrong?' (2003) 29 *Journal of Medical Ethics* 138. See also G. Dworkin, 'Markets and morals', in G. Dworkin (ed.), *Morality, Harm and the Law* (Westview, 1994).

[13] J. Radcliffe-Richards, 'Nepharious goings on: kidney sales and moral arguments' (1996) 21 *Journal of Medicine and Philosophy* 375, 391.

But she then goes on to argue that even if there is a risk of exploitation, 'that does not alter the fact that if [someone] chooses this option, all alternatives must seem worse to them'.[14] This kind of argument assumes that people will make a choice that is the best of those available, and consequently they will be at least marginally better off than they would have been had they not had the choice. Those who support organ sales then conclude that it is still better for individuals to make this choice if it improves their situation.

However, Simon Rippon claims that even just having the choice to sell can in and of itself be harming to people in poverty.[15] On his view, you 'can harm people by giving them an option that they would be better off taking', because having that option makes it more difficult for them to perform the reasoning necessary to make the best choice.[16] Once the option to sell an organ is available, people would eventually be subject to an expectation to do so if the need arose. We would move from a situation in which one cannot sell an organ (it cannot be chosen), to one in which one can only *choose not to sell* an organ, but this is still choice, and hence we can be responsible for making that choice. This can itself expose us to harms, as we could come under pressure to choose otherwise, and failing to choose to sell the organ might bring other negative consequences upon us.[17]

However, while Rippon may have a strong point, we can easily imagine situations in which it is clearly more harming to someone not to have this choice when they might desperately want it. For each person who might have sold a kidney at a low price and remained in debt (based on the examples Rippon cites), we can also imagine a mother desperate to raise funds for a potentially life-saving experimental drug for her child that the NHS will not fund. For her, the risk of health complications might be a small price to pay if selling her kidney can raise the needed funds and perhaps save her child. We can speculate either way, and we cannot know the answer, because it depends on the nature of the market, the prices, the demand and how we regulate it. We can argue that people know what is best for them, but there are many instances in which the law does not take this view, putting in place protections to help people make choices that are more likely to help them flourish. Seatbelt requirements, taxing people to pay for the NHS, and restrictions on contracts are all examples of such measures.

This debate is what Margaret Radin has called the 'Double Bind' of commodification.[18] In the context of organ markets, it means that we may harm the poor by denying them the opportunity to sell by cutting off a means to potentially alleviate their situation. But we may also harm them by giving

---

[14] J. Radcliffe-Richards and others, 'The case for allowing kidney sales' (1998) 352 *The Lancet* 1950, 1951.

[15] S. Rippon, 'Imposing options on people in poverty: the harm of a live donor organ market' (2014) 40 *Journal of Medical Ethics* 145, 145.

[16] Ibid., 146.

[17] Ibid., 148.

[18] M. Radin, 'Market-inalienability' (1987) 100 *Harvard Law Review* 1849.

them that option if it makes their situation worse in other ways, such as health or of the kind identified by Rippon.

But as Kate Greasley responds, the double bind should not be the end but the beginning of our thinking. Unlike Radcliffe-Richards and others, she comments:

> Crucially, it cannot be taken as granted that organ selling is realistically likely to improve the poverty-stricken conditions of the vendor in most (or any) cases – notwithstanding his perception that it will – let alone fully extricate him from poverty and debt.[19]

Selling organs is also not like selling other things. For one, it exposes the seller to lifelong health risks. It also involves crossing a line to which we are otherwise strongly committed – the psychological importance of maintaining our right to bodily integrity. A great deal of the law around medicine and the criminal law are focused on protecting this integrity precisely because it is psychologically important to people to be free from physical interference by others. As Rippon argues, having this eroded by the social or financial pressures that might come when organ selling is permitted would be seriously harming.[20]

Some, however, argue that permitting a market will bring it into the open, allowing us to regulate and prevent some of the harms that arise in black markets. If we think black markets are inevitable, then this could be a reason to regulate rather than prohibit. Similar arguments are made in support of laws about abortion and surrogacy, and they might be convincing in the context of organ sales as well. A regulated market could manage issues such as fair payment (including minimum pricing), recourse for sellers if buyers break their promises to pay, medical support for post-sale donors, and counselling and advice provision to help potential sellers to decide whether they wish to sell.[21]

Organs markets are often also objected to on the grounds that such a market would widen the gap between rich and poor, with the poor lacking good health as well as money. Data from the World Health Organization show that in Egypt, India and the Islamic Republic of Iran, between 58 per cent and 86 per cent of organ sellers reported a deterioration in their health status post-sale. Many also reported that their employment prospects were adversely affected as a result.[22] It is highly likely that in a market for organs, the poor will be the sellers and the rich the buyers. Therefore, these kinds of outcomes indicate that allowing a market will widen the health gap between these groups still further.

---

[19] K. Greasley, 'A legal market in organs: the problem of exploitation' (2014) 40 *Journal of Medical Ethics* 51, 52.

[20] S. Rippon, 'Imposing options on people in poverty: the harm of a live donor organ market' (2014) 40 *Journal of Medical Ethics* 145, 149.

[21] L. de Castro, 'Commodification and exploitation: arguments in favour of compensated organ donation' (2003) 29 *Journal of Medical Ethics* 142.

[22] Y. Shimazono, 'The state of the international organ trade: a provisional picture based on integration of available information' (2007) 85(12) *Bulletin of the World Health Organization* 955, 960.

To this it might be responded that we already allow the poor to work physically demanding jobs and take risks to improve their financial situations, and that we should not treat organ selling differently. However, this could equally be an argument against those practices themselves, suggesting that instead we should find better ways to protect the poor from risks and ensure they receive adequate compensation. If we recognise that we are allowing the poor to take the bulk of these risk and health burdens, usually for much lower pay than people in less menial professions, then this is no good argument for adding to those burdens. It should direct us to do more to relieve them, not add to them.

Commercialising organs can have other harmful impacts. Radin has been one of the most influential commentators on the ways commercialisation has affected how we think about persons:

> A fungible object can pass in and out of a person's possession without effect on the person as long as its market equivalent is given in exchange. … To speak of personal attributes as fungible objects – alienable 'goods' – is intuitively wrong. … We feel discomfort or even insult, and we fear degradation or even loss of the value involved when bodily integrity is conceived of as a fungible object.
>
> Systematically conceiving of personal attributes as fungible objects is threatening to personhood, because it detaches … that which is integral to the person … [I]f my bodily integrity is an integral personal attribute, not a detachable object, then hypothetically valuing my bodily integrity in money is not far removed from valuing me in money … that is inappropriate treatment of a person.[23]

Michelle Bray has applied Radin's personhood analysis to the sale of body parts, and concluded that treating body parts as saleable 'would encourage perception of body parts as interchangeable commodities and undermine the recognition of the human body as the physical embodiment of the personality'.[24] Bray has further argued that 'people selling body parts not only would lose part of themselves, but might begin to view themselves solely as a means to someone else's physical cure, instead of as an end in themselves'.[25]

Similarly, Donna Dickenson has argued:

> The body both is, and is not, the person. But it should never be only a consumer good, an obscure object of both material desire, a capital investment, a transferable resource: merely a thing. Our consciousness, dignity, energy and human essence are all embodied, caught up in our frail bodies. The body is indeed like nothing on earth: not no one's thing, but no thing at all.[26]

---

[23] M. Radin, 'Market-inalienability' (1987) 100 *Harvard Law Review* 1849, 1880–81.

[24] M. Bray, 'Personalizing personality: toward a property right in human bodies' (1990) 69 *Texas Law Review* 209, 241.

[25] Ibid., 243.

[26] D. Dickenson, *Body Shopping: the Economy Fuelled by Flesh and Blood* (Oneworld, 2008).

One response to this is that there is still a distinction between how we might value organs and how we would continue to value people. The things that make us value people are not affected by allowing them voluntarily to sell their body parts. We value them because they have the qualities of moral agents, and these are not lost when we respect one in particular of those qualities – the capacity to make their own choices. In some ways, we do them more harm by paternalistically preventing them from making their own decisions about their bodies based on their own view of the risks involved. The harms pointed to by commentators such as Bray and Dickenson are also arguably quite vague and difficult to identify, whereas the harm of people dying for lack of an organ is not.

An alternative concern, raised by others such as Thomas Murray, is the claim that it is simply inappropriate to treat human organs as something that can be traded:

> The body, in its significant manifestations, is not suitable for markets because our most important religions and secular traditions treat it as 'dignity-property' or 'sacra', as an integral part of the person who is the locus of moral concerns and moral worth. It should not be traded in markets because markets in body parts, like all markets, will be subject to inequities and abuses. But these inequities and abuses will have special significance in body markets, because it is the morally significant body (and health, and life) that is being traded off.[27]

Murray goes on to argue that 'putting a price on the priceless, even a high price, actually cheapens it. So we don't approve of selling out body parts; and the body isn't quite property'.[28] We could, however, respond that the loss of life that flows from a lack of transplant organs might speak against these concerns. It may well be true that body parts have special significance, but living people who are embedded in relationships with others have greater significance, and hence protecting those lives should trump concerns about the significance of organs.

A final objection to using markets to increase the supply of organs is that it undermines altruism. Some, such as Murray, argue that '[g]ifts of the body are one of the most significant means that mass societies have to affirm the solidarity, or community, that humans need in order to mature and to flourish as individuals'.[29] An altruism-based system of organ donation promotes a sense of

---

[27] T. Murray, 'On the human body as property: the meaning of embodiment, markets, and the meaning of strangers' (1987) 20 *Journal of Law Reform* 1055, 1088. James Harris argues that it is an affront to human dignity to commodify organs. See J. Harris, *Property and Justice* (Clarendon Press, 1996), 352.

[28] T. Murray, 'The gift of life must always remain a gift' (1986) (March) *Discover* 90, 90.

[29] T. Murray, 'On the human body as property: the meaning of embodiment, markets, and the meaning of strangers' (1987) 20 *Journal of Law Reform* 1055, 1085. Renée Fox and Judith Swazey argued in 1978 that in fact, 'the giving and receiving of a gift of enormous value … is the most significant meaning of organ transplantation', and that transplant teams were highly sensitive to this during the 1960s and 1970s: R. Fox and J. Swazey, *The Courage to Fail: A Social View of Organ Transplants and Dialysis*, 2nd rev. edn (Chicago University Press, 1978), 5.

community, which can be eroded when people give from their bodies only in exchange for money.

However, it is not necessarily true that if money exchanges are possible, people will cease to donate their organs for free. Further, there are many situations in which money changes hands yet we still consider an act to have an altruistic aspect. The caring professions, such as nursing, involve people working for a salary, but many who take on this work do so for reasons in addition to the need to earn money. For them, it can be a vocation, or a way to act altruistically towards others. The fact that it is also how they earn their living does not negate this.[30]

A MODIFIED MARKET?

One suggested solution to many of the problems of an organ market is Charles Erin and John Harris's suggestion of a monopsony model, with the NHS as a single buyer.[31] This would avoid the problems of a pure market in which demand, driven by the wealthy who need organs, and the desperation of the poor who wish to sell, determines the price. It also avoids the problems of distribution and the waste that comes when people buy organs which may not be best matched to them, causing health problems or rejection. We could include pricing mechanisms to prevent people being paid too little, and this approach would also allow us to check that sales were voluntary and not coerced.

CONCLUSION

There are clearly very strong arguments on either side of the organ sales debate, and to an extent what is needed is more evidence about some of the harms that are raised by those on both sides of the debate. One thing that cannot be disputed is that every day people die for want of a donor organ, so before rejecting any approach that would increase the supply of organs we should be convinced that that approach is worse than both this continuing loss of life and the prohibition on the poor having another option to escape their condition. As Radcliffe-Richards has written:

> There is also one further, positive, reason for keeping the trade in organs, which sounds perverse but is actually offered here more than half seriously. This is the very fact that most people do find it so profoundly shocking and distressing. It certainly is shocking; it is dreadful that people should be forced by distress and destitution into selling parts of themselves. Nevertheless, the fact remains that we seem quite capable of putting up with even worse distress as long as it is not forced on our attention in this peculiarly distasteful way. Many a Turkish peasant

---

[30] J. Herring, *Medical Law and Ethics*, 4th edn (Oxford University Press, 2012), 455.

[31] J. Harris and C. Erin, 'An ethically defensible market in organs: a single buyer like the NHS is an answer' (2002) 325 *British Medical Journal* 114.

is now presumably worse off than before we banned the trade, and the potential recipients of their kidneys may be dead; but we are not clamouring about these desperate lives and untimely deaths in the way we did about the evils of the trade.[32]

Difficult situations such as the shortage of transplant organs should compel us to think clearly about the relative harms, and not allow our own personal distaste to discourage us from permitting any approach that might in the end be best for everyone.

Debate 2
Should human body parts be treated like property?

WHY IS THERE A DEBATE?

Human organs, tissue and parts have many uses, some with which we are familiar and some which are more surprising. Whole bodies are used for anatomy teaching in some medical schools, while smaller, carefully dissected and preserved parts are held in teaching museums. Medical practitioners test blood and other tissue to help diagnose illness. Sometimes our families need access to our tissue to help diagnose their own illnesses, particularly in the case of familial cancers. Sperm and ova are the fundamental materials for creating new life, while other tissue is used to save lives through transplants and tissue treatments.[33] Medical researchers rely on access to human tissue to undertake studies into how the body and the diseases that affect it work. Outside the medical context, real human hair is used for wigs and hair extensions, while some artists use human tissue in their work. For example, artist Marc Quinn creates sculptures of his head using his own blood, titled *Self*. The most recent *Self* was bought by the National Portrait Gallery for £300,000.[34] Anyone who has ever watched the television program *CSI* will be familiar with the many ways in which human tissue can be used by police investigators to determine how a crime was committed. Not only can it be used to incriminate someone who has broken the law, tissue testing can also help to identify remains and sometimes reunite families with the bodies of those they have lost. At times, access to tissue is also needed to help provide evidence in a legal case, such as for paternity testing or demonstrating that there has been negligence on the part of a doctor.[35]

---

[32] J. Radcliffe-Richards, 'Nepharious goings on: kidney sales and moral arguments' (1996) 21 *Journal of Medicine and Philosophy* 375, 410.

[33] See further I. Goold, 'Why does it matter how we regulate the use of human body parts?' (2014) 40 *Journal of Medical Ethics* 3.

[34] A. Akbar, 'National Portrait Gallery acquires Marc Quinn's bloody head', *Independent*, 10 September 2009, available at www.independent.co.uk/arts-entertainment/art/news/national-portrait-gallery-acquires-marc-quinns-bloody-head-1785133.html.

[35] *Roche v Douglas as Administrator of the Estate of Edward Rowan (dec'd)* (2000) WASC 146; *Dobson v North Tyneside Health Authority and another* [1996] 4 All ER 474.

Given these many uses, it is not surprising that there are many individuals and groups who have a desire to possess, use or control tissue. These include medical researchers, medical practitioners, patients, families, the community and the police, among many others, all of whom have interests in human tissue. At times, their desires will conflict. It is for the law to manage such conflicts, and this is complex when we consider the psychological and emotional importance of bodies. For researchers, human tissue can provide vital insights into disease that can help create treatments to improve the health of everyone in the community. For police, access to tissue can be a crucial means of solving a case, so that a criminal can be apprehended and prevented from harming others. But this usefulness can come into conflict with the reasons why individuals might want to control who can access their tissue. For some individuals, the body is a profoundly important aspect of their self, but for others it is simply the vessel that carries them around. For families, the deceased body is a symbol of the person who is no longer here. Our tissue carries deeply personal information about us and our families in the form of DNA. It can yield information about our health, our familial relations, our past drug use and our future life expectancy. There are clear tensions here between respecting individual privacy and autonomy, and promoting the good aims of research and policing, amongst others. A regulatory framework is therefore clearly needed to manage these.

Simon Douglas and Imogen Goold[36] have described the four questions that a court should ask in determining whether a property claim can be made in relation to human material:

1. Can the biomaterial form the subject matter of a property right?
2. Should the biomaterial form the subject matter of a property right?
3. To whom would the property right be allocated?
4. Would there be any defences to the property right?

As this list shows, the question of whether human material can be property is only the first stage of a larger debate.

Most commentators agree on the need to promote individual autonomy when it comes to regulating human tissue, as the importance of the personal and privacy aspects of tissue are widely accepted. To what extent they should be protected is a matter of ongoing discussion, but the primary debate in this area of law is how best to protect individual autonomy while protecting the other interests held in tissue. The key focus of this debate in recent years has been whether the law of property is the best legal mechanism for achieving this protection.

---

[36] S. Douglas and I. Goold, 'Property in human biomaterials: a new methodology' (2017) 75 *Cambridge Law Journal* 504.

WHY IS THE DEBATE ABOUT PROPERTY?

Historically, the common law held that a human corpse could not be property.[37] In 1908, the High Court of Australia created an exception to this rule to account for situations in which it could be said someone could have a legal right to possession of a human corpse. Chief Justice Griffiths explained that 'it [did] not follow from the mere fact that a human body at death is not the subject of ownership that it [was] for ever incapable of having an owner' and that it was 'idle to contend in these days that the possession of a mummy, or of a prepared skeleton, or of a skull, or other parts of a human body is necessarily unlawful'.[38] Consequently, he found that where a body had been changed into something other than a corpse awaiting burial due to the lawful application of work or skill to preserve it, then the person who preserved it would acquire a right to possession. This came to be known as the 'work and skill exception', as was applied in a number of cases concerning the possession of corpses and body parts in the late twentieth and early twenty-first centuries in the United Kingdom.[39] In some cases, such as *R v Kelly*, the exception was applied to find that preserved anatomical specimens could be property for the purposes of theft.[40] In others, the exception was held to exist but not to apply. Doubt has also been cast in the case law on the logic behind the exception. For example, in *Dobson v North Tyneside Health Authority*, Peter Gibson LJ stated:

> I do not see how the fact that the brain was so fixed it rendered it an item to possession of which the Plaintiffs ever became entitled for the purpose of interment or any other purpose, still less that the Plaintiffs ever acquired the property in it.[41]

A number of high-profile decisions in recent years have given the debate new impetus, as these decisions appear to suggest that the courts in the UK and Australia are moving closer to accepting a much wider property approach than the limited exception. The most important of these is the decision in *Yearworth and others v North Bristol NHS Trust*, in which the UK Court of Appeal found

---

[37] On the early history of the case law, see P. Matthews, 'Whose body: people as property' (1983) 36 *Current Legal Problems* 193. For a more recent tracing of the cases, see I. Goold and M. Quigley, 'Human biomaterials: the case for a property approach' in I. Goold, K. Greasley, J. Herring and L. Skene (eds), *Persons, Parts and Property: How Should We Regulate Human Tissue in the 21st Century?* (Hart Publishing, 2014).

[38] *Doodeward v Spence* (1908) 6 CLR 406, 413, per Griffith CJ.

[39] *Dobson v North Tyneside Health Authority and another* [1996] 4 All ER 474; *R v Kelly* [1998] 3 All ER 741; *AB and others v Leeds Teaching Hospital NHS Trust* [2004] EWHC 644 (QB).

[40] *R v Kelly* [1998] 3 All ER 741.

[41] *Dobson v North Tyneside Health Authority and another* [1996] 4 All ER 474, 479.

that six men had ownership of their stored sperm that had been negligently destroyed by the facility holding it.[42]

As we saw in the previous chapter, the Human Tissue Act 1961, and later the Human Tissue Act 2004, sat alongside these case law developments and took a different approach based on the need to obtain consent to use human tissue from the person from whom it was obtained. The 1961 Act's provisions were not especially stringent, but following the organ retention revelations at the start of the 2000s, new legislation with much more strict consent requirements was created. The legislation and case law operate in tandem, and thus far the courts have not had to deal with any direct conflicts. This is partly due to the fact that the 2004 Act preserves the work and skill exception.[43]

The debate therefore partly arises from the nature of the law as it stands, which offers both approaches – consent model and property model. The deeper debate is about which approach is best, a question that has led to considerable divergence of opinion in the academic literature. Some argue in favour of a property-based approach, in which someone is accorded ownership, or at least a right to possession, of human tissue.[44] This is sometimes cast as a debate about the status of tissue, but it is better to see it as a position that supports giving someone the kind of right to which the laws that protect interests in property apply. To understand this position, we need to be clear on what it means for tissue to be property.

Property rights are rights that are good against all the world, in contrast to personal rights that can be asserted only against persons with whom one is in the necessary relationship. Contractual rights are a good example of personal rights. I can only enforce the rights I gain under a contract against the other contracting party, who is bound by the voluntary obligations that party took on when entering into it. Property rights must also be held in relation to a thing.[45] The nature of these rights is one of the prime attractions of property for some, who argue it should include human tissue. In giving the right

---

[42] *Yearworth v North Bristol NHS Trust* [2009] 3 WLR 118 (CA). In Australia two decisions have held that the widows of deceased men may have a right to possession of their husband's semen: *Bazley v Wesley Monash IVF* [2010] QSC 118; *Re the estate of the late Mark Edwards* [2011] NSWSC 478.

[43] Human Tissue Act 2004, s. 32(9)(c).

[44] See, e.g., I. Goold and M. Quigley, 'Human biomaterials: the case for a property approach' in I. Goold, K. Greasley, J. Herring and L. Skene (eds), *Persons, Parts and Property: How Should We Regulate Human Tissue in the 21st Century?* (Hart Publishing, 2014); R. Hardcastle, *Law and the Human Body: Property Rights, Ownership and Control* (Hart Publishing, 2007); S. Douglas, 'Property rights in human biological material' in I. Goold, K. Greasley, J. Herring and L. Skene (eds), *Persons, Parts and Property: How Should We Regulate Human Tissue in the 21st Century?* (Hart Publishing, 2014).

[45] Although it should be noted that this view is disputed. For a defence of the thing-relatedness of property rights, see S. Douglas, 'Property rights in human biological material' in I. Goold, K. Greasley, J. Herring and L. Skene (eds), *Persons, Parts and Property: How Should We Regulate Human Tissue in the 21st Century?* (Hart Publishing, 2014), 23.

holder a right that is good against all the world, property rules offer very strong protections. If tissue belongs to me, then for the most part no one else may interfere with it. I will have the right to possess it exclusively, and the law will protect that right against others who would steal it (through the criminal law of theft), take it without permission or damage it (through civil law actions such as conversion). As James Harris has pointed out, it is this strong protective function of property law that is being invoked when people use the language of property in a lay sense to express their belief that others should not interfere with their bodies.[46] Similarly, Ken Mason and Graeme Laurie write:

> Intuitively, it is perfectly natural for one to talk of 'my body' and to infer that, because it is 'my' body, I can determine precisely what is done to it or its parts.[47]

As Simon Douglas comments, property rules are used to protect scarce resources that are likely to be the subject of disputes about possession and control. By clarifying who may control an item, via the relative title approach, these disputes are addressed.[48] As we noted earlier, human tissue is in some contexts a scarce resource, or the subject of disputes about control, and this is one reason why a property approach is appealing. Douglas points out that human tissue, once separated from the person, is tangible, and it is possible in a practical sense to apply the rules of property to it.[49] This applicability is reflected in some of the common law decisions, such as *R v Kelly*, in which dissected, preserved body parts were found to be subject to a right to possession such that they could be stolen under the Theft Act 1968.[50] Similarly, in a string of criminal cases, the police were considered to be in legal possession of samples taken from the subjects of investigation for theft charges to be supported.[51]

Another argument in favour of a property approach is that it provides clarity about which rules of law should govern what is done with tissue. At present, the law is somewhat confused, taking as it does a consent-based approach via legislation with a limited property approach being taken by the courts. Until

---

[46] J. Harris, 'Who owns my body?' (1996) 161 *Oxford Journal of Legal Studies* 55, 62.

[47] J. Mason and G. Laurie, *Mason & McCall Smith's Law and Medical Ethics*, 7th edn (Oxford University Press, 2006), 512.

[48] S. Douglas, 'Property rights in human biological material' in I. Goold, K. Greasley, J. Herring and L. Skene (eds), *Persons, Parts and Property: How Should We Regulate Human Tissue in the 21st Century?* (Hart Publishing, 2014). See also J. Harris, *Property and Justice* (Oxford University Press, 1996).

[49] S. Douglas, 'Property rights in human biological material' in I. Goold, K. Greasley, J. Herring and L. Skene (eds), *Persons, Parts and Property: How Should We Regulate Human Tissue in the 21st Century?* (Hart Publishing, 2014). See also I. Goold, 'Sounds suspiciously like property treatment: does human tissue fit within the common law concept of property?' (2006) 7 *UTS Law Review/Santa Clara Journal of International Law*, Special joint issue 65.

[50] *R v Kelly* [1998] 3 All ER 741.

[51] *R v Rothery* [1976] Crim LR 691; *R v Turner (No. 2)* [1971] 2 All ER 441; *R v Welsh* [1974] RTR 478; *R v Herbert* (1961) 25 *Journal of Criminal Law* 163.

the *Yearworth* decision (above), the work and skill exception was the only clear way in which tissue could be property, but the *Yearworth* decision has changed this by arguably providing a much broader-based way for determining when tissue is property.[52] Depending on how the decision is subsequently interpreted, it appears that someone may obtain property rights by creating (via excising, extracting or ejaculating) tissue as a new, separate thing for their own purposes in a context in which they have rights to possess and control it.[53] Unsurprisingly, in the face of a dispute over control of tissue samples held in a biorepository that had been donated for research, a United States court turned to the law of property, specifically that concerned with possession and with gifts, to address the situation.[54] This is potentially very wide, although the decision has been criticised and may not end up having such a broad ambit.[55] Whichever way it is interpreted, even if quite broadly, the law will remain somewhat confused. A clear statement that human tissue is property would provide clarity by determining which body of laws should apply to tissue where there are no relevant legislative provisions.

A particular element of this argument is that according tissue the status of property would mean donations of tissue would be conceptualised as legal gifts or as bailments, and the rules already in place to manage such transfers could be drawn upon to regulate tissue transfers.[56] Those in favour of this approach argue that it would remove some of the ambiguity about these transfers, as it would be clear what rights were being transferred, whether the transfer was conditional and what the recipient could do with it. The rights of both the owner and the current possessor against third parties who interfered with tissue would also be clear. This would also provide researchers legitimately in possession of tissue samples with the security they need to invest time and effort in research on those samples.

---

[52] The case has been widely discussed in the academic literature: M. Quigley, 'Property: the future of human tissue?' (2009) 17 *Medical Law Review* 457; J. Lee, 'The fertile imagination of the common law: *Yearworth v North Bristol NHS Trust*' (2009) 17 *Torts Law Journal* 130; S. Harmon and G. Laurie, 'Yearworth v. North Bristol NHS Trust: property, principles, precedents, and paradigms' (2010) 69(3) *Cambridge Law Journal* 476; C. Hawes, 'Property interests in body parts: Yearworth v North Bristol NHS Trust' (2010) 73 *Modern Law Review* 119; and L. Skene, 'Proprietary interests in human bodily material: Yearworth, recent Australian cases on stored semen and their implications' (2012) 20 *Medical Law Review* 227.

[53] *Yearworth and others v North Bristol NHS Trust* [2009] 3 WLR 118 (CA).

[54] *Washington University v Catalona* (2007) 490 F 3d 667 (CA 8 Mo). For a discussion of the case and the law of gifts, see I. Goold and M. Quigley, 'Human biomaterials: the case for a property approach' in I. Goold, K. Greasley, J. Herring and L. Skene (eds), *Persons, Parts and Property: How Should We Regulate Human Tissue in the 21st Century?* (Hart Publishing, 2014).

[55] See, e.g., L. Rostill, 'The ownership that wasn't meant to be: Yearworth and property rights in human tissue' (2014) 40 *Journal of Medical Ethics* 14.

[56] I. Goold and M. Quigley, 'Human biomaterials: the case for a property approach' in I. Goold, K. Greasley, J. Herring and L. Skene (eds), *Persons, Parts and Property: How Should We Regulate Human Tissue in the 21st Century?* (Hart Publishing, 2014).

A property approach can also be the foundation for other, less individualistic ways of managing human tissue, particularly in a research context. A number of commentators have advanced the case for a charitable trust model of tissue control, where one party is the legal owner of tissue donated for research, but is bound to use it only for the beneficial purposes for which the trust was established. This approach allows for multiple researchers to use tissue, and it could be transferred to them, but constrains that use to ensure that individuals' tissue is not used in ways to which they might object.[57] Trusts, however, rest on property, and so such a model cannot be deployed unless we deem human tissue to be property.

An alternative is to invoke the device of a bailment. Under a bailment (which can be created in a range of ways), the owner does not lose ownership, but possession passes to someone else who may legitimately use the property in accordance with the wishes of the owner. Depending on the arrangement, the owner can recall the property when they wish or under certain conditions. The person in possession can defend that possession against other people, and is protected in a number of ways, while also being under a duty to take care of the item. In many ways, this could afford an appropriate way of allowing an individual to retain control of their tissue, while enabling others to use it for acceptable purposes. Such an approach also respects individual autonomy where the tissue is obtained from a living person, who may be conceptualised as the owner who bails the tissue to the bailee. In this way, the bailment approach has much in common with the consent approach. It would allow the individual to bring a claim if the tissue was improperly used or damaged. But again, bailments are arrangements that rest on the object being the subject of property rights.

Many, however, do not support a property approach to tissue. Some, such as Loane Skene, favour a modified approach that has some elements of a property model but excludes others. Skene argues that individuals should have a 'personal autonomy right', which would enable them to have a say in how their separated bodily material is used, and which would allow them to refuse, or impose conditions upon, its use. Research institutes and hospitals would be permitted to gain some proprietary interests in preserved bodily material when it comes into their possession lawfully, as this would enable them to achieve their purposes in using it.[58] Such possessory rights are important for

---

[57] See, e.g., A. Boggio, 'Charitable trusts and human research genetic databases: the way forward?' (2005) 1 *Genomics, Society and Policy* 41; D. Winickoff and R. Winickoff, 'The charitable trust as a model for genomic biobanks' (2003) 349 *New England Journal of Medicine* 1180; R. van der Graaf and J. van Delden, 'Exploring an alternative to informed consent in biobank research' in C. Lenk, N. Hoppe and K. Beier (eds), *Human Tissue Research: A European Perspective on the Ethical and Legal Challenges* (Oxford University Press, 2011).

[58] Skene's approach is outlined in a number of papers, particularly: L. Skene, 'Arguments against people legally "owning" their own bodies, body parts and tissue' (2002) 2 *Macquarie Law Journal* 165; L. Skene, 'Proprietary rights in human bodies, body parts and tissue: regulatory contexts and proposals for new laws' (2002) 22 *Legal Studies* 102.

researchers, to ensure that the samples on which they work are secure and hence that it is worth investing time in using them.

Others argue that human tissue should be excluded from the ambit of property law simply because it is inappropriate to include it. For example, Thomas Murray argues that the special and unique nature of human bodily material means it should be left outside the rules that govern chattels such as chairs and cars.[59] But if we accept that property law is precisely about protecting things that have value, as Douglas has argued, then it is the very specialness of human tissue that might suit it to being treated as property. Just as I would want to invoke the protections of its property status if my wedding ring was stolen, so I might be grateful for those protections if someone interfered with tissue taken from me in a manner to which I objected. Treating my wedding ring as property might enable them to be prosecuted for theft, or avail me of civil remedies to compensate my loss or regain my possession of the ring. None of this legal assistance would be at my disposal if I had felt my ring was too special to be property.

A stronger argument made against deeming tissue to be property is that a comprehensive legislative framework would offer better protection for the interests in tissue we want to support. Jonathan Herring and P-L. Chau have taken this position, arguing that the interconnectedness of our bodies means they do not lend themselves to a property approach.[60] They also object to the strong exclusionary control a property approach might give to one person or institution over tissue, when there are good reasons to take a more communal approach.[61] Rather, we would do better to develop a comprehensive legislative regime that provides tailored regulation suited to the particularities of bodily material, the problems posed by its regulation, and what we wish to achieve in regulating it.

Herring and Chau also argue that a legislative approach is more appropriate because it can better account for the 'complex range of interests that individuals and society can have over bodies and separated parts of bodies' than can a property model. As they point out, 'our attitudes and interests in different bodily parts differ hugely depending on the nature of the removed body part and the circumstances of its removal', and a legislative scheme can provide a more tailored, nuanced regulatory approach than property.[62] For example, in cases where a person needs access to a stored tissue sample from a family member to help identify the particular genetic mutation related to their cancer, a legislative scheme could specifically provide for such a situation, whereas

---

[59] T. Murray, 'The gift of life must always remain a gift' (1986) (March) *Discover* 90; T. Murray, 'On the human body as property: the meaning of embodiment, markets, and the meaning of strangers' (1987) 20 *Journal of Law Reform* 1055.

[60] J. Herring and P-L. Chau, 'Interconnected, inhabited and insecure: why bodies should not be property' (2014) 40 *Journal of Medical Ethics* 39; J. Herring and P-L. Chau, 'My body, your body, our bodies' (2007) 15 *Medical Law Review* 34.

[61] J. Herring and P-L. Chau, 'Interconnected, inhabited and insecure: why bodies should not be property' (2014) 40 *Journal of Medical Ethics* 39.

[62] Ibid., 39.

property would have to navigate either the hospital or the source individual's right to possession of the sample.

This leads to a further criticism of the property approach, namely that it privileges individual control over a more communal model. As we saw earlier, there are multiple, intersecting interests in human tissue, and tensions which pull in many directions. Both Murray and Herring object to property on the grounds that it places too much control over a special, communal resource in the hands of one person. For Murray, a property approach would undermine the system of altruistic giving and sharing of body parts.[63] Herring argues that there are good reasons to promote a communal approach to human tissue.[64] Property, he argues, rests on 'individualistic values that protect rights of exclusion and control'.[65] It cannot account for community interests in promoting healthcare, which are better served by avoiding such individualistic controls. Medical research is promoted by allowing wide access to tissue, something which benefits us all. A property approach makes this more difficult, and so fails to best promote the interests of the community. Donna Dickenson has made similar arguments in relation to thinking about tissue as a communal resource in her work,[66] while Loane Skene has raised significant challenges to a strong property model on the basis of the need to promote medical research.[67]

These challenges to a property model have considerable weight. We should not choose a model that undermines medical research, or our efforts at crime detection or the promotion of healthcare. But at the same time, we do need to provide individuals with protection of their bodily tissue when they have good reasons to demand such protection, whether it is to ensure their privacy or because to use it without their consent will be psychologically or emotionally damaging. Arguably, if we erode too much of the protection given by according tissue property status, then we will have departed too far from property for the model to really deserve the name. A highly modified property model would create confusion, and also the arguments from clarity and the benefits of drawing on established rules in favour of a property model would no longer hold. However, given the importance of protecting control and possession, including for those medical researchers who need to be sure they will be able to work on their samples, a legislative scheme would likely look very similar to a property approach. Lyria Bennett Moses also points out that there are

---

[63] T. Murray, 'The gift of life must always remain a gift' (1986) (March) *Discover* 90; T. Murray, 'On the human body as property: the meaning of embodiment, markets, and the meaning of strangers' (1987) 20 *Journal of Law Reform* 1055.

[64] J. Herring, 'Why we need a statute regime to regulate bodily material' in I. Goold, K. Greasley, J. Herring and L. Skene (eds), *Persons, Parts and Property: How Should We Regulate Human Tissue in the 21st Century?* (Hart Publishing, 2014).

[65] Ibid., 256.

[66] D. Dickenson, *Me Medicine vs. We Medicine: Reclaiming Biotechnology for the Common Good* (Columbia University Press, 2013).

[67] See, e.g., L. Skene, 'Proprietary rights in human bodies, body parts and tissue: regulatory contexts and proposals for new laws' (2002) 22 *Legal Studies* 102.

significant problems with *sui generis* regulatory frameworks tailored to specific areas, as they may leave a lacuna or become outdated as technology changes.[68]

How, then, should we regulate? Perhaps the answer lies somewhere between the two ends of the spectrum. Perhaps we should take the fundamentals of a property approach, but use these to inform our legislative scheme. We might draw on devices like trusts and bailments to do so. Alternatively, we could take a property approach and develop legislative provisions that cover the particular situations in which a pure property approach would be untenable or unwanted. Indeed, this latter approach is in fact what the law already does, and as Bennett Moses has argued the law of property is aptly suited to such modification.[69] There are many things that are property, but the law limits the implications of that status. Dealings with land, easements and covenants, and limits on the sale of certain goods are all examples. We could allow the availability of some property torts and their remedies (perhaps compensation for the conversion of valuable stored tissue), but restrict others where they are inappropriate (such as preventing the return of tissue that would constitute hazardous biowaste). Property law alone, like the law of consent, is unlikely to be sufficient to fully and effectively regulate human tissue use. A combination of the strengths of each is perhaps the best approach.[70]

Conclusion

In many ways, the debate about the property status of the body seems rather vexed, but it is important to recall that in many respects those on either side of the debate are in agreement. Both approaches remain focused on balancing protection of individuals with the interests of the community (which includes protecting the practices of medicine and medical research). The disagreement is primarily on what approach best enables an effective balancing of these interests.

Further Reading

Debate 1

K. Greasley, 'A legal market in organs: the problem of exploitation' (2014) 40 *Journal of Medical Ethics* 51.

J. Harris and C. Erin, 'An ethically defensible market in organs: a single buyer like the NHS is an answer' (2002) 325 *British Medical Journal* 114.

---

[68] L. Bennett Moses, 'The problem with alternatives: The importance of property law in regulating excised human tissue and *in vitro* human embryos' in I. Goold, K. Greasley, J. Herring and L. Skene (eds), *Persons, Parts and Property: How Should We Regulate Human Tissue in the 21st Century?* (Hart Publishing, 2014).

[69] Ibid.

[70] See further J. Mason and G. Laurie, 'Consent or property? Dealing with the body and its parts in the shadow of Bristol and Alder Hey' (2001) 64 *Modern Law Review* 710; L. Bennett Moses, 'The problem with alternatives: the importance of property law in regulating excised human tissue and *in vitro* human embryos' in I. Goold, K. Greasley, J. Herring and L. Skene (eds), *Persons, Parts and Property: How Should We Regulate Human Tissue in the 21st Century?* (Hart Publishing, 2014).

B. Hippen, 'In defense of a regulated market in kidneys from living vendors' (2005) 30 *Journal of Medicine and Philosophy* 593.

E. Malmqvist, 'Are bans on kidney sales unjustifiably paternalistic?' (2014) 28 *Bioethics* 110.

J. Radcliffe-Richards, 'Nepharious goings on: kidney sales and moral arguments' (1996) 21 *Journal of Medicine and Philosophy* 375.

Debate 2

S. Douglas and I. Goold, 'Property in human biomaterials: a new methodology' *Cambridge Law Journal* 75, 504.

M. Goodwin, 'Human rights, human tissue: the case of sperm as property' in R. Brownsword, E. Scotford and K. Yeung (eds), *The Oxford Handbook of Law, Regulation and Technology* (Oxford University Press, 2017).

I. Goold, K. Greasley, J. Herring and L. Skene (eds), *Persons, Parts and Property: How Should We Regulate Human Tissue in the 21st Century?* (Hart Publishing, 2014).

R. Hardcastle, *Law and the Human Body: Property Rights, Ownership and Control* (Hart Publishing, 2007).

J.W. Harris, 'Who Owns My Body?' (1996) 161 *Oxford Journal of Legal Studies* 55.

J. Herring, 'The law and the symbolic value of the body' in C. van Klink, B. van Beers and L. Poort (eds), *Symbolic Legislation Theory and Developments in Law* (Springer, 2016).

J. Herring and P-L. Chau, 'My body, your body, our bodies' (2007) 15 *Medical Law Review* 34.

J. Mason and G. Laurie, 'Consent or property? Dealing with the body and its parts in the shadow of Bristol and Alder Hey' (2001) 64 *Modern Law Review* 710.

P. Matthews, 'Whose body: people as property' (1983) 36 *Current Legal Problems* 193.

R. Nwabueze, 'Proprietary interests in organs in limbo' (2016) 36 *Legal Studies* 2.

M. Quigley, 'Property: the future of human tissue?' (2009) 17 *Medical Law Review* 457.

CHAPTER 9

Death

Debate 1
How should death be defined?

INTRODUCTION

What does it mean to say that a person is dead? It is only in recent years that this question has become an issue which has troubled lawyers and ethicists. Of course, in many cases there is really little to argue about. The person has died on any definition. However, increasingly the issue is less straightforward. Two factors in particular have made the question of the timing of death an important one.

First, increased availability and use of technologies mean that people can be kept alive in circumstances unimaginable just a few decades ago. Indeed, most biological functions can be now be performed by machines. We are not too far away from creating the recyclable body. Immortality is not simply in the realm of science fiction. Perhaps the most extreme form of preservation that is currently an option is cryogenic freezing, offering to keep a body 'alive' for centuries. The extent to which a person who is kept alive by modern technology is in fact alive is, in some cases, a complex question.

Second, the issue of the time of death has become important for the purposes of organ transplantation. If an organ is to be useable for transplant, it is important that it is as 'fresh' as possible. That means that it must be removed as early in the dying process as possible. But that then raises the question: What is death?[1] If a person is not dead until late in the process, fewer organs will be useable for transplant. However, there is a concern that some want to place death at the time convenient for organ transplant purposes rather than at the ethically appropriate moment.

The issue is not just of practical significance; it raises profound ethical and, for some, religious questions. For to decide when death occurs, we need to know what it means to be alive. And this raises the deepest of questions and the

---

[1] See generally E. Price Foley, *The Law of Life and Death* (Harvard University Press, 2011).

strongest of feelings. In this debate we will briefly set out the current law, before considering the various definitions of death and their merits and difficulties.

THE LAW

Perhaps surprisingly, given the centrality of the concept, there has been little detailed analysis of the definition of 'death' by the judiciary. In *Airedale NHS Trust v Bland*,[2] Lords Brown-Wilkinson, Goff and Keith accepted that brain stem death was the definition of 'death' for the purposes of medicine and law. Lord Keith in *Bland* held: 'In the eyes of the medical world and of the law a person is not clinically dead so long as the brain stem retains its function.' In *Re A*,[3] Johnson J held that a child, who was on a ventilator and certified as brain stem dead, was also legally dead. In reaching this decision, the judge followed the medical expert opinion, even though the parents took the view that the boy was still alive.

In short, it seems the courts have decided that the definition of 'death' is to be determined by medical experts. That clearly has an appeal to judges seeking to resolve what can be a controversial and complex subject. However, as we shall see, critics complain that defining death in medical terms is only part of the picture. Death, they say, is as much a matter of philosophy and theology as it is of medicine. In the remainder of this debate we will explore the competing definitions of death.

BRAIN DEATH

Brain stem death is widely accepted in the UK and many other European countries as the medical definition of death.[4] The brain stem is the lowest part of the brain, and connects the spinal cord with the rest of the brain. It is responsible for general wakefulness, controlling blood pressure, swallowing, body temperature and breathing. If the brain stem ceases to function then medical assistance from ventilators and the like are needed in order to breathe.

The National Health Service (NHS) has produced a guide to brain death, which states:

> There is no possibility for consciousness once brain death has occurred and in combination with inability to breathe or maintain bodily functions this constitutes death of the individual.[5]

The NHS has also produced a document setting out the tests that should be carried out before a diagnosis of brain death is given. It requires that these must be performed by two senior doctors.[6]

---

[2] *Airedale NHS Trust v Bland* [1993] 1 All ER 821, 837.
[3] *Re A* [1992] 3 *Medical Law Review* 303.
[4] C. Pallis and D. Harley, *ABC of Brain Stem Death* (BMJ Books, 1996).
[5] NHS, *Brain Death* (NHS, 2013).
[6] NHS, *Diagnosing Brain Death* (NHS, 2013).

It should be emphasised that in the case of a brain-dead patient, it is not true that all activity in the body will have ceased. Assisted breathing may take place and there may be electrical activity. Sometimes a distinction is drawn between whole brain death and brain stem death, but for all practical purposes, once there is brain stem death, the rest of the brain cannot operate.

The arguments in favour of brain stem death

The primary justification for using brain death as the medical definition of 'death' is that a person whose brain stem is dead has ceased to live in anything but a mechanical way.[7] With no brain activity, all that is left functioning is the shell of the person. The 'integrative unity' of body and mind has come to an end.[8] Without the brain stem working, separate parts of the body may still operate in a biological sense, but the body has lost its nature as a complete organism. So it is not the ceasing of the brain stem itself which is significant, so much as the consequences of that happening: the loss of consciousness and the incapacity to breathe independently.[9] These are seen as the primary functions of a person, and without them they are dead.

The objections to brain stem death

A fundamental attack on the concept of brain death is that it elevates the brain to being the essential organ of the person.[10] The body is made up of much more than the brain, opponents point out. To declare the person dead when only part of their body (the brain) is not working reveals too narrow an understanding of personhood. Alan Shewmon[11] states that homeostasis (maintenance of the internal environment of the living organism), energy balance, wound healing, fighting off infections, development of a febrile response, successful gestation of a foetus, sexual maturation and proportional growth are all capable of occurring in people who are 'brain dead'. So the fact the brain has stopped functioning does not prevent the rest of the body operating.

John Lizza,[12] in response to some of these objections, uses the example of a decapitated human being who is being kept alive. He argues that most people

---

[7] J. Dubois, 'Is organ procurement causing the death of patients?' (2012) 18 *Issues in Law and Medicine* 21.

[8] M. Potts, 'A requiem for whole brain death' (2001) 26 *Journal of Medicine and Philosophy* 491.

[9] D. Gardiner, S. Shemie, A. Manara and H. Opdam, 'International perspective on the diagnosis of death' (2012) 108 *British Journal of Anaesthesia* i14.

[10] E.g., M. Potts, P. Byrne and R. Nilges (eds), *Beyond Brain Death: The Case Against Brain Based Criteria for Human Death* (Kluwer, 2000).

[11] D. Shewmon, 'The brain and somatic integration: insights into the standard biological rationale for equating "brain death" with death' (2001) 26 *Journal of Medicine and Philosophy* 457, 467.

[12] J. Lizza, 'Commentary on "The incoherence of determining death by neurological criteria"' (2009) 19 *Kennedy Institute of Ethics Journal* 393.

would think that a decapitated person is dead, even if scientists could keep the rest of their body functioning. This indicates that when brain activity ceases, we should treat the body as dead. Whether this advances the debate might be questioned, because Franklin Miller and Robert Truog simply reply that they would regard a decapitated chicken running around as still alive.[13]

Robert Veatch[14] imagines a time in the future in which it is possible to give a person a brain transplant. He suggests that if a brain stem test were used, this would lead to such a person being classified as dead, even though they would patently be alive (the point being that their brain stem would be dead, even if someone else's was alive). One response to this argument, though, is that we can say that the body is not dead but the person is. In the case of a head transplant an interesting question arises: Who now exists – the person who had the head, or the person who had the body, or both?

It has also been objected that the brain stem death test creates too big a gap between when a person is legally dead and the understanding of death by the person in the street. A person can be classified as dead, even though their body is warm and breathing.[15] A body preserved for cryopreservation would also be regarded as dead, which supporters of that practice would oppose.[16]

THE END OF CONSCIOUSNESS

This approach puts death at an earlier time: when a person has irreversibly lost capacity for consciousness.[17] Sometimes this is known as 'higher brain death'. There may still be movements and biological functioning of the body, but without conscious control by the mind these would be of little meaning. Its use would mean that patients in a persistent vegetative state (PVS) would be regarded as dead. Robert Veatch has been a prominent supporter of this view, although it has not been accepted in any jurisdiction.[18]

The argument for end of consciousness

The argument for using end of consciousness typically starts by asking what it means to be human. To supporters, consciousness involves a sense of self and an ability to interact with others, and these abilities are at the heart of what it is

[13] F. Miller and R. Truog, 'The incoherence of determining death by neurological criteria: a reply to John Lizza' (2009) 19 *Kennedy Institute of Ethics Journal* 397.

[14] R. Veatch, *Death, Dying and the Biological Revolution* (Yale University Press, 1989), 41.

[15] H. Evans, 'Reply to: defining death: when physicians and families differ' (2002) 28 *Journal of Medical Ethics* 94.

[16] C. Cohen, 'Bioethicists must rethink the concept of death: the idea of brain death is not appropriate for cryopreservation' (2012) 67 *Clinics* 93.

[17] D. DeGrazia, 'Biology, consciousness, and the definition of death' in T. Shannon (ed.), *Death and Dying* (Rowman and Littlefield, 2004), 1.

[18] R. Veatch, *Death, Dying and the Biological Revolution* (Yale University Press, 1989).

to be a person. Without them life has lost its value. As Julian Savulescu[19] puts it, 'it is our mental life which constitutes who we are, not the machine that supports it'. In a similar vein, Tristam Engelhardt[20] is able to refer to the permanently unconscious as 'biologically living corpses'. These quotes capture the idea that even if there is a technical sense in which a person without consciousness is alive, their life *as a person* has ceased. Notably, this view typically sees death not as a question of medicine, but about our philosophical understanding of what makes human life valuable. So Jeff McMahan[21] claims that we are essentially minds or 'minded beings', and so with no mental activity we have ceased, at least in the sense that is morally significant for people.

Objections to loss of consciousness

A loss of consciousness criterion for death would lead to a far wider classification of death than used at present. For example, those in a PVS would be regarded as dead. Even more dramatically, it could classify as dead (or at least non-people) huge numbers of people with very severe mental disability if they lacked self-consciousness. The possibility that there is a question mark hanging over whether a very mentally ill person is dead may lead one to doubt the wisdom of the approach.

At the heart of the case against loss of consciousness as the marker for death is the claim that we are more than our conscious thoughts. A good example might be a person of religious faith, for whom it is important that their body is treated in line with the traditions of their religious community. Such interests may not depend on the consciousness of the individual.[22] Indeed, it might well be questioned the extent to which consciousness is key to all we value. We interact with the world with our minds and bodies in different ways, not all of them linked to our own consciousness.

An alternative critique of an approach emphasising consciousness is to challenge that concept itself. Neurophysiological progress is making us realise that what is uniquely human is shared by many other species, and that what in the past we thought to be metaphysical can be explained by biology. René Descartes thought that there was a mind–matter duality, and that the seat of consciousness could not be located in the brain. Over the years, neurophysiology has shown us that thinking, learning, emotions and other kinds of complex behaviour are most probably changes in the brain state. In short, science may be

---

[19] J. Savulescu, 'Death, us and our bodies: personal reflections' (2003) 29 *Journal of Medical Ethics* 127, 130.
[20] T. Engelhardt, 'Redefining death' in S. Youngner, R. Arnold and R. Schapiro (eds), *The Definition of Death* (Johns Hopkins University Press, 1999).
[21] J. McMahan, 'An alternative to brain death' (2006) 34 *Journal of Law, Medicine and Ethics* 44.
[22] D. DeGrazia, 'The definition of death', *The Stanford Encyclopedia of Philosophy* (Fall 2011 Edition), Edward N. Zalta (ed.), available at http://plato.stanford.edu/archives/fall2011/entries/death-definition/.

coming to the view that we humans are a very complex physiological machine like many other animals, and that the notion that humans have a special state of consciousness is highly controversial.

THE ENDING OF CARDIAC FUNCTION

Under this definition, if the heart stops beating irreversibly, the patient is dead. It is important to stress the irreversibility requirement in this test, because the heart can stop but the patient can be resuscitated. It would be nonsensical to define a person as dead every time their heart stopped, if they were then resuscitated.[23]

Justification of ending of cardiac function

In 1990 the Danish Council of Ethics preferred cessation of cardiac function over brain death as the marker of death.[24] The Council took the view that the definition of death is not a technical question but must be decided in terms of how the community as a whole understands death. It argued that the person in the street would view the stopping of the beating heart as the criterion for death, because the heart is widely seen as a symbol of life.[25] So even if the notion of the beating heart as the key to life is not logically or philosophically justifiable, it is intuitively felt to be the essential mark of life. Indeed, notably, supporters of brain stem death often refer to the fact that it is associated with cessation of breathing as a justification for using that test. The fact that this argument is used reflects the intuitive appeal of looking to cardiac function as a sign of life.

In the past, the cessation of cardiac function was the primary test for death, because there was not the technology available to assess brain activity. Hence the popularity of the old-fashioned test of putting a mirror above a person's mouth to see if any air was exhaled. Traditionally this was justified on the basis that the heart was the centre of the body and of powerful symbolic significance. Nowadays, supporters of cardiac function tend to emphasise that the cessation of the beating heart marks the point at which the body ceases to be a 'working organism'.[26] The functions of the body might include: metabolism, reproduction, sensation, locomotion. Only once all of these are no longer being performed should the body be said to have died.[27] James Bernat's definition of death as 'the permanent cessation of the critical functions of the organism as a

---

[23] D. Greer, 'Blurred lines: redefining life and death' (2012) 135 *Brain* 1332.

[24] D. Shewmon, 'The brain and somatic integration: insights into the standard biological rationale for equating "brain death" with death' (2001) 26 *Journal of Medicine and Philosophy* 457.

[25] R. Truog, 'Is it time to abandon brain death?' (1997) 27 *Hastings Center Report* 29.

[26] D. Lamb, *Death, Brain Death and Ethics* (Routledge, 1987).

[27] An extreme view is that death only occurs when every cell in the body has died, but that has few supporters and would not be practical.

whole'[28] has been very influential in the medical and legal communities. These functions do not necessarily cease on brain stem death, but they do when the heart stops beating.

With this understanding of cardiac function, the difference from the brain stem death is more limited. Indeed Mason et al.[29] suggest that it would be wrong to see brain stem death and non-breathing as two competing definitions of death. They prefer:

> to visualise the brain, the heart and the lungs as forming a 'cycle of life' which can be broken at any point; looked at in this way, there is no need to speak of two *concepts* of death – that is, cardiorespiratory death or brain death; it is simply that different criteria, and different tests, can be used for identifying that the cycle has been broken.

The cardiac function approach is used in the context of organ donation and is known as non-beating heart organ donation. It is used because once the heart has stopped beating, if there is too long a delay (as there may be to ascertain brain stem death) this may render the heart unfit for transplant. Notably this has caused controversy on the basis that the test for death used is determined by the usefulness of organs rather than a deeper concept of death.[30] Further, critics claim it can lead to the position that an organ donor will have a different test for death from a non-organ donor.

Objections to using end of cardiac function

One difficulty with using the cessation of the heartbeat as the criterion for death is that even if a patient's heart has stopped beating, medical intervention may still enable their resuscitation. Much must therefore turn on an assessment of whether there is an irreversible end of breathing. That is problematic, because in respect of a particular patient it might not be known whether the cessation of cardiac function is irreversible until further medical intervention has been used. Another difficulty is that it is also now clear that the stopping of the heart does not immediately lead to an end of brain activity. This then could lead to a person being treated as dead even though there is some form of consciousness.

Those who emphasise the beating heart as the sign of life do not have the difficulty of dealing with patients with complex mental disabilities restricting their capacity for consciousness. Their heart is undoubtedly beating and so they are alive. But if the critics of the brain stem death claim that that test elevates the

---

[28] J. Bernat, 'A defense of the whole brain concept of death' (1998) 28 *Hastings Center Report* 14, 17.

[29] J. Mason, A. McCall Smith and G. Laurie, *Law and Medical Ethics* (Oxford University Press, 2006), 466.

[30] J. Bernat, 'Life or death for the dead-donor rule?' (2013) 369 *New England Journal of Medicine* 14.

brain to being the primary function of the body, critics of the cardiac function test will complain that it elevates the heart to that role. However, Shewmon denies this, emphasising that the beating heart test is looking at whether the organism is an integrated whole: 'What is of the essence of integrative unity is neither localized nor replaceable: namely the anti-entropic mutual interaction of all the cells and tissues of the body, mediated in mammals by circulating oxygenated blood'.[31] In his view, it is not the beating heart per se which is key; it is the fact the heart pumps blood round the body, providing it with integration, that matters.

There are practical problems with the cardiac function test. It might restrict the use of organs from brain-dead patients. There would also be considerable costs in maintaining as alive people who are brain dead and currently treated as being dead. These consequences might be avoided. We might, for example, change the rule on when organs can be removed from a donor by departing from the 'dead-donor rule' and permit the removal of organs from a person still alive.[32] We could also justify the withdrawal of life support from brain-dead patients, without saying they are dead. However, these would require a major change in our treatment of living people.

DEATH AS A PROCESS

All the approaches defined so far have sought to indicate the point in time at which death occurs. An alternative approach argues that death is better seen as a process that occurs over time rather than as a one-off event.[33] Occasionally there will be a clear instant of death, where, for example, a person is blown up in an explosion. But otherwise there is no easy cut-off point at which we can mark the line between a person who is alive and a person who is dead. As one dying patient put it, 'death keeps taking a little bit of me'.[34]

Lawyers supportive of this approach will find it difficult to implement it into a legal structure. We need a definition of death for a range of purposes, such as the law of murder or withdrawal of treatment. Saying that death is a process does not provide the law with the kind of certainty required. As is often the case, the law needs to set an arbitrary point for legal purposes to produce a workable law. A good example is a speed limit of, say, 30 mph on a road. In truth 29 mph is probably no safer than 31 mph, but the law needs to draw the line somewhere, even if there is a degree of artificiality. So lawyers may

---

[31] D. Shewmon, 'The brain and somatic integration: Insights into the standard biological rationale for equating "brain death" with death' (2001) 26 *Journal of Medicine and Philosophy* 457, 473.

[32] D. DeGrazia, 'Biology, consciousness, and the definition of death' in T. Shannon (ed.), *Death and Dying* (Rowman and Littlefield, 2004), 1.

[33] A. Halevy, 'Beyond brain death?' (2001) 26 *Journal of Medicine and Philosophy* 493.

[34] Quoted in K. Kafetz, 'What happens when elderly people die' (2002) 95 *Journal of the Royal Society of Medicine* 536, 536.

comment that even if the process argument is true, as a matter of biology the law needs to be somewhat crude and adopt a clear cut-off point.

However, supporters of the 'death as a process' approach need not be dismayed by that response. While one option is to choose an arbitrary point of death, and accept it as a legal fiction,[35] there are others. We might start to separate out the 'death questions' into discrete issues for lawyers, and give different answers as to when one dies for the purposes of the law of murder, the law on organ removal or the law on cessation of treatment. In a similar vein, as Herring and Chau[36] note, it would be possible for the law to disclaim any definition of death, and simply provide answers to a range of questions (When can organs be removed? When can treatment be withdrawn?, etc.) without referring to death. Such approaches are not alien to the law. Think of the idea of adulthood. There is no clear cut-off point as to when a person becomes an adult, and instead the law makes provisions as to what age someone must be for different activities.

Another solution to the dilemma is to adopt the approach promoted by Wittgenstein[37] to the definition of some concepts and rely on 'family resemblances'. The argument is that for some concepts – in our discussions, death – we cannot produce a precise definition, but we can produce a list of features typically associated with death. This might include, David DeGrazia[38] suggests, 'unconsciousness, absence of spontaneous efforts to breathe, absence of heartbeat, inertness, lack of integrated bodily functions, incapacity to grow, and physical decay'. If all of these are present then there is death, and the more there are present, the closer the state is to death. Relying on this approach, Chiong argues:

> When some property is central to the cluster – as I've argued consciousness is – then possessing only this one property may be sufficient for membership in [the class of living things]. However, merely possessing one or several properties that are peripheral to the cluster may not be sufficient for membership. [S]ome robots are organizationally complex and functionally responsive, though intuitively not alive.[39]

Alan Shewmon and David Geffen[40] have suggested that a distinction be drawn between 'passing away' (or deceased) and 'de-animation'. Passing away would

---

[35] S. Shah, R. Truog and F. Miller, 'Death and legal fictions' (2013) 35 *Journal of Medicine and Philosophy* 256.

[36] J. Herring and P-L. Chau, 'The meaning of death' in J. Herring et al. (eds), *Death Rites and Rights* (Hart Publishing, 2007).

[37] L. Wittgenstein, *Philosophical Investigations* (Macmillan, 1953).

[38] D. DeGrazia, 'The definition of death', *The Stanford Encyclopedia of Philosophy* (Fall 2011 Edition), Edward N. Zalta (ed.), available at http://plato.stanford.edu/archives/fall2011/entries/death-definition/.

[39] W. Chiong, 'Brain death without definitions' (2005) 35 *Hastings Center Report* 20, 26.

[40] D. Shewmon and D. Geffen, 'Constructing the death elephant: a synthetic paradigm shift for the definition, criteria, and tests for death' (2010) 35 *Journal of Medicine and Philosophy* 256.

be analogous to birth: it is the being of the person in a socio-legal sense, the moment at which the person ceases to be part of the community and is no longer able to interact with the world; while de-animation would be analogous to conception: the end/beginning of the organism for biological purposes. Passing away would be used for most purposes, they suggest, including the law. De-animation would mark the point of the end of the organism as a whole, and could be used for religious purposes or ontology.

Justifications of death as a process

The argument in support of this is that there is no one moment where we can say that a person has 'died'. We can be sure by the time of putrefaction that a person is now dead, but to select one point of the process as the moment of death is artificial.

Supporters may go on to argue that looking at the different circumstances in which the definition is relevant, there is a range of interests and factors present. The arguments that might come into play in deciding when a person has died for the purposes of organ removal might be very different from those which are relevant in deciding whether a person's life-support machine can be switched off. It would be entirely sensible for the law to use one understanding of death in one context and a different one in another context.[41]

Objections to the death as a process approach

Although there is much to be said in favour of seeing death as a process, it has practical difficulties. The law, relatives and professionals require a clear point in time at which someone has died. Those caring for the patient at the end of life, whether relatives, friends or professionals, need the psychological benefit of having a single moment declared to be death. Whatever the logic of claiming that death is a process, in emotional terms we are better off using a particular moment in time.

Others will question whether we do see death as a process. To many people there is a fundamental difference between a dead person and one who is not. We are willing to treat dead bodies in a way which would be utterly unacceptable as regards those who are alive. Treating a teenager as a child and not an adult may not be a serious problem (after all, the teenager will be an adult soon), but treating an alive person as dead would be a major moral wrong. Morally, the loss of personhood is a fundamental change of status.[42] This distinction is fudged if we take the line that death is a process.

---

[41] I. Persson, 'Human death – A view from the beginning of life' (2002) 16 *Bioethics* 32, 32.

[42] R. Veatch, 'The death of whole-brain death' (2005) 30 *Journal of Medicine and Philosophy* 353.

CHOICE

Alireza Bagheri[43] has suggested that because there are so many definitions of death, and they all depend on one's theological, spiritual or political beliefs, it is best to let each person decide what they would like their definition of death to be. The proposal could be that on registering with the NHS, a patient would be asked to state which definition of death they prefer. Details of this proposal would need to be worked out. There would need to be appropriate information to enable people to make a choice. We might need to limit the choices people could make. We would not want people making absurd decisions about when they are to be treated as dead (e.g. when they reach 40!). Another difficulty might be a patient insisting on highly expensive treatment, keeping them 'alive' when they are in fact 'dead' according to any generally accepted medical standard.[44] These difficulties could be dealt with by restricting the definitions a person might use.[45] So, perhaps people would have to adopt one of, say, four models, otherwise it might become too complex. There would need to be a default option if people failed to make a selection. Provision would need to be made if people had made a choice but later departed from it. The statutory regulation for advance decisions could be used by analogy (see Chapter 3). These are all practical problems, but none seems insurmountable. The approach has been adopted in Japan and has not proved unworkable.[46]

The argument in favour

As can be seen from the debates in this chapter, people have strong views on the definition of death, and the debates reflect deeply held beliefs about the nature of life, for some touching on religious issues. Given the lack of consensus, we should allow people to select their own definition of death, rather than have it imposed by others. We already have accepted the idea that through advance decisions people can determine their future treatment, and allowing the choice of definition of death is simply an application of that.

The argument against

Some would feel that allowing choice in this area creates undesirable complexity. We do not normally allow a choice over the definition of a key term. A mother, cannot, for example, say that she regards her foetus as a person and

---

[43] A. Bagheri, 'Individual choice in the definition of death' (2007) 33 *Journal of Medical Ethics* 146.

[44] H. Evans, 'Reply to: Defining death: when physicians and families differ' (2002) 28 *Journal of Medical Ethics* 94.

[45] K. Zeiler, 'Why death-concept, death-definition, death-criterion and death-test pluralism should be allowed, even though it creates some problems' (2009) 23 *Bioethics* 450.

[46] M. Morikoa, 'Reconsidering brain death: a lesson from Japan's fifteen years of experience' (2001) 31 *Hastings Center Report* 41.

thereby grant the foetus the legal status of a person. Further, the definition of death is not just a personal matter; it raises public issues and issues for staff who must deal with a patient. The proposal might simply open the door to disputes and arguments over whether a person had understood their chosen definition, or whether they had subsequently changed their views. Arguably, a fixed definition would provide greater reassurance and clarity for all. It might be added that of course medical teams will take an individual's and their family's beliefs into account in determining a sensitive and appropriate way of dealing with a death (e.g. allowing a family to stay with a body, even though in legal terms death has taken place).

Choosing Between the Definitions

Having looked at some of the competing definitions of death, we will now highlight some of the differences between the definitions and the key issues which have led people to define death in such different ways.

David Lamb[47] has stated: 'It is as wrong to treat the living as dead as it is to treat the dead as alive.' Not everyone will agree with that, and some will claim it is far worse to treat an alive person as dead than the other way round. That is because if you are alive, you have important interests which are infringed if you die; but if you are dead, you have no interests. We explored that issue in Chapter 7. It is central to the debate here, however. If you think it is much worse to treat an alive person as dead than vice versa, you may be attracted to the argument of 'safety first': let's set the definition of death later rather than earlier, to ensure that if we make a mistake, we make the preferable one. But not everyone will agree with that. Treating a dead person as alive may be a waste of resources or delay improperly the grieving process for the family. That might argue in favour of setting the definition on the early side in dubious cases. The point is here that your reaction to Lamb's quote will affect which definition of death you will prefer.

The different definitions of death tend to group into two categories: those that emphasise life as being about conscious awareness, and those that understand the body as a living organism. The problem is that many people regard both understandings of our bodies and lives as valid.[48] One solution could be to accept that we die twice: once when we lose consciousness, and once when our biological organism comes to an end. Jeff McMahan has suggested that the correct view is that we die twice – biologically and non-biologically:

> An organism dies in the biological sense when it loses the capacity for integrated functioning. The best criterion for when this happens is probably a circulatory respiratory criterion. ... What it is important to be able to determine is when we die in

[47] D. Lamb, 'What is death?' in R. Gillon (ed.), *Principles of Health Care Ethics* (John Wiley & Sons, 1994), 1028.
[48] S. Holland, *Bioethics* (Polity, 2003), 75.

the non-biological sense – that is, when we cease to exist. If we are embodied minds, we die or cease to exist when we irreversibly lose the capacity for consciousness – or, to be more precise, when there is irreversible loss of function in those areas of the brain in which consciousness is realized. The best criterion for when this happens is a higher-brain criterion – for example, what is called 'cerebral death'.[49]

Another issue which has not received as much attention as it should is that the issue of death can be seen from the perspective of the dying person, but there are also the interests of the relatives and friends. Most of the discussion has focused on when the individual person can be said to have experienced death. However, another relevant point is to look at the issue from the point of view of those caring for the deceased. Indeed, arguably, the definition of death matters more to the family and friends than to the individual patient. A definition of death which conflicts with the perspective of the family may cause considerable grief.

While debates on the definition of death can focus on ethereal concepts, practical realities are important. We have already mentioned the importance to organ donation of the definition of death. Further, although it is rarely discussed openly, there is an important issue about rationing healthcare resources. Keeping people with minimal functioning 'alive' is an extremely expensive business. If there is no clear consensus on the definition of death, is it unreasonable to choose the cheapest definition?

CONCLUSION

As will be clear from this discussion, the debates over the definition of death can raise some deep issues. In part the difficulty is that we are using the word 'death' to mark different points in time. Clearly, a reasonable case can be made for seeing death as the loss of consciousness and interaction with others; but also as a cessation of the biological functioning. There is no right answer here. The difficulty for the law is that it must pick an understanding which achieves the goals the law seeks to promote. Those are not the same in all death questions.

Debate 2
Autonomy and death

INTRODUCTION

At the heart of many arguments in favour of allowing assisted dying is the principle of autonomy. This debate will consider how autonomy might be used to make a case in favour of permitting assisted dying, and how opponents of any such change might respond to those arguments.

---

[49] J. McMahan, *The Ethics of Killing* (Oxford University Press, 2002), 204.

Opponents of the current law claim that it fails to adequately respect people's autonomous decisions concerning their death. The law gives some limited protection to autonomy through allowing suicide[50] and through giving patients with capacity the absolute right to refuse treatment, even if doing so leads to death.[51] However, the law does not protect the autonomous wishes of those who wish or need to use the assistance of others to die. In such cases, the laws of murder and assisting and encouraging suicide[52] render assistance or positive intervention illegal. This can mean that those who lack the physical ability to commit suicide, or who cannot face doing it, are unable to put their autonomous decision into practice.

THE AUTONOMY ARGUMENT FOR BEING PERMITTED TO END ONE'S LIFE

Autonomy is the idea that people should be able to make decisions for themselves about how they wish to live their lives. Joseph Raz defines it in this way:

> The ruling idea behind the ideal of personal autonomy is that people should make their own lives. The autonomous person is a (part) author of his own life. The ideal of personal autonomy is the vision of people controlling, to some degree, their own destiny, fashioning it through successive decisions throughout their lives.[53]

The opposite of autonomy is paternalism.[54] That is where someone else decides what is best for you. It is how children are often treated. The principle of autonomy declares that a person should be free to make decisions for themselves, however foolish other people might think those decisions are. Autonomy protects people's decisions not because they are good choices, but because they are their choices. In the context of end-of-life decisions, Debbie Purdy (who brought legal proceedings to change the law on assisted dying) has written:

> I want to be in control of my life, and that means I want to be able to live it as long as I can, but I want to be able to choose what quality of life is livable; I don't want somebody else to tell me that 'the quality of your life's ok, what are you complaining about?' I want to be able to make those choices myself. I want the help and support to make it.[55]

It is generally accepted that there are exceptions to the autonomy principle. Only the decisions of an autonomous person require respect. So if someone is

---

[50] Although there is little the law could do. In the past attempted suicide was a criminal offence, but it is hard to believe that it amounted to a deterrent. The offence was abolished in s. 1 of the Suicide Act 1961.

[51] *Re B (Consent to Treatment: Capacity)* [2002] EWHC 429.

[52] Suicide Act 1961, s. 2.

[53] J. Raz, *The Morality of Freedom* (Oxford University Press, 1986), 369.

[54] See Chapter 1 for further discussion.

[55] Commission on Assisted Dying, *The Current Legal Status of Assisted Dying is Inadequate and Incoherent* ... (Demos, 2013), 70.

a child or lacks mental capacity then their decision is not protected. So, supporters of the autonomy principle are not committed to saying that a 7 year
old who wants to die when they lose their teddy has a right to have that decision respected. Also it is accepted that autonomous decisions are not respected
if doing so harms others. You cannot drive at 100 mph if you wish to, because
doing so will risk harm to others. However, supporters of assisted dying claim
that no one else would be harmed if the law were amended to allow assistance
in death. Indeed, in many cases which have come before the courts, the decision of the person seeking assistance is supported by their family. Even if it were
shown that someone would be distressed by their death, the person wishing to
die may well claim that this is insufficient to force them keep on living against
their will.

Supporters of the autonomy argument commonly claim that the weight to
be attached to an autonomous decision will depend on the seriousness of the
issue for the individual involved. A good example is the law requiring the use
of seatbelts. This is an interference in autonomy for those who would prefer
not to wear a seatbelt, but one justification is that the interference is limited.
Few people will regard seatbelt wearing as central to their life. However, it is
argued there is a particularly serious interference with autonomy if end-of-
life decisions are made. Ronald Dworkin has written: 'Making someone die
in a way that others approve, but he believes a horrifying contradiction of his
life, is a devastating, odious form of tyranny.'[56] This argument can be made
by distinguishing, as Dworkin does, between different kinds of decisions we
make. He suggests that some decisions reflect critical interests and others
reflect experiential interests. Critical interests are those which are central to
a person's identity: they reflect a person's really important values and principles. Religious principles; core ethical principles; interests which a person
would say are a central part of who they are, would all be critical interests.
By contrast, experiential interests may give someone momentary pleasure but
are not self-defining. You might enjoy the odd chocolate bar now and then,
but you would (probably!) not see chocolate bar eating as a central goal of
your life.

Using this analysis, supporters claim that decisions about a person's death
are critical interests. True, some people believe that a good death involves
struggling to live for as long as possible, while others believe it is better to die
before life becomes undignified or full of pain. But either way, how one dies is
important. The point is that each person should be free to select their mode of
dying, and if that needs the involvement of others, they should be free to act as
requested without fear of criminal prosecution.

Kate Greasley[57] has questioned whether for most people the manner of
death is a critical interest. She argues that, with a few exceptions, the exact

---

[56] R. Dworkin, *Life's Dominion* (HarperCollins, 1993), 217.

[57] K. Greasley, '*R (Purdy) v DPP* and the case for wilful blindness' (2010) 30 *Oxford Journal of Legal Studies* 301.

manner of our death is not normally regarded as a matter saying very much about a person's life. Few obituaries focus on the precise moments or nature of the death. That may well be true, but it may be no response to those for whom their manner of death is central to their life stories. Another response might be to say that control over death gives more control over life. Joseph Raz[58] has suggested that:

> inevitably shaping one's dying contributes to giving shape, contributes to the form and meaning one's life has. Those who reflect, plan and decide on the manner of their dying make their dying part of their life. And if they do so well then by integrating their dying into their life they enrich their life.
>
> It can transform one's perspective on one's life; reduce the aspects of it from which one is alienated, or those that inspire a sense of helplessness or terror. It is a change that makes one whole in generating a perspective, a way of conceiving oneself and one's life free from some of those negative aspects.

Similarly, Syme argues that '[t]he last weeks or days of a person's life are some of the most precious, because so little remains. They should not be crushed by toxic anxiety. They should be liberated from fear by the confidence of control.'[59]

In conclusion, supporters of euthanasia sometimes claim that those opposing euthanasia are attempting to impose their own ethical or religious beliefs on others.[60] There is no consensus about what makes a good life or death. Decisions about how one dies are deeply personal and will reflect a range of views. We should allow each person to decide such issues for themselves.

Arguments Against Autonomy

Those who reject the autonomy argument have three main routes open to them. We explore each of these separately.

Other principles outweigh autonomy

Some people accept that there is a right to have one's autonomous decisions respected, including death, but that such a right is trumped by other considerations. The House of Lords Select Committee stated:

> We acknowledge that there are individual cases in which euthanasia may be seen by some to be appropriate. But individual cases cannot reasonably establish the foundation of a policy which would have such serious and widespread repercussions. Moreover dying is not only a personal or individual affair. The death of a

---

[58] J. Raz, 'Death in our life', available at http://ssrn.com/abstract=2069357.

[59] R. Syme, *A Good Death: An Argument for Voluntary Euthanasia* (Melbourne University Press, 2008), 205.

[60] E. Jackson, 'In favour of the legalization of assisted dying' in E. Jackson and J. Keown, *Debating Euthanasia* (Hart Publishing, 2012).

person affects the lives of others, often in ways and to   .not be
foreseen. We believe that the issue of euthanasia is one ιιι .   .erests of
the individual cannot be separated from the interest of society as a w.. ɔle.[61]

As revealed above, in principle this is a sound argument. No one supports
the idea that autonomy allows people to do anything they want, regardless of
the harms to others. But what other interests might justify an interference in
autonomy, particularly over an issue which is (arguably) of profound importance to many people? There are several options:

(i) The interests of family members
One argument may be the interests of family members. They will suffer grief
and upset if a person is helped to die. However, while it is true that the death
of a person will inevitably affect their friends and families, it is not clear that
this will always be in a bad way. The partners of Diane Pretty, Debbie Purdy
and Tony Nicklinson, who were involved in the leading cases on assisted
dying, all supported the applicants' decisions to die. Indeed, the applicants
highlighted the harms caused to their families by the current law forbidding assisted suicide. It seems at most that the argument could be made that
there might be a case where allowing someone assistance in death would
cause great distress to a family member. It does not seem to be an argument
that assisted suicide might never be justified. Even in cases where relatives
are upset, it is not clear that that upset is sufficient harm to justify interfering
in a person's autonomous decision, particularly if it requires them to continue with a life they find unbearably painful.

(ii) Others will be pressured into 'agreeing' to assisted suicide
The argument here is that increasing some people's autonomy by giving
them the option to have an assisted death will impinge on the autonomy of
others by pressuring them into committing suicide.[62] We will not explore
this further here, because we have a separate debate specifically on the extent
to which a liberalisation of the law may lead to pressure on others (see
Debate 3 below). Nearly everyone agrees that if the law is liberalised to
permit assisted dying there need to be in place restrictions on access to
assisted dying, to ensure that people are not pressured into being killed
against their full wishes. This will be looked at later, but here we will emphasise that there is a balance to be struck. Imagine that safeguards were put
in place, but in one in a thousand cases someone slipped through the net
and was killed without their full consent. To some that is a sufficient reason
to ban assisted dying altogether. Others believe that protection of rights

---

[61] House of Lords Select Committee, *Assisted Dying for the Terminally Ill Bill* (TSO, 2005),
para. 237.
[62] K. Tomsons and S. Sherwin, 'Feminist reflections on Tracy Latimer and Su Rodriguez' in M.
Sting (ed.), *The Price of Compassion: Assisted Suicide and Euthanasia* (Broadview Press, 2010).

comes at a cost, and as long as we do our best to protect the vulnerable that is the best we can do. Further, one must remember that under the current system, vulnerable people are liable to be killed without their full consent, e.g. through the doctrine of double effect (see Chapter 10). It cannot be assumed that any change in the law will protect vulnerable people less than the current law.

We will return to these issues when considering the protection of vulnerable people in an assisted dying case in the third debate in this chapter.

(iii) Moral principles: sanctity of life

This argument is that upholding the moral principle of sanctity of life justifies an interference in autonomy. It claims that society is entitled to interfere in decisions of members in order to uphold moral principles which underpin a society. This is recognised in the European Convention on Human Rights, where in Article 8(2) 'protection of morals' is given as a reason that an interference in the right to respect for private life might be justified. What moral principle would justify restricting end-of-life decision autonomy? The most likely candidate is the principle of sanctity of life.

The principle of sanctity of life claims that no one should ever be intentionally killed. That is because every life is precious. We should never accept that a person's life is so lacking in value that we should seek to end it. Crucially for the sanctity of life view, the preciousness in a person's life exists even if the particular individual no longer values their life.[63] As Baroness Hale put it in *Purdy*: 'It is not for society to tell people what to value about their own lives. But it may be justifiable for society to insist that we value their lives even if they do not.'[64]

A powerful point made in favour of the sanctity of life approach is that it promotes the idea of human equality. Under the principle of sanctity of life, everyone's life is inherently of value. That value does not depend on your abilities, your status in society, your feelings. Everyone just has this inherent value. If you reject that argument and claim that the value of a person's life depends on their feelings, their pain levels or their disabilities, then we start saying that some lives are more precious than others. At that point we enter very dangerous territory. John Finnis claims:

> Human life is indeed the concrete reality of the human person. In sustaining human bodily life, in however impaired a condition, one is sustaining the person whose life it is. In refusing to choose to violate it, one respects the person in the most fundamental and indispensable way.[65]

---

[63] Linacre Centre, 'Submission to the House of Lords Select Committee on Medical Ethics' in L. Gormally (ed.), *Euthanasia, Clinical Practice and the Law* (Linacre Centre, 1994).

[64] *R (Purdy) v DPP* [2009] UKHL 45, para. 68.

[65] J. Finnis, 'The fragile case for euthanasia: a reply to John Harris' in J. Keown (ed.), *Euthanasia Examined* (Cambridge University Press, 1995), 32.

Yet there is a degree of ambiguity at the heart of the doctrine of sanctity of life. What exactly is this 'preciousness' which is at the heart of everyone's life? It is not surprising that the sanctity of life approach has found favour among those writing from a religious perspective. For them it is the fact God values life that gives the life its preciousness. However, there are certainly supporters of the principle who use non-religious grounds. Margaret Sommerville[66] emphasises the importance of the 'secular sacred', respecting the mysteries of life and death, which is of importance to the religious and non-religious. She also emphasises the 'deeply intuitive sense of relatedness or connectedness to other people and to the world and the universe in which we live',[67] which means that each person's life has value for the whole of society. This suggests that the source of the value need not be God but rather the wider community, or those in a relationship with the individual.[68] Emily Jackson,[69] by contrast, contends that it is impossible to have a secular understanding of the principle of sanctity of life. She argues that the principle only makes sense based on religious values. There can be no source of value outside the individual themselves, except a God. As a result, she argues the principle should play no role in secular law.

Opponents of the principle of sanctity of life generally accept that life is precious and valuable, but argue its value lies in what the individual is able to get out of life.[70] Supporters of euthanasia often take the view that there comes a point where a person's life is so wracked with pain and indignity that its special value has been lost. Ronald Dworkin, considering the position of a patient suffering from Alzheimer's, says that such a person 'is no longer capable of the acts or attachments that can give [life] value. Value cannot be poured into a life from the outside; it must be generated by the person whose life it is, and this is no longer possible for him'.[71] Such a view claims that what makes life valuable are the things that people do with it. It is the experiences people have, their relationships and activities which give life meaning. A person with no experiences (or only pain-filled ones) and no capacity for relationships has lost the goodness of life.[72]

Richard Huxtable[73] suggests that the debate over sanctity of life reflects different ways that a life can be valued. He suggests three ways:

> So first of all on the prohibitive side obviously, we have the appeal to the so-called intrinsic value of life, the idea that life itself is valuable and should not intentionally be brought to an end. On the more permissive side, of course, we've got the

---

[66] M. Sommerville, *Death Talk* (McGill-Queen's University Press, 2001).

[67] M. Sommerville, 'Deathbed disputation' (2002) 167 *Canadian Medical Association Journal* 651, 654.

[68] M. Sommerville, *Death Talk* (McGill-Queen's University Press, 2001), xiv.

[69] E. Jackson, 'Secularism, sanctity and the wrongness of killing' (2008) 3 *Biosocieties* 125.

[70] J. Harris, *The Value of Life* (Routledge, 1992).

[71] R. Dworkin, *Life's Dominion* (HarperCollins, 1993), 230.

[72] J. Glover, *Causing Death and Saving Lives* (Penguin, 1977).

[73] Quoted in Commission on Assisted Dying, *The Current Legal Status of Assisted Dying is Inadequate and Incoherent* ... (Demos, 2013), 78.

arguments that appeal to instead the instrumental value of life, in the sense that we refer to suffering and the like; so in that account we're not saying life itself is valuable, but rather that life of a sufficiently good quality is valuable. In other words life is an instrumental vehicle to other goods; if that vehicle is substantially broken maybe it's time to abandon it. But thirdly, and perhaps most prominently nowadays, we talk about the self-determined value of life whereby it's over to me to decide what counts for me or what doesn't count for me in terms of making life worth living or not.[74]

In considering the debate over the sanctity of life here are two issues to consider. First, while clearly the principle has its supporters, there are plenty in our society who do not agree with it. Given the controversy over it, can it really part of the bedrock of our society's moral principles? Should the law take sides on the debate over sanctity of life? Second, even if one accepts that life does have sanctity, a specialness independent of the feelings or experiences of the person concerned, does that specialness necessarily trump the agony a person who wishes to die is feeling? One might, in other words, take a middle view and accept there is an inherent value in life without agreeing that it creates an ultimate value that trumps whatever pain someone is going through.

One cannot make an autonomous decision to die

As mentioned earlier, supporters of autonomy accept that we only need to respect the decisions of those who have capacity to make the decision. They clearly are not claiming, therefore, that children or those lacking mental capacity should be allowed an assisted death. We shall be discussing in Debate 3 below cases where a person's mental state may be such that they cannot consent, and whether procedures can be put in place to ensure that they are not permitted access to assisted dying. However, some go further and ask whether anyone can make an autonomous decision to die. At first that might sound like an odd question, but it is not as bizarre as it at first sounds.

Could an argument be made that everyone lacks capacity to decide to die? That argument would need to rest on the claim that death is the great unknown. As we cannot know what death is like, then we lack a key piece of information necessary to make an informed decision to die. That is a somewhat questionable argument. It could be used to defeat any exercise of autonomy: you cannot know what it will be like to have a child, and so you cannot autonomously choose to become pregnant. The response to the argument is that as long as the person knows that there is much we don't know about death, they can choose to make the decision. After all, when making a decision we often choose not to know everything we could. You really *don't* want to know exactly what is in that burger …

---

[74] R. Huxtable, *Law, Ethics and Compromise at the Limits of Life* (Routledge, 2012), 112.

Autonomy does not apply to death

Some commentators argue that the principle of autonomy does not apply to death. Two arguments may be made. The first is that autonomy is about the ability to make choices. The whole point about autonomy is that we treasure the ability to control our lives. That is why a good reason for restricting autonomy is that a decision a person makes now will severely go on to limit their autonomy later on. So we do not allow people to choose to become slaves. That is because while allowing a person to be a slave would respect their autonomy now, it would severely restrict their options later in life. Well, opponents of liberalising the law will say, if this argument explains why one cannot choose to be a slave, the argument is all the stronger in relation to a decision to die. That is the ultimate denial of choice. Kate Greasley argues, having noted that even supporters of autonomy do not generally support a person's agreeing to become a slave:

> Death spells the end of all good options because it spells the end of options, period. (In this way death seems even more inimical to autonomy than enslavement; we can imagine a slave having at least some options left open to him, albeit impoverished ones.) It is difficult to see, then, that helping someone to die can ever be compatible with the value of personal autonomy, even if in so doing we are acceding to his wishes.[75]

The analogy to slavery does not convince everyone. The slave is going to be forced to act in ways they do not want to, and that is a grave violation of their autonomy. The dead person will have no wishes and so is not going to be treated against their choice. The interference in their autonomy seems much less severe than in the case of the slave.[76] But, does that argument simply reflect an over-emphasis on death? If we think that loss of autonomy is worse than death, does that not show we have forgotten there is more to life than being autonomous?

An alternative argument is that we respect autonomy because we believe it will promote human flourishing. That explains why some exercises of autonomy do not deserve respect. Alexander McCall Smith[77] has warned against seeing autonomy as a good in and of itself. He says autonomy is a good because it enables us to develop our lives as we wish in connection with other people. Euthanasia, by contrast, is not promoting personal growth; it is the end of the person. It is therefore not possible to justify euthanasia on the basis

---

[75] K. Greasley, '*R (Purdy) v DPP* and the Case for Wilful Blindness' (2010) 30 *Oxford Journal of Legal Studies* 301.

[76] M. Sjostrand, G. Helgesson, S. Eriksson and N. Juthwe, 'Autonomy-based arguments against physician-assisted suicide and euthanasia: a critique' (2013) 16 *Medicine, Health Care and Philosophy* 225.

[77] A. McCall Smith, 'Beyond autonomy' (1997) 14 *Journal of Contemporary Health Law and Policy* 23.

of autonomy. Again, that may be questioned. Ending unbearable pain may promote personal growth. It may give someone peace and the opportunity to say goodbye to their family and friends. Remember that as we will all die, it may be better to see assisted dying as a choice about when to die. Seen in this way, it is less antagonistic to autonomy than might at first appear.

Critics might reply that this overlooks the fact that a way a person dies is regarded by many as an important part of their lives. A good death is seen as a good conclusion to the end of people's lives, fitting in with the values that have determined their lives to date. So seen, it is a reasonable aspect of a person's vision of a 'good life'.

LIMITING AUTONOMY

We have left arguably the biggest difficulty for autonomy supporters to the end. This is the argument that nearly all autonomy supporters accept, that there should be some limits on who can receive assistance in death. Typically these include that the person be suffering a terminal illness and/or a permanent disability. Wayne Sumner, for example, would require a patient to have capacity, to make a free and informed request, and to have an incurable illness or experience intolerable suffering.[78]

The classic hypothetical in the debates is the love-sick 18 year old who wishes to die because the 'love of their life' has ditched them. Few people would agree that such a teenager should have assistance in committing suicide. Something like Sumner's restrictions would ensure the teenager would not be able to access assisted dying.

The difficulty is this. The principle of autonomy says we must respect the decision a person makes, even if it is one we don't agree with. This means we should support the decision of the person who wants to die, even if we think it is a bad decision. We should require simply that the person has the capacity to make the choice.

Critics, such as John Keown,[79] argue that the love-sick teenager scenario shows that supporters of euthanasia only respect the wishes of a person if they think that the decision is a reasonable one. They are not true supporters of autonomy.[80] Ronald Dworkin has responded to such arguments that:

> [w]e might very well say as a community – we bet we might be wrong, but we bet – that if the teenage lover lives another two years, maybe even two weeks, he will be very glad not to have taken his own life.[81]

---

[78] L.W. Sumner, *Assisted Death: A Study in Ethics and Law* (Oxford University Press, 2011).

[79] J. Keown, 'Against decriminalizing euthanasia, for improving care' in E. Jackson and J. Keown, *Debating Euthanasia* (Hart Publishing, 2012).

[80] Ibid.

[81] R. Dworkin, 'Euthanasia, morality, and law transcript' (1998) 31 *Loyola Los Angeles Law Review* 1147, 1151.

But this is not completely convincing. It seems to make an assumption that we know better than the person themselves. In any event, even if the love-sick teenager still decided to die after two years of thinking about it, would we still want to help them die?

Lillehammer[82] rejects the logic of this argument, saying that it is perfectly coherent to hold that euthanasia is only appropriate where the patient both competently seeks euthanasia and such a patient is terminally ill. These two requirements could be seen as 'individually necessary and jointly sufficient'.[83] But this leaves open the question of when the death is 'good'. Who can decide this apart from the person themselves?

There is no doubt that the hypothetical example of the love-sick teenager has caused some difficulties for some supporters of euthanasia. But there is a problem here for opponents of euthanasia too. Most opponents of euthanasia support the principle that if a competent person refuses life-saving treatment, their wishes should be respected. But why does autonomy dominate when the wish is not to have treatment, but not when the patient seeks active intervention to hasten death?[84] If the love-sick teenager scrapes their knee and decides to refuse all medication and allow the wound to go septic, hoping thereby to die, should we allow them to do that? This issue raises the extent to which it is justifiable to distinguish an act and an omission. Yet, as we shall see, this is a distinction many philosophers find difficult to maintain.[85]

Kevin Yuill has argued that legalising euthanasia or assisted suicide will undermine autonomy. This is because those seeking assistance will be interviewed by experts to assess their competence. That will mean doctors can 'colonize our most intimate thoughts and influence what should be the most personal decision ever made'.[86] He is concerned that:

> [l]egalising assisted suicide reduces suicide to a medical choice. What should be profound and meaningful, the most human of human actions, loses its meaning. The question of whether 'to be or not to be' becomes a medical rather than a moral question.[87]

Yuill's preferred response is to make lethal drugs more readily available so that people can commit suicide, having made their own decision. Critics will see that as irresponsible, given the links between suicide and mental illness. But it does have the strength of holding onto the principle of autonomy.

---

[82] H. Lillehammer, 'Voluntary euthanasia and the logical slippery slope argument' (2002) 61 *Cambridge Law Journal* 545.

[83] Ibid., 548.

[84] E.g. J. Keown, 'Against decriminalizing euthanasia, for improving care' in E. Jackson and J. Keown, *Debating Euthanasia* (Hart Publishing, 2012).

[85] See Chapter 10, Debate 1 for a discussion of the act/omission distinction.

[86] K. Yuill, *Assisted Suicide* (Palgrave, 2012), 9.

[87] Ibid., 84.

Scenario to ponder

In Belgium,[88] deaf twins requested suicide. They had spent all their lives together and were very close. They had both been diagnosed with an eye condition which meant they would lose their sight. If both deaf and blind, communication would become nearly impossible. The authorities authorised their assisted death.

CONCLUSION

There is no doubting the appeal of the autonomy argument. Few people like being told what to do, especially when that goes against their deeply held beliefs. Preventing someone using assistance in dying seems to require more than a claim that it goes against the moral beliefs of some. The difficulty is that the example of death pushes our belief in autonomy to the limits. We might allow people to get tattoos – after all, if they really dislike them, they can later remove them. But in the case of death, there is no going back if a person is not happy with their decision. Given the gravity of the decision, supporters of autonomy need to be completely confident that the decision represents a settled, considered and informed decision. That, we suggest, may only be true in very rare cases.

Debate 3

Protection of the vulnerable

INTRODUCTION

A major theme in the debates over assisted dying is whether any reform of the law would work against the interests of vulnerable people. This is an issue which concerns both supporters and opponents of assisted suicide. Opponents believe that a liberalisation of the law will lead to the killing of people who have not truly consented to die. Further, through coarsening of respect for the value of life, it will indirectly pressure people into volunteering to be killed.

All serious supporters of a liberalisation of the law accept that there must be limitations on who can access assisted dying. We are normally stricter about ensuring that people are fully informed and free from pressure when they make very important decisions than, for example, when they are choosing what to buy in a supermarket. That might lead us to be particularly strict about what

---

[88] J. Hall, 'Identical twins die after seeking euthanasia when they discovered they would go blind and never see each other again', *Independent*, 14 January 2013.

will count as having capacity to make the decision. It is for this reason that proposals to reform the law on assisted dying typically include a range of safeguards designed to ensure that vulnerable people are not killed without their full consent. Typical is the Assisted Dying Bill 2013, section 1:

1. Assisted dying

(1) A person who is terminally ill may request and lawfully be provided with assistance to end his or her own life.

(2) Subsection (1) only applies where the person –

(a) has a clear and settled intention to end his or her own life;

(b) has made a declaration to that effect in accordance with section 3; and

(c) on the day the declaration is made –

(i) is aged 18 or over; and

(ii) has been ordinarily resident in England and Wales for not less than one year.

2. Terminal illness

(1) For the purposes of this Act, a person is terminally ill if that person –

(a) has been diagnosed by a registered medical practitioner as having an inevitably progressive condition which cannot be reversed by treatment ('a terminal illness'); and

(b) as a consequence of that terminal illness, is reasonably expected to die within six months.

(2) Treatment which only relieves the symptoms of an inevitably progressive condition temporarily is not to be regarded as treatment which can reverse that condition.[89]

The Bill goes on to contain details, but it is notable that proponents of the change of the law have gone to considerable lengths to appease the concerns of opponents. Indeed, this reflects the fact that concerns over the vulnerable have become the major argument relied upon by the opponents of the legislation of assisted dying.

To some there is a difficult balance between ensuring the protection of the vulnerable and protecting rights of autonomy. The Assisted Dying Bill, for example, is in some ways a notably restrictive legalisation. A person with a serious debilitating condition may not be able to use it if they have more than six months to live. Tony Nicklinson,[90] who had 'locked in syndrome', might not also, for the same reason. And that is a problematic example. If anyone has a case for assisted dying you might think that Tony Nicklinson, facing decades in a condition he finds degrading, seems to have the strongest.

The problem in deciding who should have access to assisted dying is that the greater the protections for the vulnerable, the more they may impede the

---

[89] Assisted Dying Bill 2013, cl. 1 and 2.

[90] R (Nicklinson) v Ministry of Justice [2013] EWCA 961.

autonomous decision of a person who wants to die. Or maybe it is better to see this as a balancing of autonomies: the autonomy of the vulnerable, and the autonomy of the would-be deceased.

In this section we will explore further what precisely are the concerns over vulnerable people, whether they are legitimate and whether safeguards such as those in the Bill will be effective. In all these debates it is important to remember this: even if we are worried about the treatment of the vulnerable if the law is amended, does the current law protect them any better?

KINDS OF VULNERABILITY

Sometimes those in the euthanasia debate talk rather vaguely about the dangers of abuse and the protection of vulnerable people. Those concerned about abuse might accept that some people will be strong enough to resist any such pressures, but particular groups may be susceptible. The following groups may be included:

Psychologically vulnerable and end of life

John Keown[91] has claimed that many people who consent to euthanasia may in fact simply be suffering from severe pain, distress, depression or 'demoralization', and are therefore not in a position to make a rational decision. Further, it should not be forgotten that people are often expected to take decisions over their medical treatment in the alien environment of a hospital, without clothes, friends and support. Worries about the expense of being looked after and being a burden on friends and relatives can all put pressure on those making decisions.

One response to these concerns is that they can be dealt with by ensuring that the patient has time to think through the decision and is given help and support to do so; but that if a doctor determines that the person's mental state is such that they lack capacity then their decision will not be respected. The issues, however, become difficult. There are strong links (not surprisingly) between requests for assisted dying and depression.[92] As Ilana Levene and Michael Parker point out, though, there are high rates of depression among those with terminal illness anyway, and it is not clear that those who seek assisted death have higher rates of depression than those who do not.[93] So it is not proven that depression causes people to seek assisted dying. Further, they suggest that doctors are well equipped to deal with the issue, noting that in

---

[91] J. Keown, *Euthanasia, Ethics and Public Policy* (Cambridge University Press, 2002), Chapter 5.

[92] I. Levene and M. Parker, 'Prevalence of depression in granted and refused requests for euthanasia and assisted suicide: a systematic review' (2011) 37 *Journal of Medical Ethics* 205.

[93] Ibid.

the Netherlands, the majority of requests for suicide from depressed patients are rejected. This last point raises a concern. What of those who are permitted? How sure can we be that in those cases, the individuals were not responding to their depression rather than a full assessment of what was in their best interests? Levene and Parker note that there are studies showing that some of those with severe depression change their views on assisted death following treatment for depression. Indeed, there is also some evidence that many of those seeking death are suffering depression, and that once medication for depression is provided, the numbers of those seeking euthanasia falls.[94] On the other hand, if someone with depression is assumed to lack capacity then a vast section of the population will be deemed to lack capacity. Around 9 per cent of the population have depression at any given time.[95] Depression is not normally taken as a sign of lack of capacity. In part the difficulty is that there is insufficient understanding of how depression affects a person's capacity to make decisions. Biggs and Diesfeld, looking at the position of depressed people, are concerned that assisted suicide and euthanasia would only further isolate those suffering with depression, rather than forcing society to properly face up to the challenges offered by depression.[96] Maybe, or would euthanasia provide too simple a response to those with depression?

The problem is that in many of the cases where a person is likely to want to die, their decision making will be to some extent impaired. They are likely to be in pain, and in anguish. According to a leading research team at the University of Washington,[97] 90 per cent of those who die from suicide have a diagnosable mental disorder. Even if there is no functional impairment, some claim that patients do not often appreciate the effectiveness of pain relief or the availability of rehabilitative care for those with disabilities or with terminal illness, and therefore cannot make a properly informed decision.[98]

In considering these claims, we should not forget that looking at suicide attempts generally, the cases which come to court are exceptional. Most suicide cases involve people plagued by mental illness and despair. They are not carefully thought-out decisions, but suicides will often have sufficient understanding to satisfy the test for capacity under the Mental Capacity Act 2005.[99] A further issue is that evidence suggests people with terminal illnesses keep changing

[94] Royal College of Psychiatrists, *Assisted Dying for the Terminally Ill Bill – Statement from the Royal College of Psychiatrists on Physician Assisted Suicide* (RCP, 2006).

[95] Mental Health Foundation, *Mental Health Statistics* (MHF, 2013).

[96] H. Biggs and K. Diesfeld, 'Assisted suicide for people with depression: an advocate's perspective' (1995) 2 *Medical Law International* 23.

[97] Mental Health Reporting, *Facts about Mental Health and Suicide* (University of Washington, 2013).

[98] D. Coleman and S. Drake, 'A disability perspective from the United States on Ms B' (2002) 28 *Journal of Medical Ethics* 240.

[99] J. Herring, 'Escaping from the shackles of law at the end of life' (2013) 21 *Medical Law Review* 487.

their views on whether or not they want assistance in dying.[100] So abiding by a person's wish to die one day may be to work contrary to what their wishes would be the next day. The European Parliamentary Assembly, Committee on Legal Affairs and Human Rights,[101] considering such evidence, stated:

> Medical professionals working within the palliative care sector have emphasised the fragility of patients' desire for death and the rapid changes that, in their experience, may occur in response to good symptom control or psychological interventions. The dangers of acceding to rare requests for voluntary active euthanasia and physician assisted suicide should not be underestimated.

These points are important. They provide a powerful case for saying that looking at the state of mind of those wishing to die generally, a significant majority are not making a richly autonomous decision. They might have mental capacity for legal purposes, but their current wish to die may be impeded by depression; contradictory to other decisions and values they hold dear; or subject to change if suitable treatment or provision is given. However, it is not clear that this necessarily defeats the autonomy argument. At best it may persuade supporters of the autonomy argument that very few people who wish to die will have in a sufficiently rich way autonomously decided to die.

Women and end of life

Some claim that women especially will feel under pressure to consent to have their lives ended. Katrina George lists the following factors as meaning that women's choices about euthanasia may not be voluntary: 'structural inequalities and disparities in power – most evident in women's experience of violence – and social and economic disadvantage and oppressive cultural stereotypes that idealize feminine self-sacrifice and reinforce stereotyped gender roles of passivity and compliance'.[102] Callahan is concerned that the autonomous argument used to support a right to die is based on an individualised model of autonomy that places insufficient weight on our relationships and responsibilities.[103]

The difficulty is to find a way which acknowledges the impact of societal forces on women's lives, without depriving them of control over their lives. Even accepting all these pressures, are they sufficient to mean there is no autonomy? Diane Raymond recommends a more circumspect view, embracing the

---

[100] H. Chochinov, D. Tataryn and J. Clinch, 'Will to live in the terminal dying' (1999) 354 *The Lancet* 816.

[101] European Parliamentary Assembly, Committee on Legal Affairs and Human Rights, *Euthanasia* (European Union, 2003), para. I.

[102] K. George, 'A woman's choice? The gendered risks of voluntary euthanasia and physician-assisted suicide' (2008) 15 *Medical Law Review* 1, 2–3. See also S. Callahan, 'A feminist case against euthanasia' (1996) 77 *Health Progress* 21.

[103] S. Callahan, 'A feminist case against self-determined dying in assisted suicide and euthanasia' (2015) 25 *Feminism and Psychology* 109.

context and ambiguity involved from a feminist perspective by avoiding a rigid absolutism of rejecting euthanasia in all cases.[104] The feminist argument might lead to a claim that we need to work even harder to reduce the pressure complained of, rather than removing the choice of assisted dying. Evidence from jurisdictions does not suggest a marked gender divide in the numbers of men and women seeking assisted death.[105]

Culture

Perhaps the stronger case concerning the vulnerable is not that individuals might be pressured into committing suicide, but rather that we create a culture where that is expected. Kate Greasley has written of the dangers of 'the cultivation of a social environment in which controlled death is an accessible and normalized option, and in which both internal and external pressure to end one's life may consequently mount'.[106] This argument was well captured by Lord Sumption in *Nicklinson* when he talked about the 'indirect social pressure':[107]

> This refers to the problems arising from the low self-esteem of many old or severely ill and dependent people, combined with the spontaneous and negative perceptions of patients about the views of those around them. The great majority of people contemplating suicide for health-related reasons, are likely to be acutely conscious that their disabilities make them dependent on others. These disabilities may arise from illness or injury, or indeed (a much larger category) from the advancing infirmity of old age. People in this position are vulnerable. They are often afraid that their lives have become a burden to those around them. The fear may be the result of overt pressure, but may equally arise from a spontaneous tendency to place a low value on their own lives and assume that others do so too. Their feelings of uselessness are likely to be accentuated in those who were once highly active and engaged with those around them, for whom the contrast between now and then must be particularly painful. These assumptions may be mistaken but are none the less powerful for that. The legalisation of assisted suicide would be followed by its progressive normalisation, at any rate among the very old or very ill. In a world where suicide was regarded as just another optional end-of-life choice, the pressures which I have described are likely to become more powerful. It is one thing to assess some one's mental ability to form a judgment, but another to discover their true reasons for the decision which they have made and to assess the quality of those reasons. I very much doubt whether it is possible

---

[104] D. Raymond, '"Fatal practices": a feminist analysis of physician-assisted suicide and euthanasia' (1999) 14 *Hypatia* 44.

[105] A. Schafer, 'Physician assisted suicide: the great Canadian euthanasia debate' (2013) 36 *International Journal of Law and Psychiatry* 522.

[106] K. Greasley, '*R (Purdy) v DPP* and the case for wilful blindness' (2010) 30 *Oxford Journal of Legal Studies* 301.

[107] [2014] UKSC 38 at para. 89.

in the generality of cases to distinguish between those who have spontaneously formed the desire to kill themselves and those who have done so in response to real or imagined pressure arising from the impact of their disabilities on other people.

This is a very important argument. If we are honest, many of our decisions are influenced by what others do and the expectations of society. To use an example from Elizabeth Wicks, you might think you are making a free choice in having a cup of coffee at 11 o'clock, but that might in fact simply be a reflection of a tradition in your society, or the way you were brought up, or even an addiction to caffeine! But there is no escaping the fact that society is structured, and the expectations of society impact on 'our choices'. So the exercise by some people of their autonomy can create norms which impact upon the choices of others. An old person living in a care home, seeing others around them taking up the option to die, will inevitably feel a degree of pressure to take up that option, especially if the expense of the care home is eating up their savings and they feel themselves to be a burden to their relatives. This kind of background pressure, which might create a social norm or expectation, will impact on autonomy. It might particularly be a pressure felt by older people or disabled people.[108] Will we create a society where older people will feel that suicide is the appropriate thing to do, especially if they are becoming a burden to others? If there is to be a change in the law on euthanasia, we would need to do a lot more to improve the lot of older people in our society to counter that.[109]

As Lord Sumption notes, the difficulty for supporters of a liberalisation of the law is that these indirect social pressures are enormously difficult to detect in any assessment. The argument is that changes in societal norms and expectations will become adopted by people for themselves. Perhaps the message of this is that it is essential that any change in the law is accompanied by changes in societal attitudes towards older people and disabled people that ensure there is no sense in which they feel they are expected or ought to end their lives.

There have been concerns about euthanasia from those writing from a disabilities perspective; in particular that legalising euthanasia would send the message that the lives of disabled people were not worth living.[110] More often, the writings have been concerned about the way the arguments are phrased. The weight placed on autonomy is seen as misplaced by some writers, who point out that disabled people's autonomy is severely restricted.[111] Others have been concerned that opponents of euthanasia have been too quick to describe disabled people as vulnerable and easily coerced or incompetent.[112]

---

[108] E. Leipoldt, *Euthanasia and Disability Perspective: An Investigation in the Netherlands and Australia* (VDM Verlag, 2010).

[109] J. Herring, 'Escaping from the shackles of law at the end of life' (2013) 21 *Medical Law Review* 487.

[110] J. Bickenbach, 'Disability and life-ending decisions' in M. Battin, R. Rhodes and A. Silvers (eds), *Physician Assisted Suicide* (Routledge, 1998).

[111] Ibid.

[112] A. Silvers, 'Protecting the innocents from physician-assisted suicide' in M. Battin, R. Rhodes and A. Silvers (eds), *Physician Assisted Suicide* (Routledge, 1998).

SLIPPERY SLOPE IN PRACTICE

In discussions on assisted dying and vulnerable people, both sides of the debate refer to the experience from overseas. Opponents of liberalising the law claim that experience from other countries, such as the Netherlands, Belgium and some of the US (for example, Oregon),[113] show their worst fears realised. Perhaps predictably, supporters of euthanasia argue that these jurisdictions demonstrate that effective safeguards can be put in place.

We will not go into the detailed evidence from the different jurisdictions: there is fierce dispute over the correct interpretation of the statistics. However, some interesting themes have emerged from those countries which have liberalised their laws.

The first is over the medical state of those who are permitted assisted dying. All the jurisdictions impose restrictions on who can die. For example, 'lasting and unbearable' suffering or some similar requirement is required. However, such phrases are not easy to interpret. Two cases have hit the headlines which raise the issue well:

- In 2013, Nathan Verhelst, age 44, was killed under the Belgian euthanasia laws. He was suffering unbearable pain following an unsuccessful gender reassignment surgery, which he felt left him 'a monster'.
- In 2013, two twins were killed, also in Belgium.[114] They had been born deaf and spent their whole life together. Now aged 45, they were diagnosed with an eye condition which would render them blind. They felt unable to carry on living without being able to see or hear each other.

It should not be thought that such cases are common. In Belgium, too, only 7 per cent of those availing themselves of the euthanasia act have been non-terminal patients. Nevertheless, critics will point to them as examples of how the apparently strict criteria as to who can use assisted dying will be weakened. Supporters will argue that these cases show a sensitive awareness of how unbearable suffering cannot be pigeonholed into standard boxes.

A second issue is the extent to which legalisation of assisted dying becomes the normal way to die. The Netherlands provides a good example. In 2016, a total of 148,973 people died in the Netherlands.[115] Of these, 4 per cent (6,091) were reported to die legally by involving an act done with the explicit intent of hastening death.[116] In only ten cases was a case refused on the basis that the criteria were not met.

---

[113] Although there are other countries which permit assisted suicide or euthanasia, e.g. Rights of the Terminally Ill Act 1995 (Northern Territory (Australia)).

[114] T. Smets, J. Bilsen, J. Cohen, M. Rurup and L. Delines, 'Legal euthanasia in Belgium' (2009) 47 *Medical Care* 1.

[115] *Regional Euthanasia Review Committees, Annual Report 2016* (RERC, 2017).

[116] Ibid.

A third issue is the extent to which people who lack capacity are killed under the system. In the reported statistics in the Netherlands for 2016, 83 per cent (5,077 cases) concerned patients with incurable cancer, neurological disorders (such as Parkinson's disease, multiple sclerosis and motor neurone disease), cardiovascular disease or pulmonary disease. Around 2 per cent of the notifications concerned patients with dementia and around 1 per cent concerned patients with a psychiatric disorder.[117] Some will have concern about the last two categories (201 people) and question whether they involved the killing of people who lacked capacity. One child between the age of 12 and 17 was killed. Concern may also be raised at the ten cases where people were killed, but without the 'due care' criteria being met.[118] Nevertheless the fact we have these detailed statistics might indicate that the system of ending life is being carefully controlled.

A fourth issue concerns whether palliative care suffers in countries where euthanasia is practised. The issue is disputed. But it is worth noting that in 2013, Belgium ranked third among the European countries in the allocation of resources to palliative care.[119]

Inevitably, perhaps, when looking at the experience overseas, opponents of liberalisation of the law see much to be concerned about and supporters find reassurance. Lord Neuberger provided a thoughtful conclusion on the international evidence in *R (Nicklinson) v Ministry of Justice*:[120]

> It is true that the Falconer Report, supported by the reports of the two Canadian panels, states that in the Netherlands, Oregon and Switzerland there is no evidence of abuse of the law, which permits assisting a suicide in prescribed circumstances and subject to conditions. However, negative evidence is often hard to obtain, there is only a limited scope for information given the few jurisdictions where assisted suicide is lawful and the short time for which it has been lawful there, and different countries may have different potential problems. In other words, the evidence on that point plainly falls some way short of establishing that there is no risk. The most that can be said is that the Falconer commission and the Canadian panels could find no evidence of abuse.

CONCLUSION

It should also be remembered that vulnerable groups should be an issue of concern under the current law, where they can be left without treatment or provided with pain-relieving (but killing) drugs with little regulation or

---

[117] Ibid.

[118] Ibid.

[119] European Palliative Care Association, *New Indicators Demonstrate the Increasing Interest in Palliative Care throughout Europe* (NPCA, 2013).

[120] [2014] UKSC 38 at para. 88.

supervision.[121] The question is whether changing the law will lead to more or less involuntary killing. It may be that the Dutch system, which encourages a very open, explicit discussion with patients about end-of-life decisions, will bring out cases where people do not want to be killed, when previously it might have been assumed they would. That is difficult to assess. The same can be said of the question of how much the authorising of such killing will change culture and indirectly pressure vulnerable people into feeling they ought to be killed, and whether the way we treat older and disabled people reinforces or can be changed to counter that pressure.

FURTHER READING

Debate 1

J. Bernat, 'The whole-brain concept of death remains optimum public policy' (2006) 34 *Journal of Law, Medicine & Ethics* 35.

D. DeGrazia, *Human Identity and Bioethics* (Cambridge University Press, 2005).

J. Herring and P-L. Chau, 'The meaning of death' in B. Brooks-Gordon, F. Ebtehaj, J. Herring et al. (eds), *Death Rites and Rights* (Hart Publishing, 2007).

I. Persson, 'Human death – a view from the beginning of life' (2002) 16 *Bioethics* 20.

J. Savulescu, 'Death, us and our bodies: personal reflections' (2003) 29 *Journal of Medical Ethics* 127.

D. Shewmon, 'The brain and somatic integration: insights into the standard biological rationale for equating "brain death" with death' (2001) 26 *Journal of Medicine and Philosophy* 457.

R. Truog, 'Is it time to abandon brain death?' (1997) 27 *Hastings Center Report* 29.

S. Youngner and R. Arnold, 'Philosophical debates about the definition of death: who cares?' (2001) 26 *Journal of Medicine and Philosophy* 527.

Debate 2

S. Callahan, 'A feminist case against self-determined dying in assisted suicide and euthanasia' (2015) 25 *Feminism and Psychology* 109.

K. Greasley, '*R (Purdy) v DPP* and the case for wilful blindness' (2010) 30 *Oxford Journal of Legal Studies* 301.

R. Huxtable, *Law, Ethics and Compromise at the Limits of Life: To Treat or not to Treat?* (Routledge, 2013).

E. Jackson and J. Keown, *Debating Euthanasia* (Hart Publishing, 2012).

H. Lillehammer, 'Voluntary euthanasia and the logical slippery slope argument' (2002) 61 *Cambridge Law Journal* 545.

S. Smith, *End-of-Life Decisions in Medical Care: Principles and Policies for Regulating the Dying Process* (Cambridge University Press, 2012).

K. Yuill, *Assisted Suicide* (Palgrave, 2012).

---

[121] E. Jackson, 'Death, euthanasia and the medical profession' in B. Brooks-Gordon, F. Ebtehaj, J. Herring et al. (eds), *Death Rites and Rights* (Hart Publishing, 2007).

Debate 3

R. Cohen-Almagor, 'First do no harm: pressing concerns regarding euthanasia in Belgium' (2013) 36 *International Journal of Law and Psychiatry* 515.

K. George, 'A woman's choice? The gendered risks of voluntary euthanasia and physician-assisted suicide' (2008) 15 *Medical Law Review* 1.

J. Herring, 'The child must live: disability, parents and the law' in J. Herring and J. Wall (eds), *Landmark Cases in Medical Law* (Hart, 2015).

G. Lewy, *Assisted Death in Europe and America* (Oxford University Press, 2010).

C. Riddle, 'Assisted dying and disability' (2017) 31 *Bioethics* 1467.

A. Silvers, 'Protecting the innocents from physician-assisted suicide' in M. Battin, R. Rhodes and A. Silvers (eds), *Physician Assisted Suicide* (Routledge, 1998).

CHAPTER 10

Ending Life

THE CURRENT LAW

A helpful summary of the law governing the end of life was provided by Lord Sumption in *R (Nicklinson) v Ministry of Justice*:[1]

1. In law, the state is not entitled to intervene to prevent a person of full capacity who has arrived at a settled decision to take his own life from doing so. However, such a person does not have a right to call on a third party to help him to end his life.

2. A person who is legally and mentally competent is entitled to refuse food and water, and to reject any invasive manipulation of his body or other form of treatment, including artificial feeding, even though without it he will die. If he refuses, medical practitioners must comply with his wishes … A patient (or prospective patient) may express his wishes on these points by an advance decision (or 'living will').

3. A doctor may not advise a patient how to kill himself. But a doctor may give objective advice about the clinical options (such as sedation and other palliative care) which would be available if a patient were to reach a settled decision to kill himself. The doctor is in no danger of incurring criminal liability merely because he agrees in advance to palliate the pain and discomfort involved should the need for it arise. This kind of advice is no more or less than his duty. The law does not countenance assisted suicide, but it does not require medical practitioners to keep a patient in ignorance of the truth lest the truth should encourage him to kill himself. The right to give and receive information is guaranteed by article 10 of the Convention. If the law were not as I have summarised it, I have difficulty in seeing how it could comply.

4. Medical treatment intended to palliate pain and discomfort is not unlawful only because it has the incidental consequence, however foreseeable, of shortening the patient's life …

5. Whatever may be said about the clarity or lack of it in the Director [of Public Prosecution]'s published policy, the fact is that prosecutions for encouraging or assisting suicide are rare …

---

[1] *R (Nicklinson) v Ministry of Justice* [2014] UKSC 38 at para. 225.

It is a reflection of the complexity of the law, that even this authoritative summary is controversial. In particular the first point seems to overlook the fact, explored later in this chapter, that the state can be under a duty to stop a person committing suicide in certain circumstances.

In this chapter we will explore some of the distinctions which lie at the heart of the current law on ending life.

Debate 1

The act/omission distinction

An important distinction at the heart of the present law is between cases which involve an act causing a death and those which involve an omission. The distinction was emphasised in the following decision:

Leading case

Airedale NHS Trust v Bland [1993] 1 All ER 821

Tony Bland was in a persistent vegetative state following the Hillsborough Football Stadium disaster. Having been in that condition for three years, his family and medical team sought a declaration from the House of Lords that it was lawful to switch off his life-support machine. Their lordships granted the declaration. They confirmed that Tony Bland was still alive for the purposes of the law. However, the switching off of the machine would be an omission, not an act. The doctors were not required to keep the machine on, because it was not providing Tony Bland with a benefit. It was therefore lawful for them to switch it off.

Lord Goff in *Bland* summarised the current position:

> It is not lawful for a doctor to administer a drug to his patient to bring about his death, even though that course is prompted by a humanitarian desire to end his suffering, however great that suffering may be ... So to act is to cross the Rubicon which runs between – on the one hand the care of the living patient and on the other hand euthanasia – actively causing his death to avoid or to end his suffering. Euthanasia is not lawful at common law.[2]

The importance placed on the distinction between act and omission in the law on end of life is not unusual. The distinction is central to many areas of the law. Pushing someone into a lake is clearly a criminal act; walking past while someone drowns in the lake is not. You may need to pay compensation under

---

[2] *Airedale NHS Trust v Bland* [1993] 1 All ER 821, 867.

the law of tort if you drive into someone, but not if you drive past someone who is ill, ignoring their pleas to take them to the hospital.

It should not be thought that medical professionals cannot be liable for deaths following an omission. They certainly can if it is shown that their failure to act was in breach of a duty of care (i.e. that the doctor behaved unreasonably). Crucially, a doctor will never be acting in breach of a duty if they fail to provide treatment because the patient refuses to consent to it. This means a patient's autonomy rules the day in cases involving omissions. However, in cases involving acts, the fact that a patient requested a fatal dose of medication does not provide legal authorisation for the doctor.

THE JUSTIFICATION FOR THE DISTINCTION

The distinction drawn between an act and an omission is primarily supported in terms of causation. An omission cannot cause death; death is caused by the underlying medical condition. An omission may be necessary for a death, but it cannot be sufficient. No one dies from nothing. An omission can only kill by letting a different cause continue in its effect. By contrast, an act can take over authorship and full responsibility for what happens.[3] An act changes the course of events, an omission does nothing to change it.

One reason omissions are seen as having limited causal impact is because in many cases there are a host of omissions which could cause the act. If we look, for example, at the terrible events of 9/11, clearly the acts of those who flew the planes into the twin towers were causes, but were there any omissions that affected the outcome? Well, you could point to any number of omissions which 'if only' they had been done would have prevented the incident, ranging from failures of information-gathering by the CIA to plane manufacturers not inserting devices to prevent planes being flown into buildings. We could not point to any one of these and see it alone as a cause.

That said, supporters of the distinction commonly accept that there can be cases where it makes sense to say an omission has caused an event. That might be where there is a strong expectation that someone will act in a particular way and they do not. For example, if a driver of a train is expected to put the brakes on when a red light is shown and fails to do so, the failure of the driver to put the brakes on causes the accident. However, there need to be good reasons why a person's omissions should lead to their being held to have caused the result and legally responsible, when for an act, if a person has done an act causing the death, then there is no further discussion about causation required.[4]

Supporters claim this distinction between acts and omissions has a deep intuitive appeal. Philippa Foot poses the question: are we as much to blame for

---

[3] M. Stauch, 'Causal authorship and the equality principle: a defence of the acts/omissions distinction in euthanasia' (2000) 26 *Journal of Medical Ethics* 237.

[4] A. McGee, 'Ending the life of the act/omission dispute: causation in withholding and withdrawing life sustaining measures' (2011) 31 *Legal Studies* 467.

allowing people in Third World countries to starve to death as we would be for killing them by sending poisoned food?[5] She assumes that most people would see a clear distinction between these two.

This is not simply a philosophical argument based on intuition. The distinction between acts and omissions appears to be one which is shared by many healthcare professionals working in the field. One survey of UK medical practitioners suggests that 75 per cent accept a distinction between active and passive euthanasia as of important moral significance.[6] If, for these professionals, the distinction between 'letting go', which is permissible, and killing, which is not, helps them makes sense of their job, then perhaps the law should reinforce the distinction.

THE CASE AGAINST THE ACT/OMISSION DISTINCTION

However much the distinction has been accepted at a practical level, it has been far less popular among philosophers.[7] Lord Mustill was not convinced by the distinction drawn between acts and omissions, and he feared that after *Bland* the law was 'morally and intellectually misshapen', although he added: 'Still, the law is there and we must take it as it stands.'[8] Two leading medical ethicists, Beauchamp and Childress, state that:

> the distinction between killing and letting die suffers from vagueness and moral confusion. The language of killing is so thoroughly confusing – causally, legally, and morally – that it can provide little if any help in discussion of assistance in dying.[9]

The specific concerns about it are as follows.

Illogicality

First, the distinction can be said to lead to illogical results. As Lord Goff in *Bland* admitted:[10]

> [I]t can be asked why, if the doctor, by discontinuing treatment, is entitled in consequence to let his patient die, it should not be lawful to put him out of his misery straight away, in a more humane manner, by a lethal injection, rather than let him linger on in pain until he dies. But the law does not feel able to authorise

---

[5] P. Foot, *Natural Goodness* (Oxford University Press, 2001).

[6] J. Coulson, 'Till death us do part' (1996) (September) *BMA News Review* 23.

[7] E.g., F. Kamm, 'Physician-assisted suicide, euthanasia, and intending death' in M. Battin, R. Rhodes and A. Silvers (eds), *Physician Assisted Suicide* (Routledge, 1998).

[8] *Bland* [1993] 1 All ER 821, 885.

[9] T. Beauchamp and J. Childress, *Principles of Biomedical Ethics* (Oxford University Press, 2013), 65.

[10] *Bland* [1993] 1 All ER 821, 892.

euthanasia, even in circumstances such as these, for, once euthanasia is recognised as lawful in these circumstances, it is difficult to see any logical basis for excluding it in others.

Particularly topical is the practice of continuous deep sedation.[11] This involves sedating a patient by pain relief, so that they are in a coma-like state. Then food and hydration can be withdrawn and they die. This enables the medical team to claim that the death is as a result of an omission (the failure to feed or hydrate) rather than an act. Yet it might be argued that this is simply a way of manipulating the act/omission distinction to achieve death. Why not simply allow the doctors to kill the patient, if we are to allow them to undertake the rigmarole of continuous deep sedation followed by withdrawal of treatment?

Even some opponents of euthanasia are critical of the distinction between acts and omissions. To Keown,[12] the focus on acts and omissions avoids the key question: did the doctor intend to produce death? He argues that if a doctor intends to kill, they are acting wrongly. Whether the doctor intended to produce death by an act or an omission is just a detail about the method of killing, which should not carry moral weight. Although it might be asked whether the intention of a doctor should matter that much. Is what is in their mind more important than whether they have hastened death or let nature take its course?[13]

Problems in drawing the distinction

Some people criticise the distinction between acts and omissions on the basis that it can be difficult to define behaviour as an act or an omission. For example, is switching off a life-support machine an act or an omission? The House of Lords in *Bland* suggested that if the machine was switched off by the medical team, this would be an omission, while if switched off by an interloper (an unauthorised person) it would be an act. Lord Neuberger in *R (Nicklinson) v Ministry of Justice*[14] seemed troubled by the distinction and referred to 'a certain and understandable discomfort with the notion that switching a machine off actually is an omission'. To critics this response demonstrates that you can manipulate the distinction between an act and omission to reach the result you like. However, the distinction their lordships drew is not as odd as it sounds. Imagine that instead of the ventilation machine there is a team of nurses keeping the patient alive by pumping their heart, etc. The doctor tells them to stop, and they do. That is clearly an omission. We are misled by the fact

---

[11] P. Beland, 'Ethical issues around continuous deep sedation without hydration' (2012) 38 *Nursing Times* 24.

[12] J. Keown, 'Against decriminalizing euthanasia, for improving care' in E. Jackson and J. Keown, *Debating Euthanasia* (Hart Publishing, 2012).

[13] A. McGee, 'Ending the life of the act/omission dispute: causation in withholding and withdrawing life-sustaining measures' (2011) 31 *Legal Studies* 467.

[14] *R (Nicklinson) v Ministry of Justice* [2014] UKSC 38 at para. 22.

that a machine is used in the first scenario, and that pushing the switch looks like an act. However, the reality is that the doctor has stopped providing the treatment that was being performed. This is correctly seen as an omission. It also explains why the interloper is seen as doing an act: it is as if that interloper were dragging the nurses away from the patient, preventing another person providing treatment, not withdrawing the treatment previously given.

As this discussion shows, and Andrew McGee has argued,[15] determining whether something is an act or an omission requires looking at what is done *in its context*. McGee argues that doing so means that the law can draw a distinction between behaviours which look similar. He uses the example of a doctor and a lay person signing a piece of paper purporting to be a prescription for medication. They have in one sense done the same thing – 'signed a piece of paper' – but looked at in context, only the doctor has signed the prescription; the lay person has produced a fraudulent document. So too the doctor and the interloper have done the same thing – switched off the machine – but looked at in context, they have done very different things.

Some draw a contrast between switching off a ventilator (which is seen as an omission) and switching off an internal device (such as a pacemaker) (which is seen as an act). What, then, are we to make of an LVAD (left ventricular assist device, a mechanical heart pump) which is partly inside and partly outside the body?[16]

Causation problem overcome

As we have seen, supporters of the distinction claim that omissions cannot cause a result. Logically, the absence of an act cannot make something happen. In response, others claim that we regularly talk of an omission causing a result. The student failed the exam because they failed to work hard enough.[17] Much of the philosophical discussion concerning the distinction between acts and omissions has centred around a hypothetical example put forward by James Rachels:[18]

> Smith stands to gain a large inheritance if anything should happen to his 6-year-old cousin. One evening while the child is taking his bath, Smith sneaks into the bathroom and drowns the child, and then arranges things so it will look like an accident. No one is any the wiser, and Smith gets his inheritance.
>
> Jones also stands to gain if anything should happen to his 6-year-old cousin. Like Smith, Jones sneaks in to the bathroom planning to drown the child in his bath. However, just as he enters the bathroom Jones sees the child slip,

---

[15] A. McGee, 'Ending the life of the act/omission dispute: causation in withholding and withdrawing life-sustaining measures' (2011) 31 *Legal Studies* 467.

[16] F. Kraemer, 'Ontology or phenomenology? How the LVAD challenges the euthanasia debate' (2013) 27 *Bioethics* 140.

[17] E. Garrard and S. Wilkinson, 'Passive euthanasia' (2005) 31 *Journal of Medical Ethics* 64, 66.

[18] J. Rachels, *The End of Life* (Oxford University Press, 1986), 112.

hit his head, and fall face down in the water. Jones is delighted; he stands by, ready to push the child's head under if necessary, but it is not necessary. With only a little thrashing about, the child drowns all by himself, 'accidentally', as Jones watches and does nothing. No one is any the wiser and Jones gets his inheritance.

Rachels argues there is no difference between Smith and Jones in these scenarios, and this demonstrates that there is no moral difference between an act and an omission. He accepts that generally omissions are not blameworthy, but this is because omissions are normally accidental or negligent, whereas actions rarely are. A person rushing past a person drowning in a river is not normally intending that person to die, but a person who pushes another in is. He argues that the significance of his hypothetical example is that both Smith and Jones intend to kill. Where there is no difference in intention, he argues that there is no moral difference between what they have done. He goes on to point out that killing a child by deliberately starving them would be one of the cruellest ways of killing, even though it would be an omission.

CONCLUSION

There are many problems with the sharp distinction between an act and an omission. Despite these philosophical problems, many argue that the distinction provides a useful guide. It gives doctors who cease treating patients the comfort of saying they did not kill their patients, and also preserves the slippery slope argument. Even if not logical, arguably the distinction is said to be in accordance with many people's intuition.[19] McCall Smith has suggested that despite its theoretical difficulties, it provides a basis upon which many people think and act.[20] It may help medical professionals make sense of and live with the decisions they have to make. It is easier going home at night saying 'I had to let some patients go' than it is to go home saying 'I had to kill some patients tonight'. There is some value in the reassurance offered by the act/omission distinction, even if it is philosophically problematic.

It is also worth noting that generally the distinction between acts and omissions is significant. There are few cases where a killing is justified (it may be in self-defence, for example), whereas there are many cases where 'letting die' is permissible (we are not responsible for failing to ensure those starving in other countries do not die). So the distinction is useful generally in ethical analysis. The question is whether it retains its usefulness when we get to complex end-of-life decisions where the distinction between the two begins to blur.

---

[19] G. Gillett, 'Euthanasia, letting die and the pause' (1988) 14 *Journal of Medical Ethics* 61.
[20] A. McCall Smith, 'Euthanasia: the strength of the middle ground' (1999) 7 *Medical Law Review* 194.

Debate 2

The doctrine of double effect

A key distinction is drawn in the current law between intention and foresight. Lord Neuberger in *R (Nicklinson) v Ministry of Justice*[21] confirmed that 'a doctor commits no offence when treating a patient in a way which hastens death, if the purpose of the treatment is to relieve pain and suffering (the so-called "double effect")'. However, the same doctor giving the same drugs intending to kill the patient could, at least in theory, face a conviction for murder.[22] So the difference in this context between a conviction for the most serious offence in criminal law and a perfectly lawful act lies in the distinction between intention and foresight.[23] But should this distinction play such an important role in the law?

Supporters of the distinction between intention and foresight emphasise the doctrine of double effect. It plays an important role in the case *against* liberalising the law on euthanasia. Few people argue that pain-relieving drugs should not be given if appropriate, even if they will hasten death. Yet if we are to enable that practice to continue, we must distinguish it from a case where the doctor is deliberately ending the life of the patient. The doctrine provides a ready way of doing that.

In essence, the double effect doctrine holds that in some circumstances, a person who is doing an act with the purpose of producing result A, but fore-seeing that result B might well result from their actions, will be held to intend result A but not result B.[24] The exact meaning of the doctrine is disputed and there are various versions. In the legal literature the version promoted by John Keown has been particularly prominent. It quotes four principles that render it permissible to do an act which produces a bad consequence:

(1) the act one is engaged in is not itself bad,
(2) the bad consequence is not a means to the good consequence,
(3) the bad consequence is foreseen but not intended, and
(4) there is sufficiently serious reason for allowing the bad consequence to occur.[25]

Relying on this doctrine, its supporters are able to say that a doctor who gives their patient pain-relieving drugs for the purpose of pain relief, but foreseeing that they will cause death, will not be said to have intended to kill the patient. However, the doctrine has proved controversial.

---

[21] *R (Nicklinson) v Ministry of Justice* [2014] UKSC 38, para. 18.

[22] R. Huxtable, 'Get out of jail free? The doctrine of double effect in English law' (2004) 18 *Palliative Medicine* 62.

[23] C. Foster, J. Herring, K. Melham and T. Hope, 'The double effect effect' (2011) 20 *Cambridge Quarterly of Healthcare Ethics* 56.

[24] See A. McGee, 'Intention, foresight, and ending life responses and dialogue' (2013) 23 *Cambridge Quarterly of Healthcare Ethics* 77.

[25] J. Keown, *Euthanasia, Ethics and Public Policy* (Cambridge University Press, 2002), 20.

THE LINE BETWEEN INTENT AND FORESIGHT

For some commentators the line between intent (purpose) and foresight is too blurry. If you know for sure that a certain result is going to occur from your actions, can you really say you did not intend to kill? An example that commonly appears in criminal law textbooks is that of a person who puts a bomb on board a plane which has goods they have insured. Their aim is to destroy the goods, and although they foresee the pilot will be killed, that is not their intent. That seems an astonishing claim. If you know a result will occur as a result of your act and you still decide to do the act, you should not be able to escape responsibility by such sophistry.

That argument, however, is not quite as convincing as it sounds at first. Note that it would not, in fact, satisfy Keown's test for the doctrine of double effect, because the bomber does not have a good reason for doing what they are doing. The doctrine of double effect only operates where they have a sufficiently serious reason for causing the undesired harm. So the doctrine does not prevent your agreeing with 'common sense' that the bomber intended to kill the pilot.

Supporters will reply to the aeroplane example with other examples where there seems to be good reason for distinguishing between intent and foresight.[26] You may foresee that if you drink too much alcohol you will get a hangover, but that does not mean you intend it; a lecturer may foresee that their lecture will confuse their students, but this does not mean they intend to confuse them. Perhaps this last example shows again the importance of Keown's fourth requirement: the lecturer who gives the confusing lecture might be doing their best to explain a highly complex point, realising that only the best students will get it, in which case it seems particularly harsh to say that that lecturer intends to confuse the weaker students. The lecturer would be thrilled if those students were not confused, so it seems odd to say that they intend to confuse them. However, if the lecturer cannot be bothered to write a clear lecture and realises there will be confusion, and does not care, it seems more appropriate to label that as intent.

John Harris[27] has criticised the doctrine for depending too much on how one expresses a problem. He considers a scenario where a group of potholers is trapped and the only way to escape is to move a boulder, but moving the boulder will crush one person to death. You could describe this as 'intending to make an escape route, foreseeing that this will kill someone', or as 'intending to make an escape route by killing someone'. Harris suggests that the morality of an action depends on whether the action judged as a whole was right, not by how one is able to express what one is doing. Supporters would suggest that Harris is neglecting the second of the Keown's requirements: that for a side-effect to be unintended, it cannot be the means to the desired result. So you cannot kill your aunt and say you intended to gain her inheritance and foresaw,

---

[26] See, e.g., ibid., Chapter 2.
[27] J. Harris, *The Value of Law* (Oxford University Press, 1984), 44.

but did not intend, her death.[28] That is because in your plan involved the death as the means to achieve the desired result and was part of it. In Harris's example we could distinguish moving a boulder while foreseeing that doing so will kill someone, and blowing up someone who is stuck in the entrance hole. The latter is using a death to achieve an end, the former is not. Harris may think this response simply reinforces his point about huge weight being placed on the finest of distinctions.

Where does this get us? It suggests that there are some cases where even though the result was foreseen as certain it would not be appropriate to call it intention, but other cases where that seems entirely appropriate. Notably, this was precisely what the leading case in the criminal law on intention (R v Woollin[29]) states: the jury may, if they wish, find intent if the result is virtually certain and the defendant realises that. Keown's fourth criterion provides a reasonable guide to distinguish between cases where intent should be found and where it should not. But his fourth criterion has nothing to do with either foresight or purpose. Worse, it is ambiguous. Who is to decide whether the bad justified the good? How can a doctor know whether the jury will agree with them that the fourth criterion has been met? Or is there merit in the view that it is for the patient to decide whether the fourth criterion has been met?[30] At the least, these questions show the distinction between foresight and intent is only part of the picture in producing a response to the pain relief scenario.[31]

SHOULD THE DISTINCTION MATTER?

Perhaps the use of these examples and counter-examples is not particularly helpful and we need to look at the heart of the issue. Is there something about intending death which makes it worse than foreseeing that death will inevitably occur? Arguably there is. A person who is acting in the hope or expectation that another will die is showing a particular lack of respect for that person's life. They have decided to do what they can to kill. Contrast a dentist who drills a tooth intending to cause the patient pain, and the dentist who drills a tooth foreseeing that pain will occur. Their characters appear very different. Thomas Nagel explains that the person motivated by the bad effect is having their will 'guided by evil'.[32] John Finnis claims:

> There is a free choice (in the sense that matters morally) only when one is rationally motivated towards incompatible alternative possible purposes (X and Y, or X and not-X) which one considers desirable by reason of the intelligible goods

---

[28] J. Boyle, 'Medical ethics and the double effect' (2004) 25 *Theoretical Medicine and Bioethics* 51.

[29] *R v Woollin* [1999] 1 AC 82.

[30] F. Kamm, 'Physician-assisted suicide, the doctrine of double effect, and the ground of value' (1999) 109 *Ethics* 586.

[31] D. Sulmasy, 'Double effect intention is the solution, not the problem' (2000) 28 *Journal Law and Medical Ethics* 26.

[32] T. Nagel, *The View from Nowhere* (Clarendon Press, 1986).

(instrumental and basic) which they offer – and when nothing but one's choosing itself settles which alternative is chosen. In choosing one adopts a proposal to bring about certain states of affairs – one's instrumental and basic purposes – which are precisely those identified under the description which made them seem rationally appealing and choosable. And what one thus adopts is, so to speak, synthesized with one's will, that is, with oneself as an acting person. Rationally motivated choice, being for reasons, is never of a sheer particular. So one *becomes* a doer of the *sort* of thing that one saw reason to do and chose and set oneself to do and accomplish – in short, one becomes the sort of person who has *such* an intention.[33]

So too, it is claimed that the doctor who gives pain-relieving drugs desiring that the patient die is different from the doctor who wants to end the patient's pain, even if death will result.

Not everyone is convinced by this. One way of putting the counter-argument is that we accept consequences in packages. If, for example, I need a filling and I go to the dentist, I can be said to intend to have the treatment. It is true that I do not want the pain, but the pain comes with the treatment: I accept the 'package' (the treatment with the consequential pain) because I decide that even though there is pain, it will, in the long term, be preferable for me.[34] I cannot say 'I intend to have the filling but not to experience the pain', because life is not like that.

THE USE OF THE DOCTRINE FOR LAW

One difficulty for those who wish to emphasise the difference between intent and foresight is its practicability. If a doctor is found to have injected a patient with a lethal amount of a pain-relieving drug, how are we to know what their intent or foresight was? As the law stands, with its emphasis on intent, only a doctor foolish enough to admit they were intending to kill would face prosecution. Further, if a doctor wishes to give a large dose of pain-relieving drugs to a patient but seeks a lawyer's advice first, is it really sensible that the advice might be, 'You can give the injection, but make sure that at the time you are not wanting the death and focus on wanting to relieve pain'? Whatever its merits in terms of ethics, the doctrine does not provide a practical guide to medical practice.

Rodney Symes has argued that in an end-of-life case, a doctor dealing with a patient in considerable pain has intentions which are complex, ambiguous, multifactorial and uncertain.[35] He explains that if doctors are deciding whether

---

[33] J. Finnis, 'Euthanasia and justice' in J. Finnis, *Human Rights and Common Good* (Oxford University Press, 2011), 217.

[34] A. Shaw, 'Two challenges to the double effect doctrine: euthanasia and abortion' (2002) 28 *Journal of Medical Ethics* 102.

[35] R. Syme, *A Good Death: An Argument for Voluntary Euthanasia* (Melbourne University Publishing, 2008).

to give a lethal amount of drugs, it is not easy to separate out the question of whether death is a means to end the pain or whether death is a good outcome in itself. The question is often whether it is better to give the injection or require the patient to (in the words of Raymond Tallis) 'earn their death the hard way and go the whole distance along the tunnel of barbed wire'.[36]

Following on from this, Foster, Herring, Melham and Hope[37] have argued that whatever merits the doctrine of double effect may have philosophically,[38] it is not useable for the law. It fails to provide clear and workable guidance to medical professionals as regards how to behave. Simply telling them that they may foresee but not intend a result does not give them confidence they are complying with the law. The law also needs to be capable of proof in a court room. The doctrine of double effect leaves to the jury the difficult task of working out what was in the defendant's mind, and to the doctor the task of trying to persuade the jury what was in their mind. With these points in mind, the authors suggest a clear set of guidance from the NHS could be produced, setting out when pain relief can appropriately be used. This would provide clear, workable and provable advice for doctors.

Scenario to ponder

In a real case,[39] a very sick baby was taken off a ventilator. The prognosis was very poor and the parents agreed this was best for the baby. The plan was that the baby would be removed from the ventilator and handed to the parents. They would cuddle the baby while it died. Once off the ventilator the baby started having spasms and gasping (as occasionally happens in such cases). The parents were very distressed and the doctor administered a lethal injection which stopped the spasms and immediately killed the baby. Did the doctor act improperly? Is this case distinguishable from other cases of euthanasia?

CONCLUSION

As can be seen, the debates on the doctrine of double effect can raise some complex philosophical issues. As the last point highlights, it may be that such sophistication is inappropriate for the law. However, supporters will claim that the test captures something that is of value to professionals working in the area.

---

[36] R. Tallis, 'Is there a slippery slope?', *Times Literary Supplement*, 12 January 1996, 3.
[37] C. Foster, J. Herring, K. Melham and T. Hope, 'Intention and foresight – from ethics to law and back again' (2013) 22 *Cambridge Quarterly of Healthcare Ethics* 86.
[38] Which they doubt.
[39] J. Goodman, 'The case of Dr Munro: are there lessons to be learnt?' (2010) 18 *Medical Law Review* 564.

It acknowledges that they are not intending to kill people, just relieving their pain. If that is important to those working in the area, should the law reflect that?

Debate 3

How are human rights relevant in the assisted dying debate?

It is notable that human rights discourse has become a prominent feature of the debates over assisted dying.[40] Both supporters and opponents will use human rights to bolster their case. There is, perhaps, some truth in the argument that all this involves is putting the familiar arguments in a new terminology. Nevertheless we cover them here because they now play such a notable feature in court case discussions. They also bring out the issues particularly clearly. We will look at the different rights, using those in the European Convention on Human Rights, and explore how they have been used. Before doing that it is important to understand quite what is meant by a right.

DEFINING RIGHTS

There is an important difference between a right and a liberty. A liberty is a freedom to do something. You have no positive claim to receive assistance from the state or others to do the act, save that no one can legitimately interfere in your doing it. A right, by contrast, must be reflected in a duty on someone else.

This distinction explains why under the current law there is no right to commit suicide. It is true that the Suicide Act 1961 means that suicide is no longer a crime, but that does not mean that there is a right to do it. Adultery is not a crime, but there is no right to commit adultery. Lord Sumption in *R (Nicklinson) v Ministry of Justice*:[41]

> The reason for decriminalising suicide was not that suicide had become morally acceptable. It was that imposing criminal sanctions was inhumane and ineffective. It was inhumane because the old law could be enforced only against those who had tried to kill themselves but failed. The idea of taking these desperate and unhappy individuals from their hospital beds and punishing them for the attempt was as morally repugnant as the act of suicide itself. It was ineffective because assuming that they truly intended to die, criminal sanctions were incapable by definition of deterring them.

If one wanted to make a case that there should be a right to commit suicide (which, as we shall see, is an argument that can be made), more needs to be shown

---

[40] Human rights debates dominated the reasoning of the court in the two key recent decisions: *R (Nicklinson) v Ministry of Justice* [2014] UKSC 38; *R (Conway) v Secretary of State for Justice* [2017] EWCA Civ 275.
[41] [2014] UKSC 38 at para. 212.

than simply that the act is not unlawful. At most there may be a liberty (a claim to be left alone) to commit suicide, although, as we shall see, even that is doubtful.

We will now look at the key rights in the European Convention on Human Rights (ECHR), as they relate to end-of-life issues.

ARTICLE 2

Article 2 ECHR protects the right to life. It states:

1. Everyone's right to life shall be protected by law. No one shall be deprived of his life intentionally save in the execution of a sentence of a court following his conviction of a crime for which this penalty is provided by law.
2. Deprivation of life shall not be regarded as inflicted in contravention of this article when it results from the use of force which is no more than absolutely necessary:
   a. in defence of any person from unlawful violence;
   b. in order to effect a lawful arrest or to prevent the escape of a person lawfully detained;
   c. in action lawfully taken for the purpose of quelling a riot or insurrection.[42]

This is clearly important for those who argue that there is no right to die. Indeed, it seems to deny the right to euthanasia, because it sets out the circumstances in which a killing may be permitted, and euthanasia would not fit within those. The most promising argument may be that euthanasia is defending a person from the 'violence' of a medical condition and so falls into the first exception, but that seems to be stretching the language, and in any event a medical condition is hardly unlawful.

In *R (Pretty) v DPP*,[43] it was argued on Ms Pretty's behalf that the right to life in Article 2 ECHR included a right to control the manner of one's death and therefore a right to commit suicide. The House of Lords and European Court of Human Rights[44] held that Article 2 imposed a duty on the state to protect life, and this could not be taken to include a right to die. The interpretation sought by Ms Pretty involved too great a stretch of the natural meaning of the words.

Not only does Article 2 suggest there is no right to die, it imposes a positive obligation on the state to protect people from threats to their life. It requires the state to put in place laws designed to protect people's Article 2 rights. In *Pretty v UK* it was held that Article 2 positively requires the state to put in place laws protecting vulnerable people being pressured into committing suicide. This was used to justify the existence of the offence under the Suicide Act 1961 of assisting or encouraging suicide.

---

[42] European Convention on Human Rights, Art. 2 (Right to life). © Council of Europe. Reproduced with permission.
[43] *Pretty v UK* [2002] 2 FCR 97.
[44] Ibid.

Simply putting laws in place will not be sufficient to ensure compliance with Article 2. In certain circumstances public authorities have a positive duty to prevent people committing suicide. As the House of Lords made clear in *Rabone v Pennine Care Foundation Trust*,[45] where someone is in the care of a public authority (e.g. as a patient in a hospital, or as a prisoner), the public authority has a duty to take reasonable steps to prevent their committing suicide. In that case the hospital negligently released a young woman from a psychiatric hospital, who then committed suicide. The hospital trust was liable in the tort of negligence to pay compensation.

This special obligation only applies to those in the care of a local authority. *Re Z (An Adult: Capacity)*[46] explores further the obligations of a public authority which is aware that someone not in their care plans to commit suicide. These include the following:

(i)   to investigate the position of a vulnerable adult to consider what was her true position and intention;

(ii) to consider whether she was legally competent to make and carry out her decision and intention;

(iii) to consider whether any other (and if so, what) influence may be operating on her position and intention, and to ensure that she has all relevant information and knows all available options;

(iv) to consider whether she was legally competent to make and carry out her decision and intention;

(v)   to consider whether to invoke the inherent jurisdiction of the High Court so that the question of competence could be judicially investigated and determined;

(vi) in the event of the adult not being competent, to provide all such assistance as may be reasonably required both to determine and give effect to her best interests;

(vii) in the event of the adult being competent, to allow her in any lawful way to give effect to her decision, although that should not preclude the giving of advice or assistance in accordance with what are perceived to be her best interests;

(viii) where there are reasonable grounds to suspect that the commission of a criminal offence may be involved, to draw that to the attention of the police;

(ix) in very exceptional circumstances, to invoke the jurisdiction of the court under the Local Government Act 1972, section 222 (which enables a local authority to bring proceedings to a court in relation to an inhabitant in their area).

These cases seem to imply that there is generally a duty on public authorities to prevent suicide, but this needs to be balanced by what it is reasonable to expect them to do and the rights of people who have made a fully autonomous decision to kill themselves.

---

[45] *Rabone v Pennine Care Foundation Trust* [2012] UKSC 2.
[46] *Re Z (An Adult: Capacity)* [2004] EWHC 2817, para. 213.

ARTICLE 3

Article 3 ECHR states:

> No one shall be subjected to torture or to inhuman or degrading treatment or punishment.[47]

Diane Pretty argued that by prohibiting her husband from killing her, the state was inflicting torture or inhuman or degrading treatment upon her. It was held by the European Court of Human Rights that even if Ms Pretty's medical condition could be said to amount to torture, or to inhuman or degrading treatment, it could not be said that this was inflicted by the state or was as a result of treatment by the state.[48] The European Court also stated that the right under Article 3 of the Convention had to be read alongside the right to life in Article 2. It could not therefore be argued that a person had the right to be killed or helped to die under Article 3, as that would contravene the right to life under Article 2. However, in *R (Burke) v GMC*,[49] the Court of Appeal stated that Article 3 ECHR gave a right to be protected from treatment or a lack of treatment which would result in dying in avoidably distressing circumstances. This might, therefore, form the basis of an argument that a patient in agony has a right to pain-relieving drugs, even if they lead to death.[50] Arguably such a case could be dealt with under the doctrine of double effect discussed in Debate 2 above.

ARTICLE 8

The European Court of Human Rights in *Pretty v UK*[51] appeared open to the argument that the right to determine issues surrounding one's death was an aspect of private life. It was stated:

> The very essence of the Convention is respect for human dignity and human freedom. Without in any way negating the principle of sanctity of life protected under the Convention, the Court considers that it is under Article 8 that notions of the quality of life take on significance. In an era of growing medical sophistication combined with longer life expectancies, many people are concerned that they should not be forced to linger on in old age or in states of advanced physical or mental decrepitude which conflict with strongly held ideas of self and personal identity.[52]

In *R (Purdy) v DPP*,[53] it was held that a decision to commit suicide can fall within the ambit of Article 8 ECHR, which protects the right to respect for

---

[47] European Convention on Human Rights, Art. 3 (Prohibition of torture). Reproduced with the permission of the Council of Europe.

[48] *Pretty v UK* [2002] 2 FCR 97, para. 53.

[49] *R (Burke) v GMC* [2005] 3 FCR 169.

[50] J. Herring, 'Pain, human rights and the law' (2011) 2 *Managing Pain* 1.

[51] [2002] 2 FCR 97, disagreeing with the House of Lords.

[52] Ibid., para. 65.

[53] *R (Purdy) v DPP* [2012] UKHL 45.

private and family life. That decision makes it clear that the decision to commit suicide is a protected right within the European Convention, but it is a right which may be interfered with if there is sufficient justification. Later decisions of the European Court (e.g. *Haas v Switzerland*;[54] *Koch v Germany*[55]) have explained that the right includes 'an individual's right to decide in which way and at which time his or her life should end, provided that he or she was in a position freely to form his or her own will and to act accordingly'.[56] One interesting recent development in the law has been *Koch v Germany*,[57] where a man who cared for his terminally ill wife claimed that the inability for him to acquire medication to end her life infringed *his* rights to family and private life under Article 8 ECHR. The argument was accepted, but with the caveat above that the right could be justifiably interfered with.

The Article 8 right in this context does not create a positive obligation on the state to help someone commit suicide. This was confirmed in *Haas v Switzerland*.[58] There, it was held that the state was not required to supply the applicant with a particular kind of medication he wished to use to kill himself.

What we can now say is that under Article 8 ECHR, a person who is terminally ill and who has made a free and informed choice to commit suicide has a right to do so, and a right to receive assistance. However, that right may be interfered with if the interference is justified under Article 8(2). That does imply that if a person has made an undoubtedly autonomous decision to kill themselves, it would be unlawful for anyone to intervene.[59] However, if a person saw someone trying to kill themselves, they are likely to believe that the suicide lacks capacity and so they are entitled to intervene, even if their belief proves incorrect.

The decision of the House of Lords in *Purdy* was not saying that it should not be an offence to assist a person in committing suicide. Their lordships were simply stating that the law on assisting suicide needed to be sufficiently clear to enable a person to know whether they would be guilty of an offence if they were to assist a suicide. Baroness Hale indicated that the law on assisted suicide was necessary:

> Clearly, the prime object [of the law on assisted suicide] must be to protect people who are vulnerable to all sorts of pressures, both subtle and not so subtle, to consider their own lives a worthless burden to others. ... But at the same time, the object must be to protect the right to exercise a genuinely autonomous choice. The factors which tell for and against such a genuine exercise of autonomy free from pressure will be the most important.[60]

---

[54] *Haas v Switzerland* (2011) 53 EHRR 33, para. 51.

[55] *Koch v Germany* (2013) 56 EHRR 6.

[56] Ibid., para. 52.

[57] *Koch v Germany* (2013) 56 EHRR 6.

[58] *Haas v Switzerland* (2011) 53 EHRR 33, para. 51.

[59] G. Richardson, 'Mental capacity in the shadow of suicide: what can the law do?' (2013) 9 *International Journal of Law in Context* 87.

[60] *R (Purdy) v DPP* [2009] UKHL 45, para. 65.

Lord Brown, by contrast, emphasised the rights of those who wish to commit suicide. He stated:

> [S]uppose, say, a loved one, in desperate and deteriorating circumstances, who regards the future with dread and has made a fully informed, voluntary and fixed decision to die, needing another's compassionate help and support to accomplish that end (or at any rate to achieve it in the least distressing way), is assistance in *those* circumstances necessarily to be deprecated? Are there not cases in which (although no actual defence of necessity could ever arise) many might regard such conduct as if anything to be commended rather than condemned? In short, as it seems to me, there will on occasion be situations where, contrary to the assumptions underlying the Code, it would be possible to regard the conduct of the aider and abettor as altruistic rather than criminal, conduct rather to be understood out of respect for an intending suicide's rights under article 8 than discouraged so as to safeguard the right to life of others under article 2.[61]

As a result of this decision, the DPP has issued clear guidance on when an assisted suicide will be prosecuted.

It was clear from *Pretty* and *Purdy* that the precise balance under Article 8 between protecting people's right to determine the end of their life and to ensure the protection of people from being pressured into ending their lives was within the margin of appreciation for each country and so not to be determined by the European Court of Human Rights. In *R (Nicklinson) v Ministry of Justice*[62] the Supreme Court were asked to determine what was the correct balance for English and Welsh law. Tony Nicklinson claimed that the courts should declare as a matter of English law that the current law was incompatible with the European Convention (as interpreted in England). The judgment was complex and a range of views were present. The short version is that the argument was rejected by the majority. Beatson LJ has provided a helpful summary of the judgments in *R (Conway) v Secretary of State for Justice*,[63] breaking them down into three key views:

[1] Lord Sumption and Lord Hughes considered that the question of relaxation of section 2(1) was for Parliament, and that Parliament could properly conclude that a blanket ban on assisted suicide was necessary for the purposes of Article 8, and it had already done so.

[2] Lady Hale and Lord Kerr, who dissented and would have made a declaration of incompatibility, considered that, unless Parliament devised a scheme which admitted of exceptions to section 2(1), the incompatibility would persist although they recognised that Parliament might take a different view and decline to change the law, as the Human Rights Act 1998 allows.

---

[61] Ibid., para. 82. 'The Code' is a reference to Crown Prosecution Service, *The Code for Crown Prosecutors* (CPS, 2004).

[62] *R (Nicklinson) v Ministry of Justice* [2014] UKSC 38.

[63] *R (Conway) v Secretary of State for Justice* [2017] EWCA Civ 275, para. 32.

[3] The position of the remaining five justices fell in between these settled views. Lord Neuberger, Lord Mance and Lord Wilson concluded that the appeal should be disposed of in the same way but contemplated that circumstances may arise in the future in which an application for a declaration of incompatibility might succeed.

So, the majority in *Nicklinson* was that it was not appropriate, at least at that point in time, for the courts to issue a declaration of incompatibility as the matter was better left to Parliament. After that decision several private members' bills were presented to Parliament which attempted to liberalise the law on assisted dying. They were all decisively rejected. In *R (Conway) v Secretary of State* the issue returned to the court. The case turned on whether when in *Nicklinson* the Supreme Court said that a declaration of incompatibility could only be considered if the matter was not dealt with by Parliament, they meant Parliament needed to consider the issue or whether they meant Parliament needed to change the law. At the time of writing the litigation is ongoing. The Court of Appeal[64] have confirmed it is at least arguable that the courts are now in a position to make a declaration of incompatibility. However, subsequently Burnett J in *R (Conway) v Secretary of State*[65] in the High Court refused the application, explaining:

> Parliament has reconsidered the issue of assisted dying following the decision of the Supreme Court in *Nicklinson*, as that court encouraged it to do. Both the House of Commons and the House of Lords have debated the matter in the context of bills proposing a relaxation of the strict application of section 2(1). The result is that Parliament has decided, at least for the moment, not to provide for legislative exceptions to section 2(1) of the 1961 Act.

No doubt the litigation and the arguments will continue. However, it should be noted that even if Mr Conway wins the most the courts can do is to declare the law incompatible with the European Convention and require Parliament to debate the issue. Most constitutional lawyers accept that Parliament is entitled to still take the view that no reform is needed.

ARTICLE 14

This article of the European Convention on Human Rights prohibits discrimination on various grounds, including disability. Article 14 can only be used when another Convention right is interfered with in a discriminatory way. It was argued in *Pretty v UK*[66] that to allow people who were physically capable of committing suicide to do so, but to prohibit those physically incapable of committing suicide from arranging for another person to assist them to do so, amounted

---

[64] Ibid.

[65] *R (Conway) v Secretary of State for Justice* [2017] EWHC 640 (Admin), para. 5.

[66] *Pretty v UK* [2002] 2 FCR 97.

to discrimination on the grounds of disability contrary to Article 14 ECHR. The European Court of Human Rights accepted that Ms Pretty was discriminated against in this way, but held that there were objective and reasonable justifications for the discrimination, namely, that any law that permitted assisted suicide could lead to vulnerable people being manipulated into killing themselves.

This argument appears the most promising of the human rights arguments if the law is to be liberalised. This is because a particularly strong justification is required in order to justify discrimination, and concerns over hypothetical vulnerable people may be insufficient. Although these arguments were dismissed in *Pretty*, they were done so with relatively little analysis. It may be that in future decisions the issue will be looked at in more detail.

CONCLUSION

In truth, both sides of the debate can draw on human rights arguments. What the discussion does highlight is the tension between the rights of those who wish autonomously to die, and the interests of those who might be killed without full consent if the law was liberalised. In the future it may be the discrimination argument which is emphasised by those seeking a more permissible law, while the right to life will be drawn on by those seeking to resist any change. We may see, too, with the increased emphasis on mental health, stronger arguments being made for an effective anti-suicide strategy, to do something to combat the horrifyingly high suicide rates, especially among young people. That is an issue that sometimes gets lost in the heat of the arguments over euthanasia.

FURTHER READING

Debate 1

H. Kuhse and P. Singer, 'Killing and letting die' in J. Harris (ed.), *Bioethics* (Oxford University Press, 2001).

A. McGee, 'Ending the life of the act/omission dispute: causation in withholding and withdrawing life-sustaining measures' (2011) 31 *Legal Studies* 467.

A. McGee, 'Does withdrawing life-sustaining treatment cause death or allow the patient to die?' (2015) 22 *Medical Law Review* 26.

F. Miller, R. Truog and D. Brock, 'Moral fictions and medical ethics' (2010) 24 *Bioethics* 453.

A. Mullock and R. Heywood, 'The value of life in English law: revered but not sacred?'(2016) 36 *Legal Studies* 258.

M. Stauch, 'Causal authorship and the equality principle: a defence of the acts/omissions distinction in euthanasia' (2000) 26 *Journal of Medical Ethics* 237.

Debate 2

C. Foster, J. Herring, K. Melham and T. Hope, 'Intention and foresight – from ethics to law and back again' (2013) 22 *Cambridge Quarterly of Healthcare Ethics* 86.

F. Kamm, 'Physician-assisted suicide, the doctrine of double effect, and the ground of value' (1999) 109 *Ethics* 586.

A. McGee, 'Intention, foresight, and ending life responses and dialogue' (2013) 23 *Cambridge Quarterly of Healthcare Ethics* 77.

A. Shaw, 'Two challenges to the double effect doctrine: euthanasia and abortion' (2002) 28 *Journal of Medical Ethics* 102.

R. Syme, *A Good Death: An Argument for Voluntary Euthanasia* (Melbourne University Publishing, 2008).

Debate 3

J. Herring, 'Ending Life' in J. Laing and J. McHale (eds), *Principles of Medical Law* (Oxford University Press, 2017).

P. Lewis, *Assisted Dying and Legal Change* (Oxford University Press, 2007).

G. Richardson, 'Mental capacity in the shadow of suicide: what can the law do?' (2013) 9 *International Journal of Law in Context* 87.

E. Wicks, *The Right to Life and Conflicting Interests* (Oxford University Press, 2010).

CPI Antony Rowe

Chippenham, UK

2018-06-04 12:40